Nature's Daily Guide to Success

The lunar cycle has an important influence on our lives, the effects are listed in the columns.
Easy to follow advice for every given day.

Discover more about the lunar cycle and it's effects in the reference book "Nature's Daily Guide". ISBN 978-0-9854637-8-6

Nature's Daily Guide
The Influence of the Lunar Cycle

• Considering the effect the moon has on certain body parts, you can maximize the results from medicines, supplements, and detox measures.

• If you incorporate the lunar cycle, you will improve and get the most benefit from body, nail and hair care.

• Get the best growth from your plants, optimize your harvest, and take advantage of sustainable gardening methods when you garden according to the moon's rhythm.

• Plan your business meetings on days when people are most open for negotiating, networking, and exchanging ideas. Learn about the days when it's advisable to focus on financial matters or routine work.

• Plan parties and activities when you and others enjoy them the most. Know in advance what will work best for family and social time, hobbies, exercises, and other leisure activities.

• Enjoy inspiring aphorisms on every page.

• The moon passes through a zodiac sign during the given days, activating the characteristics of the zodiac sign. The resulting influences are listed for easy use in the advice columns above.

• Qualities of the given zodiac sign.

• Space for your personal notes.

• Doing housework in tune with nature and the lunar cycle will get you the best results for your efforts. Use the most favorable time for your work and visible results will be proof of your success.

• Discover simple ways to improve your diet. Know which fruits and vegetables benefit your body the most. Eat anything you like, but optimize the timing!

• Positive affirmations improve your well-being.

• Based on the declination of the moon all gardening work is unfavorable for the day.

• Benefit from the qualities of the waxing and the waning moon phases.

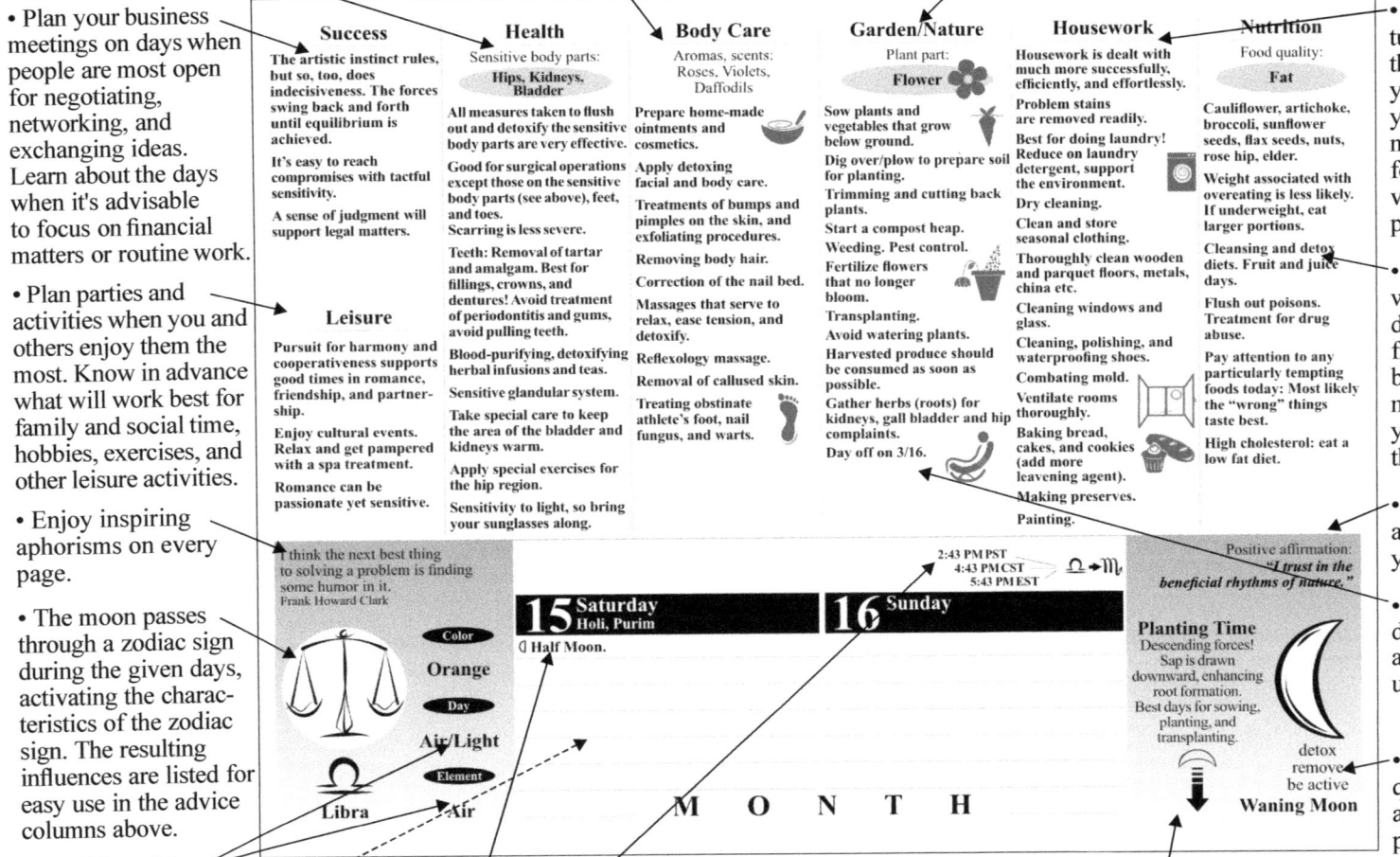

Success

The artistic instinct rules, but so, too, does indecisiveness. The forces swing back and forth until equilibrium is achieved.

It's easy to reach compromises with tactful sensitivity.

A sense of judgment will support legal matters.

Leisure

Pursuit for harmony and cooperativeness supports good times in romance, friendship, and partner-ship.

Enjoy cultural events. Relax and get pampered with a spa treatment.

Romance can be passionate yet sensitive.

Health

Sensitive body parts:
Hips, Kidneys, Bladder

All measures taken to flush out and detoxify the sensitive body parts are very effective.

Good for surgical operations except those on the sensitive body parts (see above), feet, and toes.

Scarring is less severe.

Teeth: Removal of tartar and amalgam. Best for fillings, crowns, and dentures! Avoid treatment of periodontitis and gums, avoid pulling teeth.

Blood-purifying, detoxifying herbal infusions and teas.

Sensitive glandular system.

Take special care to keep the area of the bladder and kidneys warm.

Apply special exercises for the hip region.

Sensitivity to light, so bring your sunglasses along.

Body Care

Aromas, scents:
Roses, Violets, Daffodils

Prepare home-made ointments and cosmetics.

Apply detoxing facial and body care.

Treatments of bumps and pimples on the skin, and exfoliating procedures.

Removing body hair.

Correction of the nail bed.

Massages that serve to relax, ease tension, and detoxify.

Reflexology massage.

Removal of callused skin.

Treating obstinate athlete's foot, nail fungus, and warts.

Garden/Nature

Plant part:
Flower

Sow plants and vegetables that grow below ground.

Dig over/plow to prepare soil for planting.

Trimming and cutting back plants.

Start a compost heap.

Weeding. Pest control.

Fertilize flowers that no longer bloom.

Transplanting.

Avoid watering plants.

Harvested produce should be consumed as soon as possible.

Gather herbs (roots) for kidneys, gall bladder and hip complaints.

Day off on 3/16.

Housework

Housework is dealt with much more successfully, efficiently, and effortlessly.

Problem stains are removed readily.

Best for doing laundry! Reduce on laundry detergent, support the environment.

Dry cleaning.

Clean and store seasonal clothing.

Thoroughly clean wooden and parquet floors, metals, china etc.

Cleaning windows and glass.

Cleaning, polishing, and waterproofing shoes.

Combating mold.

Ventilate rooms thoroughly.

Baking bread, cakes, and cookies (add more leavening agent).

Making preserves.

Painting.

Nutrition

Food quality:
Fat

Cauliflower, artichoke, broccoli, sunflower seeds, flax seeds, nuts, rose hip, elder.

Weight associated with overeating is less likely. If underweight, eat larger portions.

Cleansing and detox diets. Fruit and juice days.

Flush out poisons. Treatment for drug abuse.

Pay attention to any particularly tempting foods today: Most likely the "wrong" things taste best.

High cholesterol: eat a low fat diet.

I think the next best thing to solving a problem is finding some humor in it.
Frank Howard Clark

Color — Orange
Day
Air/Light
Element — Air
Libra

15 Saturday
Holi, Purim
☽ Half Moon.

16 Sunday

2:43 PM PST
4:43 PM CST
5:43 PM EST
♎ → ♏

M O N T H

Positive affirmation:
"I trust in the beneficial rhythms of nature."

Planting Time
Descending forces!
Sap is drawn downward, enhancing root formation. Best days for sowing, planting, and transplanting.

detox
remove
be active
Waning Moon

• Half Moon marks the midpoint of waxing and waning moon phases.

• The exact times the moon moves in and out of a sign are shown in three different time zones: Eastern (EDT), Central(CDT) and Pacific Daylight Time (PDT) and respectively the daylight savings times.

• Ascending and descending forces reign in nature supporting planting and harvesting.

Easy to use!

How to best utilize the information in the advice columns:

Success

Considering the effect of the lunar cycle enables you to plan ahead to best utilize all opportunities, possibilities, and activities. You may have experienced a great many times that on some days work goes easier and more efficiently than on other days.

Knowing the subtle influence of the lunar cycle, any goal-oriented activity can be scheduled optimally to avoid any negative influences and achieve the most successful results while saving time, effort, and money.

Leisure

What is the best day for a successful party event? Have more fun! Plan parties and activities when you and others enjoy them the most. Know in advance what will work best for family and social time, hobbies, exercises, and other leisure activities in life.

Health

In the course of the lunar cycle every body part and organ gets affected, listed daily as **'sensitive body parts'**. Knowing this you can plan ahead to improve your health: Whatever you do for the well-being of the sensitive body parts during that day is even more beneficial. Beware that everything that puts a special burden or strain on the 'sensitive body parts' is more harmful. If possible avoid any surgery on these parts.

During waxing moon all measures taken to supply nutrient materials and strengthen the body are more effective. When the moon is on the wane all measures taken to flush out and detoxify are more successful.

All this advice is based on century old knowledge to support and strengthen your health and well-being.

Body Care

You may have wondered why on some days your hair just doesn't retain its form, or why the same body treatments seem to yield different results on different days?

The lunar cycle has an effect on body, nail, and hair care. Massages are more effective during certain periods of the lunar cycle. Washing hair during the time the moon travels in Pisces may result in dandruff. Knowing all the details enables you to pick the best dates for your visit to the hair dresser. You will also save on hair restorers.

There is an old farmer's rule of cutting and filing fingernails and toenails any Friday after sunset. The result of that rule is healthy and strong nails.

Scents are assigned to each zodiac sign. Improve your well-being by surrounding yourself with these soothing scents.

Garden/Nature

For centuries gardeners and farmers all over the world used these powerful guidelines successfully.

The lunar cycle has an effect on each part of a plant: **roots, leaves, fruits or blossoms**. Pick the right timing for great results. For example, when planting leafy vegetables such as lettuce, spinach or cabbage, choose a leaf day for best results.

If you consider the lunar effect on plants, your plants will grow better, your harvest will be plentiful, and pests will be reduced or completely avoided. Weeding, fertilizing, and watering will be less frequent but more effective.

There are many opportunities to coordinate your agenda for the kind of work you want to do. Consider as well that on New Moon and Full Moon weather changes are more likely.

House Work

Doing housework in tune with nature and the lunar cycle will get you the best results for your efforts. It's like magic!

Housework is dealt with much more successfully, efficiently, and effortlessly during the waning moon. For example, problem stains are removed readily. Reduce your use of cleaners and save money. You will also be supporting the environment, since waste water is broken down much better. Get the best results with baking, cooking, and preserving foods.

Improve and refine your methods. Use the most favorable time for your work and visible results will be proof of your success, saving you time for the things you enjoy most.

Discover more in the reference book "Nature's Daily Guide. The Influence of the Lunar Cycle."

Nutrition

Discover simple ways to improve your diet. Know which fruits and vegetables benefit your body the most. Eat anything you like, but optimize the timing!

The food components of **protein, salt, fat, and carbohydrate** are linked to the elements of the zodiac signs on any given day. Healthy bodies absorb and digest the assigned food component the best, while sensitive or sick bodies may not fare well with the same food component. Observe how your body digests the assigned food components on any given day and factor this in for your choice of foods.

During waxing moon it's most beneficial to strengthen the body. Weight gain is easier than during waning moon, stimulants and vitamins are more effective as well. The waning moon phase is best for measures to detoxify the body.

Introduction

The moon governs the oceans on earth, it rules the tides. All of nature is affected by the lunar cycle. Since our human bodies consist to 80 per cent of water, the moon influences us as well. Powers activated by the moon affect us more than the powers activated by the sun.

Many of the ancient calendars followed the position of the moon. This knowledge has been used for centuries in all aspects of life. Generations of farmer's and people living close to nature observed these rules of nature, guided by the moon. You'll find plenty of valuable, easy to use information. You will know, what, when, and how to do the best. Plan your actions, revise your results, use your time, work, and money effectively. Improve and live a better, healthier, and more successful life.

Nature's Almanac 2025:
Nature's Daily Guide to Success.
Copyright © Edith Stadig, Raya Publishing LLC
service@rayapublishing.com
www.rayapublishing.com
ISBN 979-8-9864777-3-2
Author and Designer: Edith Stadig.
Originally published since 1997: **"Mein Leben mit dem Mondrhythmus"** by Clebitady Verlag in Rutesheim, Germany

Notice

This calendar book is intended as a reference volume only, not as a medical manual. The information given here is designed to help you make informed decisions about your health. It is not intended as a substitute for any treatment that may have been prescribed by your doctor. If you suspect that you have a medical problem, we urge you to seek competent medical help.

Reference list and further reading
Stadig, E.: Nature's Daily Guide: The Influence of the Lunar Cycle, 2018
Paungger, J./Poppe, T.: Guided by the Moon: Living in Harmony with the Lunar Cycles, 2002
The Power of Timing: Living in Harmony with Natural and Lunar Cycles, 2013
Thun, M.: The Biodynamic Year: Increasing Yield, Quality and Flavour: 100 Helpful Tips for the Gardener or Smallholder, 2010

How to use the calendar section on the bottom section of each page:

Zodiac Signs

Each pages depicts the position of the moon in the various zodiac signs.

Similar to the sun, the moon also travels through all of the zodiac signs. The moon only takes 28 days for all zodiac signs. This is called the lunar cycle.

Because it takes the moon 2 to 3 days to pass through a zodiac sign this calendar is divided in 1-3 days per page, considering the zodiac sign the moon is in, as well as the periods of waxing and waning moon.

Each zodiac sign represents certain characteristics which are activated while the moon passes through the sign. All characteristics and resulting influences are listed for easy use in the advice columns.

Beneath each picture of a zodiac sign, you find the matching astrological symbol.

Color

Colors apply to the lunar cycle and the position of the moon in each zodiac sign. Experiment with matching or complimentary colors in your daily outfit. Watch their effects on your well-being. The colors may also be applied to color therapy.

Day and Element

Each zodiac sign correlates with one of the **elements:** fire, earth, air, or water.

Linked to the elements of fire, earth, air, and water, every day reveals a different quality: Warm, Cool, Air/Light, or Wetness. As the moon travels through the signs these qualities are activated.

Summarized for a quick overview of the day, you find the effects listed in detail in the columns.

Calendar

The calendar is based on the waxing and waning moon phases as well as the moon passing through the zodiac signs. The moon takes 2 to 3 days to travel through a sign, and the same characteristics apply for these days. The exact times the moon moves in and out of a sign are shown in three different time zones: Eastern (EDT), Central (CDT), and Pacific Daylight Time (PDT), and respectively the daylight savings times EST, CST and PST. For all other US time zones please add hours accordingly.

Deviations occur on New Moon or Full Moon days and are listed accordingly. The highlighted tips for New Moon and Full Moon are effective only on the day of New Moon or Full Moon, with the exception of the advice on vaccinations (see below).

New Moon Day

On New Moon the body detoxifies most efficiently, but ingestion of food likely slows down. A day of fasting promotes health and can prevent illnesses. It's the best day to drop bad habits, change directions if necessary, confirm your resolutions, and finalize new decisions. Body and mind are more likely to stay calm and balanced in the face of changes, withdrawal, or loss.

Full Moon Day

A day of fasting promotes health and can prevent illnesses. Be cautious since the body utilizes nutrition most effectively during this time, it acts the same on any artificial flavors, additives, stimulants, drugs, as well as poisonous substances. Wounds might bleed more profusely than other times. Recovery after surgery is impeded. Vaccinations are unfavorable in the 3 days before or on Full Moon. The body is more likely to retain water. Healing herbs collected have greater curative power.

Ancient Rule: No meat on Wednesdays and Fridays.

Planting Time, Harvest Time, or Turning Points.

While the moon travels in Cancer, Leo, Virgo, Libra, and Scorpio, descending forces draw the sap downward in all plants, enhancing root formation. Hence these days are best for any sowing, planting, and transplanting of all plants, and harvesting of root plants.

When the moon travels in Capricorn, Aquarius, Pisces, Aries, and Taurus, ascending forces are raising the sap upward, enhancing plant growth above ground and resulting in the most juicy fruits and vegetables. This is a good time for harvesting any plant that grows above ground and for harvesting fruit and vegetables for storage.

Transitioning from ascending to descending forces and vice versa, both forces are at work, resulting in neutralizing effects on each other and preventing both harvesting and planting from yielding the best results.

Waxing Moon

The time of the waxing moon is best used to rest, recover, regroup, and gather strength. Since the body readily absorbs during this time, you are more likely to gain weight even with regular amount of food intake. Everything that is supplied to build up and strengthen the body is most effective. The closer it is to Full Moon the stronger the impact of the forces.

Waning Moon

Detoxify, remove, and be active. The body is ready to detoxify and cleanse, and weight gain associated with overeating is less likely. Housework yields better results. Dirt and spots are removed more easily. The closer to New Moon the stronger the impact of the forces.

You find the effects listed in detail in the columns.

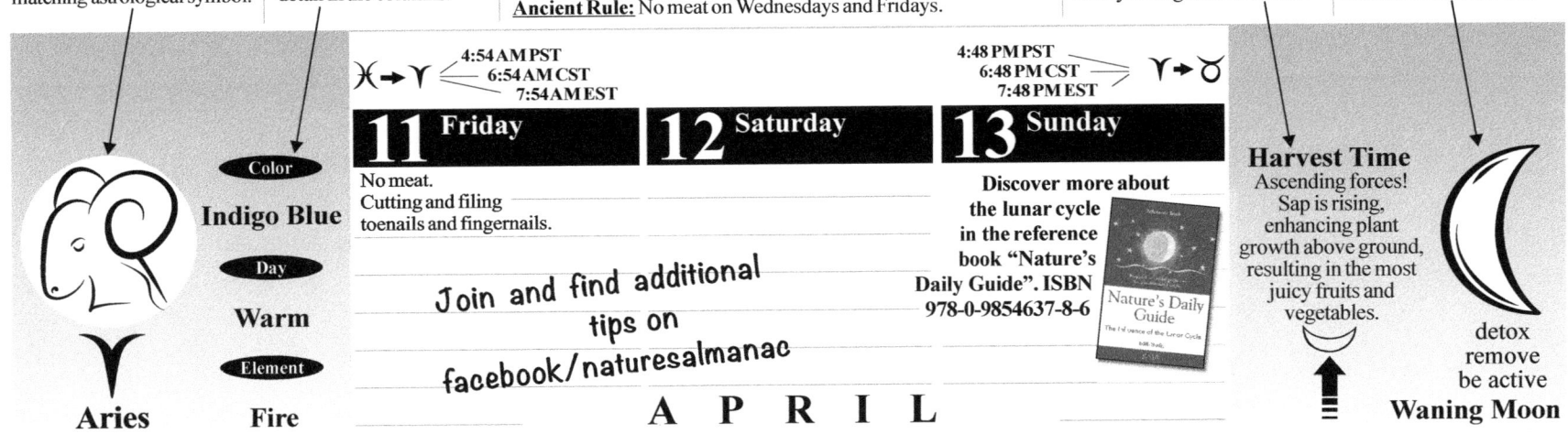

Color — **Indigo Blue**

Day — **Warm**

Element — **Fire**

Aries — **Fire**

4:54 AM PST / 6:54 AM CST / 7:54 AM EST

4:48 PM PST / 6:48 PM CST / 7:48 PM EST

11 Friday
No meat.
Cutting and filing toenails and fingernails.

12 Saturday

13 Sunday
Discover more about the lunar cycle in the reference book "Nature's Daily Guide". ISBN 978-0-9854637-8-6

Nature's Daily Guide — The Influence of the Lunar Cycle

Join and find additional tips on facebook/naturesalmanac

A P R I L

Harvest Time
Ascending forces! Sap is rising, enhancing plant growth above ground, resulting in the most juicy fruits and vegetables.

detox remove be active
Waning Moon

Overview 2025

Mercury is retrograde from 3/15 to 4/6/25, from 7/18 to 8/10/25, and from 11/9 to 11/28/25.

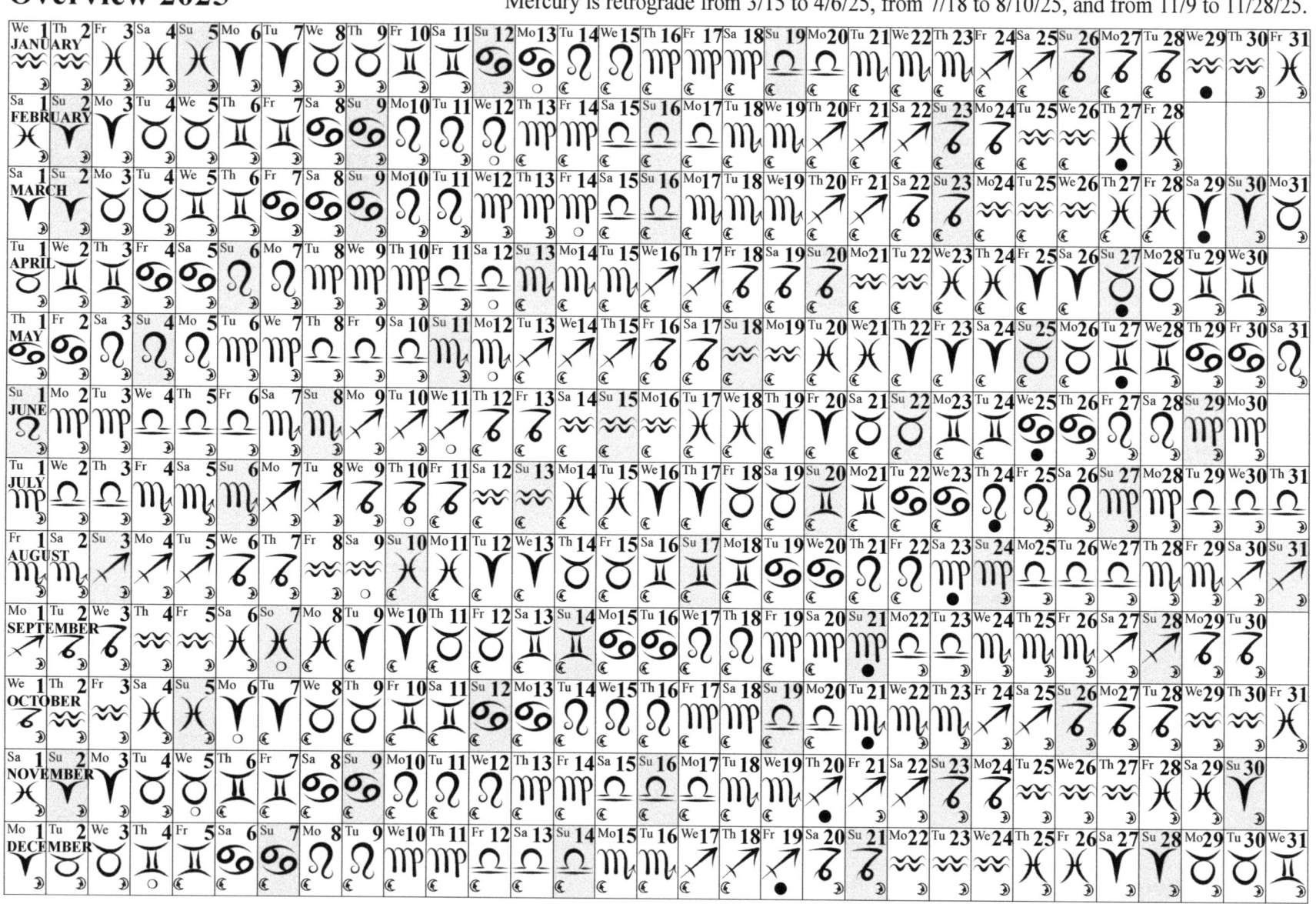

♈-Aries ♉-Taurus ♊-Gemini ♋-Cancer ♌-Leo ♍-Virgo ♎-Libra ♏-Scorpio ♐-Sagittarius ♑-Capricorn ♒-Aquarius ♓-Pisces

Success

Inspiration, optimism, and impatience. Rational thinking, creativity and imagination spark new ideas and inspire planning for the future.

Shying away from routine tasks people will feel more drawn to anything new.

Instead of gridlocked structures choose new possibilities.

Leisure

Inspiration and optimism will boost friendship, social gatherings, and parties.

Express your creativity and imagination. Dwell in dreams and utopian ideas. It is easier now to perceive intuitive thoughts.

Health

Sensitive body parts:

Lower Legs, Veins

All measures taken to supply nutrient materials and strengthen the sensitive body parts are very effective.

Healing ointments are easily absorbed.

Sensitive glandular system.

Avoid inflammation of the veins. Apply ointments to lower legs, and rest legs in a raised position.

Varicose veins: Avoid long periods of standing.

While exercising go easy on the ankles.

Sensitivity to light, so bring your sunglasses along.

Body Care

Aromas, scents: Cyclamen, Peach, Wild Roses

Treatments with firming and moisturizing creams are more effective.

Massages that serve to regenerate, and strengthen, perhaps aided with beneficial massage oils.

Correcting and cutting ingrown nails.

Hair dyes applied now, will look more vibrant.

Garden/Nature

Plant part:

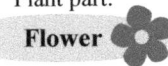
Flower

Avoid watering plants.

Harvested produce is well suitable for storage.

Gather herbs for vein diseases.

Housework

Light housework only.

Ventilate rooms thoroughly.

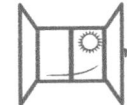

Baking cakes and cookies. Dough rises faster. (Except on New Moon)

Making preserves.

Nutrition

Food quality:

Fat

Cauliflower, artichoke, broccoli, sunflower seeds, flax seeds, nuts, rose hip, elder.

Weight gain: avoid indulging in rich foods. If overweight, eat smaller portions.

Supply nutrient materials to strengthen the body. Focus on foods that contain essential minerals and vitamins.

Stimulants and vitamins are more effective.

Pay attention to any particularly tempting foods today: Most likely the "wrong" things taste best.

High cholesterol: eat a low fat diet.

We wish all readers a Happy New Year!

Positive affirmation:
"I am safe."

Harvest Time
Ascending forces! Sap is rising, enhancing plant growth above ground, resulting in the most juicy fruits and vegetables.

gather strength rest, recover buildup
Waxing Moon

2:51 AM PST
4:51 AM CST
5:51 AM EST

1 Wednesday New Year's Day	**2** Thursday Last Day of Chanukah
No meat.	

J A N U A R Y

Nobody can bring you peace but yourself.
Ralph Waldo Emerson

Color
Bright/ Dark Blue

Day
Air/Light

Element

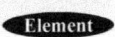

Air    **Aquarius**

Success

Sensibility, intuition, and helpfulness.

Where possible, retreating is more favorable than dealing with business matters.

Dissolve restrictions, be patient and wait. Be aware that people can be more easily influenced.

Leisure

Your helpfulness will boost friendships.

Enjoy dancing or swimming, or watch a movie that will inspire your fantasies and imagination.

Retreat, relax, and recover.

Romance can be gentle and coziness will prevail.

If you plan outdoor excursions, be prepared for a shower here and there.

Health

Sensitive body parts:

Feet and Toes

All measures taken to supply nutrient materials and strengthen the sensitive body parts are very effective.

Healing ointments are easily absorbed.

Sensitive nervous system.

Drugs have a much stronger effect on your body. Monitor closely what you put into your body.

Lymphatic therapy.

Sluggishness or fatigue may occur in the transition into the next Zodiac sign of Aries.

Body Care

Aromas, scents: Magnolia, Amaryllis, Clary Sage

Treatments with firming and moisturizing creams are more effective.

Massages that serve to regenerate, and strengthen, perhaps aided with beneficial massage oils. Reflexology massage. Carry out with special care, people are more sensitive.

Correcting and cutting ingrown nails.

Foot bath.

No haircuts, hair becomes shaggy and unmanageable. Avoid washing your hair. Dandruff could develop.

Garden/Nature

Plant part:

Leaf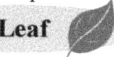

Watering all indoor and outdoor plants.

Sow plants, herbs, and vegetables that grow and flourish above ground, and leaf vegetables.

Transplanting.

Mowing lawns.

Avoid pruning fruit trees and bushes.

Harvested produce should be consumed as soon as possible.

Gather herbs for foot complaints.

Housework

Light housework only.

Ventilate rooms briefly and rapidly. Don't air mattresses.

Any dirt and spots are easily removed in the laundry.

Avoid painting, as paint will take very long to dry.

Preserving and storing should be avoided.

Nutrition

Food quality:

Carbohydrate

Lettuce, spinach, lamb's lettuce, Endive, parsley, leek, cabbage (Brussels sprouts, kale, Chinese cabbage), all leafy herbs, asparagus, mushrooms, cress, Swiss chard, rhubarb.

Weight gain: avoid indulging in rich foods. If overweight, eat smaller portions and avoid carbohydrates.

Supply nutrient materials to strengthen the body. Focus on foods that contain essential minerals and vitamins.

Caffeine, alcohol, drugs, certain foods, and stimulants have a much stronger effect.

Positive affirmation:
"I am safe."

Harvest Time
Ascending forces! Sap is rising, enhancing plant growth above ground, resulting in the most juicy fruits and vegetables.

gather strength
rest, recover
buildup
Waxing Moon

7:22 AM PST
9:22 AM CST
10:22 AM EST

11:02 AM PST
1:02 PM CST
2:02 PM EST

♒ → ♓   ♓ → ♈

3 Friday   **4 Saturday**   **5 Sunday**

No meat. Cutting and filing toenails and fingernails.

The unexamined life is not worth living.
Socrates

Color
Blueish White
Day
Wetness
Element
Water

Pisces

J A N U A R Y

Success

Things get going and the way straight ahead seems the best.

People feel energetic, courageous, assertive, and at times anxious.

Good time for meetings and sales talks but impatience and selfishness do not favor teamwork.

Leisure

An enterprising spirit and spontaneity move people to enjoy outings, sports, competitions, cultural events, and travels.

Romance can be very passionate.

Good days for outings, even with cloudy skies the air still feels somewhat warm. Drying effect, get plenty to drink.

Health

Sensitive body parts:

Head, Brain, Eyes

All measures taken to supply nutrient materials and strengthen the sensitive body parts are very effective.

Healing ointments are easily absorbed.

Sensitive sense organs.

If you suffer from migraines drink plenty of water, and avoid coffee, chocolate, and sugar.

Body Care

Aromas, scents: Cloves, Peppermint, Thyme

Treatments with firming and moisturizing creams are more effective.

Massages that serve to regenerate, and strengthen, perhaps aided with beneficial massage oils.

Correcting and cutting ingrown nails.

Eye compresses for strained eyes.

Any kind of hair care. Hair dyes applied now, will look more vibrant.

Garden/Nature

Plant part:

Fruit

Sow plants and vegetables that grow and flourish above ground, especially fruit and tomatoes.

Sowing and planting anything that is supposed to grow fast and for immediate use.

Grafting onto fruit trees.

Cultivating grains.

Transplanting.

Harvesting and storing grains, vegetables, potatoes, fruit, and tomatoes.

Gather herbs for eye complaints and headaches.

Day off on 1/6.

Housework

Light housework only.

Ventilate sufficiently.

Preserving fruit.

Freezing fruit and vegetables.

Baking bread, cakes, and cookies. Dough rises faster. (Except on New Moon)

Suitable for making cheese.

Nutrition

Food quality:

Protein

Beans, peas, corn, tomatoes, pumpkin, lentils, soybeans, cucumber, eggplant, zucchini, berries, fruit, chili, bell pepper, figs, avocado, melon, olives.

Weight gain: avoid indulging in rich foods. If overweight, eat smaller portions.

Supply nutrient materials to strengthen the body. Focus on foods that contain essential minerals and vitamins.

Stimulants and vitamins are more effective.

Drink plenty of water.

Positive affirmation: *"I am safe."*

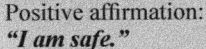

Harvest Time
Ascending forces! Sap is rising, enhancing plant growth above ground, resulting in the most juicy fruits and vegetables.

gather strength rest, recover buildup

Waxing Moon

6 Monday Epiphany

☾ Half Moon.

7 Tuesday Orthodox Christmas Day

Get busy living or get busy dying.
Stephen King

Color

Indigo Blue

Day

Warm

Element

Fire   **Aries**

J A N U A R Y

Success

Realism and material security are important. Persistence comes easy, thoughts and reactions are slower.

Assess financial areas.

Conservative tendencies may make people want to stay away from risk taking.

Leisure

Relax at a picnic/feast. Enjoy culinary pleasures and hobbies.

The earth feels cold to the touch, so take slightly warmer clothes.

Health

Sensitive body parts:

Head and Neck

All measures taken to supply nutrient materials and strengthen the sensitive body parts are very effective.

Healing ointments are easily absorbed.

Sensitive blood circulation.

Organs of speech, jaws, teeth, tonsils, thyroid gland, neck, and vocal chords get easily affected. Keep neck warm. On cold days ears should be protected. Sensitivity to noise.

High blood pressure: Avoid salty foods.

Massages, lymphatic therapy, and chiropractic treatment to release blockages.

Body Care

Aromas, scents: Geranium, Jasmine, Rose

Treatments with firming and moisturizing creams are more effective.

Massages that serve to regenerate, and strengthen, perhaps aided with beneficial massage oils.

Correcting and cutting ingrown nails.

Hair dyes applied now, will look more vibrant.

Garden/Nature

Plant part:

Root

Sow plants, herbs, and vegetables that grow and flourish above ground.

Sowing and planting trees, bushes, hedges, and root vegetables. Everything grows slowly and lasts well.

Transplanting.

Harvesting and storing root vegetables. Harvested produce is well suited for storage.

Gather herbs for sinus issues, sore throat, and ear complaints.

Housework

Light housework only.

Air rooms only briefly.

Preserving root vegetables.

Nutrition

Food quality:

Salt

Garlic, carrots, red beets, reddish, rutabaga, sugar beet, celery, potatoes, onions, kohlrabi.

Weight gain: avoid indulging in rich foods. If overweight, eat smaller portions.

Supply nutrient materials to strengthen the body. Focus on foods that contain essential minerals and vitamins.

Stimulants and vitamins are more effective.

Avoid large quantities of salty foods like bacon, ham, salted herring, fatty cheese, and the like.

Positive affirmation:
"I am safe."

Harvest Time
Ascending forces! Sap is rising, enhancing plant growth above ground, resulting in the most juicy fruits and vegetables.

gather strength rest, recover buildup

Waxing Moon

8 Wednesday

No meat.

9 Thursday

5:08 PM PST
7:08 PM CST
8:08 PM EST
♉ → ♊

J A N U A R Y

If you want to live a happy life, tie it to a goal, not to people or things.
Albert Einstein

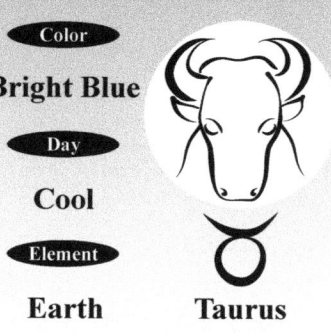

Color
Bright Blue

Day
Cool

Element
Earth

Taurus

Success

Open mindedness and curiosity. A changeable and hectic time.

Good time for talking, negotiating, networking, and exchanging ideas as well as for meetings of a nonbinding nature, conferences, and studies.

Leisure

Good time for family gatherings, parties, and short trips.

People enjoy stimulating their minds with reading and studying. Attending theater performances is a preferred enjoyment. Enhance friendships.

Stretching exercises.

Be prepared for sudden changes in weather or climate.

Health

Sensitive body parts:

Shoulders, Arms, Hands, Lungs

All measures taken to supply nutrient materials and strengthen the sensitive body parts are very effective.

Healing ointments are easily absorbed. Applying herbal ointments to the shoulders for rheumatic gout and alike.

Sensitive glandular system.

Make sure you are dressed warm enough in cool weather.

Exercises for shoulders. Breathing exercises.

Avoid having any teeth pulled.

Sensitivity to light, bring your sunglasses along.

Massages, lymphatic therapy, and chiropractic treatment to release blockages.

Body Care

Aromas, scents: Lavender, Lemon Balm, Magnolia, Verbena

Treatments with firming and moisturizing creams are more effective.

Massages that serve to regenerate, and strengthen, perhaps aided with beneficial massage oils.

Correcting and cutting ingrown nails.

Hair dyes applied now, will look more vibrant.

Garden/Nature

Plant part:

Flower

Sow plants, herbs, and vegetables that grow and flourish above ground.

Sowing and planting any creeping or climbing plants, flowers, and medicinal herbs.

Transplanting.

Avoid watering plants.

Gather herbs for tensions in the shoulder and lung complaints.

Changes in weather are more likely.

Housework

Light housework only.

Ventilate rooms thoroughly.

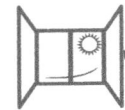

Making preserves.

Baking cakes and cookies. Dough rises faster. (Except on New Moon)

Nutrition

Food quality:

Fat

Cauliflower, artichoke, broccoli, sunflower seeds, flax seeds, nuts, rose hip, elder.

Weight gain: avoid indulging in rich foods. If overweight, eat smaller portions.

Supply nutrient materials to strengthen the body. Focus on foods that contain essential minerals and vitamins.

Stimulants and vitamins are more effective.

Pay attention to any particularly tempting foods today: Most likely the "wrong" things taste best.

High cholesterol: eat a low fat diet.

Positive affirmation:
"I am safe."

Turning Point

Transition of ascending to descending forces. Both forces are at work and neutralize each other.

gather strength rest, recover buildup

Waxing Moon

8:25 PM PST
10:25 PM CST
11:25 PM EST

10 Friday

No meat. Cutting and filing toenails and fingernails.

11 Saturday

J A N U A R Y

Money and success don't change people; they merely amplify what is already there.
Will Smith

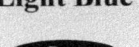 Color

Light Blue

 Day

Air/Light

 Element

Air

Gemini

Success

Feelings, sensitivity, and cooperativeness. Many are overly sensitive, so beware of treading on someone's toes.

Be cautious if you are easily influenced.

During negotiations make use of the cognitive ability of your senses.

Leisure

Relax within your close family.

Retreat to your safe haven and enjoy your fantasy while reading or listening to music. The inner world becomes more colorful than the outer.

Romance can be gentle. Deep feelings will prevail.

If you plan outdoor excursions, be prepared for a shower here and there.

Health

Sensitive body parts:
Chest, Lungs, Liver, Stomach, Gall Bladder

All measures taken to supply nutrient materials and strengthen the sensitive body parts are very effective.

Healing ointments are easily absorbed.

Sensitive nervous system.

Be cautious with alcohol since the liver is very sensitive.

Stomach could play up and cause gas and heartburn.

Rheumatism: Don't air bedding outside, damp will remain in the bedding.

Lymphatic therapy.

○ *Full Moon: Avoid any surgery and vaccination if possible.*

Body Care

Aromas, scents:
Lilac, Lilies of the Valley, Lilies, Violets

Treatments with firming and moisturizing creams are more effective.

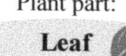

Massages that serve to regenerate, and strengthen, perhaps aided with beneficial massage oils.

Correcting and cutting ingrown nails.

No haircuts, hair becomes shaggy and unmanageable. Avoid washing your hair.

Garden/Nature

Plant part:
Leaf

Watering all indoor and outdoor plants.

Sow plants, herbs, and vegetables that grow and flourish above ground, leaf vegetables (no lettuce).

Transplanting.

Trimming and cutting back plants. Avoid pruning fruit trees and bushes.

Cut trees, garlands, pick flowers to dry; they will last longer.

Sowing and mowing lawns.

Setting up a compost heap.

Gather herbs for bronchitis, stomach, liver, and gall bladder complaints.

Unfavorable for harvesting, storing, and preserving.

○ *Full Moon: Weather and climate changes. Herbs are most powerful.*

Housework

Light housework only.

Ventilate rooms briefly and rapidly. Don't air mattresses.

Any dirt and spots are easily removed in the laundry.

Avoid painting, as paint will take very long to dry.

○ *Full Moon: Avoid doing laundry, cleaning windows, making preserves, painting.*

Nutrition

Food quality:
Carbohydrate

Lettuce, spinach, lamb's lettuce, Endive, parsley, leek, cabbage (Brussels sprouts, kale, Chinese cabbage), all leafy herbs, asparagus, mushrooms, cress, Swiss chard, rhubarb.

Weight gain: avoid indulging in rich foods. If overweight, eat smaller portions and avoid carbohydrates. Moodiness may make you want to eat more than is healthy.

Supply nutrient materials to strengthen the body. Focus on foods that contain essential minerals and vitamins. Stimulants and vitamins are more effective.

If you get stomach troubles easily, avoid heavy meals.

○ *Full Moon: A day of fasting.*

Positive affirmation:
"I am safe."

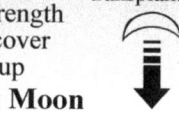

Planting Time
Descending forces! Sap is drawn downward, enhancing root formation. Best days for sowing, planting, and transplanting.

gather strength rest, recover buildup
Waxing Moon

12 Sunday

13 Monday

○ **Full Moon** 2:28 PM PST, 4:28 PM CST, 5:28 PM EST

J A N U A R Y

Flowers always make people better, happier, and more helpful; they are sunshine, food and medicine for the soul.
Luther Burbank

Color

Green

Day

Wetness

Element

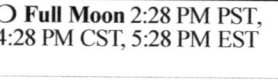

Water   **Cancer**

Success

Determination reigns, and risks are taken more often. Master your tasks with more self-confidence and creativity.

Limits appear to be more easily surmountable.

Auspicious day for sales, advertising, and publicity.

Leisure

Zest for life is in the air. People want to have a fun time, enjoy parties, musical events, movies, etc.

Possessive feelings can harm a relationship. Romance can be very passionate.

Outings: even with cloudy skies the air still feels somewhat warm. Drying effect, get plenty to drink.

Danger of sudden storms, not only in the sky.

Health

Sensitive body parts:
Heart, Back, Diaphragm, Circulation, Arteries

All measures taken to flush out and detoxify the sensitive body parts are very effective.

Good for surgery, except on the sensitive body parts (see above), knees, bones, joints, and skin.
Scarring is less severe.

Teeth: Removal of tartar and amalgam. Best for fillings, crowns, and dentures!

Blood-purifying, detoxifying herbal infusions and teas.

Sensitive sense organs.

Back and heart problems are more likely to occur.

Avoid overstraining of the heart and circulation with unusual physical activities.

Expect sleepless nights.

Body Care

Aromas, scents:
Hibiscus, Oleander, Rose

Prepare home-made ointments and cosmetics.

Apply detoxing facial and body care.

Treatments of bumps and pimples on the skin, and exfoliating procedures.

Removing body hair.

Correction of the nail bed.

Massages that serve to relax, ease tension, and detoxify.

Reflexology massage.

Removal of callused skin.

Treating obstinate athlete's foot, nail fungus, and warts.

Good days for haircuts, hair becomes stronger. But be aware that if you get a perm, curls will become quite frizzy. Baby's first haircut.

Garden/Nature

Plant part:
Fruit

Sowing plants and vegetables that grow below ground.

Sowing and planting fruit. Also sow and plant vegetables that are highly perishable. Plant trees and bushes. Sow lawns.

Dig over/plow to prepare soil for planting.

Trimming and cutting back plants. Pruning of fruit trees and bushes.
Transplanting.
Not suitable for fertilizing. Weeding. Pest Control.

Harvested produce should be consumed as soon as possible.

Gather herbs (roots) for heart and circulation complaints.

Start compost heap.

Housework

Housework is dealt with much more successfully, efficiently, and effortlessly.

Problem stains are removed readily.

Best for doing laundry!

Dry cleaning.

Thoroughly clean wooden and parquet floors, metals, china, etc.

Cleaning windows and glass.

Cleaning, polishing, and waterproofing shoes.

Combating mold.

Ventilate rooms sufficiently.
Air beds.

Suitable for making cheese.

Preserving and freezing fruit and vegetables.

Baking bread, cakes, and cookies (use more leavening agent).

Avoid painting.

Nutrition

Food quality:
Protein

Beans, peas, corn, tomatoes, pumpkin, lentils, soybeans, cucumber, eggplant, zucchini, berries, fruit, chili, bell pepper, figs, avocado, melon, olives.

Weight associated with overeating is less likely. If underweight, eat larger portions.

Cleansing and detox diets. Fruit and juice days.

Flush out poisons. Treatment for drug abuse.

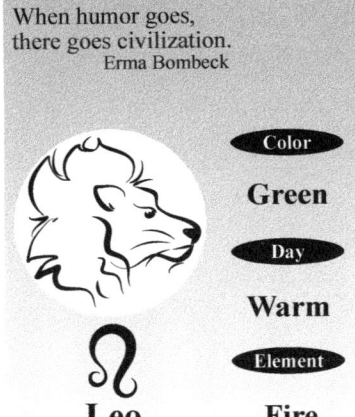

When humor goes, there goes civilization.
Erma Bombeck

Color
Green

Day
Warm

Element
Fire

♌
Leo

♋ ➔ ♌
1:13 AM PST
3:13 AM CST
4:13 AM EST

14 Tuesday Orthodox New Year, Makar Sankranti

15 Wednesday
No meat.

J A N U A R Y

Planting Time
Descending forces!
Sap is drawn downward, enhancing root formation.
Best days for sowing, planting, and transplanting.

detox
remove
be active

Waning Moon

Success

Good time for details, organization, routine, concentration, and duty.

Take care of financial and administrative tasks.

Prepare for future success now with realistic and critical assessment.

Leisure

Enjoy a nature walk.

Good time for health regimes. Improve your health with stretching exercises and yoga.

The earth feels cold to the touch, so take slightly warmer clothes.

Health

Sensitive body parts:
Digestive Organs, Nerves, Spleen, Pancreas

All measures taken to flush out and detoxify the sensitive body parts are very effective.

Good for surgery, except on the sensitive body parts (see above), knees, bones, joints, and skin.
Scarring is less severe.
Teeth: Removal of tartar and amalgam. Best for fillings, crowns, and dentures!
Avoiding treatment of periodontitis and gums.
Blood-purifying, detoxifying herbal infusions and teas.
Sensitive blood circulation.
For a sensitive digestive system, a wholesome diet is recommended.
Dress slightly warmer.
High blood pressure:
Avoid salty foods.
Massages, lymphatic therapy, and chiropractic treatment to release blockages.

Body Care

Aromas, scents:
Lavender, Spruce Needles, Sage, Meadow Flowers

Prepare home-made ointments and cosmetics.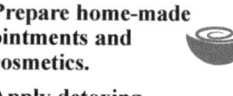

Apply detoxing facial and body care.

Treatments of bumps and pimples on the skin, and exfoliating procedures.

Removing body hair.

Correction of the nail bed.

Massages that serve to relax, ease tension, and detoxify.

Reflexology massage.

Removal of callused skin.

Treating obstinate athlete's foot, nail fungus, and warts.

Best for haircuts because it retains its shape longer.
Perms turn out best.

Garden/Nature

Plant part:
Root

Best for sowing and planting, except lettuce.

Plant trees which are supposed to grow very tall. Plant hedges and bushes that are meant to grow very fast.

Planting and re-potting balcony and indoor plants.

Dig over/plow to prepare soil for planting.

Trimming and cutting back plants. Planting cuttings.

Spread fertilizer and manure. Fertilize flowers with poorly formed roots.

Start a compost heap.

Transplanting. Mulching.

Weeding. Pest control (vermin in the soil).

Avoid harvesting and storing.

Gather herbs (roots) for digestive organs, pancreas, and nervous complaints.

Housework

Housework is dealt with much more successfully, efficiently, and effortlessly.

Problem stains are removed readily.

Best for doing laundry! Reduce on laundry detergent, support the environment.

Dry cleaning.

Thoroughly clean wooden and parquet floors, metals, china etc.

Cleaning, polishing, and waterproofing shoes.

Combating mold.

Air rooms only briefly.

Painting.

Making pickles, preserves, and cheese yields suboptimal results and should be avoided.

Nutrition

Food quality:
Salt

Garlic, carrots, red beets, reddish, rutabaga, sugar beet, celery, potatoes, onions, kohlrabi.

Weight associated with overeating is less likely. If underweight, eat larger portions.

Cleansing and detox diets. Fruit and juice days.

Flush out poisons. Treatment for drug abuse.

Avoid large quantities of salty foods like bacon, ham, salted herring, fatty cheese, and the like. Avoid heavy and greasy foods.

If life were predictable it would cease to be life, and be without flavor.
Eleanor Roosevelt

Virgo

Color: **Yellow**

Day: **Cool**

Element: **Earth**

Ω → ♍ 8:47 AM PST / 10:47 AM CST / 11:47 AM EST

7:34 PM PST / 9:34 PM CST / 10:34 PM EST ♍ → ♎

16 Thursday

17 Friday
No meat. Cutting and filing toenails and fingernails.

18 Saturday

J A N U A R Y

Positive affirmation:
"I am safe."

Planting Time
Descending forces! Sap is drawn downward, enhancing root formation.
Best days for sowing, planting, and transplanting.

detox
remove
be active

Waning Moon

Success

The artistic instinct rules, but so, too, does indecisiveness. The forces swing back and forth until equilibrium is achieved.

It's easy to reach compromises with tactful sensitivity.

A sense of judgment will support legal matters.

Leisure

Pursuit for harmony and cooperativeness supports good times in romance, friendship, and partnership.

Enjoy cultural events. Relax and get pampered with a spa treatment.

Romance can be passionate yet sensitive.

Health

Sensitive body parts:

Hips, Kidneys, Bladder

All measures taken to flush out and detoxify the sensitive body parts are very effective.

Good for surgery, except on the sensitive body parts (see above), knees, bones, joints, skin, lower legs, and veins. Scarring is less severe.

Teeth: Removal of tartar and amalgam. Best for fillings, crowns, and dentures! Avoid treatment of periodontitis and gums, avoid pulling teeth.

Blood-purifying, detoxifying herbal infusions and teas.

Sensitive glandular system.

Take special care to keep the area of the bladder and kidneys warm.

Apply special exercises for the hip region.

Sensitivity to light, so bring your sunglasses along.

Body Care

Aromas, scents: Roses, Violets, Daffodils

Prepare home-made ointments and cosmetics.

Apply detoxing facial and body care.

Treatments of bumps and pimples on the skin, and exfoliating procedures.

Removing body hair.

Correction of the nail bed.

Massages that serve to relax, ease tension, and detoxify.

Reflexology massage.

Removal of callused skin.

Treating obstinate athlete's foot, nail fungus, and warts.

Garden/Nature

Plant part:

Flower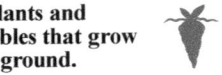

Sow plants and vegetables that grow below ground.

Dig over/plow to prepare soil for planting.

Trimming and cutting back plants.

Start a compost heap.

Weeding. Pest control.

Fertilize flowers that no longer bloom.

Transplanting.

Avoid watering plants.

Harvested produce should be consumed as soon as possible.

Gather herbs (roots) for kidneys, gall bladder and hip complaints.

Day off on 1/19.

Housework

Housework is dealt with much more successfully, efficiently, and effortlessly.

Problem stains are removed readily.

Best for doing laundry! Reduce on laundry detergent, support the environment.

Dry cleaning.

Clean and store seasonal clothing.

Thoroughly clean wooden and parquet floors, metals, china etc.

Cleaning windows and glass.

Cleaning, polishing, and waterproofing shoes.

Combating mold.

Ventilate rooms thoroughly.

Baking bread, cakes, and cookies (add more leavening agent).

Making preserves.

Painting.

Nutrition

Food quality:

Fat

Cauliflower, artichoke, broccoli, sunflower seeds, flax seeds, nuts, rose hip, elder.

Weight associated with overeating is less likely. If underweight, eat larger portions.

Cleansing and detox diets. Fruit and juice days.

Flush out poisons. Treatment for drug abuse.

Pay attention to any particularly tempting foods today: Most likely the "wrong" things taste best.

High cholesterol: eat a low fat diet.

Discover more about the lunar cycle and it's effects in the reference book "Nature's Daily Guide". ISBN 978-0-9854637-8-6

Nature's Daily Guide
The Influence of the Lunar Cycle

Whatever you can do or dream you can, begin it. For boldness has genius, power and magic in it.
Johann Wolfgang von Goethe

Color
Orange

Day
Air/Light

Element

Libra **Air**

19 Sunday

20 Monday
Martin Luther King Day (US)

J A N U A R Y

Planting Time
Descending forces! Sap is drawn downward, enhancing root formation. Best days for sowing, planting, and transplanting.

detox
remove
be active

Waning Moon

Success

Critical and superstitious behavior emerges, especially pertaining to money.

A penetrating power will strengthen your capacity to act.

An increased perception opens our interest for the essentials and helps to discover hidden potentials.

Leisure

Relax within your close family, with meditation, and relaxation exercises.

A longing to feel safe will be nurtured if you focus on habits and rituals. An increased sensitivity will help to enjoy every moment.

Romance can be very passionate.

If you plan outdoor excursions, be prepared for a shower here and there.

Health

Sensitive body parts:

Sex organs, Ureter

All measures taken to flush out and detoxify the sensitive body parts are very effective.

Good for surgical operations except those on the sensitive body parts (see above), lower legs, and veins. Scarring is less severe.

Teeth: Removal of tartar and amalgam. Best for fillings, crowns, and dentures!

Blood-purifying, detoxifying herbal infusions and teas.

Sensitive nervous system.

Female disorders: As a preventative measure apply hip baths using yarrow.

Pregnancy: Avoid any exertion, miscarriages are more likely.

Keep region of the pelvis, kidneys, and feet warm to prevent infection of the bladder and kidneys.

Lymphatic therapy.

Body Care

Aromas, scents:
Anemone, Cornflower
Oregano, Thuja

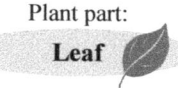

Prepare home-made ointments and cosmetics.

Apply detoxing facial and body care.

Treatments of bumps and pimples on the skin, and exfoliating procedures.

Removing body hair.

Correction of the nail bed.

Massages that serve to relax, ease tension, and detoxify.

Reflexology massage.

Removal of callused skin.

Treating obstinate athlete's foot, nail fungus, and warts.

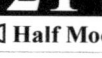

Garden/Nature

Plant part:

Leaf

Water plants.

Fertilize flowers and meadows, no vegetables.

Sow plants and vegetables that grow below ground, leaf vegetables, and lettuce.

Sowing, planting, harvesting, and drying every kind of medicinal herbs.

Dig over/plow to prepare soil for planting.

Trimming and cutting back plants. Transplanting. Weeding. Pest control. Start a compost heap.

Mowing lawns.

Harvested produce should be consumed as soon as possible.

Avoid cutting down trees, danger of bark beetles.

Housework

Housework is dealt with much more successfully, efficiently, and effortlessly.

Problem stains are removed readily.

Best for doing laundry! Reduce on laundry detergent, support the environment.

Dry cleaning.

Thoroughly clean wooden and parquet floors, metals, china etc.

Cleaning, polishing, and waterproofing shoes.

Combating mold.

Ventilate rooms briefly and rapidly.

Avoid painting.

Nutrition

Food quality:

Carbohydrate

Lettuce, spinach, lamb's lettuce, Endive, parsley, leek, cabbage (Brussels sprouts, kale, Chinese cabbage), all leafy herbs, asparagus, mushrooms, cress, Swiss chard, rhubarb.

Weight associated with overeating is less likely. If underweight, eat larger portions.

Cleansing and detox diets. Fruit and juice days.

Flush out poisons. Treatment for drug abuse.

The great obstacle is not ignorance but the illusion of knowledge.
Daniel Boorstin

Scorpio

Color
Red
Day
Wetness
Element
Water

Ω →♏ 8:21 AM PST
10:21 AM CST
11:21 AM EST

8:30 PM PST
10:30 PM CST
11:30 PM EST ♏ →♐

21 Tuesday
☽ Half Moon.

22 Wednesday
No meat.

23 Thursday

Positive affirmation:
"I am safe."

Planting Time
Descending forces!
Sap is drawn downward, enhancing root formation.
Best days for sowing, planting, and transplanting.

detox
remove
be active
Waning Moon

J A N U A R Y

Success

Inquisitiveness and exuberant inspiration lead to new horizons. Insight and love for truth reign.

Bringing together is more important than splitting asunder.

Expansive forces will assist in legal matters, discussions, and debates.

Leisure

Expansion feels great, and travel, short trips, and outings are most welcome. A competitive spirit excites any sports event.

Talk things out when necessary.

Romance can be very passionate.

Good days for outings; even with cloudy skies the air still feels somewhat warm. Drying effect, get plenty to drink.

Health

Sensitive body parts:

Thighs and Veins

All measures taken to flush out and detoxify the sensitive body parts are very effective.

Good for surgical operations except those on the sensitive body parts (see above), lower legs. Scarring is less severe.

Teeth: Removal of tartar and amalgam. Best for fillings, crowns, and dentures!

Blood-purifying, detoxifying herbal infusions and tea.

Sensitive sense organs.

Pains often arise in the sciatic nerve, veins, the small of the back, and thighs.

Avoid overstraining the body with unusual physical activities.

Body Care

Aromas, scents: Calendula (Marigold), Geranium, Rosemary

Prepare home-made ointments and cosmetics.

Apply detoxing facial and body care.

Treatments of bumps and pimples on the skin, and exfoliating procedures.

Removing body hair.

Correction of the nail bed.

Massages that serve to relax, ease tension, and detoxify.

Reflexology massage.

Removal of callused skin.

Treating obstinate athlete's foot, nail fungus, and warts.

Garden/Nature

Plant part:

Fruit

Sowing plants and vegetables that grow below ground.

Dig over/plow to prepare soil for planting.

Trimming and cutting back plants.

Pruning of fruit trees and bushes.

Cultivating grains, particularly corn.

Fertilize grains, vegetables, and fruit.

Combating pests above ground.

Weeding.

Gather herbs (roots) for vein diseases.

Avoid hoeing and harrowing.

Start a compost heap.

Housework

Housework is dealt with much more successfully, efficiently, and effortlessly.

Problem stains are removed readily.

Best for doing laundry!

Dry cleaning.

Thoroughly clean wooden and parquet floors, metals, china, etc.

Cleaning windows and glass.

Cleaning, polishing, and waterproofing shoes.

Combating mold.

Ventilate rooms sufficiently. Air beds.

Suitable for making cheese.

Preserving and freezing fruit and vegetables.

Baking bread, cakes, and cookies (use more leavening agent).

Painting.

Nutrition

Food quality:

Protein

Beans, peas, corn, tomatoes, pumpkin, lentils, soybeans, cucumber, eggplant, zucchini, berries, fruit, chili, bell pepper, figs, avocado, melon, olives.

Weight associated with overeating is less likely. If underweight, eat larger portions.

Cleansing and detox diets. Fruit and juice days.

Flush out poisons. Treatment for drug abuse.

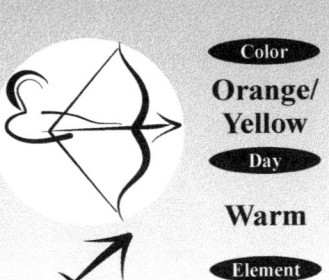

If one way be better than another, that you may be sure is nature's way.
Aristotle

Color
Orange/ Yellow

Day
Warm

Element

Sagittarius **Fire**

24 Friday

No meat. Cutting and filing toenails and fingernails.

25 Saturday

J A N U A R Y

Turning Point

Transition of descending to ascending forces. Both forces are at work and neutralize each other.

detox remove be active

Waning Moon

Success

Career and business are in the foreground now and thinking becomes clear and serious, but somewhat inflexible.

Perseverance and reasoning assist in financial matters, planning, and contracts.

The values of tradition, authority, and discipline impact our endeavors.

Leisure

Money is not likely to be wasted in a shopping spree.

Many are drawn to enjoy cultural events.

The earth feels cold to the touch, so take slightly warmer clothes.

Health

Sensitive body parts:

Knees, Joints, Bones, Skin

All measures taken to flush out and detoxify the sensitive body parts are very effective.

Good for surgery, except on the sensitive body parts (see above), lower legs, and veins. Scarring is less severe.

Teeth: Removal of tartar and amalgam. Best for fillings, crowns, and dentures!

Blood-purifying, detoxifying herbal infusions and teas.

Sensitive blood circulation.

Avoid overstraining bones and knees, and apply gentle stretching exercises only.

Problems with meniscus: Don't overstrain.

Dress slightly warmer.

High blood pressure: Avoid salty foods.

Massages, lymphatic therapy, and chiropractic treatment to release blockages.

Body Care

Aromas, scents:

Cedar, Juniper

Prepare home-made ointments and cosmetics.

Apply detoxing facial and body care.

Treatments of bumps and pimples on the skin, and exfoliating procedures.

Remove body hair, it may not grow back.

Correction of the nail bed.

Massages that serve to relax, ease tension, and detoxify.

Reflexology massage.

Treating obstinate athlete's foot, nail fungus, and warts.

Cutting and filing toenails and fingernails will make the nails grow stronger over time.

Garden/Nature

Plant part: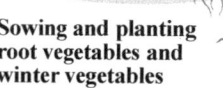

Root

Sowing and planting root vegetables and winter vegetables

Weeding. Harrowing weeds. Dig over to prepare soil. Trimming and cutting back plants.
Clear and thin out plants, forest edges, and hedges. Plant cuttings.
Spread fertilizer and manure.
Start a compost heap.
Combat vermin.

Fertilize flowers with poorly formed roots.

Mulching.

Harvest produce is suitable for storage. Harvest root vegetables.

Gather herbs (roots) for bone, joint, and skin diseases.

Housework

Housework is dealt with much more successfully, efficiently, and effortlessly.

Problem stains are removed readily.

Best for doing laundry! Reduce on laundry detergent, support the environment.

Avoid dry cleaning, as the fabric may develop unwanted glossy blotches.

Thoroughly clean wooden and parquet floors, metals, china etc.

Cleaning, polishing, and waterproofing shoes.

Combating mold.

Air rooms only briefly.

Painting.

Preserving root vegetables. Slice cabbage now to ferment into sauerkraut.

Nutrition

Food quality:

Salt

Garlic, carrots, red beets, reddish, rutabaga, sugar beet, celery, potatoes, onions, kohlrabi.

Weight associated with overeating is less likely. If underweight, eat larger portions.

Cleansing and detox diets. Fruit and juice days.

Flush out poisons. Treatment for drug abuse.

Avoid large quantities of salty foods like bacon, ham, salted herring, fatty cheese, and the like. Avoid heavy and greasy foods.

Birds sing after a storm; why shouldn't people feel as free to delight in whatever remains to them?
Rose Kennedy

Capricorn

Color: **Yellow**

Day: **Cool**

Element: **Earth**

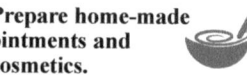

5:44 AM PST
7:44 AM CST
8:44 AM EST

26 Sunday

27 Monday
Isra and Mi'raj

11:33 AM PST
1:33 PM CST
2:33 PM EST

28 Tuesday

J A N U A R Y

Positive affirmation:
"I am safe."

Harvest Time
Ascending forces! Sap is rising, enhancing plant growth above ground, resulting in the most juicy fruits and vegetables.

detox
remove
be active

Waning Moon

Success

Inspiration, optimism, and impatience. Rational thinking, creativity and imagination spark new ideas and inspire planning for the future.

Shying away from routine tasks people will feel more drawn to anything new.

Instead of gridlocked structures choose new possibilities.

● *New Moon: Confirm your resolutions. Finalize new decisions. Drop bad habits.*

Leisure

Inspiration and optimism will boost friendship, social gatherings, and parties.

Express your creativity and imagination. Dwell in dreams and utopian ideas. It is easier now to perceive intuitive thoughts.

Health

Sensitive body parts:

Lower Legs, Veins

All measures taken to supply nutrient materials and strengthen the sensitive body parts are very effective.

Healing ointments are easily absorbed.

Sensitive glandular system.

Avoid inflammation of the veins. Apply ointments to lower legs, and rest legs in a raised position.

Varicose veins: Avoid long periods of standing.

While exercising go easy on the ankles.

Sensitivity to light, so bring your sunglasses along.

● *New Moon: Avoid any surgery if possible.*

Body Care

Aromas, scents: Cyclamen, Peach, Wild Roses

Treatments with firming and moisturizing creams are more effective.

Massages that serve to regenerate, and strengthen, perhaps aided with beneficial massage oils.

Correcting and cutting ingrown nails.

Hair dyes applied now, will look more vibrant.

Garden/Nature

Plant part:

Flower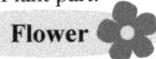

Avoid watering plants.

Harvested produce is well suitable for storage.

Gather herbs for vein diseases.

● *New Moon: Change of weather is likely. Care for sickly plants.*

Housework

Light housework only.

Ventilate rooms thoroughly.

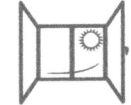

Baking cakes and cookies. Dough rises faster. (Except on New Moon)

Making preserves.

Nutrition

Food quality:

Fat

Cauliflower, artichoke, broccoli, sunflower seeds, flax seeds, nuts, rose hip, elder.

Weight gain: avoid indulging in rich foods. If overweight, eat smaller portions.

Supply nutrient materials to strengthen the body. Focus on foods that contain essential minerals and vitamins.

Stimulants and vitamins are more effective.

Pay attention to any particularly tempting foods today: Most likely the "wrong" things taste best.

High cholesterol: eat a low fat diet.

● *New Moon: A day of fasting.*

Positive affirmation:
"I trust for the best to develop."

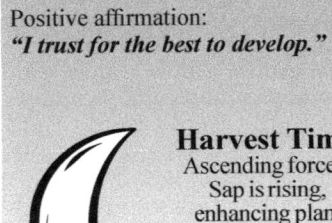

Harvest Time
Ascending forces! Sap is rising, enhancing plant growth above ground, resulting in the most juicy fruits and vegetables.

gather strength rest, recover buildup

Waxing Moon

2:54 PM PST
4:54 PM CST
5:54 PM EST

29 Wednesday
Chinese New Year
● **New Moon** 4:37 AM PST, 6:37 AM CST, 7:37 AM EST
No meat.

30 Thursday

J A N U A R Y

The pursuit of truth and beauty is a sphere of activity in which we are permitted to remain children all our lives.
Albert Einstein

Color
Bright/ Dark Blue

Day
Air/Light

Element

Air

Aquarius

Success

Sensibility, intuition, and helpfulness.

Where possible, retreating is more favorable than dealing with business matters.

Dissolve restrictions, be patient and wait. Be aware that people can be more easily influenced.

Leisure

Your helpfulness will boost friendships.

Enjoy dancing or swimming, or watch a movie that will inspire your fantasies and imagination.

Retreat, relax, and recover.

Romance can be gentle and coziness will prevail.

If you plan outdoor excursions, be prepared for a shower here and there.

Health

Sensitive body parts:

Feet and Toes

All measures taken to supply nutrient materials and strengthen the sensitive body parts are very effective.

Healing ointments are easily absorbed.

Sensitive nervous system.

Drugs have a much stronger effect on your body. Monitor closely what you put into your body.

Lymphatic therapy.

Sluggishness or fatigue may occur in the transition into the next Zodiac sign of Aries.

Body Care

Aromas, scents: Magnolia, Amaryllis, Clary Sage

Treatments with firming and moisturizing creams are more effective.

Massages that serve to regenerate, and strengthen, perhaps aided with beneficial massage oils. Reflexology massage. Carry out with special care, people are more sensitive.

Correcting and cutting ingrown nails.

Foot bath.

No haircuts, hair becomes shaggy and unmanageable. Avoid washing your hair. Dandruff could develop.

Garden/Nature

Plant part:

Leaf

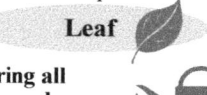

Watering all indoor and outdoor plants.

Sow plants, herbs, and vegetables that grow and flourish above ground, and leaf vegetables.

Transplanting.

Mowing lawns.

Avoid pruning fruit trees and bushes.

Harvested produce should be consumed as soon as possible.

Gather herbs for foot complaints.

Housework

Light housework only.

Ventilate rooms briefly and rapidly. Don't air mattresses.

Any dirt and spots are easily removed in the laundry.

Avoid painting, as paint will take very long to dry.

Preserving and storing should be avoided.

Nutrition

Food quality:

Carbohydrate

Lettuce, spinach, lamb's lettuce, Endive, parsley, leek, cabbage (Brussels sprouts, kale, Chinese cabbage), all leafy herbs, asparagus, mushrooms, cress, Swiss chard, rhubarb.

Weight gain: avoid indulging in rich foods. If overweight, eat smaller portions and avoid carbohydrates.

Supply nutrient materials to strengthen the body. Focus on foods that contain essential minerals and vitamins.

Caffeine, alcohol, drugs, certain foods, and stimulants have a much stronger effect.

Positive affirmation:
"I trust for the best to develop."

Harvest Time
Ascending forces! Sap is rising, enhancing plant growth above ground, resulting in the most juicy fruits and vegetables.

gather strength
rest, recover
buildup
Waxing Moon

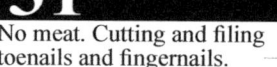

5:11 PM PST
7:11 PM CST ⟩)(→ ♈
8:11 PM EST

31 Friday

No meat. Cutting and filing toenails and fingernails.

1 Saturday
National Freedom Day

JANUARY/FEBRUARY

Everything has beauty, but not everyone sees it.
Confucius

Color
Blueish White

Day

Wetness

Element

Water

Pisces

Success

Things get going and the way straight ahead seems the best.

People feel energetic, courageous, assertive, and at times anxious.

Good time for meetings and sales talks but impatience and selfishness do not favor teamwork.

Leisure

An enterprising spirit and spontaneity move people to enjoy outings, sports, competitions, cultural events, and travels.

Romance can be very passionate.

Good days for outings, even with cloudy skies the air still feels somewhat warm. Drying effect, get plenty to drink.

Health

Sensitive body parts:

Head, Brain, Eyes

All measures taken to supply nutrient materials and strengthen the sensitive body parts are very effective.

Healing ointments are easily absorbed.

Sensitive sense organs.

If you suffer from migraines drink plenty of water, and avoid coffee, chocolate, and sugar.

Body Care

Aromas, scents: Cloves, Peppermint, Thyme

Treatments with firming and moisturizing creams are more effective.

Massages that serve to regenerate, and strengthen, perhaps aided with beneficial massage oils.

Correcting and cutting ingrown nails.

Eye compresses for strained eyes.

Any kind of hair care. Hair dyes applied now, will look more vibrant.

Garden/Nature

Plant part:

Fruit

Sow plants and vegetables that grow and flourish above ground, especially fruit and tomatoes.

Sowing and planting anything that is supposed to grow fast and for immediate use.

Grafting onto fruit trees.

Cultivating grains.

Transplanting.

Harvesting and storing grains, vegetables, potatoes, fruit, and tomatoes.

Gather herbs for eye complaints and headaches.

Day off on 2/2.

Housework

Light housework only.

Ventilate sufficiently.

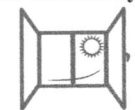

Preserving fruit.

Freezing fruit and vegetables.

Baking bread, cakes, and cookies. Dough rises faster. (Except on New Moon)

Suitable for making cheese.

Nutrition

Food quality:

Protein

Beans, peas, corn, tomatoes, pumpkin, lentils, soybeans, cucumber, eggplant, zucchini, berries, fruit, chili, bell pepper, figs, avocado, melon, olives.

Weight gain: avoid indulging in rich foods. If overweight, eat smaller portions.

Supply nutrient materials to strengthen the body. Focus on foods that contain essential minerals and vitamins.

Stimulants and vitamins are more effective.

Drink plenty of water.

Positive affirmation:
"I trust for the best to develop."

Harvest Time
Ascending forces! Sap is rising, enhancing plant growth above ground, resulting in the most juicy fruits and vegetables.

gather strength rest, recover buildup
Waxing Moon

7:35 PM PST
9:35 PM CST
10:35 PM EST ⟶ ♈ ➔ ♉

2 Sunday
Groundhog Day

3 Monday

F E B R U A R Y

If there is no struggle, there is no progress.
Frederick Douglass

 Color
Indigo Blue

 Day
Warm

Element
Fire   **Aries** ♈

Success

Realism and material security are important. Persistence comes easy, thoughts and reactions are slower.

Assess financial areas.

Conservative tendencies may make people want to stay away from risk taking.

Leisure

Relax at a picnic/feast. Enjoy culinary pleasures and hobbies.

The earth feels cold to the touch, so take slightly warmer clothes.

Health

Sensitive body parts:

Head and Neck

All measures taken to supply nutrient materials and strengthen the sensitive body parts are very effective.

Healing ointments are easily absorbed.

Sensitive blood circulation.

Organs of speech, jaws, teeth, tonsils, thyroid gland, neck, and vocal chords get easily affected. Keep neck warm. On cold days ears should be protected. Sensitivity to noise.

High blood pressure: Avoid salty foods.

Massages, lymphatic therapy, and chiropractic treatment to release blockages.

Body Care

Aromas, scents: Geranium, Jasmine, Rose

Treatments with firming and moisturizing creams are more effective.

Massages that serve to regenerate, and strengthen, perhaps aided with beneficial massage oils.

Correcting and cutting ingrown nails.

Hair dyes applied now, will look more vibrant.

Garden/Nature

Plant part: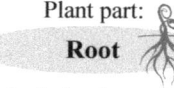

Root

Sow plants, herbs, and vegetables that grow and flourish above ground.

Sowing and planting trees, bushes, hedges, and root vegetables. Everything grows slowly and lasts well.

Transplanting.

Harvesting and storing root vegetables. Harvested produce is well suited for storage.

Gather herbs for sinus issues, sore throat, and ear complaints.

Housework

Light housework only.

Air rooms only briefly.

Preserving root vegetables.

Nutrition

Food quality:

Salt

Garlic, carrots, red beets, reddish, rutabaga, sugar beet, celery, potatoes, onions, kohlrabi.

Weight gain: avoid indulging in rich foods. If overweight, eat smaller portions.

Supply nutrient materials to strengthen the body. Focus on foods that contain essential minerals and vitamins.

Stimulants and vitamins are more effective.

Avoid large quantities of salty foods like bacon, ham, salted herring, fatty cheese, and the like.

Positive affirmation:
"I trust for the best to develop."

Harvest Time
Ascending forces! Sap is rising, enhancing plant growth above ground, resulting in the most juicy fruits and vegetables.

gather strength rest, recover buildup
Waxing Moon

4 Tuesday

5 Wednesday

☽ **Half Moon.** No meat.

Experience is one thing you can't get for nothing.
Oscar Wilde

Color
Bright Blue

Day
Cool

Element
Earth

Taurus

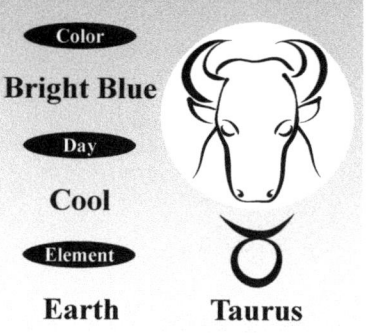

F E B R U A R Y

Success

Open mindedness and curiosity. A changeable and hectic time.

Good time for talking, negotiating, networking, and exchanging ideas as well as for meetings of a nonbinding nature, conferences, and studies.

Leisure

Good time for family gatherings, parties, and short trips.

People enjoy stimulating their minds with reading and studying. Attending theater performances is a preferred enjoyment. Enhance friendships.

Stretching exercises.

Be prepared for sudden changes in weather or climate.

Health

Sensitive body parts:

Shoulders, Arms, Hands, Lungs

All measures taken to supply nutrient materials and strengthen the sensitive body parts are very effective.

Healing ointments are easily absorbed. Applying herbal ointments to the shoulders for rheumatic gout and alike.

Sensitive glandular system.

Make sure you are dressed warm enough in cool weather.

Exercises for shoulders. Breathing exercises.

Avoid having any teeth pulled.

Sensitivity to light, bring your sunglasses along.

Massages, lymphatic therapy, and chiropractic treatment to release blockages.

Body Care

Aromas, scents:
Lavender, Lemon Balm, Magnolia, Verbena

Treatments with firming and moisturizing creams are more effective.

Massages that serve to regenerate, and strengthen, perhaps aided with beneficial massage oils.

Correcting and cutting ingrown nails.

Hair dyes applied now, will look more vibrant.

Garden/Nature

Plant part:

Flower

Sow plants, herbs, and vegetables that grow and flourish above ground.

Sowing and planting any creeping or climbing plants, flowers, and medicinal herbs.

Transplanting.

Avoid watering plants.

Gather herbs for tensions in the shoulder and lung complaints.

Changes in weather are more likely.

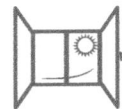

Discover more about the lunar cycle and it's effects in the reference book "Nature's Daily Guide". ISBN 978-0-9854637-8-6

Housework

Light housework only.

Ventilate rooms thoroughly.

Making preserves.

Baking cakes and cookies. Dough rises faster. (Except on New Moon)

Nutrition

Food quality:

Fat

Cauliflower, artichoke, broccoli, sunflower seeds, flax seeds, nuts, rose hip, elder.

Weight gain: avoid indulging in rich foods. If overweight, eat smaller portions.

Supply nutrient materials to strengthen the body. Focus on foods that contain essential minerals and vitamins.

Stimulants and vitamins are more effective.

Pay attention to any particularly tempting foods today: Most likely the "wrong" things taste best.

High cholesterol: eat a low fat diet.

Positive affirmation:
"I trust for the best to develop."

Turning Point

Transition of ascending to descending forces. Both forces are at work and neutralize each other.

gather strength rest, recover buildup

Waxing Moon

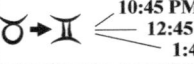

10:45 PM PST Wednesday
12:45 AM CST
1:45 AM EST

6 Thursday

7 Friday

No meat. Cutting and filing toenails and fingernails.

The key is to keep company only with people who uplift you, whose presence calls forth your best.
Epictetus

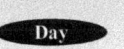
Color
Light Blue

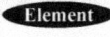
Day
Air/Light

Element

Air   **Gemini**

F E B R U A R Y

Success

Feelings, sensitivity, and cooperativeness. Many are overly sensitive, so beware of treading on someone's toes.

Be cautious if you are easily influenced.

During negotiations make use of the cognitive ability of your senses.

Leisure

Relax within your close family.

Retreat to your safe haven and enjoy your fantasy while reading or listening to music. The inner world becomes more colorful than the outer.

Romance can be gentle. Deep feelings will prevail.

If you plan outdoor excursions, be prepared for a shower here and there.

Health

Sensitive body parts:

Chest, Lungs, Liver, Stomach, Gall Bladder

All measures taken to supply nutrient materials and strengthen the sensitive body parts are very effective.

Healing ointments are easily absorbed.

Sensitive nervous system.

Be cautious with alcohol since the liver is very sensitive.

Stomach could play up and cause gas and heartburn.

Rheumatism: Don't air bedding outside, damp will remain in the bedding.

Lymphatic therapy.

Body Care

Aromas, scents:
Lilac, Lilies of the Valley, Lilies, Violets

Treatments with firming and moisturizing creams are more effective.

Massages that serve to regenerate, and strengthen, perhaps aided with beneficial massage oils.

Correcting and cutting ingrown nails.

No haircuts, hair becomes shaggy and unmanageable. Avoid washing your hair.

Garden/Nature

Plant part:

Leaf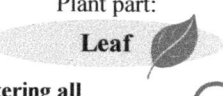

Watering all indoor and outdoor plants.

Sow plants, herbs, and vegetables that grow and flourish above ground, leaf vegetables (no lettuce).

Transplanting.

Trimming and cutting back plants. Avoid pruning fruit trees and bushes.

Cut trees, garlands, pick flowers to dry; they will last longer.

Sowing and mowing lawns.

Setting up a compost heap.

Gather herbs for bronchitis, stomach, liver, and gall bladder complaints.

Unfavorable for harvesting, storing, and preserving.

Housework

Light housework only.

Ventilate rooms briefly and rapidly. Don't air mattresses.

Any dirt and spots are easily removed in the laundry.

Avoid painting, as paint will take very long to dry.

Nutrition

Food quality:

Carbohydrate

Lettuce, spinach, lamb's lettuce, Endive, parsley, leek, cabbage (Brussels sprouts, kale, Chinese cabbage), all leafy herbs, asparagus, mushrooms, cress, Swiss chard, rhubarb.

Weight gain: avoid indulging in rich foods. If overweight, eat smaller portions and avoid carbohydrates. Moodiness may make you want to eat more than is healthy.

Supply nutrient materials to strengthen the body. Focus on foods that contain essential minerals and vitamins. Stimulants and vitamins are more effective.

If you get stomach troubles easily, avoid heavy meals.

Positive affirmation:
"I trust for the best to develop."

3:05 AM PST
♊ ➞ ♋ 5:05 AM CST
6:05 AM EST

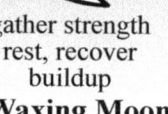

Planting Time
Descending forces! Sap is drawn downward, enhancing root formation. Best days for sowing, planting, and transplanting.

gather strength rest, recover buildup
Waxing Moon

8 Saturday

9 Sunday

There's no money in poetry, but then there's no poetry in money, either.
Robert Graves

Color
Green

Day
Wetness

Element
Water

Cancer

F E B R U A R Y

Success

Determination reigns, and risks are taken more often. Master your tasks with more self-confidence and creativity.

Limits appear to be more easily surmountable.

Auspicious day for sales, advertising, and publicity.

Leisure

Zest for life is in the air. People want to have a fun time, enjoy parties, musical events, movies, etc.

Possessive feelings can harm a relationship. Romance can be very passionate.

Outings: even with cloudy skies the air still feels somewhat warm. Drying effect, get plenty to drink.

Danger of sudden storms, not only in the sky.

Health

Sensitive body parts:
Heart, Back, Diaphragm, Circulation, Arteries

All measures taken to supply nutrient materials and strengthen the sensitive body parts are very effective.

Healing ointments are easily absorbed.

Sensitive sense organs.

Back and heart problems are more likely to occur.

Avoid over straining of the heart and circulation with unusual physical activities.

Expect sleepless nights.

Body Care

Aromas, scents:
Hibiscus, Oleander, Rose

Treatments with firming and moisturizing creams are more effective.

Massages that serve to regenerate, and strengthen, perhaps aided with beneficial massage oils.

Correcting and cutting ingrown nails.

Good days for haircuts, hair becomes stronger. But be aware that if you get a perm, curls will become quite frizzy. Baby's first haircut.

Garden/Nature

Plant part:

Fruit

Sow plants and vegetables that grow and flourish above ground. Sowing and planting fruit. Also sow and plant vegetables that are highly perishable. Plant trees and bushes. Sow lawns.

Transplanting. Grafting onto fruit trees.

Trimming and cutting back plants.

Best for cultivating grains on wet fields.

Dig over/plow to prepare soil for planting.

Setting up a compost heap.

Not suitable for fertilizing.

Harvested produce should be consumed as soon as possible.

Gather herbs for heart and circulation complaints.

Housework

Light housework only.

Ventilate sufficiently.

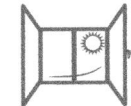

Freezing fruit and vegetables.

Baking bread, cakes, and cookies. Dough rises faster. (Except on New Moon)

Suitable for making cheese.

Avoid painting.

Nutrition

Food quality:
Protein

Beans, peas, corn, tomatoes, pumpkin, lentils, soybeans, cucumber, eggplant, zucchini, berries, fruit, chili, bell pepper, figs, avocado, melon, olives.

Weight gain: avoid indulging in rich foods. If overweight, eat smaller portions.

Supply nutrient materials to strengthen the body. Focus on foods that contain essential minerals and vitamins.

Stimulants and vitamins are more effective.

Positive affirmation:
"I trust for the best to develop."

Planting Time
Descending forces! Sap is drawn downward, enhancing root formation. Best days for sowing, planting, and transplanting.

gather strength rest, recover buildup

Waxing Moon

♋ → ♌
9:02 AM PST
11:02 AM CST
12:02 PM EST

10 Monday

11 Tuesday

F E B R U A R Y

All gardening is landscape painting.
William Kent

Color: **Green**

Day: **Warm**

Element: **Fire**

Leo ♌

Success

Determination reigns, and risks are taken more often. Master your tasks with more self-confidence and creativity.

Limits appear to be more easily surmountable.

Auspicious day for sales, advertising, and publicity.

Leisure

Zest for life is in the air. People want to have a fun time, enjoy parties, musical events, movies, etc.

Possessive feelings can harm a relationship. Romance can be very passionate.

Outings: even with cloudy skies the air still feels somewhat warm. Drying effect, get plenty to drink.

Danger of sudden storms, not only in the sky.

Health

Sensitive body parts:
Heart, Back, Diaphragm, Circulation, Arteries

All measures taken to flush out and detoxify the sensitive body parts are very effective.

Scarring is less severe.

Teeth: Removal of tartar and amalgam. Best for fillings, crowns, and dentures!

Blood-purifying, detoxifying herbal infusions and teas.

Sensitive sense organs.

Back and heart problems are more likely to occur.

Avoid overstraining of the heart and circulation with unusual physical activities.

Expect sleepless nights.

○ *Full Moon: Avoid any surgery and vaccination if possible.*

Body Care

Aromas, scents:
Hibiscus, Oleander, Rose

Prepare home-made ointments and cosmetics.

Apply detoxing facial and body care.

Treatments of bumps and pimples on the skin, and exfoliating procedures.

Removing body hair.

Correction of the nail bed.

Massages that serve to relax, ease tension, and detoxify.

Reflexology massage.

Removal of callused skin.

Treating obstinate athlete's foot, nail fungus, and warts.

Good days for haircuts, hair becomes stronger. But be aware that if you get a perm, curls will become quite frizzy. Baby's first haircut.

Garden/Nature

Plant part:
Fruit

Sowing plants and vegetables that grow below ground.

Sowing and planting fruit. Also sow and plant vegetables that are highly perishable. Plant trees and bushes. Sow lawns.

Dig over/plow to prepare soil for planting.

Trimming and cutting back plants. Pruning of fruit trees and bushes. Transplanting. Not suitable for fertilizing. Weeding. Pest Control.

Harvested produce should be consumed as soon as possible.

Gather herbs (roots) for heart and circulation complaints.

Start compost heap.

○ *Full Moon: Weather and climate changes. Herbs are most powerful.*

Housework

Housework is dealt with much more successfully, efficiently, and effortlessly.

Problem stains are removed readily.

Dry cleaning.

Thoroughly clean wooden and parquet floors, metals, china, etc.

Cleaning, polishing, and waterproofing shoes.

Combating mold.

Ventilate rooms sufficiently. Air beds.

Suitable for making cheese.

Freezing fruit and vegetables.

Baking bread, cakes, and cookies (use more leavening agent).

○ *Full Moon: Avoid doing laundry, cleaning windows, making preserves, painting.*

Nutrition

Food quality:
Protein

Beans, peas, corn, tomatoes, pumpkin, lentils, soybeans, cucumber, eggplant, zucchini, berries, fruit, chili, bell pepper, figs, avocado, melon, olives.

Weight associated with overeating is less likely. If underweight, eat larger portions.

Cleansing and detox diets. Fruit and juice days.

Flush out poisons. Treatment for drug abuse.

○ *Full Moon: A day of fasting.*

If we have no peace, it is because we have forgotten that we belong to each other.
Mother Teresa

Color
Green

Day
Warm

Element
Fire

♌ **Leo**

5:08 PM PST
7:08 PM CST
8:08 PM EST
♌ → ♍

12 Wednesday
Lincoln's Birthday (US)

○ **Full Moon** 5:55 AM PST, 7:55 AM CST, 8:55 AM EST
No meat.

F E B R U A R Y

Positive affirmation:
"I trust for the best to develop."

Planting Time
Descending forces! Sap is drawn downward, enhancing root formation. Best days for sowing, planting, and transplanting.

detox remove be active
Waning Moon

Success

Good time for details, organization, routine, concentration, and duty.

Take care of financial and administrative tasks.

Prepare for future success now with realistic and critical assessment.

Leisure

Enjoy a nature walk.

Good time for health regimes. Improve your health with stretching exercises and yoga.

The earth feels cold to the touch, so take slightly warmer clothes.

Health

Sensitive body parts:
Digestive Organs, Nerves, Spleen, Pancreas

All measures taken to flush out and detoxify the sensitive body parts are very effective.

Good for surgery, except on the sensitive body parts (see above), lower legs, and veins. Scarring is less severe.

Teeth: Removal of tartar and amalgam. Best for fillings, crowns, and dentures! Avoiding treatment of periodontitis and gums.

Blood-purifying, detoxifying herbal infusions and teas.

Sensitive blood circulation.

For a sensitive digestive system, a wholesome diet is recommended.

Dress slightly warmer.

High blood pressure: Avoid salty foods.

Massages, lymphatic therapy, and chiropractic treatment to release blockages.

Body Care

Aromas, scents:
Lavender, Spruce Needles, Sage, Meadow Flowers

Prepare home-made ointments and cosmetics.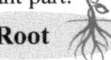

Apply detoxing facial and body care.

Treatments of bumps and pimples on the skin, and exfoliating procedures.

Removing body hair.

Correction of the nail bed.

Massages that serve to relax, ease tension, and detoxify.

Reflexology massage.

Removal of callused skin.

Treating obstinate athlete's foot, nail fungus, and warts.

Best for haircuts because it retains its shape longer. Perms turn out best.

Garden/Nature

Plant part:
Root

Best for sowing and planting, except lettuce.

Plant trees which are supposed to grow very tall. Plant hedges and bushes that are meant to grow very fast.

Planting and re-potting balcony and indoor plants.

Dig over/plow to prepare soil for planting.

Trimming and cutting back plants. Planting cuttings.

Spread fertilizer and manure. Fertilize flowers with poorly formed roots.

Start a compost heap.

Transplanting. Mulching.

Weeding. Pest control (vermin in the soil).

Avoid harvesting and storing.

Gather herbs (roots) for digestive organs, pancreas, and nervous complaints.

Housework

Housework is dealt with much more successfully, efficiently, and effortlessly.

Problem stains are removed readily.

Best for doing laundry! Reduce on laundry detergent, support the environment.

Dry cleaning.

Thoroughly clean wooden and parquet floors, metals, china etc.

Cleaning, polishing, and waterproofing shoes.

Combating mold.

Air rooms only briefly.

Painting.

Making pickles, preserves, and cheese yields suboptimal results and should be avoided.

Nutrition

Food quality:
Salt

Garlic, carrots, red beets, reddish, rutabaga, sugar beet, celery, potatoes, onions, kohlrabi.

Weight associated with overeating is less likely. If underweight, eat larger portions.

Cleansing and detox diets. Fruit and juice days.

Flush out poisons. Treatment for drug abuse.

Avoid large quantities of salty foods like bacon, ham, salted herring, fatty cheese, and the like. Avoid heavy and greasy foods.

To keep the body in good health is a duty... otherwise we shall not be able to keep our mind strong and clear.
Buddha

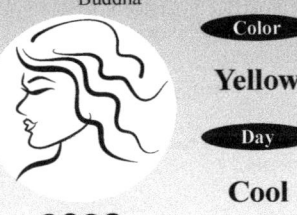

Color — Yellow

Day — Cool

Element — Earth

♍ Virgo

13 Thursday
Tu B'Shevat

14 Friday Valentine's Day, Laylat al Bara'at
No meat. Cutting and filing toenails and fingernails.

F E B R U A R Y

Positive affirmation:
"I trust for the best to develop."

Planting Time
Descending forces! Sap is drawn downward, enhancing root formation. Best days for sowing, planting, and transplanting.

detox remove be active

Waning Moon

Success

The artistic instinct rules, but so, too, does indecisiveness. The forces swing back and forth until equilibrium is achieved.

It's easy to reach compromises with tactful sensitivity.

A sense of judgment will support legal matters.

Leisure

Pursuit for harmony and cooperativeness supports good times in romance, friendship, and partnership.

Enjoy cultural events. Relax and get pampered with a spa treatment.

Romance can be passionate yet sensitive.

Health

Sensitive body parts:

Hips, Kidneys, Bladder

All measures taken to flush out and detoxify the sensitive body parts are very effective.

Good for surgical operations except those on the sensitive body parts (see above), lower legs, and veins. Scarring is less severe.

Teeth: Removal of tartar and amalgam. Best for fillings, crowns, and dentures! Avoid treatment of periodontitis and gums, avoid pulling teeth.

Blood-purifying, detoxifying herbal infusions and teas.

Sensitive glandular system.

Take special care to keep the area of the bladder and kidneys warm.

Apply special exercises for the hip region.

Sensitivity to light, so bring your sunglasses along.

Body Care

Aromas, scents: Roses, Violets, Daffodils

Prepare home-made ointments and cosmetics.

Apply detoxing facial and body care.

Treatments of bumps and pimples on the skin, and exfoliating procedures.

Removing body hair.

Correction of the nail bed.

Massages that serve to relax, ease tension, and detoxify.

Reflexology massage.

Removal of callused skin.

Treating obstinate athlete's foot, nail fungus, and warts.

Garden/Nature

Plant part:

Flower

Sow plants and vegetables that grow below ground.

Dig over/plow to prepare soil for planting.

Trimming and cutting back plants.

Start a compost heap.

Weeding. Pest control.

Fertilize flowers that no longer bloom.

Transplanting.

Avoid watering plants.

Harvested produce should be consumed as soon as possible.

Gather herbs (roots) for kidneys, gall bladder and hip complaints.

Day off on 2/16.

Housework

Housework is dealt with much more successfully, efficiently, and effortlessly.

Problem stains are removed readily.

Best for doing laundry! Reduce on laundry detergent, support the environment.

Dry cleaning.

Clean and store seasonal clothing.

Thoroughly clean wooden and parquet floors, metals, china etc.

Cleaning windows and glass.

Cleaning, polishing, and waterproofing shoes.

Combating mold.

Ventilate rooms thoroughly.

Baking bread, cakes, and cookies (add more leavening agent).

Making preserves.

Painting.

Nutrition

Food quality:

Fat

Cauliflower, artichoke, broccoli, sunflower seeds, flax seeds, nuts, rose hip, elder.

Weight associated with overeating is less likely. If underweight, eat larger portions.

Cleansing and detox diets. Fruit and juice days.

Flush out poisons. Treatment for drug abuse.

Pay attention to any particularly tempting foods today: Most likely the "wrong" things taste best.

High cholesterol: eat a low fat diet.

I think the next best thing to solving a problem is finding some humor in it.
Frank Howard Clark

Color Orange

Day Air/Light

Element

Libra — Air

MP ➔ ♎
3:46 AM PST
5:46 AM CST
6:46 AM EST

♎ ➔ ♏
4:20 PM PST
6:20 PM CST
7:20 PM EST

15 Saturday

16 Sunday

17 Monday President's Day (US)

F E B R U A R Y

Planting Time
Descending forces! Sap is drawn downward, enhancing root formation. Best days for sowing, planting, and transplanting.

detox remove be active

Waning Moon

Success

Critical and superstitious behavior emerges, especially pertaining to money.

A penetrating power will strengthen your capacity to act.

An increased perception opens our interest for the essentials and helps to discover hidden potentials.

Leisure

Relax within your close family, with meditation, and relaxation exercises.

A longing to feel safe will be nurtured if you focus on habits and rituals. An increased sensitivity will help to enjoy every moment.

Romance can be very passionate.

If you plan outdoor excursions, be prepared for a shower here and there.

Health

Sensitive body parts:

Sex organs, Ureter

All measures taken to flush out and detoxify the sensitive body parts are very effective.

Good for surgical operations except those on the sensitive body parts (see above), lower legs, and veins. Scarring is less severe.

Teeth: Removal of tartar and amalgam. Best for fillings, crowns, and dentures!

Blood-purifying, detoxifying herbal infusions and teas.

Sensitive nervous system.

Female disorders: As a preventative measure apply hip baths using yarrow.

Pregnancy: Avoid any exertion, miscarriages are more likely.

Keep region of the pelvis, kidneys, and feet warm to prevent infection of the bladder and kidneys.

Lymphatic therapy.

Body Care

Aromas, scents:
Anemone, Cornflower
Oregano, Thuja

Prepare home-made ointments and cosmetics.

Apply detoxing facial and body care.

Treatments of bumps and pimples on the skin, and exfoliating procedures.

Removing body hair.

Correction of the nail bed.

Massages that serve to relax, ease tension, and detoxify.

Reflexology massage.

Removal of callused skin.

Treating obstinate athlete's foot, nail fungus, and warts.

Garden/Nature

Plant part:
Leaf

Water plants.

Fertilize flowers and meadows, no vegetables.

Sow plants and vegetables that grow below ground, leaf vegetables, and lettuce.

Sowing, planting, harvesting, and drying every kind of medicinal herbs.

Dig over/plow to prepare soil for planting.

Trimming and cutting back plants. Transplanting. Weeding. Pest control. Start a compost heap.

Mowing lawns.

Harvested produce should be consumed as soon as possible.

Avoid cutting down trees, danger of bark beetles.

Housework

Housework is dealt with much more successfully, efficiently, and effortlessly.

Problem stains are removed readily.

Best for doing laundry! Reduce on laundry detergent, support the environment.

Dry cleaning.

Thoroughly clean wooden and parquet floors, metals, china etc.

Cleaning, polishing, and waterproofing shoes.

Combating mold.

Ventilate rooms briefly and rapidly.

Avoid painting.

Nutrition

Food quality:
Carbohydrate

Lettuce, spinach, lamb's lettuce, Endive, parsley, leek, cabbage (Brussels sprouts, kale, Chinese cabbage), all leafy herbs, asparagus, mushrooms, cress, Swiss chard, rhubarb.

Weight associated with overeating is less likely. If underweight, eat larger portions.

Cleansing and detox diets. Fruit and juice days.

Flush out poisons. Treatment for drug abuse.

If you don't have a goal that's anchored in your heart, then you're going to give up.
Craig Miller

Scorpio ♏

Color **Red**

Day **Wetness**

Element **Water**

18 Tuesday

19 Wednesday

No meat.

F E B R U A R Y

Positive affirmation:
"I trust for the best to develop."

Planting Time
Descending forces!
Sap is drawn downward, enhancing root formation.
Best days for sowing, planting, and transplanting.

detox
remove
be active

Waning Moon

Success

Inquisitiveness and exuberant inspiration lead to new horizons. Insight and love for truth reign.

Bringing together is more important than splitting asunder.

Expansive forces will assist in legal matters, discussions, and debates.

Leisure

Expansion feels great, and travel, short trips, and outings are most welcome. A competitive spirit excites any sports event.

Talk things out when necessary.

Romance can be very passionate.

Good days for outings; even with cloudy skies the air still feels somewhat warm. Drying effect, get plenty to drink.

Health

Sensitive body parts:

Thighs and Veins

All measures taken to flush out and detoxify the sensitive body parts are very effective.

Good for surgical operations except those on the sensitive body parts (see above), feet, and toes. Scarring is less severe.

Teeth: Removal of tartar and amalgam. Best for fillings, crowns, and dentures!

Blood-purifying, detoxifying herbal infusions and tea.

Sensitive sense organs.

Pains often arise in the sciatic nerve, veins, the small of the back, and thighs.

Avoid overstraining the body with unusual physical activities.

Body Care

Aromas, scents: Calendula (Marigold), Geranium, Rosemary

Prepare home-made ointments and cosmetics.

Apply detoxing facial and body care.

Treatments of bumps and pimples on the skin, and exfoliating procedures.

Removing body hair.

Correction of the nail bed.

Massages that serve to relax, ease tension, and detoxify.

Reflexology massage.

Removal of callused skin.

Treating obstinate athlete's foot, nail fungus, and warts.

Garden/Nature

Plant part:

Fruit

Sowing plants and vegetables that grow below ground.

Dig over/plow to prepare soil for planting.

Trimming and cutting back plants.

Pruning of fruit trees and bushes.

Cultivating grains, particularly corn.

Fertilize grains, vegetables, and fruit.

Combating pests above ground.

Weeding.

Gather herbs (roots) for vein diseases.

Avoid hoeing and harrowing.

Start a compost heap.

Housework

Housework is dealt with much more successfully, efficiently, and effortlessly.

Problem stains are removed readily.

Best for doing laundry!

Dry cleaning.

Thoroughly clean wooden and parquet floors, metals, china, etc.

Cleaning windows and glass.

Cleaning, polishing, and waterproofing shoes.

Combating mold.

Ventilate rooms sufficiently. Air beds.

Suitable for making cheese.

Preserving and freezing fruit and vegetables.

Baking bread, cakes, and cookies (use more leavening agent).

Painting.

Nutrition

Food quality:

Protein

Beans, peas, corn, tomatoes, pumpkin, lentils, soybeans, cucumber, eggplant, zucchini, berries, fruit, chili, bell pepper, figs, avocado, melon, olives.

Weight associated with overeating is less likely. If underweight, eat larger portions.

Cleansing and detox diets. Fruit and juice days.

Flush out poisons. Treatment for drug abuse.

Beauty is eternity gazing at itself in a mirror.
Khalil Gibran

Sagittarius

Color
Orange/Yellow

Day
Warm

Element
Fire

4:56 AM PST
6:56 AM CST
7:56 AM EST

3:10 PM PST
5:10 PM CST
6:10 PM EST

20 Thursday
☽ Half Moon.

21 Friday
No meat. Cutting and filing toenails and fingernails.

22 Saturday

F E B R U A R Y

Positive affirmation:
"I trust for the best to develop."

Turning Point

Transition of descending to ascending forces. Both forces are at work and neutralize each other.

detox remove be active

Waning Moon

Success

Career and business are in the foreground now and thinking becomes clear and serious, but somewhat inflexible.

Perseverance and reasoning assist in financial matters, planning, and contracts.

The values of tradition, authority, and discipline impact our endeavors.

Leisure

Money is not likely to be wasted in a shopping spree.

Many are drawn to enjoy cultural events.

The earth feels cold to the touch, so take slightly warmer clothes.

Health

Sensitive body parts:

Knees, Joints, Bones, Skin

All measures taken to flush out and detoxify the sensitive body parts are very effective.

Good for surgical operations except those on the sensitive body parts (see above), feet, and toes. Scarring is less severe.

Teeth: Removal of tartar and amalgam. Best for fillings, crowns, and dentures!

Blood-purifying, detoxifying herbal infusions and teas.

Sensitive blood circulation.

Avoid overstraining bones and knees, and apply gentle stretching exercises only.

Problems with meniscus: Don't overstrain.

Dress slightly warmer.

High blood pressure: Avoid salty foods.

Massages, lymphatic therapy, and chiropractic treatment to release blockages.

Body Care

Aromas, scents:

Cedar, Juniper

Prepare home-made ointments and cosmetics.

Apply detoxing facial and body care.

Treatments of bumps and pimples on the skin, and exfoliating procedures.

Remove body hair, it may not grow back.

Correction of the nail bed.

Massages that serve to relax, ease tension, and detoxify.

Reflexology massage.

Treating obstinate athlete's foot, nail fungus, and warts.

Cutting and filing toenails and fingernails will make the nails grow stronger over time.

Garden/Nature

Plant part:

Root

Sowing and planting root vegetables and winter vegetables

Weeding. Harrowing weeds. Dig over to prepare soil. Trimming and cutting back plants.
Clear and thin out plants, forest edges, and hedges. Plant cuttings.
Spread fertilizer and manure.
Start a compost heap.
Combat vermin.

Fertilize flowers with poorly formed roots.

Mulching.

Harvest produce is suitable for storage. Harvest root vegetables.

Gather herbs (roots) for bone, joint, and skin diseases.

Housework

Housework is dealt with much more successfully, efficiently, and effortlessly.

Problem stains are removed readily.

Best for doing laundry! Reduce on laundry detergent, support the environment.

Avoid dry cleaning, as the fabric may develop unwanted glossy blotches.

Thoroughly clean wooden and parquet floors, metals, china etc.

Cleaning, polishing, and waterproofing shoes.

Combating mold.

Air rooms only briefly.

Painting.

Preserving root vegetables. Slice cabbage now to ferment into sauerkraut.

Nutrition

Food quality:

Salt

Garlic, carrots, red beets, reddish, rutabaga, sugar beet, celery, potatoes, onions, kohlrabi.

Weight associated with overeating is less likely. If underweight, eat larger portions.

Cleansing and detox diets. Fruit and juice days.

Flush out poisons. Treatment for drug abuse.

Avoid large quantities of salty foods like bacon, ham, salted herring, fatty cheese, and the like. Avoid heavy and greasy foods.

I go to nature to be soothed and healed, and to have my senses put in order.
John Burroughs

Capricorn

Color — **Yellow**

Day — **Cool**

Element — **Earth**

9:41 PM PST
11:41 PM CST
Tuesday 12:41 AM EST

23 Sunday

24 Monday

F E B R U A R Y

Positive affirmation:
"I trust for the best to develop."

Harvest Time
Ascending forces! Sap is rising, enhancing plant growth above ground, resulting in the most juicy fruits and vegetables.

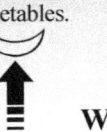

detox
remove
be active

Waning Moon

Success

Inspiration, optimism, and impatience. Rational thinking, creativity and imagination spark new ideas and inspire planning for the future.

Shying away from routine tasks people will feel more drawn to anything new.

Instead of gridlocked structures choose new possibilities.

Leisure

Inspiration and optimism will boost friendship, social gatherings, and parties.

Express your creativity and imagination. Dwell in dreams and utopian ideas. It is easier now to perceive intuitive thoughts.

Health

Sensitive body parts:

Lower Legs, Veins

All measures taken to flush out and detoxify the sensitive body parts are very effective.

Good for surgery, except on the sensitive body parts (see above), feet, and toes. Scarring is less severe.

Teeth: Removal of tartar and amalgam. Best for fillings, crowns, and dentures!

Blood-purifying, detoxifying herbal infusions and teas.

Sensitive glandular system.

Avoid inflammation of the veins. Apply ointments to lower legs, and rest legs in a raised position.

Varicose veins: Avoid long periods of standing.

While exercising go easy on the ankles.

Sensitivity to light, so bring your sunglasses along.

Body Care

Aromas, scents: Cyclamen, Peach, Wild Roses

Prepare home-made ointments and cosmetics.

Apply detoxing facial and body care.

Treatments of bumps and pimples on the skin, and exfoliating procedures.

Removing body hair.

Correction of the nail bed.

Massages that serve to relax, ease tension, and detoxify.

Reflexology massage.

Removal of callused skin.

Treating obstinate athlete's foot, nail fungus, and warts.

Garden/Nature

Plant part:

Flower

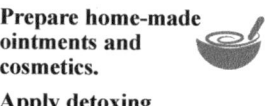

Fertilize flowers that no longer bloom.

Dig over/plow to prepare soil for planting.

Trimming and cutting back plants.

Hoeing and harrowing; weeds can be left to rot.

Pest control.

Start a compost heap.

Avoid watering plants.

Avoid transplanting sprouts.

Harvested produce is well suitable for storage.

Gather herbs (roots) for vein diseases.

Housework

Housework is dealt with much more successfully, efficiently, and effortlessly.

Problem stains are removed readily.

Best for doing laundry! Reduce on laundry detergent, support the environment.

Dry cleaning.

Clean and store seasonal clothing.

Best suited for a spring cleaning: Thoroughly clean wooden and parquet floors, metals, china etc.

Cleaning windows and glass.

Cleaning, polishing, and waterproofing shoes.

Combating mold.

Ventilate rooms thoroughly.

Baking bread, cakes, and cookies (add more leavening agent).

Making preserves.

Painting.

Nutrition

Food quality:

Fat

Cauliflower, artichoke, broccoli, sunflower seeds, flax seeds, nuts, rose hip, elder.

Weight associated with overeating is less likely. If underweight, eat larger portions.

Cleansing and detox diets. Fruit and juice days.

Flush out poisons. Treatment for drug abuse.

Pay attention to any particularly tempting foods today: Most likely the "wrong" things taste best.

High cholesterol: eat a low fat diet.

Come forth into the light of things, let nature be your teacher.
William Wordsworth

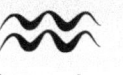

Color
Bright/ Dark Blue

Day

Air/Light

Element

Aquarius   **Air**

25 Tuesday Maha Shivaratri	**26** Wednesday
	No meat.

Positive affirmation:
"I trust for the best to develop."

Harvest Time
Ascending forces! Sap is rising, enhancing plant growth above ground, resulting in the most juicy fruits and vegetables.

detox remove be active
Waning Moon

F E B R U A R Y

Success

Sensibility, intuition, and helpfulness.

Where possible, retreating is more favorable than dealing with business matters.

Dissolve restrictions, be patient and wait. Be aware that people can be more easily influenced.

● *New Moon: Confirm your resolutions. Finalize new decisions. Drop bad habits.*

Leisure

Your helpfulness will boost friendships.

Enjoy dancing or swimming, or watch a movie that will inspire your fantasies and imagination.

Retreat, relax, and recover.

Romance can be gentle and coziness will prevail.

If you plan outdoor excursions, be prepared for a shower here and there.

Health

Sensitive body parts:

Feet and Toes

All measures taken to flush out and detoxify the sensitive body parts are very effective.

Scarring is less severe.

Teeth: Removal of tartar and amalgam. Best for fillings, crowns, and dentures!

Blood-purifying, detoxifying herbal infusions and teas.

Sensitive nervous system.

Drugs have a much stronger effect on your body. Monitor closely what you put into your body.

Lymphatic therapy.

Sluggishness or fatigue may occur in the transition into the next Zodiac sign of Aries.

● *New Moon: Avoid any surgery if possible.*

Body Care

Aromas, scents: Magnolia, Amaryllis, Clary Sage

Prepare home-made ointments and cosmetics.

Apply detoxing facial and body care.

Treatments of bumps and pimples on the skin, and exfoliating procedures.

Removing body hair.

Correction of the nail bed.

Massages that serve to relax, ease tension, and detoxify. Reflexology massage. Carry out with special care, people are more sensitive.

Removal of callused skin.

Treating obstinate athlete's foot, nail fungus, and warts.

Foot bath.

No haircuts, hair becomes shaggy and unmanageable. Avoid washing your hair.

Garden/Nature

Plant part:

Leaf

Water plants.

Fertilize flowers.

Sow plants and vegetables that grow below ground, potatoes, leaf vegetables, and lettuce.

Dig over/plow to prepare soil for planting.
Trimming and cutting back plants.
Start a compost heap.

Mowing lawns.

Pest control. Weeding.

Harvested produce should be consumed as soon as possible.

Gather herbs for foot complaints.

● *New Moon: Change of weather is likely. Care for sickly plants.*

Housework

Housework is dealt with much more successfully, efficiently, and effortlessly.

Problem stains are removed readily.

Best for doing laundry! Reduce on laundry detergent, support the environment.

Dry cleaning.

Clean and store seasonal clothing.

Thoroughly clean wooden and parquet floors, metals, china etc.

Cleaning, polishing, and waterproofing shoes.

Combating mold.

Ventilate rooms briefly and rapidly.

Avoid painting.

Preserving and storing should be avoided.

Nutrition

Food quality:

Carbohydrate

Lettuce, spinach, lamb's lettuce, Endive, parsley, leek, cabbage (Brussels sprouts, kale, Chinese cabbage), all leafy herbs, asparagus, mushrooms, cress, Swiss chard, rhubarb.

Weight associated with overeating is less likely. If underweight, eat larger portions.

Cleansing and detox diets. Fruit and juice days.

Flush out poisons. Treatment for drug abuse.

Caffeine, alcohol, drugs, certain foods, and stimulants have a much stronger effect.

● *New Moon: A day of fasting.*

Life belongs to the living, and he who lives must be prepared for changes.
Johann Wolfgang von Goethe

Positive affirmation:
"I trust for the best to develop."

Color
Blueish White
Day
Wetness
Element

Pisces **Water**

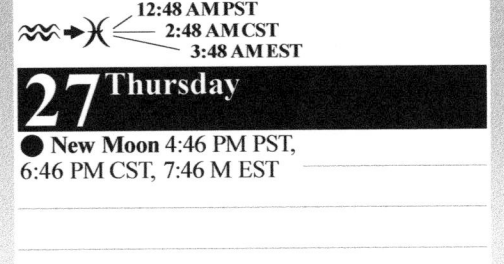

♒ → ♓
12:48 AM PST
2:48 AM CST
3:48 AM EST

27 Thursday

● New Moon 4:46 PM PST, 6:46 PM CST, 7:46 M EST

F E B R U A R Y

Harvest Time
Ascending forces! Sap is rising, enhancing plant growth above ground, resulting in the most juicy fruits and vegetables.

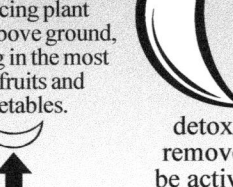

detox remove be active

Waning Moon

Success

Sensibility, intuition, and helpfulness.

Where possible, retreating is more favorable than dealing with business matters.

Dissolve restrictions, be patient and wait. Be aware that people can be more easily influenced.

Leisure

Your helpfulness will boost friendships.

Enjoy dancing or swimming, or watch a movie that will inspire your fantasies and imagination.

Retreat, relax, and recover.

Romance can be gentle and coziness will prevail.

If you plan outdoor excursions, be prepared for a shower here and there.

Health

Sensitive body parts:

Feet and Toes

All measures taken to supply nutrient materials and strengthen the sensitive body parts are very effective.

Healing ointments are easily absorbed.

Sensitive nervous system.

Drugs have a much stronger effect on your body. Monitor closely what you put into your body.

Lymphatic therapy.

Sluggishness or fatigue may occur in the transition into the next Zodiac sign of Aries.

Body Care

Aromas, scents: Magnolia, Amaryllis, Clary Sage

Treatments with firming and moisturizing creams are more effective.

Massages that serve to regenerate, and strengthen, perhaps aided with beneficial massage oils. Reflexology massage. Carry out with special care, people are more sensitive.

Correcting and cutting ingrown nails.

Foot bath.

No haircuts, hair becomes shaggy and unmanageable. Avoid washing your hair. Dandruff could develop.

Garden/Nature

Plant part:

Leaf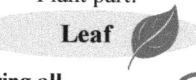

Watering all indoor and outdoor plants.

Sow plants, herbs, and vegetables that grow and flourish above ground, and leaf vegetables.

Transplanting.

Mowing lawns.

Avoid pruning fruit trees and bushes.

Harvested produce should be consumed as soon as possible.

Gather herbs for foot complaints.

Housework

Light housework only.

Ventilate rooms briefly and rapidly. Don't air mattresses.

Any dirt and spots are easily removed in the laundry.

Avoid painting, as paint will take very long to dry.

Preserving and storing should be avoided.

Nutrition

Food quality:

Carbohydrate

Lettuce, spinach, lamb's lettuce, Endive, parsley, leek, cabbage (Brussels sprouts, kale, Chinese cabbage), all leafy herbs, asparagus, mushrooms, cress, Swiss chard, rhubarb.

Weight gain: avoid indulging in rich foods. If overweight, eat smaller portions and avoid carbohydrates.

Supply nutrient materials to strengthen the body. Focus on foods that contain essential minerals and vitamins.

Caffeine, alcohol, drugs, certain foods, and stimulants have a much stronger effect.

Positive affirmation:
"I trust in the beneficial rhythms of nature."

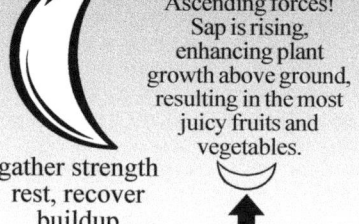

Harvest Time
Ascending forces! Sap is rising, enhancing plant growth above ground, resulting in the most juicy fruits and vegetables.

gather strength
rest, recover
buildup
Waxing Moon

28 Friday

No meat. Cutting and filing toenails and fingernails.

F E B R U A R Y

Experience enables you to recognize a mistake when you make it again.
Franklin P. Jones

Color
Blueish White

Day
Wetness

Element
Water

Pisces

Success

Things get going and the way straight ahead seems the best.

People feel energetic, courageous, assertive, and at times anxious.

Good time for meetings and sales talks but impatience and selfishness do not favor teamwork.

Leisure

An enterprising spirit and spontaneity move people to enjoy outings, sports, competitions, cultural events, and travels.

Romance can be very passionate.

Good days for outings, even with cloudy skies the air still feels somewhat warm. Drying effect, get plenty to drink.

Health

Sensitive body parts:

Head, Brain, Eyes

All measures taken to supply nutrient materials and strengthen the sensitive body parts are very effective.

Healing ointments are easily absorbed.

Sensitive sense organs.

If you suffer from migraines drink plenty of water, and avoid coffee, chocolate, and sugar.

Body Care

Aromas, scents: Cloves, Peppermint, Thyme

Treatments with firming and moisturizing creams are more effective.

Massages that serve to regenerate, and strengthen, perhaps aided with beneficial massage oils.

Correcting and cutting ingrown nails.

Eye compresses for strained eyes.

Any kind of hair care. Hair dyes applied now, will look more vibrant.

Garden/Nature

Plant part:

Fruit

Sow plants and vegetables that grow and flourish above ground, especially fruit and tomatoes.

Sowing and planting anything that is supposed to grow fast and for immediate use.

Grafting onto fruit trees.

Cultivating grains.

Transplanting.

Harvesting and storing grains, vegetables, potatoes, fruit, and tomatoes.

Gather herbs for eye complaints and headaches.

Day off on 3/2.

Housework

Light housework only.

Ventilate sufficiently.

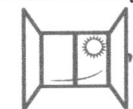

Preserving fruit.

Freezing fruit and vegetables.

Baking bread, cakes, and cookies. Dough rises faster. (Except on New Moon)

Suitable for making cheese.

Nutrition

Food quality:

Protein

Beans, peas, corn, tomatoes, pumpkin, lentils, soybeans, cucumber, eggplant, zucchini, berries, fruit, chili, bell pepper, figs, avocado, melon, olives.

Weight gain: avoid indulging in rich foods. If overweight, eat smaller portions.

Supply nutrient materials to strengthen the body. Focus on foods that contain essential minerals and vitamins.

Stimulants and vitamins are more effective.

Drink plenty of water.

Positive affirmation:
"I see the best in myself and others."

Harvest Time
Ascending forces! Sap is rising, enhancing plant growth above ground, resulting in the most juicy fruits and vegetables.

gather strength rest, recover buildup

Waxing Moon

♓ ➜ ♈ 1:53 AM PST
3:53 AM CST
4:53 AM EST

1 Saturday	**2** Sunday
Ramadan starts	

M A R C H

Where we love is home – home that our feet may leave, but not our hearts.
Oliver Wendell Holmes

 Color

Indigo Blue

 Day

Warm

Element

Fire ♈ **Aries**

Success

Realism and material security are important. Persistence comes easy, thoughts and reactions are slower.

Assess financial areas.

Conservative tendencies may make people want to stay away from risk taking.

Leisure

Relax at a picnic/feast. Enjoy culinary pleasures and hobbies.

The earth feels cold to the touch, so take slightly warmer clothes.

Health

Sensitive body parts:

Head and Neck

All measures taken to supply nutrient materials and strengthen the sensitive body parts are very effective.

Healing ointments are easily absorbed.

Sensitive blood circulation.

Organs of speech, jaws, teeth, tonsils, thyroid gland, neck, and vocal chords get easily affected. Keep neck warm. On cold days ears should be protected. Sensitivity to noise.

High blood pressure: Avoid salty foods.

Massages, lymphatic therapy, and chiropractic treatment to release blockages.

Body Care

Aromas, scents: Geranium, Jasmine, Rose

Treatments with firming and moisturizing creams are more effective.

Massages that serve to regenerate, and strengthen, perhaps aided with beneficial massage oils.

Correcting and cutting ingrown nails.

Hair dyes applied now, will look more vibrant.

Garden/Nature

Plant part:

Root

Sow plants, herbs, and vegetables that grow and flourish above ground.

Sowing and planting trees, bushes, hedges, and root vegetables. Everything grows slowly and lasts well.

Transplanting.

Harvesting and storing root vegetables. Harvested produce is well suited for storage.

Gather herbs for sinus issues, sore throat, and ear complaints.

Housework

Light housework only.

Air rooms only briefly.

Preserving root vegetables.

Nutrition

Food quality:

Salt

Garlic, carrots, red beets, reddish, rutabaga, sugar beet, celery, potatoes, onions, kohlrabi.

Weight gain: avoid indulging in rich foods. If overweight, eat smaller portions.

Supply nutrient materials to strengthen the body. Focus on foods that contain essential minerals and vitamins.

Stimulants and vitamins are more effective.

Avoid large quantities of salty foods like bacon, ham, salted herring, fatty cheese, and the like.

Positive affirmation:
"I trust in the beneficial rhythms of nature."

Harvest Time
Ascending forces! Sap is rising, enhancing plant growth above ground, resulting in the most juicy fruits and vegetables.

gather strength
rest, recover
buildup
Waxing Moon

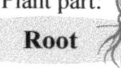
♈ → ♉ 2:38 AM PDT
4:38 AM CST
5:38 AM EST

3 Monday

4 Tuesday
Mardi Gras, Fat Tuesday

M A R C H

Small deeds done are better than great deeds planned.
Peter Marshall

Color
Bright Blue

Day
Cool

Element
Earth

Taurus

Success

Open mindedness and curiosity. A changeable and hectic time.

Good time for talking, negotiating, networking, and exchanging ideas as well as for meetings of a nonbinding nature, conferences, and studies.

Leisure

Good time for family gatherings, parties, and short trips.

People enjoy stimulating their minds with reading and studying. Attending theater performances is a preferred enjoyment. Enhance friendships.

Stretching exercises.

Be prepared for sudden changes in weather or climate.

Health

Sensitive body parts:

Shoulders, Arms, Hands, Lungs

All measures taken to supply nutrient materials and strengthen the sensitive body parts are very effective.

Healing ointments are easily absorbed. Applying herbal ointments to the shoulders for rheumatic gout and alike.

Sensitive glandular system.

Make sure you are dressed warm enough in cool weather.

Exercises for shoulders. Breathing exercises.

Avoid having any teeth pulled.

Sensitivity to light, bring your sunglasses along.

Massages, lymphatic therapy, and chiropractic treatment to release blockages.

Body Care

Aromas, scents: Lavender, Lemon Balm, Magnolia, Verbena

Treatments with firming and moisturizing creams are more effective.

Massages that serve to regenerate, and strengthen, perhaps aided with beneficial massage oils.

Correcting and cutting ingrown nails.

Hair dyes applied now, will look more vibrant.

Garden/Nature

Plant part:

Flower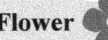

Sow plants, herbs, and vegetables that grow and flourish above ground.

Sowing and planting any creeping or climbing plants, flowers, and medicinal herbs.

Transplanting.

Avoid watering plants.

Gather herbs for tensions in the shoulder and lung complaints.

Changes in weather are more likely.

Housework

Light housework only.

Ventilate rooms thoroughly.

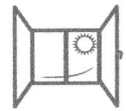

Making preserves.

Baking cakes and cookies. Dough rises faster. (Except on New Moon)

Nutrition

Food quality:

Fat

Cauliflower, artichoke, broccoli, sunflower seeds, flax seeds, nuts, rose hip, elder.

Weight gain: avoid indulging in rich foods. If overweight, eat smaller portions.

Supply nutrient materials to strengthen the body. Focus on foods that contain essential minerals and vitamins.

Stimulants and vitamins are more effective.

Pay attention to any particularly tempting foods today: Most likely the "wrong" things taste best.

High cholesterol: eat a low fat diet.

Positive affirmation:
"I trust in the beneficial rhythms of nature."

Turning Point

Transition of ascending to descending forces. Both forces are at work and neutralize each other.

gather strength rest, recover buildup
Waxing Moon

☿ ➔ ♊
4:30 AM PST
6:30 AM CST
7:30 AM EST

5 Wednesday
Ash Wednesday

No meat.

6 Thursday

☽ Half Moon.

M A R C H

Genuine poetry can communicate before it is understood.
T. S. Eliot

Color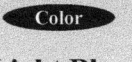
Light Blue

Day
Air/Light

Element
Air

Gemini

Success

Feelings, sensitivity, and cooperativeness. Many are overly sensitive, so beware of treading on someone's toes.

Be cautious if you are easily influenced.

During negotiations make use of the cognitive ability of your senses.

Leisure

Relax within your close family.

Retreat to your safe haven and enjoy your fantasy while reading or listening to music. The inner world becomes more colorful than the outer.

Romance can be gentle. Deep feelings will prevail.

If you plan outdoor excursions, be prepared for a shower here and there.

Health

Sensitive body parts:
Chest, Lungs, Liver, Stomach, Gall Bladder

All measures taken to supply nutrient materials and strengthen the sensitive body parts are very effective.

Healing ointments are easily absorbed.

Sensitive nervous system.

Be cautious with alcohol since the liver is very sensitive.

Stomach could play up and cause gas and heartburn.

Rheumatism: Don't air bedding outside, damp will remain in the bedding.

Lymphatic therapy.

Body Care

Aromas, scents:
Lilac, Lilies of the Valley, Lilies, Violets

Treatments with firming and moisturizing creams are more effective.

Massages that serve to regenerate, and strengthen, perhaps aided with beneficial massage oils.

Correcting and cutting ingrown nails.

No haircuts, hair becomes shaggy and unmanageable. Avoid washing your hair.

Garden/Nature

Plant part:
Leaf

Watering all indoor and outdoor plants.

Sow plants, herbs, and vegetables that grow and flourish above ground, leaf vegetables (no lettuce).

Transplanting.

Trimming and cutting back plants. Avoid pruning fruit trees and bushes.

Cut trees, garlands, pick flowers to dry; they will last longer.

Sowing and mowing lawns.

Setting up a compost heap.

Gather herbs for bronchitis, stomach, liver, and gall bladder complaints.

Unfavorable for harvesting, storing, and preserving.

Housework

Light housework only.

Ventilate rooms briefly and rapidly. Don't air mattresses.

Any dirt and spots are easily removed in the laundry.

Avoid painting, as paint will take very long to dry.

Nutrition

Food quality:
Carbohydrate

Lettuce, spinach, lamb's lettuce, Endive, parsley, leek, cabbage (Brussels sprouts, kale, Chinese cabbage), all leafy herbs, asparagus, mushrooms, cress, Swiss chard, rhubarb.

Weight gain: avoid indulging in rich foods. If overweight, eat smaller portions and avoid carbohydrates. Moodiness may make you want to eat more than is healthy.

Supply nutrient materials to strengthen the body. Focus on foods that contain essential minerals and vitamins. Stimulants and vitamins are more effective.

If you get stomach troubles easily, avoid heavy meals.

Positive affirmation:
"I trust in the beneficial rhythms of nature."

Planting Time
Descending forces! Sap is drawn downward, enhancing root formation. Best days for sowing, planting, and transplanting.

gather strength rest, recover buildup
Waxing Moon

Ⅱ➔♋   8:30 AM PST
10:30 AM CST
11:30 AM EST

4:00 PM PDT
6:00 PM CDT   ♋➔♌
7:00 PM EDT

7 Friday
No meat. Cutting and filing toenails and fingernails.

8 Saturday

9 Sunday Daylight Saving Time starts

M A R C H

If you can dream it, you can do it.
Walt Disney

Color — **Green**

Day — **Wetness**

Element — **Water**

Cancer

Success

Determination reigns, and risks are taken more often. Master your tasks with more self-confidence and creativity.

Limits appear to be more easily surmountable.

Auspicious day for sales, advertising, and publicity.

Leisure

Zest for life is in the air. People want to have a fun time, enjoy parties, musical events, movies, etc.

Possessive feelings can harm a relationship. Romance can be very passionate.

Outings: even with cloudy skies the air still feels somewhat warm. Drying effect, get plenty to drink.

Danger of sudden storms, not only in the sky.

Health

Sensitive body parts:
Heart, Back, Diaphragm, Circulation, Arteries

All measures taken to supply nutrient materials and strengthen the sensitive body parts are very effective.

Healing ointments are easily absorbed.

Sensitive sense organs.

Back and heart problems are more likely to occur.

Avoid over straining of the heart and circulation with unusual physical activities.

Expect sleepless nights.

Body Care

Aromas, scents:
Hibiscus, Oleander, Rose

Treatments with firming and moisturizing creams are more effective.

Massages that serve to regenerate, and strengthen, perhaps aided with beneficial massage oils.

Correcting and cutting ingrown nails.

Good days for haircuts, hair becomes stronger. But be aware that if you get a perm, curls will become quite frizzy. Baby's first haircut.

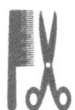

Garden/Nature

Plant part:

Fruit

Sow plants and vegetables that grow and flourish above ground. Sowing and planting fruit. Also sow and plant vegetables that are highly perishable. Plant trees and bushes. Sow lawns.

Transplanting. Grafting onto fruit trees.

Trimming and cutting back plants.

Best for cultivating grains on wet fields.

Dig over/plow to prepare soil for planting.

Setting up a compost heap.

Not suitable for fertilizing.

Harvested produce should be consumed as soon as possible.

Gather herbs for heart and circulation complaints.

Housework

Light housework only.

Ventilate sufficiently.

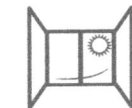

Freezing fruit and vegetables.

Baking bread, cakes, and cookies. Dough rises faster. (Except on New Moon)

Suitable for making cheese.

Avoid painting.

Nutrition

Food quality:
Protein

Beans, peas, corn, tomatoes, pumpkin, lentils, soybeans, cucumber, eggplant, zucchini, berries, fruit, chili, bell pepper, figs, avocado, melon, olives.

Weight gain: avoid indulging in rich foods. If overweight, eat smaller portions.

Supply nutrient materials to strengthen the body. Focus on foods that contain essential minerals and vitamins.

Stimulants and vitamins are more effective.

Positive affirmation:
"I trust in the beneficial rhythms of nature."

Planting Time
Descending forces! Sap is drawn downward, enhancing root formation. Best days for sowing, planting, and transplanting.

gather strength rest, recover buildup
Waxing Moon

10 Monday

11 Tuesday

M A R C H

A weed is a plant that has mastered every survival skill except for learning how to grow in rows.
Doug Larson

Color
Green

Day
Warm

Element
Fire

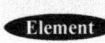

Leo

Success

Good time for details, organization, routine, concentration, and duty.

Take care of financial and administrative tasks.

Prepare for future success now with realistic and critical assessment.

Leisure

Enjoy a nature walk.

Good time for health regimes. Improve your health with stretching exercises and yoga.

The earth feels cold to the touch, so take slightly warmer clothes.

Health

Sensitive body parts:
Digestive Organs, Nerves, Spleen, Pancreas

All measures taken to supply nutrient materials and strengthen the sensitive body parts are very effective.

Healing ointments are easily absorbed.

Sensitive blood circulation.

For a sensitive digestive system, a wholesome diet is recommended.

Dress slightly warmer.

High blood pressure: Avoid salty foods.

Massages, lymphatic therapy, and chiropractic treatment to release blockages.

Body Care

Aromas, scents:
Lavender, Spruce Needles, Sage, Meadow Flowers

Treatments with firming and moisturizing creams are more effective.

Massages that serve to regenerate, and strengthen, perhaps aided with beneficial massage oils.

Correcting and cutting ingrown nails.

Best for haircuts because it retains its shape longer. Perms turn out best. Hair dyes applied now, will look more vibrant.

Garden/Nature

Plant part: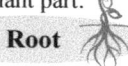
Root

Best for sowing and planting, except lettuce.

Plant trees which are supposed to grow very tall. Plant hedges and bushes that are meant to grow very fast.

Sowing lawns.

Planting and re-potting balcony and indoor plants.

Transplanting.

Trimming and cutting back plants.

Planting cuttings.

Start a compost heap.

Avoid harvesting and storing.

Gather herbs (roots) for digestive organs, pancreas, and nervous complaints.

Housework

Light housework only.

Air rooms only briefly.

Making pickles, preserves, and cheese yields suboptimal results and should be avoided.

Nutrition

Food quality:
Salt

Garlic, carrots, red beets, reddish, rutabaga, sugar beet, celery, potatoes, onions, kohlrabi.

Weight gain: avoid indulging in rich foods. If overweight, eat smaller portions.

Supply nutrient materials to strengthen the body. Focus on foods that contain essential minerals and vitamins.

Stimulants and vitamins are more effective.

Avoid large quantities of salty foods like bacon, ham, salted herring, fatty cheese, and the like. Avoid heavy and greasy foods.

Positive affirmation:
"I trust in the beneficial rhythms of nature."

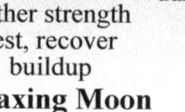

Planting Time
Descending forces! Sap is drawn downward, enhancing root formation. Best days for sowing, planting, and transplanting.

gather strength rest, recover buildup
Waxing Moon

♌ → ♍ 12:57 AM PDT
2:57 AM CDT
3:57 AM EDT

12 Wednesday

No meat.

13 Thursday

M A R C H

Color
Yellow

Day
Cool

Element
Earth

♍ **Virgo**

Success

Good time for details, organization, routine, concentration, and duty.

Take care of financial and administrative tasks.

Prepare for future success now with realistic and critical assessment.

Leisure

Enjoy a nature walk.

Good time for health regimes. Improve your health with stretching exercises and yoga.

The earth feels cold to the touch, so take slightly warmer clothes.

Health

Sensitive body parts:
Digestive Organs, Nerves, Spleen, Pancreas

All measures taken to flush out and detoxify the sensitive body parts are very effective.

Scarring is less severe.

Teeth: Removal of tartar and amalgam. Best for fillings, crowns, and dentures! Avoiding treatment of periodontitis and gums.

Blood-purifying, detoxifying herbal infusions and teas.

Sensitive blood circulation.

For a sensitive digestive system, a wholesome diet is recommended.

Dress slightly warmer.

High blood pressure: Avoid salty foods.

Massages, lymphatic therapy, and chiropractic treatment to release blockages.

○ *Full Moon: Avoid any surgery and vaccination if possible.*

Body Care

Aromas, scents:
Lavender, Spruce Needles, Sage, Meadow Flowers

Prepare home-made ointments and cosmetics.

Apply detoxing facial and body care.

Treatments of bumps and pimples on the skin, and exfoliating procedures.

Removing body hair.

Correction of the nail bed.

Massages that serve to relax, ease tension, and detoxify.

Reflexology massage.

Removal of callused skin.

Treating obstinate athlete's foot, nail fungus, and warts.

Best for haircuts because it retains its shape longer. Perms turn out best.

Garden/Nature

Plant part:
Root

Best for sowing and planting, except lettuce.

Plant trees which are supposed to grow very tall. Plant hedges and bushes that are meant to grow very fast.

Planting and re-potting balcony and indoor plants.

Dig over/plow to prepare soil for planting.

Trimming and cutting back plants. Planting cuttings.

Spread fertilizer and manure. Fertilize flowers with poorly formed roots.

Start a compost heap.

Transplanting. Mulching.

Weeding. Pest control (vermin in the soil).

Avoid harvesting and storing.

Gather herbs (roots) for digestive organs, pancreas, and nervous complaints.

○ *Full Moon: Weather and climate changes. Herbs are most powerful.*

Housework

Housework is dealt with much more successfully, efficiently, and effortlessly.

Problem stains are removed readily.

Dry cleaning.

Thoroughly clean wooden and parquet floors, metals, china etc.

Cleaning, polishing, and waterproofing shoes.

Combating mold.

Air rooms only briefly.

Making pickles, and cheese yields suboptimal results and should be avoided.

○ *Full Moon: Avoid doing laundry, cleaning windows, making preserves, painting.*

Nutrition

Food quality:
Salt

Garlic, carrots, red beets, reddish, rutabaga, sugar beet, celery, potatoes, onions, kohlrabi.

Weight associated with overeating is less likely. If underweight, eat larger portions.

Cleansing and detox diets. Fruit and juice days.

Flush out poisons. Treatment for drug abuse.

Avoid large quantities of salty foods like bacon, ham, salted herring, fatty cheese, and the like. Avoid heavy and greasy foods.

○ *Full Moon: A day of fasting.*

The way you think, the way you behave, the way you eat, can influence your life by 30 to 50 years.
Deepak Chopra

Color
Yellow

Day
Cool

Element
Earth

♍ **Virgo**

12:00 PM PDT
2:00 PM CDT ♍➔♎
3:00 PM EDT

14 Friday

○ **Full Moon** 11:56 PM PDT Thursday, 1:56 AM CDT, 2:56 AM EDT
Lunar Eclipse 12:00 AM PDT 2:00 PM CDT, 3:00 PM EDT

M A R C H

Positive affirmation:
"I trust in the beneficial rhythms of nature."

Planting Time
Descending forces! Sap is drawn downward, enhancing root formation. Best days for sowing, planting, and transplanting.

detox
remove
be active

Waning Moon

Success

The artistic instinct rules, but so, too, does indecisiveness. The forces swing back and forth until equilibrium is achieved.

It's easy to reach compromises with tactful sensitivity.

A sense of judgment will support legal matters.

Leisure

Pursuit for harmony and cooperativeness supports good times in romance, friendship, and partnership.

Enjoy cultural events. Relax and get pampered with a spa treatment.

Romance can be passionate yet sensitive.

Health

Sensitive body parts:

Hips, Kidneys, Bladder

All measures taken to flush out and detoxify the sensitive body parts are very effective.

Good for surgical operations except those on the sensitive body parts (see above), feet, and toes.
Scarring is less severe.

Teeth: Removal of tartar and amalgam. Best for fillings, crowns, and dentures! Avoid treatment of periodontitis and gums, avoid pulling teeth.

Blood-purifying, detoxifying herbal infusions and teas.

Sensitive glandular system.

Take special care to keep the area of the bladder and kidneys warm.

Apply special exercises for the hip region.

Sensitivity to light, so bring your sunglasses along.

Body Care

Aromas, scents: Roses, Violets, Daffodils

Prepare home-made ointments and cosmetics.

Apply detoxing facial and body care.

Treatments of bumps and pimples on the skin, and exfoliating procedures.

Removing body hair.

Correction of the nail bed.

Massages that serve to relax, ease tension, and detoxify.

Reflexology massage.

Removal of callused skin.

Treating obstinate athlete's foot, nail fungus, and warts.

Garden/Nature

Plant part:

Flower

Sow plants and vegetables that grow below ground.

Dig over/plow to prepare soil for planting.

Trimming and cutting back plants.

Start a compost heap.

Weeding. Pest control.

Fertilize flowers that no longer bloom.

Transplanting.

Avoid watering plants.

Harvested produce should be consumed as soon as possible.

Gather herbs (roots) for kidneys, gall bladder and hip complaints.

Day off on 3/16.

Housework

Housework is dealt with much more successfully, efficiently, and effortlessly.

Problem stains are removed readily.

Best for doing laundry! Reduce on laundry detergent, support the environment.

Dry cleaning.

Clean and store seasonal clothing.

Thoroughly clean wooden and parquet floors, metals, china etc.

Cleaning windows and glass.

Cleaning, polishing, and waterproofing shoes.

Combating mold.

Ventilate rooms thoroughly.

Baking bread, cakes, and cookies (add more leavening agent).

Making preserves.

Painting.

Nutrition

Food quality:

Fat

Cauliflower, artichoke, broccoli, sunflower seeds, flax seeds, nuts, rose hip, elder.

Weight associated with overeating is less likely. If underweight, eat larger portions.

Cleansing and detox diets. Fruit and juice days.

Flush out poisons. Treatment for drug abuse.

Pay attention to any particularly tempting foods today: Most likely the "wrong" things taste best.

High cholesterol: eat a low fat diet.

I still get wildly enthusiastic about little things... I play with leaves. I skip down the street and run against the wind.
Leo Buscaglia

Color
Orange

Day
Air/Light

Element

Libra   **Air**

15 Saturday
Holi, Purim

16 Sunday

Positive affirmation:
"I trust in the beneficial rhythms of nature."

Planting Time
Descending forces! Sap is drawn downward, enhancing root formation. Best days for sowing, planting, and transplanting.

detox remove be active

Waning Moon

M A R C H

Success

Critical and superstitious behavior emerges, especially pertaining to money.

A penetrating power will strengthen your capacity to act.

An increased perception opens our interest for the essentials and helps to discover hidden potentials.

Leisure

Relax within your close family, with meditation, and relaxation exercises.

A longing to feel safe will be nurtured if you focus on habits and rituals. An increased sensitivity will help to enjoy every moment.

Romance can be very passionate.

If you plan outdoor excursions, be prepared for a shower here and there.

Health

Sensitive body parts:

Sex organs, Ureter

All measures taken to flush out and detoxify the sensitive body parts are very effective.

Good for surgical operations except those on the sensitive body parts (see above), feet, and toes.
Scarring is less severe.

Teeth: Removal of tartar and amalgam. Best for fillings, crowns, and dentures!

Blood-purifying, detoxifying herbal infusions and teas.

Sensitive nervous system.

Female disorders: As a preventative measure apply hip baths using yarrow.

Pregnancy: Avoid any exertion, miscarriages are more likely.

Keep region of the pelvis, kidneys, and feet warm to prevent infection of the bladder and kidneys.

Lymphatic therapy.

Body Care

Aromas, scents:
Anemone, Cornflower
Oregano, Thuja

Prepare home-made ointments and cosmetics.

Apply detoxing facial and body care.

Treatments of bumps and pimples on the skin, and exfoliating procedures.

Removing body hair.

Correction of the nail bed.

Massages that serve to relax, ease tension, and detoxify.

Reflexology massage.

Removal of callused skin.

Treating obstinate athlete's foot, nail fungus, and warts.

Garden/Nature

Plant part:

Leaf

Water plants.
Fertilize flowers and meadows, no vegetables.

Sow plants and vegetables that grow below ground, leaf vegetables, and lettuce.

Sowing, planting, harvesting, and drying every kind of medicinal herbs.

Dig over/plow to prepare soil for planting.

Trimming and cutting back plants. Transplanting. Weeding. Pest control. Start a compost heap.

Mowing lawns.

Harvested produce should be consumed as soon as possible.

Avoid cutting down trees, danger of bark beetles.

Housework

Housework is dealt with much more successfully, efficiently, and effortlessly.

Problem stains are removed readily.

Best for doing laundry! Reduce on laundry detergent, support the environment.

Dry cleaning.

Thoroughly clean wooden and parquet floors, metals, china etc.

Cleaning, polishing, and waterproofing shoes.

Combating mold.

Ventilate rooms briefly and rapidly.

Avoid painting.

Nutrition

Food quality:

Carbohydrate

Lettuce, spinach, lamb's lettuce, Endive, parsley, leek, cabbage (Brussels sprouts, kale, Chinese cabbage), all leafy herbs, asparagus, mushrooms, cress, Swiss chard, rhubarb.

Weight associated with overeating is less likely. If underweight, eat larger portions.

Cleansing and detox diets. Fruit and juice days.

Flush out poisons. Treatment for drug abuse.

Force always attracts men of low morality.
Albert Einstein

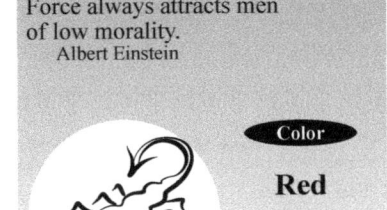

Scorpio ♏

Color — **Red**

Day — **Wetness**

Element — **Water**

12:32 AM PDT
2:32 AM CDT
3:32 AM EDT
♎ → ♏

3:18 PM PDT
5:18 PM CDT
6:18 PM EST
♏ → ♐

17 Monday
St. Patrick's Day

18 Tuesday

19 Wednesday
No meat.

MARCH

Positive affirmation:
"I trust in the beneficial rhythms of nature."

Planting Time
Descending forces!
Sap is drawn downward, enhancing root formation.
Best days for sowing, planting, and transplanting.

detox
remove
be active

Waning Moon

Success

Inquisitiveness and exuberant inspiration lead to new horizons. Insight and love for truth reign.

Bringing together is more important than splitting asunder.

Expansive forces will assist in legal matters, discussions, and debates.

Leisure

Expansion feels great, and travel, short trips, and outings are most welcome. A competitive spirit excites any sports event.

Talk things out when necessary.

Romance can be very passionate.

Good days for outings; even with cloudy skies the air still feels somewhat warm. Drying effect, get plenty to drink.

Health

Sensitive body parts:

Thighs and Veins

All measures taken to flush out and detoxify the sensitive body parts are very effective.

Good for surgical operations except those on the sensitive body parts (see above), feet, and toes. Scarring is less severe.

Teeth: Removal of tartar and amalgam. Best for fillings, crowns, and dentures!

Blood-purifying, detoxifying herbal infusions and tea.

Sensitive sense organs.

Pains often arise in the sciatic nerve, veins, the small of the back, and thighs.

Avoid overstraining the body with unusual physical activities.

Body Care

Aromas, scents: Calendula (Marigold), Geranium, Rosemary

Prepare home-made ointments and cosmetics.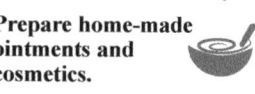

Apply detoxing facial and body care.

Treatments of bumps and pimples on the skin, and exfoliating procedures.

Removing body hair.

Correction of the nail bed.

Massages that serve to relax, ease tension, and detoxify.

Reflexology massage.

Removal of callused skin.

Treating obstinate athlete's foot, nail fungus, and warts.

Garden/Nature

Plant part:

Fruit

Sowing plants and vegetables that grow below ground.

Dig over/plow to prepare soil for planting.

Trimming and cutting back plants.

Pruning of fruit trees and bushes.

Cultivating grains, particularly corn.

Fertilize grains, vegetables, and fruit.

Combating pests above ground.

Weeding.

Gather herbs (roots) for vein diseases.

Avoid hoeing and harrowing.

Start a compost heap.

Housework

Housework is dealt with much more successfully, efficiently, and effortlessly.

Problem stains are removed readily.

Best for doing laundry!

Dry cleaning.

Thoroughly clean wooden and parquet floors, metals, china, etc.

Cleaning windows and glass.

Cleaning, polishing, and waterproofing shoes.

Combating mold.

Ventilate rooms sufficiently. Air beds.

Suitable for making cheese.

Preserving and freezing fruit and vegetables.

Baking bread, cakes, and cookies (use more leavening agent).

Painting.

Nutrition

Food quality:

Protein

Beans, peas, corn, tomatoes, pumpkin, lentils, soybeans, cucumber, eggplant, zucchini, berries, fruit, chili, bell pepper, figs, avocado, melon, olives.

Weight associated with overeating is less likely. If underweight, eat larger portions.

Cleansing and detox diets. Fruit and juice days.

Flush out poisons. Treatment for drug abuse.

Deep in their roots,
all flowers keep the light.
Theodore Roethke

Sagittarius

Color
Orange/Yellow

Day
Warm

Element
Fire

20 Thursday
Spring Equinox

21 Friday

No meat. Cutting and filing toenails and fingernails.

Turning Point
Transition of descending to ascending forces. Both forces are at work and neutralize each other.

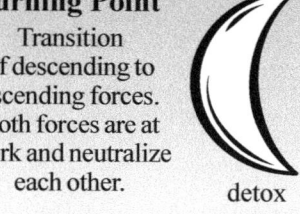
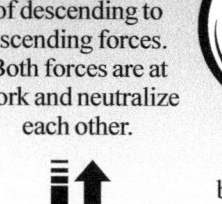

detox
remove
be active

Waning Moon

M A R C H

Success

Career and business are in the foreground now and thinking becomes clear and serious, but somewhat inflexible.

Perseverance and reasoning assist in financial matters, planning, and contracts.

The values of tradition, authority, and discipline impact our endeavors.

Leisure

Money is not likely to be wasted in a shopping spree.

Many are drawn to enjoy cultural events.

The earth feels cold to the touch, so take slightly warmer clothes.

Health

Sensitive body parts:
Knees, Joints, Bones, Skin

All measures taken to flush out and detoxify the sensitive body parts are very effective.

Good for surgery, except on the sensitive body parts (see above), head, brain, and eyes. Scarring is less severe.

Teeth: Removal of tartar and amalgam. Best for fillings, crowns, and dentures!

Blood-purifying, detoxifying herbal infusions and teas.

Sensitive blood circulation.

Avoid overstraining bones and knees, and apply gentle stretching exercises only.

Problems with meniscus: Don't overstrain.

Dress slightly warmer.

High blood pressure: Avoid salty foods.

Massages, lymphatic therapy, and chiropractic treatment to release blockages.

Body Care

Aromas, scents:
Cedar, Juniper

Prepare home-made ointments and cosmetics.

Apply detoxing facial and body care.

Treatments of bumps and pimples on the skin, and exfoliating procedures.

Remove body hair, it may not grow back.

Correction of the nail bed.

Massages that serve to relax, ease tension, and detoxify.

Reflexology massage.

Treating obstinate athlete's foot, nail fungus, and warts.

Cutting and filing toenails and fingernails will make the nails grow stronger over time.

Garden/Nature

Plant part:
Root

Sowing and planting root vegetables and winter vegetables

Weeding. Harrowing weeds. Dig over to prepare soil. Trimming and cutting back plants.
Clear and thin out plants, forest edges, and hedges.
Plant cuttings.
Spread fertilizer and manure.
Start a compost heap.
Combat vermin.

Fertilize flowers with poorly formed roots.

Mulching.

Harvest produce is suitable for storage. Harvest root vegetables.

Gather herbs (roots) for bone, joint, and skin diseases.

Housework

Housework is dealt with much more successfully, efficiently, and effortlessly.

Problem stains are removed readily.

Best for doing laundry! Reduce on laundry detergent, support the environment.

Avoid dry cleaning, as the fabric may develop unwanted glossy blotches.

Thoroughly clean wooden and parquet floors, metals, china etc.

Cleaning, polishing, and waterproofing shoes.

Combating mold.

Air rooms only briefly.

Painting.

Preserving root vegetables. Slice cabbage now to ferment into sauerkraut.

Nutrition

Food quality:
Salt

Garlic, carrots, red beets, reddish, rutabaga, sugar beet, celery, potatoes, onions, kohlrabi.

Weight associated with overeating is less likely. If underweight, eat larger portions.

Cleansing and detox diets. Fruit and juice days.

Flush out poisons. Treatment for drug abuse.

Avoid large quantities of salty foods like bacon, ham, salted herring, fatty cheese, and the like. Avoid heavy and greasy foods.

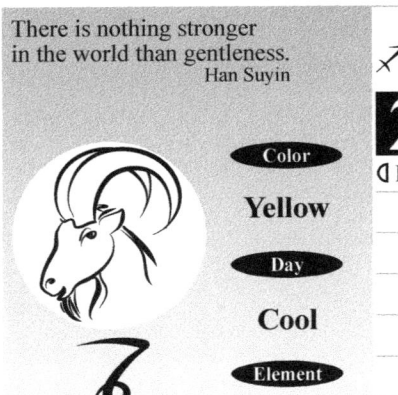

There is nothing stronger in the world than gentleness.
Han Suyin

Color — **Yellow**
Day — **Cool**
Element — **Earth**

Capricorn

12:30 AM PDT
2:30 AM CDT
3:30 AM EDT

22 Saturday

☽ Half Moon.

23 Sunday

M A R C H

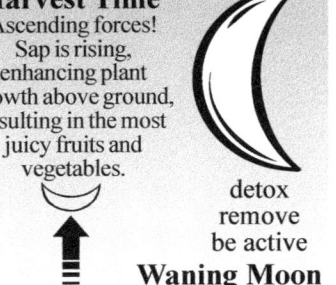

Harvest Time
Ascending forces! Sap is rising, enhancing plant growth above ground, resulting in the most juicy fruits and vegetables.

detox remove be active

Waning Moon

Success

Inspiration, optimism, and impatience. Rational thinking, creativity and imagination spark new ideas and inspire planning for the future.

Shying away from routine tasks people will feel more drawn to anything new.

Instead of gridlocked structures choose new possibilities.

Leisure

Inspiration and optimism will boost friendship, social gatherings, and parties.

Express your creativity and imagination. Dwell in dreams and utopian ideas. It is easier now to perceive intuitive thoughts.

Health

Sensitive body parts:

Lower Legs, Veins

All measures taken to flush out and detoxify the sensitive body parts are very effective.

Good for surgery, except on the sensitive body parts (see above), head, brain, and eyes. Scarring is less severe.

Teeth: Removal of tartar and amalgam. Best for fillings, crowns, and dentures!

Blood-purifying, detoxifying herbal infusions and teas.

Sensitive glandular system.

Avoid inflammation of the veins. Apply ointments to lower legs, and rest legs in a raised position.

Varicose veins: Avoid long periods of standing.

While exercising go easy on the ankles.

Sensitivity to light, so bring your sunglasses along.

Body Care

Aromas, scents: Cyclamen, Peach, Wild Roses

Prepare home-made ointments and cosmetics.

Apply detoxing facial and body care.

Treatments of bumps and pimples on the skin, and exfoliating procedures.

Removing body hair.

Correction of the nail bed.

Massages that serve to relax, ease tension, and detoxify.

Reflexology massage.

Removal of callused skin.

Treating obstinate athlete's foot, nail fungus, and warts.

Garden/Nature

Plant part:

Flower

Fertilize flowers that no longer bloom.

Dig over/plow to prepare soil for planting.

Trimming and cutting back plants.

Hoeing and harrowing; weeds can be left to rot.

Pest control.

Start a compost heap.

Avoid watering plants.

Avoid transplanting sprouts.

Harvested produce is well suitable for storage.

Gather herbs (roots) for vein diseases.

Housework

Housework is dealt with much more successfully, efficiently, and effortlessly.

Problem stains are removed readily.

Best for doing laundry! Reduce on laundry detergent, support the environment.

Dry cleaning.

Clean and store seasonal clothing.

Best suited for a spring cleaning: Thoroughly clean wooden and parquet floors, metals, china etc.

Cleaning windows and glass.

Cleaning, polishing, and waterproofing shoes.

Combating mold.

Ventilate rooms thoroughly.

Baking bread, cakes, and cookies (add more leavening agent).

Making preserves.

Painting.

Nutrition

Food quality:

Fat

Cauliflower, artichoke, broccoli, sunflower seeds, flax seeds, nuts, rose hip, elder.

Weight associated with overeating is less likely. If underweight, eat larger portions.

Cleansing and detox diets. Fruit and juice days.

Flush out poisons. Treatment for drug abuse.

Pay attention to any particularly tempting foods today: Most likely the "wrong" things taste best.

High cholesterol: eat a low fat diet.

Never believe that a few caring people can't change the world. For, indeed, that's all who ever have.
Margaret Mead

Color
Bright/Dark Blue

Day
Air/Light

Element

Aquarius   Air

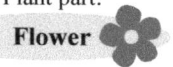

8:26 AM PDT
10:26 AM CDT
11:26 AM EDT

24 Monday

25 Tuesday

12:33 PM PDT
2:33 PM CDT
3:33 PM EDT

26 Wednesday

No meat.

Harvest Time
Ascending forces! Sap is rising, enhancing plant growth above ground, resulting in the most juicy fruits and vegetables.

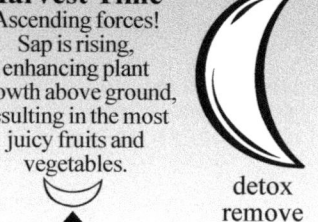

detox remove be active

Waning Moon

M A R C H

Success

Sensibility, intuition, and helpfulness.

Where possible, retreating is more favorable than dealing with business matters.

Dissolve restrictions, be patient and wait. Be aware that people can be more easily influenced.

Leisure

Your helpfulness will boost friendships.

Enjoy dancing or swimming, or watch a movie that will inspire your fantasies and imagination.

Retreat, relax, and recover.

Romance can be gentle and coziness will prevail.

If you plan outdoor excursions, be prepared for a shower here and there.

Health

Sensitive body parts:

Feet and Toes

All measures taken to flush out and detoxify the sensitive body parts are very effective.

Good for surgical operations except those on the sensitive body parts (see above), head, brain, and eyes.
Scarring is less severe.

Teeth: Removal of tartar and amalgam. Best for fillings, crowns, and dentures!

Blood-purifying, detoxifying herbal infusions and teas.

Sensitive nervous system.

Drugs have a much stronger effect on your body.
Monitor closely what you put into your body.

Lymphatic therapy.

Sluggishness or fatigue may occur in the transition into the next Zodiac sign of Aries.

Body Care

Aromas, scents:
Magnolia, Amaryllis, Clary Sage

Prepare home-made ointments and cosmetics.

Apply detoxing facial and body care.

Treatments of bumps and pimples on the skin, and exfoliating procedures.

Removing body hair.

Correction of the nail bed.

Massages that serve to relax, ease tension, and detoxify. Reflexology massage. Carry out with special care, people are more sensitive.

Removal of callused skin.

Treating obstinate athlete's foot, nail fungus, and warts.

Foot bath.

No haircuts, hair becomes shaggy and unmanageable. Avoid washing your hair.

Garden/Nature

Plant part:

Leaf

Water plants.

Fertilize flowers.

Sow plants and vegetables that grow below ground, potatoes, leaf vegetables, and lettuce.

Dig over/plow to prepare soil for planting.
Trimming and cutting back plants.
Start a compost heap.

Mowing lawns.

Pest control. Weeding.

Harvested produce should be consumed as soon as possible.

Gather herbs for foot complaints.

Housework

Housework is dealt with much more successfully, efficiently, and effortlessly.

Problem stains are removed readily.

Best for doing laundry! Reduce on laundry detergent, support the environment.

Dry cleaning.

Clean and store seasonal clothing.

Thoroughly clean wooden and parquet floors, metals, china etc.

Cleaning, polishing, and waterproofing shoes.

Combating mold.

Ventilate rooms briefly and rapidly.

Avoid painting.

Preserving and storing should be avoided.

Nutrition

Food quality:

Carbohydrate

Lettuce, spinach, lamb's lettuce, Endive, parsley, leek, cabbage (Brussels sprouts, kale, Chinese cabbage), all leafy herbs, asparagus, mushrooms, cress, Swiss chard, rhubarb.

Weight associated with overeating is less likely. If underweight, eat larger portions.

Cleansing and detox diets. Fruit and juice days.

Flush out poisons. Treatment for drug abuse.

Caffeine, alcohol, drugs, certain foods, and stimulants have a much stronger effect.

Everything has been said before, but since nobody listens we have to keep going back and beginning all over again.
Andre Gide

Pisces

Color
Blueish White

Day
Wetness

Element
Water

1:37 PM PDT
3:37 PM CDT
4:37 PM EDT
♓ → ♈

27 Thursday

28 Friday

No meat. Cutting and filing toenails and fingernails.

M A R C H

Harvest Time
Ascending forces! Sap is rising, enhancing plant growth above ground, resulting in the most juicy fruits and vegetables.

detox
remove
be active
Waning Moon

Success

Things get going and the way straight ahead seems the best.

People feel energetic, courageous, assertive, and at times anxious.

Good time for meetings and sales talks but impatience and selfishness do not favor teamwork.

● *New Moon: Confirm your resolutions. Finalize new decisions. Drop bad habits.*

Leisure

An enterprising spirit and spontaneity move people to enjoy outings, sports, competitions, cultural events, and travels.

Romance can be very passionate.

Good days for outings, even with cloudy skies the air still feels somewhat warm. Drying effect, get plenty to drink.

Health

Sensitive body parts:

Head, Brain, Eyes

All measures taken to supply nutrient materials and strengthen the sensitive body parts are very effective.

Healing ointments are easily absorbed.

Sensitive sense organs.

If you suffer from migraines drink plenty of water, and avoid coffee, chocolate, and sugar.

● *New Moon: Avoid any surgery if possible.*

Body Care

Aromas, scents: Cloves, Peppermint, Thyme

Treatments with firming and moisturizing creams are more effective.

Massages that serve to regenerate, and strengthen, perhaps aided with beneficial massage oils.

Correcting and cutting ingrown nails.

Eye compresses for strained eyes.

Any kind of hair care. Hair dyes applied now, will look more vibrant.

Garden/Nature

Plant part:

Fruit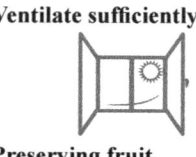

Sow plants and vegetables that grow and flourish above ground, especially fruit and tomatoes.

Sowing and planting anything that is supposed to grow fast and for immediate use.

Grafting onto fruit trees.

Cultivating grains.

Transplanting.

Harvesting and storing grains, vegetables, potatoes, fruit, and tomatoes.

Gather herbs for eye complaints and headaches.

Day off on 3/29.

● *New Moon: Change of weather is likely. Care for sickly plants.*

Housework

Light housework only.

Ventilate sufficiently.

Preserving fruit.

Freezing fruit and vegetables.

Baking bread, cakes, and cookies. Dough rises faster. (Except on New Moon)

Suitable for making cheese.

Nutrition

Food quality:

Protein

Beans, peas, corn, tomatoes, pumpkin, lentils, soybeans, cucumber, eggplant, zucchini, berries, fruit, chili, bell pepper, figs, avocado, melon, olives.

Weight gain: avoid indulging in rich foods. If overweight, eat smaller portions.

Supply nutrient materials to strengthen the body. Focus on foods that contain essential minerals and vitamins.

Stimulants and vitamins are more effective.

Drink plenty of water.

● *New Moon: A day of fasting.*

Positive affirmation:
"I trust in love that is all-encompassing."

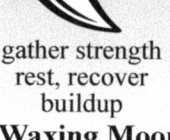

Harvest Time
Ascending forces! Sap is rising, enhancing plant growth above ground, resulting in the most juicy fruits and vegetables.

gather strength rest, recover buildup
Waxing Moon

29 **Saturday**
● **New Moon** 3:59 AM PDT
5:59 AM CDT, 6:59 AM EDT
Solar Eclipse 3:49 AM PDT
5:49 AM CDT, 6:49 AM EDT

1:17 PM PDT
3:17 PM CDT
4:17 PM EDT
♈ ➙ ♉

30 **Sunday**

M A R C H

The fellow that owns his own home is always just coming out of a hardware store.
Kin Hubbard

Color
Indigo Blue

Day
Warm

Element
Fire

♈

Aries

Success

Realism and material security are important. Persistence comes easy, thoughts and reactions are slower.

Assess financial areas.

Conservative tendencies may make people want to stay away from risk taking.

Leisure

Relax at a picnic/feast. Enjoy culinary pleasures and hobbies.

The earth feels cold to the touch, so take slightly warmer clothes.

Health

Sensitive body parts:

Head and Neck

All measures taken to supply nutrient materials and strengthen the sensitive body parts are very effective.

Healing ointments are easily absorbed.

Sensitive blood circulation.

Organs of speech, jaws, teeth, tonsils, thyroid gland, neck, and vocal chords get easily affected. Keep neck warm. On cold days ears should be protected. Sensitivity to noise.

High blood pressure: Avoid salty foods.

Massages, lymphatic therapy, and chiropractic treatment to release blockages.

Body Care

Aromas, scents: Geranium, Jasmine, Rose

Treatments with firming and moisturizing creams are more effective.

Massages that serve to regenerate, and strengthen, perhaps aided with beneficial massage oils.

Correcting and cutting ingrown nails.

Hair dyes applied now, will look more vibrant.

Garden/Nature

Plant part:

Root

Sow plants, herbs, and vegetables that grow and flourish above ground.

Sowing and planting trees, bushes, hedges, and root vegetables. Everything grows slowly and lasts well.

Transplanting.

Harvesting and storing root vegetables. Harvested produce is well suited for storage.

Gather herbs for sinus issues, sore throat, and ear complaints.

Housework

Light housework only.

Air rooms only briefly.

Preserving root vegetables.

Nutrition

Food quality:

Salt

Garlic, carrots, red beets, reddish, rutabaga, sugar beet, celery, potatoes, onions, kohlrabi.

Weight gain: avoid indulging in rich foods. If overweight, eat smaller portions.

Supply nutrient materials to strengthen the body. Focus on foods that contain essential minerals and vitamins.

Stimulants and vitamins are more effective.

Avoid large quantities of salty foods like bacon, ham, salted herring, fatty cheese, and the like.

Positive affirmation:
"I trust in love that is all-encompassing."

Harvest Time
Ascending forces! Sap is rising, enhancing plant growth above ground, resulting in the most juicy fruits and vegetables.

gather strength rest, recover buildup
Waxing Moon

1:27 PM PDT
3:27 PM CDT
4:37 PM EDT
♉ → ♊

31	Monday
	Eid al-Fitr

1	Tuesday
	April Fool's Day

MARCH / APRIL

Quality is not an act, it is a habit.
Aristotle

Color — **Bright Blue**

Day — **Cool**

Element — **Earth**

Taurus

Success

Open mindedness and curiosity. A changeable and hectic time.

Good time for talking, negotiating, networking, and exchanging ideas as well as for meetings of a nonbinding nature, conferences, and studies.

Leisure

Good time for family gatherings, parties, and short trips.

People enjoy stimulating their minds with reading and studying. Attending theater performances is a preferred enjoyment. Enhance friendships.

Stretching exercises.

Be prepared for sudden changes in weather or climate.

Health

Sensitive body parts:

Shoulders, Arms, Hands, Lungs

All measures taken to supply nutrient materials and strengthen the sensitive body parts are very effective.

Healing ointments are easily absorbed. Applying herbal ointments to the shoulders for rheumatic gout and alike.

Sensitive glandular system.

Make sure you are dressed warm enough in cool weather.

Exercises for shoulders. Breathing exercises.

Avoid having any teeth pulled.

Sensitivity to light, bring your sunglasses along.

Massages, lymphatic therapy, and chiropractic treatment to release blockages.

Body Care

Aromas, scents: Lavender, Lemon Balm, Magnolia, Verbena

Treatments with firming and moisturizing creams are more effective.

Massages that serve to regenerate, and strengthen, perhaps aided with beneficial massage oils.

Correcting and cutting ingrown nails.

Hair dyes applied now, will look more vibrant.

Garden/Nature

Plant part:

Flower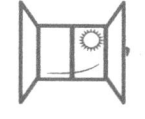

Sow plants, herbs, and vegetables that grow and flourish above ground.

Sowing and planting any creeping or climbing plants, flowers, and medicinal herbs.

Transplanting.

Avoid watering plants.

Gather herbs for tensions in the shoulder and lung complaints.

Changes in weather are more likely.

Housework

Light housework only.

Ventilate rooms thoroughly.

Making preserves.

Baking cakes and cookies. Dough rises faster. (Except on New Moon)

Nutrition

Food quality:

Fat

Cauliflower, artichoke, broccoli, sunflower seeds, flax seeds, nuts, rose hip, elder.

Weight gain: avoid indulging in rich foods. If overweight, eat smaller portions.

Supply nutrient materials to strengthen the body. Focus on foods that contain essential minerals and vitamins.

Stimulants and vitamins are more effective.

Pay attention to any particularly tempting foods today: Most likely the "wrong" things taste best.

High cholesterol: eat a low fat diet.

Positive affirmation:
"I trust in love that is all-encompassing."

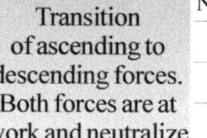

Turning Point
Transition of ascending to descending forces. Both forces are at work and neutralize each other.

gather strength rest, recover buildup
Waxing Moon

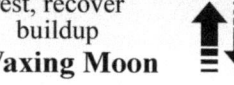

2 Wednesday
No meat.

3:51 PM PDT
5:51 PM CDT
6:51 PM EDT
♊ ➔ ♋

3 Thursday

A P R I L

You can't build a reputation on what you are going to do.
Henry Ford

Color
Light Blue

Day
Air/Light

Element
Air

Gemini

Success

Feelings, sensitivity, and cooperativeness. Many are overly sensitive, so beware of treading on someone's toes.

Be cautious if you are easily influenced.

During negotiations make use of the cognitive ability of your senses.

Leisure

Relax within your close family.

Retreat to your safe haven and enjoy your fantasy while reading or listening to music. The inner world becomes more colorful than the outer.

Romance can be gentle. Deep feelings will prevail.

If you plan outdoor excursions, be prepared for a shower here and there.

Health

Sensitive body parts:
Chest, Lungs, Liver, Stomach, Gall Bladder

All measures taken to supply nutrient materials and strengthen the sensitive body parts are very effective.

Healing ointments are easily absorbed.

Sensitive nervous system.

Be cautious with alcohol since the liver is very sensitive.

Stomach could play up and cause gas and heartburn.

Rheumatism: Don't air bedding outside, damp will remain in the bedding.

Lymphatic therapy.

Body Care

Aromas, scents:
Lilac, Lilies of the Valley, Lilies, Violets

Treatments with firming and moisturizing creams are more effective.

Massages that serve to regenerate, and strengthen, perhaps aided with beneficial massage oils.

Correcting and cutting ingrown nails.

No haircuts, hair becomes shaggy and unmanageable. Avoid washing your hair.

Garden/Nature

Plant part:
Leaf

 Watering all indoor and outdoor plants.

Sow plants, herbs, and vegetables that grow and flourish above ground, leaf vegetables (no lettuce).

Transplanting.

Trimming and cutting back plants. Avoid pruning fruit trees and bushes.

Cut trees, garlands, pick flowers to dry; they will last longer.

Sowing and mowing lawns.

Setting up a compost heap.

Gather herbs for bronchitis, stomach, liver, and gall bladder complaints.

Unfavorable for harvesting, storing, and preserving.

Housework

Light housework only.

Ventilate rooms briefly and rapidly. Don't air mattresses.

Any dirt and spots are easily removed in the laundry.

Avoid painting, as paint will take very long to dry.

Nutrition

Food quality:
Carbohydrate

Lettuce, spinach, lamb's lettuce, Endive, parsley, leek, cabbage (Brussels sprouts, kale, Chinese cabbage), all leafy herbs, asparagus, mushrooms, cress, Swiss chard, rhubarb.

Weight gain: avoid indulging in rich foods. If overweight, eat smaller portions and avoid carbohydrates. Moodiness may make you want to eat more than is healthy.

Supply nutrient materials to strengthen the body. Focus on foods that contain essential minerals and vitamins. Stimulants and vitamins are more effective.

If you get stomach troubles easily, avoid heavy meals.

Positive affirmation:
"I trust in love that is all-encompassing."

Planting Time
Descending forces! Sap is drawn downward, enhancing root formation. Best days for sowing, planting, and transplanting.

gather strength
rest, recover
buildup
Waxing Moon

9:35 PM PDT
11:35 PM CDT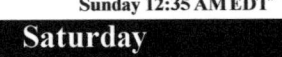
Sunday 12:35 AM EDT

4 Friday	**5** Saturday
	Rama Navani

☾ **Half Moon.**
No meat. Cutting and filing toenails and fingernails.

A P R I L

I don't believe you have to be better than everybody else.
I believe you have to be better than you ever thought you could be.
Ken Venturi

Color
Green

Day
Wetness

Element
Water

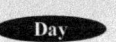

Cancer

Success

Determination reigns, and risks are taken more often. Master your tasks with more self-confidence and creativity.

Limits appear to be more easily surmountable.

Auspicious day for sales, advertising, and publicity.

Leisure

Zest for life is in the air. People want to have a fun time, enjoy parties, musical events, movies, etc.

Possessive feelings can harm a relationship. Romance can be very passionate.

Outings: even with cloudy skies the air still feels somewhat warm. Drying effect, get plenty to drink.

Danger of sudden storms, not only in the sky.

Health

Sensitive body parts:
Heart, Back, Diaphragm, Circulation, Arteries

All measures taken to supply nutrient materials and strengthen the sensitive body parts are very effective.

Healing ointments are easily absorbed.

Sensitive sense organs.

Back and heart problems are more likely to occur.

Avoid over straining of the heart and circulation with unusual physical activities.

Expect sleepless nights.

Body Care

Aromas, scents:
Hibiscus, Oleander, Rose

Treatments with firming and moisturizing creams are more effective.

Massages that serve to regenerate, and strengthen, perhaps aided with beneficial massage oils.

Correcting and cutting ingrown nails.

Good days for haircuts, hair becomes stronger. But be aware that if you get a perm, curls will become quite frizzy. Baby's first haircut.

Garden/Nature

Plant part:
Fruit

Sow plants and vegetables that grow and flourish above ground. Sowing and planting fruit. Also sow and plant vegetables that are highly perishable. Plant trees and bushes. Sow lawns.

Transplanting. Grafting onto fruit trees.

Trimming and cutting back plants.

Best for cultivating grains on wet fields.

Dig over/plow to prepare soil for planting.

Setting up a compost heap.

Not suitable for fertilizing.

Harvested produce should be consumed as soon as possible.

Gather herbs for heart and circulation complaints.

Housework

Light housework only.

Ventilate sufficiently.

Freezing fruit and vegetables.

Baking bread, cakes, and cookies. Dough rises faster. (Except on New Moon)

Suitable for making cheese.

Avoid painting.

Nutrition

Food quality:
Protein

Beans, peas, corn, tomatoes, pumpkin, lentils, soybeans, cucumber, eggplant, zucchini, berries, fruit, chili, bell pepper, figs, avocado, melon, olives.

Weight gain: avoid indulging in rich foods. If overweight, eat smaller portions.

Supply nutrient materials to strengthen the body. Focus on foods that contain essential minerals and vitamins.

Stimulants and vitamins are more effective.

Positive affirmation:
"I trust in love that is all-encompassing."

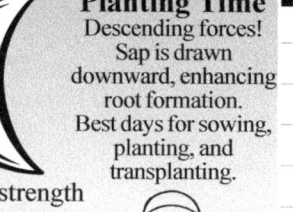

Planting Time
Descending forces! Sap is drawn downward, enhancing root formation. Best days for sowing, planting, and transplanting.

gather strength rest, recover buildup
Waxing Moon

6 Sunday

7 Monday

A P R I L

It takes more than just a good looking body. You've got to have the heart and soul to go with it.
Epictetus

Color — **Green**
Day — **Warm**
Element — **Fire**

Leo

Success

Good time for details, organization, routine, concentration, and duty.

Take care of financial and administrative tasks.

Prepare for future success now with realistic and critical assessment.

Leisure

Enjoy a nature walk.

Good time for health regimes. Improve your health with stretching exercises and yoga.

The earth feels cold to the touch, so take slightly warmer clothes.

Health

Sensitive body parts:
Digestive Organs, Nerves, Spleen, Pancreas

All measures taken to supply nutrient materials and strengthen the sensitive body parts are very effective.

Healing ointments are easily absorbed.

Sensitive blood circulation.

For a sensitive digestive system, a wholesome diet is recommended.

Dress slightly warmer.

High blood pressure: Avoid salty foods.

Massages, lymphatic therapy, and chiropractic treatment to release blockages.

Body Care

Aromas, scents:
Lavender, Spruce Needles, Sage, Meadow Flowers

Treatments with firming and moisturizing creams are more effective.

Massages that serve to regenerate, and strengthen, perhaps aided with beneficial massage oils.

Correcting and cutting ingrown nails.

Best for haircuts because it retains its shape longer. Perms turn out best. Hair dyes applied now, will look more vibrant.

Garden/Nature

Plant part:
Root

Best for sowing and planting, except lettuce.

Plant trees which are supposed to grow very tall. Plant hedges and bushes that are meant to grow very fast.

Sowing lawns.

Planting and re-potting balcony and indoor plants.

Transplanting.

Trimming and cutting back plants.

Planting cuttings.

Start a compost heap.

Avoid harvesting and storing.

Gather herbs (roots) for digestive organs, pancreas, and nervous complaints.

Housework

Light housework only.

Air rooms only briefly.

Making pickles, preserves, and cheese yields suboptimal results and should be avoided.

Nutrition

Food quality:
Salt

Garlic, carrots, red beets, reddish, rutabaga, sugar beet, celery, potatoes, onions, kohlrabi.

Weight gain: avoid indulging in rich foods. If overweight, eat smaller portions.

Supply nutrient materials to strengthen the body. Focus on foods that contain essential minerals and vitamins.

Stimulants and vitamins are more effective.

Avoid large quantities of salty foods like bacon, ham, salted herring, fatty cheese, and the like. Avoid heavy and greasy foods.

Positive affirmation:
"I trust in love that is all-encompassing."

Planting Time
Descending forces! Sap is drawn downward, enhancing root formation. Best days for sowing, planting, and transplanting.

gather strength rest, recover buildup
Waxing Moon

Ω → ℳ
6:41 AM PDT
8:41 AM CDT
9:41 AM EDT

6:13 PM PDT
8:13 PM CDT
9:13 PM EDT
ℳ → Ω

8 Tuesday   **9** Wednesday   **10** Thursday

No meat.

A P R I L

Humor distorts nothing, and only false gods are laughed off their earthly pedestals.
Agnes Repplier

Color
Yellow

Day
Cool

Element
Earth

ℳ
Virgo

Success

The artistic instinct rules, but so, too, does indecisiveness. The forces swing back and forth until equilibrium is achieved.

It's easy to reach compromises with tactful sensitivity.

A sense of judgment will support legal matters.

Leisure

Pursuit for harmony and cooperativeness supports good times in romance, friendship, and partnership.

Enjoy cultural events. Relax and get pampered with a spa treatment.

Romance can be passionate yet sensitive.

Health

Sensitive body parts:

Hips, Kidneys, Bladder

All measures taken to supply nutrient materials and strengthen the sensitive body parts are very effective.

Healing ointments are easily absorbed.

Sensitive glandular system.

Take special care to keep the area of bladder and kidneys warm.

Apply special exercises for the hip region.

Avoid having any teeth pulled.

Sensitivity to light, bring your sunglasses along.

○ *Full Moon: Avoid any surgery and vaccination if possible.*

Body Care

Aromas, scents: Roses, Violets, Daffodils

Treatments with firming and moisturizing creams are more effective.

Massages that serve to regenerate, and strengthen, perhaps aided with beneficial massage oils.

Correcting and cutting ingrown nails.

Hair dyes applied now, will look more vibrant.

Garden/Nature

Plant part:

Flower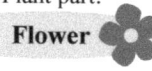

Sow plants and vegetables that grow and flourish above ground, specially flowers, and medicinal herbs.

Transplanting.

Trimming and cutting back plants.

Avoid watering plants.

Start a compost heap.

Harvested produce should be consumed as soon as possible.

Gather herbs for kidneys, gall bladder, and hip complaints.

Day off on 4/11.

○ *Full Moon: Weather and climate changes. Herbs are most powerful.*

Housework

Light housework only.

Ventilate rooms thoroughly.

Baking cakes and cookies. Dough rises faster. (Except on New Moon)

○ *Full Moon: Avoid doing laundry, cleaning windows, making preserves, painting.*

Nutrition

Food quality:

Fat

Cauliflower, artichoke, broccoli, sunflower seeds, flax seeds, nuts, rose hip, elder.

Weight gain: avoid indulging in rich foods. If overweight, eat smaller portions.

Supply nutrient materials to strengthen the body. Focus on foods that contain essential minerals and vitamins.

Stimulants and vitamins are more effective.

Pay attention to any particularly tempting foods today: Most likely the "wrong" things taste best.

High cholesterol: eat a low fat diet.

○ *Full Moon: A day of fasting.*

Positive affirmation:
"I trust in love that is all-encompassing."

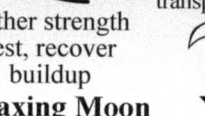

Planting Time
Descending forces! Sap is drawn downward, enhancing root formation. Best days for sowing, planting, and transplanting.

gather strength rest, recover buildup

Waxing Moon

11 Friday

No meat. Cutting and filing toenails and fingernails.

12 Saturday

○ **Full Moon** 3:23 PM PDT, 5:23 PM CDT, 6:23 PM EDT

There is always an easy solution to every human problem – neat, plausible and wrong.
H. L. Mencken

Color

Orange

Day

Air/Light

Element

Air   **Libra**

A P R I L

Success

Critical and superstitious behavior emerges, especially pertaining to money.

A penetrating power will strengthen your capacity to act.

An increased perception opens our interest for the essentials and helps to discover hidden potentials.

Leisure

Relax within your close family, with meditation, and relaxation exercises.

A longing to feel safe will be nurtured if you focus on habits and rituals. An increased sensitivity will help to enjoy every moment.

Romance can be very passionate.

If you plan outdoor excursions, be prepared for a shower here and there.

Health

Sensitive body parts:

Sex organs, Ureter

All measures taken to flush out and detoxify the sensitive body parts are very effective.

Good for surgical operations except those on the sensitive body parts (see above), head, brain, and eyes. Scarring is less severe.

Teeth: Removal of tartar and amalgam. Best for fillings, crowns, and dentures!

Blood-purifying, detoxifying herbal infusions and teas.

Sensitive nervous system.

Female disorders: As a preventative measure apply hip baths using yarrow.

Pregnancy: Avoid any exertion, miscarriages are more likely.

Keep region of the pelvis, kidneys, and feet warm to prevent infection of the bladder and kidneys.

Lymphatic therapy.

Body Care

Aromas, scents:
Anemone, Cornflower
Oregano, Thuja

Prepare home-made ointments and cosmetics.

Apply detoxing facial and body care.

Treatments of bumps and pimples on the skin, and exfoliating procedures.

Removing body hair.

Correction of the nail bed.

Massages that serve to relax, ease tension, and detoxify.

Reflexology massage.

Removal of callused skin.

Treating obstinate athlete's foot, nail fungus, and warts.

Garden/Nature

Plant part:

Leaf

Water plants.

Fertilize flowers and meadows, no vegetables.

Sow plants and vegetables that grow below ground, leaf vegetables, and lettuce.

Sowing, planting, harvesting, and drying every kind of medicinal herbs.

Dig over/plow to prepare soil for planting.

Trimming and cutting back plants. Transplanting. Weeding. Pest control. Start a compost heap.

Mowing lawns.

Harvested produce should be consumed as soon as possible.

Avoid cutting down trees, danger of bark beetles.

Housework

Housework is dealt with much more successfully, efficiently, and effortlessly.

Problem stains are removed readily.

Best for doing laundry! Reduce on laundry detergent, support the environment.

Dry cleaning.

Thoroughly clean wooden and parquet floors, metals, china etc.

Cleaning, polishing, and waterproofing shoes.

Combating mold.

Ventilate rooms briefly and rapidly.

Avoid painting.

Nutrition

Food quality:

Carbohydrate

Lettuce, spinach, lamb's lettuce, Endive, parsley, leek, cabbage (Brussels sprouts, kale, Chinese cabbage), all leafy herbs, asparagus, mushrooms, cress, Swiss chard, rhubarb.

Weight associated with overeating is less likely. If underweight, eat larger portions.

Cleansing and detox diets. Fruit and juice days.

Flush out poisons. Treatment for drug abuse.

Music is a higher revelation than all wisdom and philosophy.
Ludwig van Beethoven

Scorpio

Color	**Red**
Day	**Wetness**
Element	**Water**

♎→♏ 6:55 AM PDT
8:55 AM CDT
9:55 AM EDT

7:38 PM PDT
9:38 PM CDT
10:38 PM EDT ♏→♐

13 Sunday Palm Sunday

14 Monday

15 Tuesday

A P R I L

Planting Time
Descending forces! Sap is drawn downward, enhancing root formation. Best days for sowing, planting, and transplanting.

detox
remove
be active

Waning Moon

Success

Inquisitiveness and exuberant inspiration lead to new horizons. Insight and love for truth reign.

Bringing together is more important than splitting asunder.

Expansive forces will assist in legal matters, discussions, and debates.

Leisure

Expansion feels great, and travel, short trips, and outings are most welcome. A competitive spirit excites any sports event.

Talk things out when necessary.

Romance can be very passionate.

Good days for outings; even with cloudy skies the air still feels somewhat warm. Drying effect, get plenty to drink.

Health

Sensitive body parts:

Thighs and Veins

All measures taken to flush out and detoxify the sensitive body parts are very effective.

Good for surgical operations except those on the sensitive body parts (see above), head, brain, and eyes.
Scarring is less severe.

Teeth: Removal of tartar and amalgam. Best for fillings, crowns, and dentures!

Blood-purifying, detoxifying herbal infusions and tea.

Sensitive sense organs.

Pains often arise in the sciatic nerve, veins, the small of the back, and thighs.

Avoid overstraining the body with unusual physical activities.

Body Care

Aromas, scents:
Calendula (Marigold), Geranium, Rosemary

Prepare home-made ointments and cosmetics.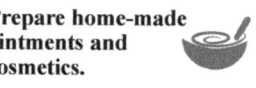

Apply detoxing facial and body care.

Treatments of bumps and pimples on the skin, and exfoliating procedures.

Removing body hair.

Correction of the nail bed.

Massages that serve to relax, ease tension, and detoxify.

Reflexology massage.

Removal of callused skin.

Treating obstinate athlete's foot, nail fungus, and warts.

Garden/Nature

Plant part:

Fruit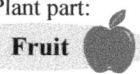

Sowing plants and vegetables that grow below ground.

Dig over/plow to prepare soil for planting.

Trimming and cutting back plants.

Pruning of fruit trees and bushes.

Cultivating grains, particularly corn.

Fertilize grains, vegetables, and fruit.

Combating pests above ground.

Weeding.

Gather herbs (roots) for vein diseases.

Avoid hoeing and harrowing.

Start a compost heap.

Housework

Housework is dealt with much more successfully, efficiently, and effortlessly.

Problem stains are removed readily.

Best for doing laundry!

Dry cleaning.

Thoroughly clean wooden and parquet floors, metals, china, etc.

Cleaning windows and glass.

Cleaning, polishing, and waterproofing shoes.

Combating mold.

Ventilate rooms sufficiently. Air beds.

Suitable for making cheese.

Preserving and freezing fruit and vegetables.

Baking bread, cakes, and cookies (use more leavening agent).

Painting.

Nutrition

Food quality:

Protein

Beans, peas, corn, tomatoes, pumpkin, lentils, soybeans, cucumber, eggplant, zucchini, berries, fruit, chili, bell pepper, figs, avocado, melon, olives.

Weight associated with overeating is less likely. If underweight, eat larger portions.

Cleansing and detox diets. Fruit and juice days.

Flush out poisons. Treatment for drug abuse.

How strange that nature does not knock, and yet does not intrude!
Emily Dickinson

Sagittarius

Color
Orange/ Yellow

Day
Warm

Element
Fire

16 Wednesday

No meat.

17 Thursday

Positive affirmation:
"I trust in love that is all-encompassing."

Turning Point
Transition of descending to ascending forces. Both forces are at work and neutralize each other.

detox remove be active

Waning Moon

Success

Career and business are in the foreground now and thinking becomes clear and serious, but somewhat inflexible.

Perseverance and reasoning assist in financial matters, planning, and contracts.

The values of tradition, authority, and discipline impact our endeavors.

Leisure

Money is not likely to be wasted in a shopping spree.

Many are drawn to enjoy cultural events.

The earth feels cold to the touch, so take slightly warmer clothes.

Health

Sensitive body parts:

Knees, Joints, Bones, Skin

All measures taken to flush out and detoxify the sensitive body parts are very effective.

Good for surgery, except on the sensitive body parts (see above), head, brain, and eyes. Scarring is less severe.

Teeth: Removal of tartar and amalgam. Best for fillings, crowns, and dentures!

Blood-purifying, detoxifying herbal infusions and teas.

Sensitive blood circulation.

Avoid overstraining bones and knees, and apply gentle stretching exercises only.

Problems with meniscus: Don't overstrain.

Dress slightly warmer.

High blood pressure: Avoid salty foods.

Massages, lymphatic therapy, and chiropractic treatment to release blockages.

Body Care

Aromas, scents:

Cedar, Juniper

Prepare home-made ointments and cosmetics.

Apply detoxing facial and body care.

Treatments of bumps and pimples on the skin, and exfoliating procedures.

Remove body hair, it may not grow back.

Correction of the nail bed.

Massages that serve to relax, ease tension, and detoxify.

Reflexology massage.

Treating obstinate athlete's foot, nail fungus, and warts.

Cutting and filing toenails and fingernails will make the nails grow stronger over time.

Garden/Nature

Plant part:

Root

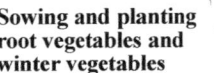

Sowing and planting root vegetables and winter vegetables

Weeding. Harrowing weeds. Dig over to prepare soil. Trimming and cutting back plants.
Clear and thin out plants, forest edges, and hedges. Plant cuttings.
Spread fertilizer and manure.
Start a compost heap.
Combat vermin.

Fertilize flowers with poorly formed roots.

Mulching.

Harvest produce is suitable for storage. Harvest root vegetables.

Gather herbs (roots) for bone, joint, and skin diseases.

Housework

Housework is dealt with much more successfully, efficiently, and effortlessly.

Problem stains are removed readily.

Best for doing laundry! Reduce on laundry detergent, support the environment.

Avoid dry cleaning, as the fabric may develop unwanted glossy blotches.

Thoroughly clean wooden and parquet floors, metals, china etc.

Cleaning, polishing, and waterproofing shoes.

Combating mold.

Air rooms only briefly.

Painting.

Preserving root vegetables. Slice cabbage now to ferment into sauerkraut.

Nutrition

Food quality:

Salt

Garlic, carrots, red beets, reddish, rutabaga, sugar beet, celery, potatoes, onions, kohlrabi.

Weight associated with overeating is less likely. If underweight, eat larger portions.

Cleansing and detox diets. Fruit and juice days.

Flush out poisons. Treatment for drug abuse.

Avoid large quantities of salty foods like bacon, ham, salted herring, fatty cheese, and the like. Avoid heavy and greasy foods.

Autumn is a second spring when every leaf is a flower.
Albert Camus

Color — **Yellow**
Day — **Cool**
Element — **Earth**

Capricorn

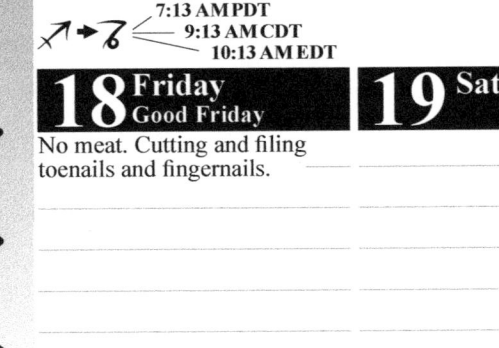

7:13 AM PDT
9:13 AM CDT
10:13 AM EDT

4:23 PM PDT
6:32 PM CDT
7:32 PM EDT

18 Friday — Good Friday
No meat. Cutting and filing toenails and fingernails.

19 Saturday

20 Sunday Easter, Passover Final Day
Half Moon.

A P R I L

Harvest Time
Ascending forces! Sap is rising, enhancing plant growth above ground, resulting in the most juicy fruits and vegetables.

detox
remove
be active

Waning Moon

Success

Inspiration, optimism, and impatience. Rational thinking, creativity and imagination spark new ideas and inspire planning for the future.

Shying away from routine tasks people will feel more drawn to anything new.

Instead of gridlocked structures choose new possibilities.

Leisure

Inspiration and optimism will boost friendship, social gatherings, and parties.

Express your creativity and imagination. Dwell in dreams and utopian ideas. It is easier now to perceive intuitive thoughts.

Health

Sensitive body parts:

Lower Legs, Veins

All measures taken to flush out and detoxify the sensitive body parts are very effective.

Good for surgery, except on the sensitive body parts (see above), head, and neck. Scarring is less severe.

Teeth: Removal of tartar and amalgam. Best for fillings, crowns, and dentures!

Blood-purifying, detoxifying herbal infusions and teas.

Sensitive glandular system.

Avoid inflammation of the veins. Apply ointments to lower legs, and rest legs in a raised position.

Varicose veins: Avoid long periods of standing.

While exercising go easy on the ankles.

Sensitivity to light, so bring your sunglasses along.

Body Care

Aromas, scents:
Cyclamen, Peach, Wild Roses

Prepare home-made ointments and cosmetics.

Apply detoxing facial and body care.

Treatments of bumps and pimples on the skin, and exfoliating procedures.

Removing body hair.

Correction of the nail bed.

Massages that serve to relax, ease tension, and detoxify.

Reflexology massage.

Removal of callused skin.

Treating obstinate athlete's foot, nail fungus, and warts.

Garden/Nature

Plant part:

Flower

Fertilize flowers that no longer bloom.

Dig over/plow to prepare soil for planting.

Trimming and cutting back plants.

Hoeing and harrowing; weeds can be left to rot.

Pest control.

Start a compost heap.

Avoid watering plants.

Avoid transplanting sprouts.

Harvested produce is well suitable for storage.

Gather herbs (roots) for vein diseases.

Housework

Housework is dealt with much more successfully, efficiently, and effortlessly.

Problem stains are removed readily.

Best for doing laundry! Reduce on laundry detergent, support the environment.

Dry cleaning.

Clean and store seasonal clothing.

Best suited for a spring cleaning: Thoroughly clean wooden and parquet floors, metals, china etc.

Cleaning windows and glass.

Cleaning, polishing, and waterproofing shoes.

Combating mold.

Ventilate rooms thoroughly.

Baking bread, cakes, and cookies (add more leavening agent).

Making preserves.

Painting.

Nutrition

Food quality:

Fat

Cauliflower, artichoke, broccoli, sunflower seeds, flax seeds, nuts, rose hip, elder.

Weight associated with overeating is less likely. If underweight, eat larger portions.

Cleansing and detox diets. Fruit and juice days.

Flush out poisons. Treatment for drug abuse.

Pay attention to any particularly tempting foods today: Most likely the "wrong" things taste best.

High cholesterol: eat a low fat diet.

Tears are often the telescope by which men see far into heaven.
Henry Ward Beecher

Positive affirmation:
"I trust in love that is all-encompassing."

21 **Monday**
Easter Monday (CAN)

22 **Tuesday**
Earth Day

Color

Bright/ Dark Blue

Day

Air/Light

Element

Aquarius   **Air**

A P R I L

Harvest Time
Ascending forces! Sap is rising, enhancing plant growth above ground, resulting in the most juicy fruits and vegetables.

detox
remove
be active

Waning Moon

Success

Sensibility, intuition, and helpfulness.

Where possible, retreating is more favorable than dealing with business matters.

Dissolve restrictions, be patient and wait. Be aware that people can be more easily influenced.

Leisure

Your helpfulness will boost friendships.

Enjoy dancing or swimming, or watch a movie that will inspire your fantasies and imagination.

Retreat, relax, and recover.

Romance can be gentle and coziness will prevail.

If you plan outdoor excursions, be prepared for a shower here and there.

Health

Sensitive body parts:

Feet and Toes

All measures taken to flush out and detoxify the sensitive body parts are very effective.

Good for surgical operations except those on the sensitive body parts (see above), head, and neck.
Scarring is less severe.

Teeth: Removal of tartar and amalgam. Best for fillings, crowns, and dentures!

Blood-purifying, detoxifying herbal infusions and teas.

Sensitive nervous system.

Drugs have a much stronger effect on your body. Monitor closely what you put into your body.

Lymphatic therapy.

Sluggishness or fatigue may occur in the transition into the next Zodiac sign of Aries.

Body Care

Aromas, scents:
Magnolia, Amaryllis, Clary Sage

Prepare home-made ointments and cosmetics.

Apply detoxing facial and body care.

Treatments of bumps and pimples on the skin, and exfoliating procedures.

Removing body hair.

Correction of the nail bed.

Massages that serve to relax, ease tension, and detoxify. Reflexology massage. Carry out with special care, people are more sensitive.

Removal of callused skin.

Treating obstinate athlete's foot, nail fungus, and warts.

Foot bath.

No haircuts, hair becomes shaggy and unmanageable. Avoid washing your hair.

Garden/Nature

Plant part:

Leaf

Water plants.

Fertilize flowers.

Sow plants and vegetables that grow below ground, potatoes, leaf vegetables, and lettuce.

Dig over/plow to prepare soil for planting.
Trimming and cutting back plants.
Start a compost heap.

Mowing lawns.

Pest control. Weeding.

Harvested produce should be consumed as soon as possible.

Gather herbs for foot complaints.

Housework

Housework is dealt with much more successfully, efficiently, and effortlessly.

Problem stains are removed readily.

Best for doing laundry! Reduce on laundry detergent, support the environment.

Dry cleaning.

Clean and store seasonal clothing.

Thoroughly clean wooden and parquet floors, metals, china etc.

Cleaning, polishing, and waterproofing shoes.

Combating mold.

Ventilate rooms briefly and rapidly.

Avoid painting.

Preserving and storing should be avoided.

Nutrition

Food quality:

Carbohydrate

Lettuce, spinach, lamb's lettuce, Endive, parsley, leek, cabbage (Brussels sprouts, kale, Chinese cabbage), all leafy herbs, asparagus, mushrooms, cress, Swiss chard, rhubarb.

Weight associated with overeating is less likely. If underweight, eat larger portions.

Cleansing and detox diets. Fruit and juice days.

Flush out poisons. Treatment for drug abuse.

Caffeine, alcohol, drugs, certain foods, and stimulants have a much stronger effect.

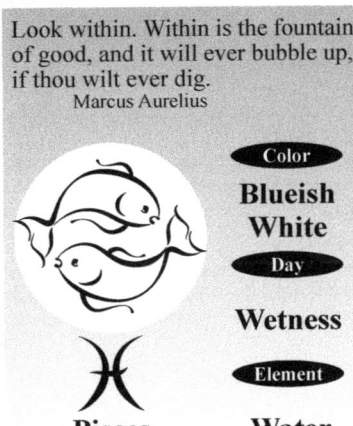

Look within. Within is the fountain of good, and it will ever bubble up, if thou wilt ever dig.
Marcus Aurelius

Color
Blueish White

Day
Wetness

Element

Pisces   **Water**

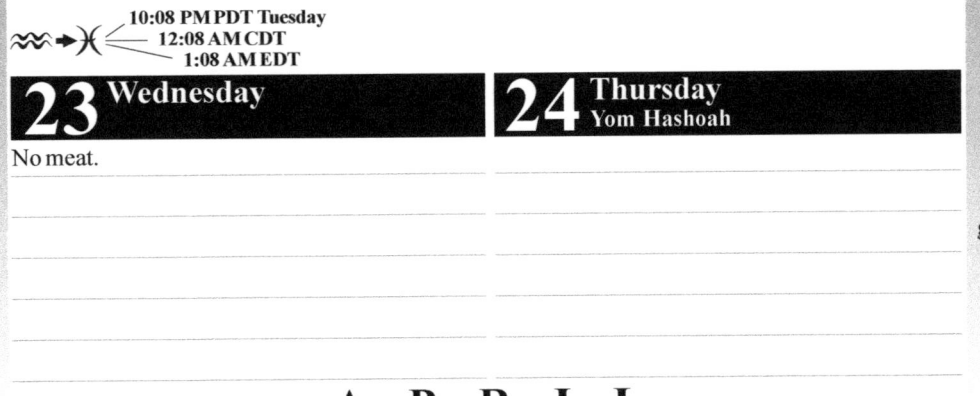

10:08 PM PDT Tuesday
≈≈ → ⫶ ← 12:08 AM CDT
1:08 AM EDT

23 Wednesday

No meat.

24 Thursday
Yom Hashoah

A P R I L

Harvest Time
Ascending forces! Sap is rising, enhancing plant growth above ground, resulting in the most juicy fruits and vegetables.

detox
remove
be active

Waning Moon

Success

Things get going and the way straight ahead seems the best.

People feel energetic, courageous, assertive, and at times anxious.

Good time for meetings and sales talks but impatience and selfishness do not favor teamwork.

Leisure

An enterprising spirit and spontaneity move people to enjoy outings, sports, competitions, cultural events, and travels.

Romance can be very passionate.

Good days for outings, even with cloudy skies the air still feels somewhat warm. Drying effect, get plenty to drink.

Health

Sensitive body parts:

Head, Brain, Eyes

All measures taken to flush out and detoxify the sensitive body parts are very effective.

Good for surgery, except on the sensitive body parts (see above), and neck.

Scarring is less severe.

Teeth: Removal of tartar and amalgam. Best for fillings, crowns, and dentures! Avoiding treatment of periodontitis and gums.

Blood-purifying, detoxifying herbal infusions and teas.

Sensitive sense organs.

If you suffer from migraines drink plenty of water, and avoid coffee, chocolate, and sugar.

Body Care

Aromas, scents: Cloves, Peppermint, Thyme

Prepare home-made ointments and cosmetics.

Apply detoxing facial and body care.

Treatments of bumps and pimples on the skin, and exfoliating procedures.

Removing body hair.

Correction of the nail bed.

Massages that serve to relax, ease tension, and detoxify.

Reflexology massage.

Removal of callused skin.

Treating obstinate athlete's foot, nail fungus, and warts.

Eye compresses to relieve strained eyes.

Any kind of hair care.

Garden/Nature

Plant part:

Fruit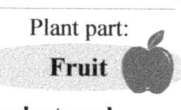

Sowing plants and vegetables that grow below ground. Sowing and planting anything that is supposed to grow fast. Sowing and planting fruit and tomatoes. Dig over/plow the soil to prepare for planting. Spreading manure. Fertilizing grains, vegetables, and fruit. Weeding. Pest control. Pruning of fruit trees and bushes. Harvesting and storing grains, vegetables, potatoes, fruits, and tomatoes. Start a compost heap. Gather herbs (roots) for eye complaints and headaches. Day off on 4/26.

Housework

Housework is dealt with much more successfully, efficiently, and effortlessly.

Problem stains are removed readily.

Best for doing laundry!

Dry cleaning.

Clean and store seasonal clothing.

Thoroughly clean wooden and parquet floors, metals, china, etc.

Cleaning windows and glass.

Cleaning, polishing, and waterproofing shoes.

Combating mold.

Ventilate rooms sufficiently. Air beds.

Suitable for making cheese.

Preserving and freezing fruit and vegetables.

Baking bread, cakes, and cookies (use more leavening agent).

Painting.

Nutrition

Food quality:

Protein

Beans, peas, corn, tomatoes, pumpkin, lentils, soybeans, cucumber, eggplant, zucchini, berries, fruit, chili, bell pepper, figs, avocado, melon, olives.

Weight associated with overeating is less likely. If underweight, eat larger portions.

Cleansing and detox diets. Fruit and juice days.

Flush out poisons. Treatment for drug abuse.

Drink plenty of water.

All experience is an arch, to build upon.
Henry B. Adams

Color
Indigo Blue

Day

Warm

Element

Aries   Fire

♓ → ♈ ← 12:25 AM PDT
                   2:25 AM CDT
                   3:25 AM EDT

25 Friday
Arbor Day

No meat. Cutting and filing toenails and fingernails.

26 Saturday

A P R I L

Harvest Time
Ascending forces! Sap is rising, enhancing plant growth above ground, resulting in the most juicy fruits and vegetables.

detox remove be active

Waning Moon

Success

Realism and material security are important. Persistence comes easy, thoughts and reactions are slower.

Assess financial areas.

Conservative tendencies may make people want to stay away from risk taking.

● *New Moon: Confirm your resolutions. Finalize new decisions. Drop bad habits.*

Leisure

Relax at a picnic/feast. Enjoy culinary pleasures and hobbies.

The earth feels cold to the touch, so take slightly warmer clothes.

Health

Sensitive body parts:

Head and Neck

All measures taken to flush out and detoxify the sensitive body parts are very effective. Scarring is less severe. Teeth: Removal of tartar and amalgam. Best for fillings, crowns, and dentures! Avoiding treatment of periodontitis and gums. Blood-purifying, detoxifying herbal infusions and teas. Sensitive blood circulation. Organs of speech, jaws, teeth, tonsils, thyroid gland, neck, and vocal chords get easily affected. Keep neck warm. On cold days ears should be protected. Sensitivity to noise. High blood pressure: Avoid salty foods. Massages, lymphatic therapy, and chiropractic treatment to release blockages.

● *New Moon: Avoid any surgery if possible.*

Body Care

Aromas, scents: Geranium, Jasmine, Rose

Prepare home-made ointments and cosmetics.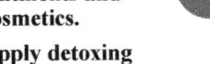

Apply detoxing facial and body care.

Treatments of bumps and pimples on the skin, and exfoliating procedures.

Removing body hair.

Correction of the nail bed.

Massages that serve to relax, ease tension, and detoxify.

Reflexology massage.

Removal of callused skin.

Treating obstinate athlete's foot, nail fungus, and warts.

Garden/Nature

Plant part: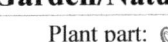

Root

Sow plants and vegetables that grow below ground. Everything grows slowly and lasts well.

Dig over to prepare soil.

Trimming/cutting back plants. Weeding. Mulching.

Start a compost heap.

Combat vermin found in the soil.

Spread fertilizer and liquid manure.

Fertilize flowers with poorly formed roots.

Harvested produce is well suited for storage. Harvesting root vegetables.

Gather herbs (roots) for sinus issues, sore throat, and ear complaints.

● *New Moon: Change of weather is likely. Care for sickly plants.*

Housework

Housework is dealt with much more successfully, efficiently, and effortlessly.

Problem stains are removed readily.

Best for doing laundry! Reduce on laundry detergent, support the environment.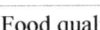

Dry cleaning.

Clean and store seasonal clothing.

Thoroughly clean wooden and parquet floors, metals, china etc.

Cleaning, polishing, and waterproofing shoes.

Combating mold.

Air rooms only briefly.

Painting.

Preserving root vegetables.

Nutrition

Food quality:

Salt

Garlic, carrots, red beets, reddish, rutabaga, sugar beet, celery, potatoes, onions, kohlrabi.

Weight associated with overeating is less likely. If underweight, eat larger portions.

Cleansing and detox diets. Fruit and juice days.

Flush out poisons. Treatment for drug abuse.

Avoid large quantities of salty foods like bacon, ham, salted herring, fatty cheese, and the like.

● *New Moon: A day of fasting.*

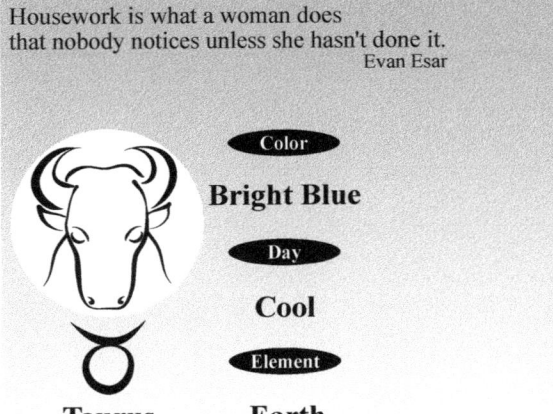

Housework is what a woman does that nobody notices unless she hasn't done it.
Evan Esar

Color **Bright Blue**

Day **Cool**

Element **Earth**

Taurus

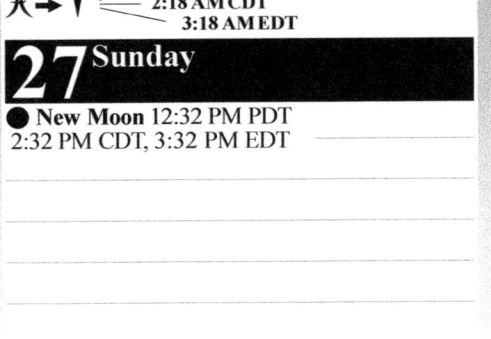

♓ ➝ ♈
12:18 AM PDT
2:18 AM CDT
3:18 AM EDT

27 Sunday

● New Moon 12:32 PM PDT
2:32 PM CDT, 3:32 PM EDT

A P R I L

Positive affirmation:
"I trust in love that is all-encompassing."

Harvest Time
Ascending forces! Sap is rising, enhancing plant growth above ground, resulting in the most juicy fruits and vegetables.

detox remove be active

Waning Moon

Success

Realism and material security are important. Persistence comes easy, thoughts and reactions are slower.

Assess financial areas.

Conservative tendencies may make people want to stay away from risk taking.

Leisure

Relax at a picnic/feast. Enjoy culinary pleasures and hobbies.

The earth feels cold to the touch, so take slightly warmer clothes.

Health

Sensitive body parts:

Head and Neck

All measures taken to supply nutrient materials and strengthen the sensitive body parts are very effective.

Healing ointments are easily absorbed.

Sensitive blood circulation.

Organs of speech, jaws, teeth, tonsils, thyroid gland, neck, and vocal chords get easily affected. Keep neck warm. On cold days ears should be protected. Sensitivity to noise.

High blood pressure: Avoid salty foods.

Massages, lymphatic therapy, and chiropractic treatment to release blockages.

Body Care

Aromas, scents: Geranium, Jasmine, Rose

Treatments with firming and moisturizing creams are more effective.

Massages that serve to regenerate, and strengthen, perhaps aided with beneficial massage oils.

Correcting and cutting ingrown nails.

Hair dyes applied now, will look more vibrant.

Garden/Nature

Plant part:

Root

Sow plants, herbs, and vegetables that grow and flourish above ground.

Sowing and planting trees, bushes, hedges, and root vegetables. Everything grows slowly and lasts well.

Transplanting.

Harvesting and storing root vegetables. Harvested produce is well suited for storage.

Gather herbs for sinus issues, sore throat, and ear complaints.

Housework

Light housework only.

Air rooms only briefly.

Preserving root vegetables.

Nutrition

Food quality:

Salt

Garlic, carrots, red beets, reddish, rutabaga, sugar beet, celery, potatoes, onions, kohlrabi.

Weight gain: avoid indulging in rich foods. If overweight, eat smaller portions.

Supply nutrient materials to strengthen the body. Focus on foods that contain essential minerals and vitamins.

Stimulants and vitamins are more effective.

Avoid large quantities of salty foods like bacon, ham, salted herring, fatty cheese, and the like.

Positive affirmation:
"I trust in deep healing."

Harvest Time
Ascending forces! Sap is rising, enhancing plant growth above ground, resulting in the most juicy fruits and vegetables.

gather strength rest, recover buildup

Waxing Moon

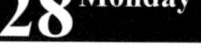

28 Monday

A P R I L

Believe in yourself! Have faith in your abilities! Without a humble but reasonable confidence in your own powers you cannot be successful or happy.
Norman Vincent Peale

Color
Bright Blue

Day
Cool

Element
Earth

Taurus

Success

Open mindedness and curiosity. A changeable and hectic time.

Good time for talking, negotiating, networking, and exchanging ideas as well as for meetings of a nonbinding nature, conferences, and studies.

Leisure

Good time for family gatherings, parties, and short trips.

People enjoy stimulating their minds with reading and studying. Attending theater performances is a preferred enjoyment. Enhance friendships.

Stretching exercises.

Be prepared for sudden changes in weather or climate.

Health

Sensitive body parts:

Shoulders, Arms, Hands, Lungs

All measures taken to supply nutrient materials and strengthen the sensitive body parts are very effective.

Healing ointments are easily absorbed. Applying herbal ointments to the shoulders for rheumatic gout and alike.

Sensitive glandular system.

Make sure you are dressed warm enough in cool weather.

Exercises for shoulders. Breathing exercises.

Avoid having any teeth pulled.

Sensitivity to light, bring your sunglasses along.

Massages, lymphatic therapy, and chiropractic treatment to release blockages.

Body Care

Aromas, scents: Lavender, Lemon Balm, Magnolia, Verbena

Treatments with firming and moisturizing creams are more effective.

Massages that serve to regenerate, and strengthen, perhaps aided with beneficial massage oils.

Correcting and cutting ingrown nails.

Hair dyes applied now, will look more vibrant.

Garden/Nature

Plant part:

Flower

Sow plants, herbs, and vegetables that grow and flourish above ground.

Sowing and planting any creeping or climbing plants, flowers, and medicinal herbs.

Transplanting.

Avoid watering plants.

Gather herbs for tensions in the shoulder and lung complaints.

Changes in weather are more likely.

Housework

Light housework only.

Ventilate rooms thoroughly.

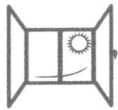

Making preserves.

Baking cakes and cookies. Dough rises faster. (Except on New Moon)

Nutrition

Food quality:

Fat

Cauliflower, artichoke, broccoli, sunflower seeds, flax seeds, nuts, rose hip, elder.

Weight gain: avoid indulging in rich foods. If overweight, eat smaller portions.

Supply nutrient materials to strengthen the body. Focus on foods that contain essential minerals and vitamins.

Stimulants and vitamins are more effective.

Pay attention to any particularly tempting foods today: Most likely the "wrong" things taste best.

High cholesterol: eat a low fat diet.

Positive affirmation:
"I trust in deep healing."

Turning Point
Transition of ascending to descending forces. Both forces are at work and neutralize each other.

gather strength rest, recover buildup
Waxing Moon

11:36 PM PDT Monday
1:36 AM CDT
2:36 AM EDT

29 Tuesday

30 Wednesday
No meat.

A P R I L

Problems are not stop signs, they are guidelines.
Robert H. Schuller

Color
Light Blue

Day
Air/Light

Element
Air

Gemini

Success

Feelings, sensitivity, and cooperativeness. Many are overly sensitive, so beware of treading on someone's toes.

Be cautious if you are easily influenced.

During negotiations make use of the cognitive ability of your senses.

Leisure

Relax within your close family.

Retreat to your safe haven and enjoy your fantasy while reading or listening to music. The inner world becomes more colorful than the outer.

Romance can be gentle. Deep feelings will prevail.

If you plan outdoor excursions, be prepared for a shower here and there.

Health

Sensitive body parts:
Chest, Lungs, Liver, Stomach, Gall Bladder

All measures taken to supply nutrient materials and strengthen the sensitive body parts are very effective.

Healing ointments are easily absorbed.

Sensitive nervous system.

Be cautious with alcohol since the liver is very sensitive.

Stomach could play up and cause gas and heartburn.

Rheumatism: Don't air bedding outside, damp will remain in the bedding.

Lymphatic therapy.

Body Care

Aromas, scents:
Lilac, Lilies of the Valley, Lilies, Violets

Treatments with firming and moisturizing creams are more effective.

Massages that serve to regenerate, and strengthen, perhaps aided with beneficial massage oils.

Correcting and cutting ingrown nails.

No haircuts, hair becomes shaggy and unmanageable. Avoid washing your hair.

Garden/Nature

Plant part:
Leaf

Watering all indoor and outdoor plants.

Sow plants, herbs, and vegetables that grow and flourish above ground, leaf vegetables (no lettuce).

Transplanting.

Trimming and cutting back plants. Avoid pruning fruit trees and bushes.

Cut trees, garlands, pick flowers to dry; they will last longer.

Sowing and mowing lawns.

Setting up a compost heap.

Gather herbs for bronchitis, stomach, liver, and gall bladder complaints.

Unfavorable for harvesting, storing, and preserving.

Housework

Light housework only.

Ventilate rooms briefly and rapidly. Don't air mattresses.

Any dirt and spots are easily removed in the laundry.

Avoid painting, as paint will take very long to dry.

Nutrition

Food quality:
Carbohydrate

Lettuce, spinach, lamb's lettuce, Endive, parsley, leek, cabbage (Brussels sprouts, kale, Chinese cabbage), all leafy herbs, asparagus, mushrooms, cress, Swiss chard, rhubarb.

Weight gain: avoid indulging in rich foods. If overweight, eat smaller portions and avoid carbohydrates. Moodiness may make you want to eat more than is healthy.

Supply nutrient materials to strengthen the body. Focus on foods that contain essential minerals and vitamins. Stimulants and vitamins are more effective.

If you get stomach troubles easily, avoid heavy meals.

Positive affirmation:
"I trust in deep healing."

Planting Time
Descending forces! Sap is drawn downward, enhancing root formation. Best days for sowing, planting, and transplanting.

gather strength rest, recover buildup
Waxing Moon

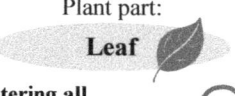

12:24 AM PDT
2:24 AM CDT
3:24 AM EDT

1 Thursday
May Day

2 Friday
National Day of Prayer

No meat. Cutting and filing toenails and fingernails.

M A Y

Wherever you are – be all there.
Jim Elliot

Color
Green

Day
Wetness

Element
Water

Cancer

Success

Determination reigns, and risks are taken more often. Master your tasks with more self-confidence and creativity.

Limits appear to be more easily surmountable.

Auspicious day for sales, advertising, and publicity.

Leisure

Zest for life is in the air. People want to have a fun time, enjoy parties, musical events, movies, etc.

Possessive feelings can harm a relationship. Romance can be very passionate.

Outings: even with cloudy skies the air still feels somewhat warm. Drying effect, get plenty to drink.

Danger of sudden storms, not only in the sky.

Health

Sensitive body parts:
Heart, Back, Diaphragm, Circulation, Arteries

All measures taken to supply nutrient materials and strengthen the sensitive body parts are very effective.

Healing ointments are easily absorbed.

Sensitive sense organs.

Back and heart problems are more likely to occur.

Avoid over straining of the heart and circulation with unusual physical activities.

Expect sleepless nights.

Body Care

Aromas, scents:
Hibiscus, Oleander, Rose

Treatments with firming and moisturizing creams are more effective.

Massages that serve to regenerate, and strengthen, perhaps aided with beneficial massage oils.

Correcting and cutting ingrown nails.

Good days for haircuts, hair becomes stronger. But be aware that if you get a perm, curls will become quite frizzy. Baby's first haircut.

Garden/Nature

Plant part:
Fruit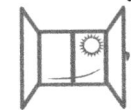

Sow plants and vegetables that grow and flourish above ground. Sowing and planting fruit. Also sow and plant vegetables that are highly perishable. Plant trees and bushes. Sow lawns.

Transplanting. Grafting onto fruit trees.

Trimming and cutting back plants.

Best for cultivating grains on wet fields.

Dig over/plow to prepare soil for planting.

Setting up a compost heap.

Not suitable for fertilizing.

Harvested produce should be consumed as soon as possible.

Gather herbs for heart and circulation complaints.

Housework

Light housework only.

Ventilate sufficiently.

Freezing fruit and vegetables.

Baking bread, cakes, and cookies. Dough rises faster. (Except on New Moon)

Suitable for making cheese.

Avoid painting.

Nutrition

Food quality:
Protein

Beans, peas, corn, tomatoes, pumpkin, lentils, soybeans, cucumber, eggplant, zucchini, berries, fruit, chili, bell pepper, figs, avocado, melon, olives.

Weight gain: avoid indulging in rich foods. If overweight, eat smaller portions.

Supply nutrient materials to strengthen the body. Focus on foods that contain essential minerals and vitamins.

Stimulants and vitamins are more effective.

Positive affirmation:
"I trust in deep healing."

Planting Time
Descending forces! Sap is drawn downward, enhancing root formation. Best days for sowing, planting, and transplanting.

gather strength rest, recover buildup
Waxing Moon

♋ → ♌
4:30 AM PDT
6:30 AM CDT
7:30 AM EDT

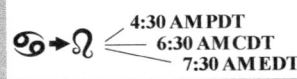

3 Saturday	**4** Sunday	**5** Monday Cinco de Mayo

☽ Half Moon.

12:41 PM PDT
2:41 PM CDT
3:41 PM EDT
♌ → ♍

M A Y

Music in the soul can be heard by the universe.
Lao Tzu

 Color
Green

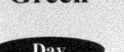 Day
Warm

 Element

Fire

 Leo

Success

Good time for details, organization, routine, concentration, and duty.

Take care of financial and administrative tasks.

Prepare for future success now with realistic and critical assessment.

Leisure

Enjoy a nature walk.

Good time for health regimes. Improve your health with stretching exercises and yoga.

The earth feels cold to the touch, so take slightly warmer clothes.

Health

Sensitive body parts:
Digestive Organs, Nerves, Spleen, Pancreas

All measures taken to supply nutrient materials and strengthen the sensitive body parts are very effective.

Healing ointments are easily absorbed.

Sensitive blood circulation.

For a sensitive digestive system, a wholesome diet is recommended.

Dress slightly warmer.

High blood pressure: Avoid salty foods.

Massages, lymphatic therapy, and chiropractic treatment to release blockages.

Body Care

Aromas, scents:
Lavender, Spruce Needles, Sage, Meadow Flowers

Treatments with firming and moisturizing creams are more effective.

Massages that serve to regenerate, and strengthen, perhaps aided with beneficial massage oils.

Correcting and cutting ingrown nails.

Best for haircuts because it retains its shape longer. Perms turn out best. Hair dyes applied now, will look more vibrant.

Garden/Nature

Plant part:
Root

Best for sowing and planting, except lettuce.

Plant trees which are supposed to grow very tall. Plant hedges and bushes that are meant to grow very fast.

Sowing lawns.

Planting and re-potting balcony and indoor plants.

Transplanting.

Trimming and cutting back plants.

Planting cuttings.

Start a compost heap.

Avoid harvesting and storing.

Gather herbs (roots) for digestive organs, pancreas, and nervous complaints.

Housework

Light housework only.

Air rooms only briefly.

Making pickles, preserves, and cheese yields suboptimal results and should be avoided.

Nutrition

Food quality:
Salt

Garlic, carrots, red beets, reddish, rutabaga, sugar beet, celery, potatoes, onions, kohlrabi.

Weight gain: avoid indulging in rich foods. If overweight, eat smaller portions.

Supply nutrient materials to strengthen the body. Focus on foods that contain essential minerals and vitamins.

Stimulants and vitamins are more effective.

Avoid large quantities of salty foods like bacon, ham, salted herring, fatty cheese, and the like. Avoid heavy and greasy foods.

Positive affirmation:
"I trust in deep healing."

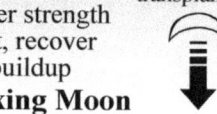

Planting Time
Descending forces! Sap is drawn downward, enhancing root formation. Best days for sowing, planting, and transplanting.

gather strength rest, recover buildup
Waxing Moon

6 Tuesday	**7** Wednesday
	No meat.

M A Y

Everyone chases after happiness, not noticing that happiness is right at their heels.
Bertolt Brecht

Color
Yellow

Day
Cool

Element
Earth

♍ **Virgo**

Success

The artistic instinct rules, but so, too, does indecisiveness. The forces swing back and forth until equilibrium is achieved.

It's easy to reach compromises with tactful sensitivity.

A sense of judgment will support legal matters.

Leisure

Pursuit for harmony and cooperativeness supports good times in romance, friendship, and partnership.

Enjoy cultural events. Relax and get pampered with a spa treatment.

Romance can be passionate yet sensitive.

Health

Sensitive body parts:

Hips, Kidneys, Bladder

All measures taken to supply nutrient materials and strengthen the sensitive body parts are very effective.

Healing ointments are easily absorbed.

Sensitive glandular system.

Take special care to keep the area of bladder and kidneys warm.

Apply special exercises for the hip region.

Avoid having any teeth pulled.

Sensitivity to light, bring your sunglasses along.

Body Care

Aromas, scents: Roses, Violets, Daffodils

Treatments with firming and moisturizing creams are more effective.

Massages that serve to regenerate, and strengthen, perhaps aided with beneficial massage oils.

Correcting and cutting ingrown nails.

Hair dyes applied now, will look more vibrant.

Garden/Nature

Plant part:

Flower

Sow plants and vegetables that grow and flourish above ground, specially flowers, and medicinal herbs.

Transplanting.

Trimming and cutting back plants.

Avoid watering plants.

Start a compost heap.

Harvested produce should be consumed as soon as possible.

Gather herbs for kidneys, gall bladder, and hip complaints.

Day off on 5/9.

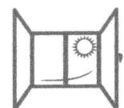

Housework

Light housework only.

Ventilate rooms thoroughly.

Baking cakes and cookies. Dough rises faster. (Except on New Moon)

Nutrition

Food quality:

Fat

Cauliflower, artichoke, broccoli, sunflower seeds, flax seeds, nuts, rose hip, elder.

Weight gain: avoid indulging in rich foods. If overweight, eat smaller portions.

Supply nutrient materials to strengthen the body. Focus on foods that contain essential minerals and vitamins.

Stimulants and vitamins are more effective.

Pay attention to any particularly tempting foods today: Most likely the "wrong" things taste best.

High cholesterol: eat a low fat diet.

Positive affirmation:
"I trust in deep healing."

gather strength rest, recover buildup
Waxing Moon

Planting Time
Descending forces! Sap is drawn downward, enhancing root formation. Best days for sowing, planting, and transplanting.

	12:07 AM PDT
ℏ→♎	2:07 AM CDT
	3:07 AM EDT

8 Thursday

9 Friday

No meat. Cutting and filing toenails and fingernails.

12:59 PM PDT	
2:59 PM CDT	♎→♏
3:59 PM EDT	

10 Saturday

M A Y

Everywhere is within walking distance if you have the time.
Steven Wright

Color
Orange

Day
Air/Light

Element
Air

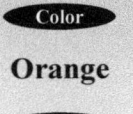

Libra

Success

Critical and superstitious behavior emerges, especially pertaining to money.

A penetrating power will strengthen your capacity to act.

An increased perception opens our interest for the essentials and helps to discover hidden potentials.

Leisure

Relax within your close family, with meditation, and relaxation exercises.

A longing to feel safe will be nurtured if you focus on habits and rituals. An increased sensitivity will help to enjoy every moment.

Romance can be very passionate.

If you plan outdoor excursions, be prepared for a shower here and there.

Health

Sensitive body parts:

Sex organs, Ureter

All measures taken to supply nutrient materials and strengthen the sensitive body parts are very effective.

Healing ointments are easily absorbed. Applying herbal ointments to the shoulders for rheumatic gout and alike.

Sensitive nervous system.

Female disorders: As a preventative measure apply hip baths using yarrow.

Pregnancy: Avoid any exertion, miscarriages are more likely.

Keep region of the pelvis, kidneys, and feet warm to prevent infection of the bladder and kidneys.

Lymphatic therapy.

Body Care

Aromas, scents:
Anemone, Cornflower
Oregano, Thuja

Treatments with firming and moisturizing creams are more effective.

Massages that serve to regenerate, and strengthen, perhaps aided with beneficial massage oils.

Correcting and cutting ingrown nails.

Hair dyes applied now, will look more vibrant.

Garden/Nature

Plant part:

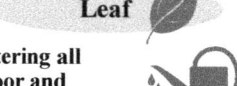

Leaf

Watering all indoor and outdoor plants.

Sow plants, herbs, and vegetables that grow and flourish above ground, leaf vegetables (no lettuce).

Sowing, planting, harvesting, and drying every kind of medicinal herbs.

Transplanting.

Trimming and cutting back plants.

Combating slugs and snails. Mowing lawns.

Start a compost heap.

Avoid pruning fruit trees and bushes. Avoid cutting down any trees.

Harvested produce should be consumed as soon as possible.

Housework

Light housework only.

Ventilate rooms briefly and rapidly. Don't air mattresses.

Any dirt and spots are easily removed in the laundry.

Avoid painting, as paint will take very long to dry.

Nutrition

Food quality:

Carbohydrate

Lettuce, spinach, lamb's lettuce, Endive, parsley, leek, cabbage (Brussels sprouts, kale, Chinese cabbage), all leafy herbs, asparagus, mushrooms, cress, Swiss chard, rhubarb.

Weight gain: avoid indulging in rich foods. If overweight, eat smaller portions and avoid carbohydrates.

Supply nutrient materials to strengthen the body. Focus on foods that contain essential minerals and vitamins. Stimulants and vitamins are more effective.

Positive affirmation:
"I trust in deep healing."

Planting Time
Descending forces!
Sap is drawn downward, enhancing root formation. Best days for sowing, planting, and transplanting.

gather strength
rest, recover
buildup
Waxing Moon

11 **Sunday**
Mother's Day

M A Y

Those who cannot remember the past are condemned to repeat it.
George Santayana

Color
Red

Day
Wetness

Element
Water   **Scorpio**

Success

Critical and superstitious behavior emerges, especially pertaining to money.

A penetrating power will strengthen your capacity to act.

An increased perception opens our interest for the essentials and helps to discover hidden potentials.

Leisure

Relax within your close family, with meditation, and relaxation exercises.

A longing to feel safe will be nurtured if you focus on habits and rituals. An increased sensitivity will help to enjoy every moment.

Romance can be very passionate.

If you plan outdoor excursions, be prepared for a shower here and there.

Health

Sensitive body parts:

Sex organs, Ureter

All measures taken to flush out and detoxify the sensitive body parts are very effective.

Scarring is less severe.

Teeth: Removal of tartar and amalgam. Best for fillings, crowns, and dentures!

Blood-purifying, detoxifying herbal infusions and teas.

Sensitive nervous system.

Female disorders: As a preventative measure apply hip baths using yarrow.

Pregnancy: Avoid any exertion, miscarriages are more likely.

Keep region of the pelvis, kidneys, and feet warm to prevent infection of the bladder and kidneys.

Lymphatic therapy.

○ *Full Moon: Avoid any surgery and vaccination if possible.*

Body Care

Aromas, scents:
Anemone, Cornflower
Oregano, Thuja

Prepare home-made ointments and cosmetics.

Apply detoxing facial and body care.

Treatments of bumps and pimples on the skin, and exfoliating procedures.

Removing body hair.

Correction of the nail bed.

Massages that serve to relax, ease tension, and detoxify.

Reflexology massage.

Removal of callused skin.

Treating obstinate athlete's foot, nail fungus, and warts.

Garden/Nature

Plant part:
Leaf

Water plants.

Fertilize flowers and meadows, no vegetables.

Sow plants and vegetables that grow below ground, leaf vegetables, and lettuce.

Sowing, planting, harvesting, and drying every kind of medicinal herbs.

Dig over/plow to prepare soil for planting.

Trimming and cutting back plants. Transplanting. Weeding. Pest control. Start a compost heap.

Mowing lawns.

Harvested produce should be consumed as soon as possible.

Avoid cutting down trees, danger of bark beetles.

○ *Full Moon: Weather and climate changes. Herbs are most powerful.*

Housework

Housework is dealt with much more successfully, efficiently, and effortlessly.

Problem stains are removed readily.

Dry cleaning.

Thoroughly clean wooden and parquet floors, metals, china etc.

Cleaning, polishing, and waterproofing shoes.

Combating mold.

Ventilate rooms briefly and rapidly.

○ *Full Moon: Avoid doing laundry, cleaning windows, making preserves, painting.*

Nutrition

Food quality:
Carbohydrate

Lettuce, spinach, lamb's lettuce, Endive, parsley, leek, cabbage (Brussels sprouts, kale, Chinese cabbage), all leafy herbs, asparagus, mushrooms, cress, Swiss chard, rhubarb.

Weight associated with overeating is less likely. If underweight, eat larger portions.

Cleansing and detox diets. Fruit and juice days.

Flush out poisons. Treatment for drug abuse.

○ *Full Moon: A day of fasting.*

Hope is the only bee
that makes honey without flowers.
Robert Green Ingersoll

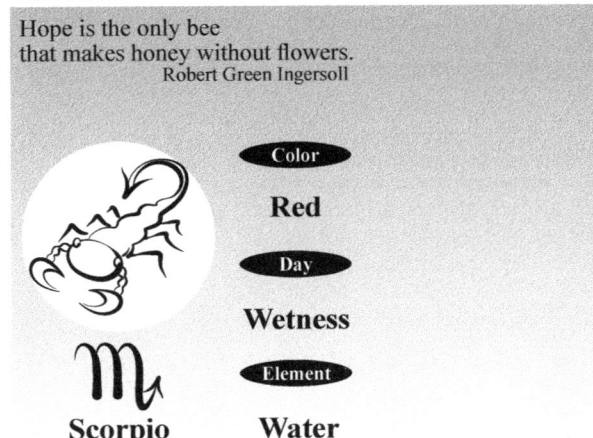

Color

Red

Day

Wetness

Element

Scorpio

Water

12 **Monday**

○ **Full Moon** 8:57 AM PDT,
10:57 AM CDT, 11:57 AM EDT

M   A   Y

Planting Time
Descending forces!
Sap is drawn
downward, enhancing
root formation.
Best days for sowing,
planting, and
transplanting.

detox
remove
be active

Waning Moon

Success

Inquisitiveness and exuberant inspiration lead to new horizons. Insight and love for truth reign.

Bringing together is more important than splitting asunder.

Expansive forces will assist in legal matters, discussions, and debates.

Leisure

Expansion feels great, and travel, short trips, and outings are most welcome. A competitive spirit excites any sports event.

Talk things out when necessary.

Romance can be very passionate.

Good days for outings; even with cloudy skies the air still feels somewhat warm. Drying effect, get plenty to drink.

Health

Sensitive body parts:

Thighs and Veins

All measures taken to flush out and detoxify the sensitive body parts are very effective.

Good for surgical operations except those on the sensitive body parts (see above), head, and neck. Scarring is less severe.

Teeth: Removal of tartar and amalgam. Best for fillings, crowns, and dentures!

Blood-purifying, detoxifying herbal infusions and tea.

Sensitive sense organs.

Pains often arise in the sciatic nerve, veins, the small of the back, and thighs.

Avoid overstraining the body with unusual physical activities.

Body Care

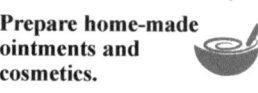

Aromas, scents:
Calendula (Marigold), Geranium, Rosemary

Prepare home-made ointments and cosmetics.

Apply detoxing facial and body care.

Treatments of bumps and pimples on the skin, and exfoliating procedures.

Removing body hair.

Correction of the nail bed.

Massages that serve to relax, ease tension, and detoxify.

Reflexology massage.

Removal of callused skin.

Treating obstinate athlete's foot, nail fungus, and warts.

Garden/Nature

Plant part:

Fruit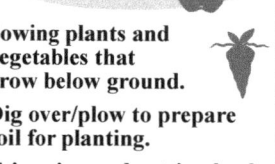

Sowing plants and vegetables that grow below ground.

Dig over/plow to prepare soil for planting.

Trimming and cutting back plants.

Pruning of fruit trees and bushes.

Cultivating grains, particularly corn.

Fertilize grains, vegetables, and fruit.

Combating pests above ground.

Weeding.

Gather herbs (roots) for vein diseases.

Avoid hoeing and harrowing.

Start a compost heap.

Housework

Housework is dealt with much more successfully, efficiently, and effortlessly.

Problem stains are removed readily.

Best for doing laundry!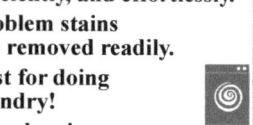

Dry cleaning.

Thoroughly clean wooden and parquet floors, metals, china, etc.

Cleaning windows and glass.

Cleaning, polishing, and waterproofing shoes.

Combating mold.

Ventilate rooms sufficiently. Air beds.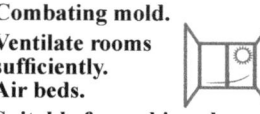

Suitable for making cheese.

Preserving and freezing fruit and vegetables.

Baking bread, cakes, and cookies (use more leavening agent).

Painting.

Nutrition

Food quality:

Protein

Beans, peas, corn, tomatoes, pumpkin, lentils, soybeans, cucumber, eggplant, zucchini, berries, fruit, chili, bell pepper, figs, avocado, melon, olives.

Weight associated with overeating is less likely. If underweight, eat larger portions.

Cleansing and detox diets. Fruit and juice days.

Flush out poisons. Treatment for drug abuse.

Only the educated are free.
Epictetus

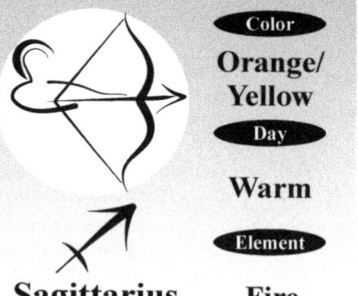

Sagittarius

Color
Orange/Yellow

Day
Warm

Element
Fire

m → ↗ 1:36 AM PDT
              3:36 AM CDT
              4:36 AM EDT

12:59 PM PDT
2:59 PM CDT   ↗ → ♑
3:59 PM EDT

13 Tuesday

14 Wednesday
No meat.

15 Thursday

M A Y

Turning Point
Transition of descending to ascending forces. Both forces are at work and neutralize each other.

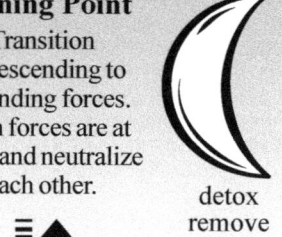

detox remove be active

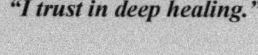
Waning Moon

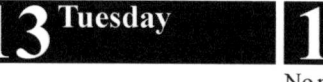

Success

Career and business are in the foreground now and thinking becomes clear and serious, but somewhat inflexible.

Perseverance and reasoning assist in financial matters, planning, and contracts.

The values of tradition, authority, and discipline impact our endeavors.

Leisure

Money is not likely to be wasted in a shopping spree.

Many are drawn to enjoy cultural events.

The earth feels cold to the touch, so take slightly warmer clothes.

Health

Sensitive body parts:
Knees, Joints, Bones, Skin

All measures taken to flush out and detoxify the sensitive body parts are very effective.

Good for surgery, except on the sensitive body parts (see above), head, and neck. Scarring is less severe.

Teeth: Removal of tartar and amalgam. Best for fillings, crowns, and dentures!

Blood-purifying, detoxifying herbal infusions and teas.

Sensitive blood circulation.

Avoid overstraining bones and knees, and apply gentle stretching exercises only.

Problems with meniscus: Don't overstrain.

Dress slightly warmer.

High blood pressure: Avoid salty foods.

Massages, lymphatic therapy, and chiropractic treatment to release blockages.

Body Care

Aromas, scents:
Cedar, Juniper

Prepare home-made ointments and cosmetics.

Apply detoxing facial and body care.

Treatments of bumps and pimples on the skin, and exfoliating procedures.

Remove body hair, it may not grow back.

Correction of the nail bed.

Massages that serve to relax, ease tension, and detoxify.

Reflexology massage.

Treating obstinate athlete's foot, nail fungus, and warts.

Cutting and filing toenails and fingernails will make the nails grow stronger over time.

Garden/Nature

Plant part:
Root

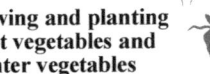

Sowing and planting root vegetables and winter vegetables

Weeding. Harrowing weeds. Dig over to prepare soil. Trimming and cutting back plants.
Clear and thin out plants, forest edges, and hedges. Plant cuttings.
Spread fertilizer and manure.
Start a compost heap.
Combat vermin.

Fertilize flowers with poorly formed roots.

Mulching.

Harvest produce is suitable for storage. Harvest root vegetables.

Gather herbs (roots) for bone, joint, and skin diseases.

Housework

Housework is dealt with much more successfully, efficiently, and effortlessly.

Problem stains are removed readily.

Best for doing laundry! Reduce on laundry detergent, support the environment.

Avoid dry cleaning, as the fabric may develop unwanted glossy blotches.

Thoroughly clean wooden and parquet floors, metals, china etc.

Cleaning, polishing, and waterproofing shoes.

Combating mold.

Air rooms only briefly.

Painting.

Preserving root vegetables. Slice cabbage now to ferment into sauerkraut.

Nutrition

Food quality:
Salt

Garlic, carrots, red beets, reddish, rutabaga, sugar beet, celery, potatoes, onions, kohlrabi.

Weight associated with overeating is less likely. If underweight, eat larger portions.

Cleansing and detox diets. Fruit and juice days.

Flush out poisons. Treatment for drug abuse.

Avoid large quantities of salty foods like bacon, ham, salted herring, fatty cheese, and the like. Avoid heavy and greasy foods.

Joy descends gently upon us like the evening dew, and does not patter down like a hailstorm.
Jean Paul

Color
Yellow

Day
Cool

Element
Earth

Capricorn

16 Friday
Lag BaOmer

No meat. Cutting and filing toenails and fingernails.

17 Saturday
Armed Forces Day (US)

M A Y

Positive affirmation:
"I trust in the deep healing."

Harvest Time
Ascending forces! Sap is rising, enhancing plant growth above ground, resulting in the most juicy fruits and vegetables.

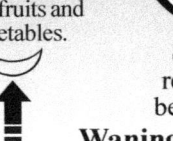

detox remove be active

Waning Moon

Success

Inspiration, optimism, and impatience. Rational thinking, creativity and imagination spark new ideas and inspire planning for the future.

Shying away from routine tasks people will feel more drawn to anything new.

Instead of gridlocked structures choose new possibilities.

Leisure

Inspiration and optimism will boost friendship, social gatherings, and parties.

Express your creativity and imagination. Dwell in dreams and utopian ideas. It is easier now to perceive intuitive thoughts.

Health

Sensitive body parts:

Lower Legs, Veins

All measures taken to flush out and detoxify the sensitive body parts are very effective.

Good for surgery, except on the sensitive body parts (see above), head, and neck. Scarring is less severe.

Teeth: Removal of tartar and amalgam. Best for fillings, crowns, and dentures!

Blood-purifying, detoxifying herbal infusions and teas.

Sensitive glandular system.

Avoid inflammation of the veins. Apply ointments to lower legs, and rest legs in a raised position.

Varicose veins: Avoid long periods of standing.

While exercising go easy on the ankles.

Sensitivity to light, so bring your sunglasses along.

Body Care

Aromas, scents: Cyclamen, Peach, Wild Roses

Prepare home-made ointments and cosmetics.

Apply detoxing facial and body care.

Treatments of bumps and pimples on the skin, and exfoliating procedures.

Removing body hair.

Correction of the nail bed.

Massages that serve to relax, ease tension, and detoxify.

Reflexology massage.

Removal of callused skin.

Treating obstinate athlete's foot, nail fungus, and warts.

Garden/Nature

Plant part:

Flower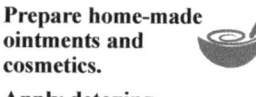

Fertilize flowers that no longer bloom.

Dig over/plow to prepare soil for planting.

Trimming and cutting back plants.

Hoeing and harrowing; weeds can be left to rot.

Pest control.

Start a compost heap.

Avoid watering plants.

Avoid transplanting sprouts.

Harvested produce is well suitable for storage.

Gather herbs (roots) for vein diseases.

Housework

Housework is dealt with much more successfully, efficiently, and effortlessly.

Problem stains are removed readily.

Best for doing laundry! Reduce on laundry detergent, support the environment.

Dry cleaning.

Clean and store seasonal clothing.

Best suited for a spring cleaning: Thoroughly clean wooden and parquet floors, metals, china etc.

Cleaning windows and glass.

Cleaning, polishing, and waterproofing shoes.

Combating mold.

Ventilate rooms thoroughly.

Baking bread, cakes, and cookies (add more leavening agent).

Making preserves.

Painting.

Nutrition

Food quality:

Fat

Cauliflower, artichoke, broccoli, sunflower seeds, flax seeds, nuts, rose hip, elder.

Weight associated with overeating is less likely. If underweight, eat larger portions.

Cleansing and detox diets. Fruit and juice days.

Flush out poisons. Treatment for drug abuse.

Pay attention to any particularly tempting foods today: Most likely the "wrong" things taste best.

High cholesterol: eat a low fat diet.

He that would live in peace and at ease must not speak all he knows or all he sees.
Benjamin Franklin

Color
Bright/ Dark Blue

Day
Air/Light

Element

Aquarius   **Air**

10:31 PM PDT Saturday
12:31 AM CDT
1:31 AM EDT

18 Sunday

19 Monday
Victoria Day (CAN)

M A Y

Positive affirmation:
"I trust in deep healing."

Harvest Time
Ascending forces! Sap is rising, enhancing plant growth above ground, resulting in the most juicy fruits and vegetables.

detox remove be active
Waning Moon

Success

Sensibility, intuition, and helpfulness.

Where possible, retreating is more favorable than dealing with business matters.

Dissolve restrictions, be patient and wait. Be aware that people can be more easily influenced.

Leisure

Your helpfulness will boost friendships.

Enjoy dancing or swimming, or watch a movie that will inspire your fantasies and imagination.

Retreat, relax, and recover.

Romance can be gentle and coziness will prevail.

If you plan outdoor excursions, be prepared for a shower here and there.

Health

Sensitive body parts:

Feet and Toes

All measures taken to flush out and detoxify the sensitive body parts are very effective.

Good for surgical operations except those on the sensitive body parts (see above), head, and neck.
Scarring is less severe.

Teeth: Removal of tartar and amalgam. Best for fillings, crowns, and dentures!

Blood-purifying, detoxifying herbal infusions and teas.

Sensitive nervous system.

Drugs have a much stronger effect on your body. Monitor closely what you put into your body.

Lymphatic therapy.

Sluggishness or fatigue may occur in the transition into the next Zodiac sign of Aries.

Body Care

Aromas, scents:
Magnolia, Amaryllis, Clary Sage

Prepare home-made ointments and cosmetics.

Apply detoxing facial and body care.

Treatments of bumps and pimples on the skin, and exfoliating procedures.

Removing body hair.

Correction of the nail bed.

Massages that serve to relax, ease tension, and detoxify. Reflexology massage. Carry out with special care, people are more sensitive.

Removal of callused skin.

Treating obstinate athlete's foot, nail fungus, and warts.

Foot bath.

No haircuts, hair becomes shaggy and unmanageable. Avoid washing your hair.

Garden/Nature

Plant part:

Leaf

Water plants.

Fertilize flowers.

Sow plants and vegetables that grow below ground, potatoes, leaf vegetables, and lettuce.

Dig over/plow to prepare soil for planting.
Trimming and cutting back plants.
Start a compost heap.

Mowing lawns.

Pest control. Weeding.

Harvested produce should be consumed as soon as possible.

Gather herbs for foot complaints.

Housework

Housework is dealt with much more successfully, efficiently, and effortlessly.

Problem stains are removed readily.

Best for doing laundry! Reduce on laundry detergent, support the environment.

Dry cleaning.

Clean and store seasonal clothing.

Thoroughly clean wooden and parquet floors, metals, china etc.

Cleaning, polishing, and waterproofing shoes.

Combating mold.

Ventilate rooms briefly and rapidly.

Avoid painting.

Preserving and storing should be avoided.

Nutrition

Food quality:

Carbohydrate

Lettuce, spinach, lamb's lettuce, Endive, parsley, leek, cabbage (Brussels sprouts, kale, Chinese cabbage), all leafy herbs, asparagus, mushrooms, cress, Swiss chard, rhubarb.

Weight associated with overeating is less likely. If underweight, eat larger portions.

Cleansing and detox diets. Fruit and juice days.

Flush out poisons. Treatment for drug abuse.

Caffeine, alcohol, drugs, certain foods, and stimulants have a much stronger effect.

Put your heart, mind, and soul into even your smallest acts. This is the secret of success.
Swami Shivananda

Pisces

Color
Blueish White

Day
Wetness

Element
Water

≋ ➔ ⟩⟨ 5:30 AM PDT
7:30 AM CDT
8:30 AM EDT

20 Tuesday
☾ Half Moon.

21 Wednesday
No meat.

M A Y

Harvest Time
Ascending forces! Sap is rising, enhancing plant growth above ground, resulting in the most juicy fruits and vegetables.

detox remove be active

Waning Moon

Success

Things get going and the way straight ahead seems the best.

People feel energetic, courageous, assertive, and at times anxious.

Good time for meetings and sales talks but impatience and selfishness do not favor teamwork.

Leisure

An enterprising spirit and spontaneity move people to enjoy outings, sports, competitions, cultural events, and travels.

Romance can be very passionate.

Good days for outings, even with cloudy skies the air still feels somewhat warm. Drying effect, get plenty to drink.

Health

Sensitive body parts:

Head, Brain, Eyes

All measures taken to flush out and detoxify the sensitive body parts are very effective.

Good for surgery, except on the sensitive body parts (see above), shoulders, arms, hands, and lungs.

Scarring is less severe.

Teeth: Removal of tartar and amalgam. Best for fillings, crowns, and dentures! Avoiding treatment of periodontitis and gums.

Blood-purifying, detoxifying herbal infusions and teas.

Sensitive sense organs.

If you suffer from migraines drink plenty of water, and avoid coffee, chocolate, and sugar.

Body Care

Aromas, scents: Cloves, Peppermint, Thyme

Prepare home-made ointments and cosmetics.

Apply detoxing facial and body care.

Treatments of bumps and pimples on the skin, and exfoliating procedures.

Removing body hair.

Correction of the nail bed.

Massages that serve to relax, ease tension, and detoxify.

Reflexology massage.

Removal of callused skin.

Treating obstinate athlete's foot, nail fungus, and warts.

Eye compresses to relieve strained eyes.

Any kind of hair care.

Garden/Nature

Plant part:

Fruit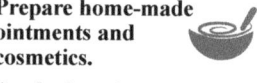

Sowing plants and vegetables that grow below ground.

Sowing and planting anything that is supposed to grow fast. Sowing and planting fruit and tomatoes.

Dig over/plow the soil to prepare for planting.

Spreading manure. Fertilizing grains, vegetables, and fruit.

Weeding. Pest control.

Pruning of fruit trees and bushes.

Harvesting and storing grains, vegetables, potatoes, fruits, and tomatoes.

Start a compost heap.

Gather herbs (roots) for eye complaints and headaches.

Day off on 5/23.

Housework

Housework is dealt with much more successfully, efficiently, and effortlessly.

Problem stains are removed readily.

Best for doing laundry!

Dry cleaning.

Clean and store seasonal clothing.

Thoroughly clean wooden and parquet floors, metals, china, etc.

Cleaning windows and glass.

Cleaning, polishing, and waterproofing shoes.

Combating mold.

Ventilate rooms sufficiently. Air beds.

Suitable for making cheese.

Preserving and freezing fruit and vegetables.

Baking bread, cakes, and cookies (use more leavening agent).

Painting.

Nutrition

Food quality:

Protein

Beans, peas, corn, tomatoes, pumpkin, lentils, soybeans, cucumber, eggplant, zucchini, berries, fruit, chili, bell pepper, figs, avocado, melon, olives.

Weight associated with overeating is less likely. If underweight, eat larger portions.

Cleansing and detox diets. Fruit and juice days.

Flush out poisons. Treatment for drug abuse.

Drink plenty of water.

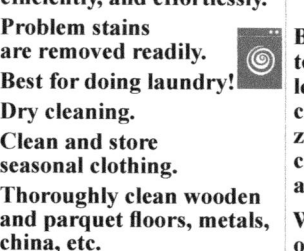

Be thine own palace, or the world's thy jail.
John Donne

Color: **Indigo Blue**

Day: **Warm**

Element: **Fire**

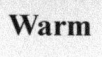

Aries

$\mathcal{H} \rightarrow \Upsilon$ 9:27 AM PDT / 11:27 AM CDT / 12:27 PM EDT

10:39 AM PDT / 12:39 PM CDT / 1:39 PM EDT $\Upsilon \rightarrow \aleph$

22 Thursday

23 Friday
No meat. Cutting and filing toenails and fingernails.

24 Saturday

M A Y

Harvest Time
Ascending forces! Sap is rising, enhancing plant growth above ground, resulting in the most juicy fruits and vegetables.

detox remove be active

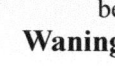

Waning Moon

Success

Realism and material security are important. Persistence comes easy, thoughts and reactions are slower.

Assess financial areas.

Conservative tendencies may make people want to stay away from risk taking.

Leisure

Relax at a picnic/feast. Enjoy culinary pleasures and hobbies.

The earth feels cold to the touch, so take slightly warmer clothes.

Health

Sensitive body parts:

Head and Neck

All measures taken to flush out and detoxify the sensitive body parts are very effective.
Good for surgery, except on the sensitive body parts (see above), shoulders, arms, hands, and lungs.
Scarring is less severe.
Teeth: Removal of tartar and amalgam. Best for fillings, crowns, and dentures!
Avoiding treatment of periodontitis and gums.
Blood-purifying, detoxifying herbal infusions and teas.
Sensitive blood circulation.
Organs of speech, jaws, teeth, tonsils, thyroid gland, neck, and vocal chords get easily affected. On cold days ears should be protected. Sensitivity to noise.
High blood pressure: Avoid salty foods.
Massages, lymphatic therapy, and chiropractic treatment to release blockages.

Body Care

Aromas, scents: Geranium, Jasmine, Rose

Prepare home-made ointments and cosmetics.

Apply detoxing facial and body care.

Treatments of bumps and pimples on the skin, and exfoliating procedures.

Removing body hair.

Correction of the nail bed.

Massages that serve to relax, ease tension, and detoxify.

Reflexology massage.

Removal of callused skin.

Treating obstinate athlete's foot, nail fungus, and warts.

Garden/Nature

Plant part:
Root

Sow plants and vegetables that grow below ground.
Everything grows slowly and lasts well.
Dig over to prepare soil.
Trimming/cutting back plants. Weeding. Mulching.
Start a compost heap.
Combat vermin found in the soil.
Spread fertilizer and liquid manure.
Fertilize flowers with poorly formed roots.
Harvested produce is well suited for storage.
Harvesting root vegetables.
Gather herbs (roots) for sinus issues, sore throat, and ear complaints.

Housework

Housework is dealt with much more successfully, efficiently, and effortlessly.

Problem stains are removed readily.

Best for doing laundry! Reduce on laundry detergent, support the environment.

Dry cleaning.

Clean and store seasonal clothing.

Thoroughly clean wooden and parquet floors, metals, china etc.

Cleaning, polishing, and waterproofing shoes.

Combating mold.

Air rooms only briefly.

Painting.

Preserving root vegetables.

Nutrition

Food quality:

Salt

Garlic, carrots, red beets, reddish, rutabaga, sugar beet, celery, potatoes, onions, kohlrabi.

Weight associated with overeating is less likely. If underweight, eat larger portions.

Cleansing and detox diets. Fruit and juice days.

Flush out poisons. Treatment for drug abuse.

Avoid large quantities of salty foods like bacon, ham, salted herring, fatty cheese, and the like.

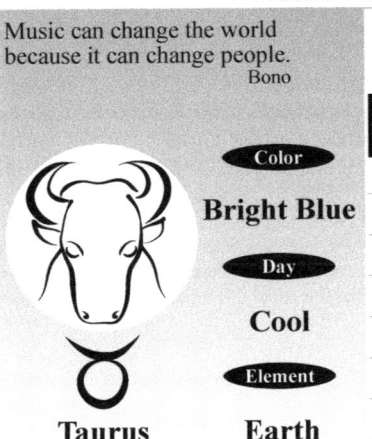

Color — **Bright Blue**

Day — **Cool**

Element — **Earth**

Taurus

10:23 AM PDT
12:23 PM CDT
1:23 PM EDT ♉ ➔ ♊

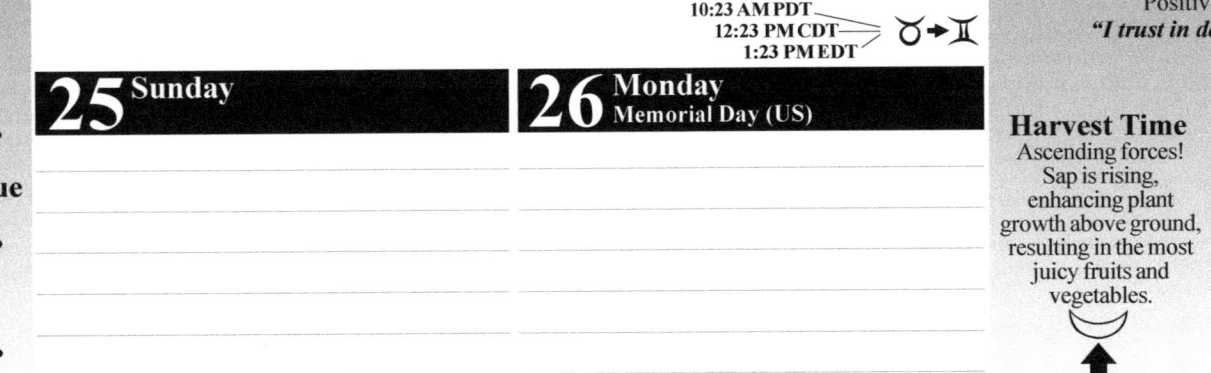

25 Sunday

26 Monday
Memorial Day (US)

M A Y

Positive affirmation:
"I trust in deep healing."

Harvest Time
Ascending forces! Sap is rising, enhancing plant growth above ground, resulting in the most juicy fruits and vegetables.

detox
remove
be active

Waning Moon

Success

Open mindedness and curiosity. A changeable and hectic time.

Good time for talking, negotiating, networking, and exchanging ideas as well as for meetings of a nonbinding nature, conferences, and studies.

● *New Moon: Confirm your resolutions. Finalize new decisions. Drop bad habits.*

Leisure

Good time for family gatherings, parties, and short trips.

People enjoy stimulating their minds with reading and studying. Attending theater performances is a preferred enjoyment. Enhance friendships.

Stretching exercises.

Be prepared for sudden changes in weather or climate.

Health

Sensitive body parts:

Shoulders, Arms, Hands, Lungs

All measures taken to flush out and detoxify the sensitive body parts are very effective.

Scarring is less severe.

Teeth: Removal of tartar and amalgam. Best for fillings, crowns, and dentures! Avoid having any teeth pulled.

Blood-purifying, detoxifying herbal infusions and teas.

Sensitive glandular system.

Make sure you are dressed warm enough in cool weather.

Exercises for shoulders. Breathing exercises.

Sensitivity to light, bring your sunglasses along.

Massages, lymphatic therapy, and chiropractic treatment to release blockages.

● *New Moon: Avoid any surgery if possible.*

Body Care

Aromas, scents: Lavender, Lemon Balm, Magnolia, Verbena

Prepare home-made ointments and cosmetics.

Apply detoxing facial and body care.

Treatments of bumps and pimples on the skin, and exfoliating procedures.

Removing body hair.

Correction of the nail bed.

Massages that serve to relax, ease tension, and detoxify.

Reflexology massage.

Removal of callused skin.

Treating obstinate athlete's foot, nail fungus, and warts.

Garden/Nature

Plant part:

Flower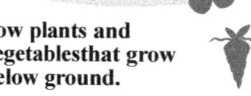

Sow plants and vegetablesthat grow below ground.

Trimming and cutting back plants.

Start a compost heap.

Weeding. Pest control.

Fertilize flowers that no longer bloom.

Avoid watering plants.

Changes in weather are more likely.

Gather herbs (roots) for tensions in the shoulder and lung complaints.

● *New Moon: Change of weather is likely. Care for sickly plants.*

Housework

Housework is dealt with much more successfully, efficiently, and effortlessly.

Problem stains are removed readily.

Best for doing laundry! Reduce on laundry detergent, support the environment.

Dry cleaning.

Clean and store seasonal clothing.

Thoroughly clean wooden and parquet floors, metals, china etc.

Cleaning windows and glass.

Cleaning, polishing, and waterproofing shoes.

Combating mold.

Ventilate rooms thoroughly.

Baking bread, cakes, and cookies (add more leavening agent).

Making preserves.

Painting.

Nutrition

Food quality:

Fat

Cauliflower, artichoke, broccoli, sunflower seeds, flax seeds, nuts, rose hip, elder.

Weight associated with overeating is less likely. If underweight, eat larger portions.

Cleansing and detox diets. Fruit and juice days.

Flush out poisons. Treatment for drug abuse.

Pay attention to any particularly tempting foods today: Most likely the "wrong" things taste best.

High cholesterol: eat a low fat diet.

● *New Moon: A day of fasting.*

If you wait for the perfect moment when all is safe and assured, it may never arrive. Mountains will not be climbed, races won, or lasting happiness achieved.
Maurice Chevalier

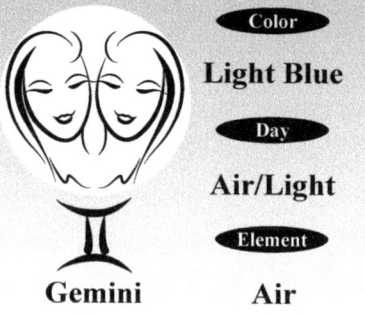

Color
Light Blue

Day
Air/Light

Element

Gemini   **Air**

27 **Tuesday**
Laylat al-Qadr
● **New Moon 8:04 PM PDT,**
10:04 PM CDT, 11:04 PM EDT

M A Y

Positive affirmation:
"I trust in deep healing."

Turning Point

Transition of ascending to descending forces. Both forces are at work and neutralize each other.

detox remove be active

Waning Moon

Success

Open mindedness and curiosity. A changeable and hectic time.

Good time for talking, negotiating, networking, and exchanging ideas as well as for meetings of a nonbinding nature, conferences, and studies.

Leisure

Good time for family gatherings, parties, and short trips.

People enjoy stimulating their minds with reading and studying. Attending theater performances is a preferred enjoyment. Enhance friendships.

Stretching exercises.

Be prepared for sudden changes in weather or climate.

Health

Sensitive body parts:

Shoulders, Arms, Hands, Lungs

All measures taken to supply nutrient materials and strengthen the sensitive body parts are very effective.

Healing ointments are easily absorbed. Applying herbal ointments to the shoulders for rheumatic gout and alike.

Sensitive glandular system.

Make sure you are dressed warm enough in cool weather.

Exercises for shoulders. Breathing exercises.

Avoid having any teeth pulled.

Sensitivity to light, bring your sunglasses along.

Massages, lymphatic therapy, and chiropractic treatment to release blockages.

Body Care

Aromas, scents: Lavender, Lemon Balm, Magnolia, Verbena

Treatments with firming and moisturizing creams are more effective.

Massages that serve to regenerate, and strengthen, perhaps aided with beneficial massage oils.

Correcting and cutting ingrown nails.

Hair dyes applied now, will look more vibrant.

Garden/Nature

Plant part:

Flower

Sow plants, herbs, and vegetables that grow and flourish above ground.

Sowing and planting any creeping or climbing plants, flowers, and medicinal herbs.

Transplanting.

Avoid watering plants.

Gather herbs for tensions in the shoulder and lung complaints.

Changes in weather are more likely.

Housework

Light housework only.

Ventilate rooms thoroughly.

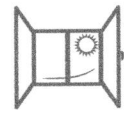

Making preserves.

Baking cakes and cookies. Dough rises faster. (Except on New Moon)

Nutrition

Food quality:

Fat

Cauliflower, artichoke, broccoli, sunflower seeds, flax seeds, nuts, rose hip, elder.

Weight gain: avoid indulging in rich foods. If overweight, eat smaller portions.

Supply nutrient materials to strengthen the body. Focus on foods that contain essential minerals and vitamins.

Stimulants and vitamins are more effective.

Pay attention to any particularly tempting foods today: Most likely the "wrong" things taste best.

High cholesterol: eat a low fat diet.

Positive affirmation:
"I trust my inner guidance."

Turning Point

Transition of ascending to descending forces. Both forces are at work and neutralize each other.

gather strength rest, recover buildup
Waxing Moon

10:34 AM PDT
12:34 PM CDT
1:34 PM EDT

28 Wednesday

No meat.

M A Y

When you reach the end of your rope, tie a knot in it and hang on.
Thomas Jefferson

 Color

Light Blue

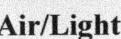 Day

Air/Light

 Element

Air

Gemini

Success

Feelings, sensitivity, and cooperativeness. Many are overly sensitive, so beware of treading on someone's toes.

Be cautious if you are easily influenced.

During negotiations make use of the cognitive ability of your senses.

Leisure

Relax within your close family.

Retreat to your safe haven and enjoy your fantasy while reading or listening to music. The inner world becomes more colorful than the outer.

Romance can be gentle. Deep feelings will prevail.

If you plan outdoor excursions, be prepared for a shower here and there.

Health

Sensitive body parts:
Chest, Lungs, Liver, Stomach, Gall Bladder

All measures taken to supply nutrient materials and strengthen the sensitive body parts are very effective.

Healing ointments are easily absorbed.

Sensitive nervous system.

Be cautious with alcohol since the liver is very sensitive.

Stomach could play up and cause gas and heartburn.

Rheumatism: Don't air bedding outside, damp will remain in the bedding.

Lymphatic therapy.

Body Care

Aromas, scents:
Lilac, Lilies of the Valley, Lilies, Violets

Treatments with firming and moisturizing creams are more effective.

Massages that serve to regenerate, and strengthen, perhaps aided with beneficial massage oils.

Correcting and cutting ingrown nails.

No haircuts, hair becomes shaggy and unmanageable. Avoid washing your hair.

Garden/Nature

Plant part:
Leaf

Watering all indoor and outdoor plants.

Sow plants, herbs, and vegetables that grow and flourish above ground, leaf vegetables (no lettuce).

Transplanting.

Trimming and cutting back plants. Avoid pruning fruit trees and bushes.

Cut trees, garlands, pick flowers to dry; they will last longer.

Sowing and mowing lawns.

Setting up a compost heap.

Gather herbs for bronchitis, stomach, liver, and gall bladder complaints.

Unfavorable for harvesting, storing, and preserving.

Housework

Light housework only.

Ventilate rooms briefly and rapidly. Don't air mattresses.

Any dirt and spots are easily removed in the laundry.

Avoid painting, as paint will take very long to dry.

Nutrition

Food quality:
Carbohydrate

Lettuce, spinach, lamb's lettuce, Endive, parsley, leek, cabbage (Brussels sprouts, kale, Chinese cabbage), all leafy herbs, asparagus, mushrooms, cress, Swiss chard, rhubarb.

Weight gain: avoid indulging in rich foods. If overweight, eat smaller portions and avoid carbohydrates. Moodiness may make you want to eat more than is healthy.

Supply nutrient materials to strengthen the body. Focus on foods that contain essential minerals and vitamins. Stimulants and vitamins are more effective.

If you get stomach troubles easily, avoid heavy meals.

Positive affirmation:
"I trust my inner guidance."

Planting Time
Descending forces! Sap is drawn downward, enhancing root formation. Best days for sowing, planting, and transplanting.

gather strength rest, recover buildup
Waxing Moon

1:18 PM PDT
3:18 PM CDT
4:18 PM EDT
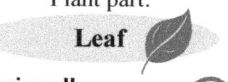

29 Thursday
Ascension Day

30 Friday

No meat. Cutting and filing toenails and fingernails.

M A Y

Don't wait around for other people to be happy for you. Any happiness you get you've got to make yourself.
Alice Walker

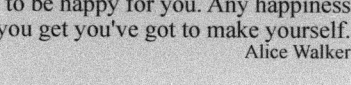

Color
Green

Day

Wetness

Element

Water

Cancer

Success

Determination reigns, and risks are taken more often. Master your tasks with more self-confidence and creativity.

Limits appear to be more easily surmountable.

Auspicious day for sales, advertising, and publicity.

Leisure

Zest for life is in the air. People want to have a fun time, enjoy parties, musical events, movies, etc.

Possessive feelings can harm a relationship. Romance can be very passionate.

Outings: even with cloudy skies the air still feels somewhat warm. Drying effect, get plenty to drink.

Danger of sudden storms, not only in the sky.

Health

Sensitive body parts:

Heart, Back, Diaphragm, Circulation, Arteries

All measures taken to supply nutrient materials and strengthen the sensitive body parts are very effective.

Healing ointments are easily absorbed.

Sensitive sense organs.

Back and heart problems are more likely to occur.

Avoid over straining of the heart and circulation with unusual physical activities.

Expect sleepless nights.

Body Care

Aromas, scents:
Hibiscus,
Oleander, Rose

Treatments with firming and moisturizing creams are more effective.

Massages that serve to regenerate, and strengthen, perhaps aided with beneficial massage oils.

Correcting and cutting ingrown nails.

Good days for haircuts, hair becomes stronger. But be aware that if you get a perm, curls will become quite frizzy. Baby's first haircut.

Garden/Nature

Plant part:
Fruit

Sow plants and vegetables that grow and flourish above ground. Sowing and planting fruit. Also sow and plant vegetables that are highly perishable. Plant trees and bushes. Sow lawns.

Transplanting. Grafting onto fruit trees.

Trimming and cutting back plants.

Best for cultivating grains on wet fields.

Dig over/plow to prepare soil for planting.

Setting up a compost heap.

Not suitable for fertilizing.

Harvested produce should be consumed as soon as possible.

Gather herbs for heart and circulation complaints.

Housework

Light housework only.

Ventilate sufficiently.

Freezing fruit and vegetables.

Baking bread, cakes, and cookies. Dough rises faster. (Except on New Moon)

Suitable for making cheese.

Avoid painting.

Nutrition

Food quality:
Protein

Beans, peas, corn, tomatoes, pumpkin, lentils, soybeans, cucumber, eggplant, zucchini, berries, fruit, chili, bell pepper, figs, avocado, melon, olives.

Weight gain: avoid indulging in rich foods. If overweight, eat smaller portions.

Supply nutrient materials to strengthen the body. Focus on foods that contain essential minerals and vitamins.

Stimulants and vitamins are more effective.

Positive affirmation:
"I trust my inner guidance."

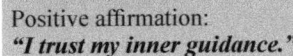

Planting Time
Descending forces! Sap is drawn downward, enhancing root formation. Best days for sowing, planting, and transplanting.

gather strength rest, recover buildup
Waxing Moon

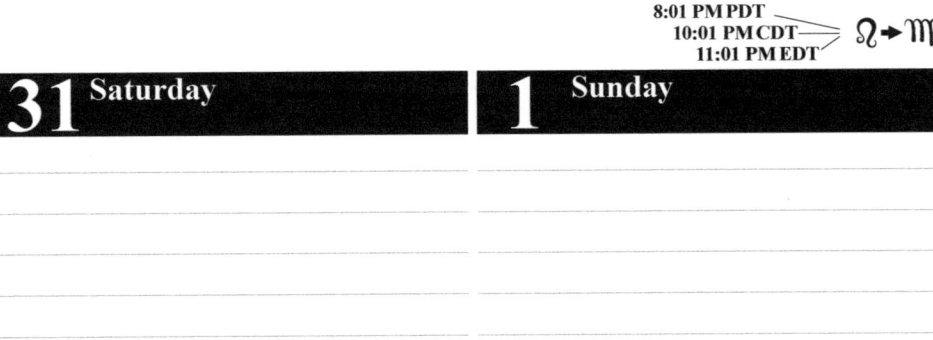

8:01 PM PDT
10:01 PM CDT ⟶ ♌ ➜ ♍
11:01 PM EDT

31 Saturday

1 Sunday

M A Y / J U N E

Love is trembling happiness.
Khalil Gibran

Color
Green

Day
Warm

Element
Fire

♌
Leo

Success

Good time for details, organization, routine, concentration, and duty.

Take care of financial and administrative tasks.

Prepare for future success now with realistic and critical assessment.

Leisure

Enjoy a nature walk.

Good time for health regimes. Improve your health with stretching exercises and yoga.

The earth feels cold to the touch, so take slightly warmer clothes.

Health

Sensitive body parts:
Digestive Organs, Nerves, Spleen, Pancreas

All measures taken to supply nutrient materials and strengthen the sensitive body parts are very effective.

Healing ointments are easily absorbed.

Sensitive blood circulation.

For a sensitive digestive system, a wholesome diet is recommended.

Dress slightly warmer.

High blood pressure: Avoid salty foods.

Massages, lymphatic therapy, and chiropractic treatment to release blockages.

Body Care

Aromas, scents: Lavender, Spruce Needles, Sage, Meadow Flowers

Treatments with firming and moisturizing creams are more effective.

Massages that serve to regenerate, and strengthen, perhaps aided with beneficial massage oils.

Correcting and cutting ingrown nails.

Best for haircuts because it retains its shape longer. Perms turn out best. Hair dyes applied now, will look more vibrant.

Garden/Nature

Plant part:
Root

Best for sowing and planting, except lettuce.

Plant trees which are supposed to grow very tall. Plant hedges and bushes that are meant to grow very fast.

Sowing lawns.

Planting and re-potting balcony and indoor plants.

Transplanting.

Trimming and cutting back plants.

Planting cuttings.

Start a compost heap.

Avoid harvesting and storing.

Gather herbs (roots) for digestive organs, pancreas, and nervous complaints.

Housework

Light housework only.

Air rooms only briefly.

Making pickles, preserves, and cheese yields suboptimal results and should be avoided.

Nutrition

Food quality:
Salt

Garlic, carrots, red beets, reddish, rutabaga, sugar beet, celery, potatoes, onions, kohlrabi.

Weight gain: avoid indulging in rich foods. If overweight, eat smaller portions.

Supply nutrient materials to strengthen the body. Focus on foods that contain essential minerals and vitamins.

Stimulants and vitamins are more effective.

Avoid large quantities of salty foods like bacon, ham, salted herring, fatty cheese, and the like. Avoid heavy and greasy foods.

Positive affirmation:
"I trust my inner guidance."

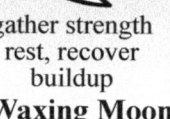

Planting Time
Descending forces! Sap is drawn downward, enhancing root formation. Best days for sowing, planting, and transplanting.

gather strength rest, recover buildup

Waxing Moon

2 Monday
Shavuot
☾ Half Moon.

3 Tuesday

J U N E

He is richest who is content with the least, for content is the wealth of nature.
Socrates

Color
Yellow

Day
Cool

Element
Earth

Virgo

Success

The artistic instinct rules, but so, too, does indecisiveness. The forces swing back and forth until equilibrium is achieved.

It's easy to reach compromises with tactful sensitivity.

A sense of judgment will support legal matters.

Leisure

Pursuit for harmony and cooperativeness supports good times in romance, friendship, and partnership.

Enjoy cultural events. Relax and get pampered with a spa treatment.

Romance can be passionate yet sensitive.

Health

Sensitive body parts:

Hips, Kidneys, Bladder

All measures taken to supply nutrient materials and strengthen the sensitive body parts are very effective.

Healing ointments are easily absorbed.

Sensitive glandular system.

Take special care to keep the area of bladder and kidneys warm.

Apply special exercises for the hip region.

Avoid having any teeth pulled.

Sensitivity to light, bring your sunglasses along.

Body Care

Aromas, scents: Roses, Violets, Daffodils

Treatments with firming and moisturizing creams are more effective.

Massages that serve to regenerate, and strengthen, perhaps aided with beneficial massage oils.

Correcting and cutting ingrown nails.

Hair dyes applied now, will look more vibrant.

Garden/Nature

Plant part:

Flower

Sow plants and vegetables that grow and flourish above ground, specially flowers, and medicinal herbs.

Transplanting.

Trimming and cutting back plants.

Avoid watering plants.

Start a compost heap.

Harvested produce should be consumed as soon as possible.

Gather herbs for kidneys, gall bladder, and hip complaints.

Day off on 6/5.

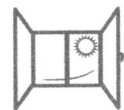

Housework

Light housework only.

Ventilate rooms thoroughly.

Baking cakes and cookies. Dough rises faster. (Except on New Moon)

Nutrition

Food quality:

Fat

Cauliflower, artichoke, broccoli, sunflower seeds, flax seeds, nuts, rose hip, elder.

Weight gain: avoid indulging in rich foods. If overweight, eat smaller portions.

Supply nutrient materials to strengthen the body. Focus on foods that contain essential minerals and vitamins.

Stimulants and vitamins are more effective.

Pay attention to any particularly tempting foods today: Most likely the "wrong" things taste best.

High cholesterol: eat a low fat diet.

Positive affirmation:
"I trust my inner guidance."

Planting Time
Descending forces! Sap is drawn downward, enhancing root formation. Best days for sowing, planting, and transplanting.

gather strength rest, recover buildup
Waxing Moon

♍→♎ 6:39 AM PDT
8:39 AM CDT
9:39 AM EDT

7:24 AM PDT
9:24 PM CDT   ♎→♏
10:24 PM EDT

4 Wednesday
No meat.

5 Thursday

6 Friday
D-Day (US)
No meat. Cutting and filing toenails and fingernails.

J U N E

Tolerance of intolerance is cowardice.
Ayaan Hirsi Ali

Color — **Orange**

Day — **Air/Light**

Element — **Air**   **Libra**

Success

Critical and superstitious behavior emerges, especially pertaining to money.

A penetrating power will strengthen your capacity to act.

An increased perception opens our interest for the essentials and helps to discover hidden potentials.

Leisure

Relax within your close family, with meditation, and relaxation exercises.

A longing to feel safe will be nurtured if you focus on habits and rituals. An increased sensitivity will help to enjoy every moment.

Romance can be very passionate.

If you plan outdoor excursions, be prepared for a shower here and there.

Health

Sensitive body parts:

Sex organs, Ureter

All measures taken to supply nutrient materials and strengthen the sensitive body parts are very effective.

Healing ointments are easily absorbed. Applying herbal ointments to the shoulders for rheumatic gout and alike.

Sensitive nervous system.

Female disorders: As a preventative measure apply hip baths using yarrow.

Pregnancy: Avoid any exertion, miscarriages are more likely.

Keep region of the pelvis, kidneys, and feet warm to prevent infection of the bladder and kidneys.

Lymphatic therapy.

Body Care

Aromas, scents:
Anemone, Cornflower
Oregano, Thuja

Treatments with firming and moisturizing creams are more effective.

Massages that serve to regenerate, and strengthen, perhaps aided with beneficial massage oils.

Correcting and cutting ingrown nails.

Hair dyes applied now, will look more vibrant.

Garden/Nature

Plant part:

Leaf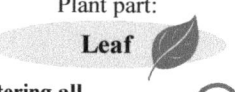

Watering all indoor and outdoor plants.

Sow plants, herbs, and vegetables that grow and flourish above ground, leaf vegetables (no lettuce).

Sowing, planting, harvesting, and drying every kind of medicinal herbs.

Transplanting.

Trimming and cutting back plants.
Combating slugs and snails.
Mowing lawns.

Start a compost heap.

Avoid pruning fruit trees and bushes. Avoid cutting down any trees.

Harvested produce should be consumed as soon as possible.

Housework

Light housework only.

Ventilate rooms briefly and rapidly. Don't air mattresses.

Any dirt and spots are easily removed in the laundry.

Avoid painting, as paint will take very long to dry.

Nutrition

Food quality:

Carbohydrate

Lettuce, spinach, lamb's lettuce, Endive, parsley, leek, cabbage (Brussels sprouts, kale, Chinese cabbage), all leafy herbs, asparagus, mushrooms, cress, Swiss chard, rhubarb.

Weight gain: avoid indulging in rich foods. If overweight, eat smaller portions and avoid carbohydrates.

Supply nutrient materials to strengthen the body. Focus on foods that contain essential minerals and vitamins. Stimulants and vitamins are more effective.

Positive affirmation:
"I trust my inner guidance."

Planting Time
Descending forces!
Sap is drawn downward, enhancing root formation.
Best days for sowing, planting, and transplanting.

gather strength
rest, recover
buildup
Waxing Moon

7 Saturday Eid al-Adha	**8** Sunday Pentecost

J U N E

Forget not that the earth delights to feel your bare feet and the winds long to play with your hair.
Khalil Gibran

Color
Red

Day

Wetness

Element

Water

Scorpio

Success

Inquisitiveness and exuberant inspiration lead to new horizons. Insight and love for truth reign.

Bringing together is more important than splitting asunder.

Expansive forces will assist in legal matters, discussions, and debates.

Leisure

Expansion feels great, and travel, short trips, and outings are most welcome. A competitive spirit excites any sports event.

Talk things out when necessary.

Romance can be very passionate.

Good days for outings; even with cloudy skies the air still feels somewhat warm. Drying effect, get plenty to drink.

Health

Sensitive body parts:

Thighs and Veins

All measures taken to supply nutrient materials and strengthen the sensitive body parts are very effective.

Healing ointments are easily absorbed.

Sensitive sense organs.

Pains often arise in the sciatic nerve, veins, the small of the back, and thighs.

Avoid overstraining the body with unusual physical activities.

Body Care

Aromas, scents:
Calendula (Marigold), Geranium, Rosemary

Treatments with firming and moisturizing creams are more effective.

Massages that serve to regenerate, and strengthen, perhaps aided with beneficial massage oils.

Correcting and cutting ingrown nails.

Hair dyes applied now, will look more vibrant.

Garden/Nature

Plant part:

Fruit

Sow plants and vegetables that grow and flourish above ground.

Sowing and planting fruit and vegetables that grow tall, and tomatoes, but no lettuce.

Transplanting.

Grafting onto fruit trees.

Cultivating grains, particularly corn.

Gather herbs for vein diseases.

Housework

Light housework only.

Ventilate sufficiently.

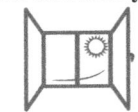

Freezing fruit and vegetables.

Baking bread, cakes, and cookies. Dough rises faster. (Except on New Moon)

Suitable for making cheese.

Making preserves.

Nutrition

Food quality:

Protein

Beans, peas, corn, tomatoes, pumpkin, lentils, soybeans, cucumber, eggplant, zucchini, berries, fruit, chili, bell pepper, figs, avocado, melon, olives.

Weight gain: avoid indulging in rich foods. If overweight, eat smaller portions.

Supply nutrient materials to strengthen the body. Focus on foods that contain essential minerals and vitamins.

Stimulants and vitamins are more effective.

Positive affirmation:
"I trust my inner guidance."

Turning Point
Transition of descending to ascending forces. Both forces are at work and neutralize each other.

gather strength rest, recover buildup
Waxing Moon

7:57 AM PDT
9:57 AM CDT
10:57 AM EDT

9 Monday

10 Tuesday

J U N E

Your present circumstances don't determine where you can go; they merely determine where you start.
Nido Qubein

Color
Orange/ Yellow

Day
Warm

Element

Fire   **Sagittarius**

Success

Inquisitiveness and exuberant inspiration lead to new horizons. Insight and love for truth reign.

Bringing together is more important than splitting asunder.

Expansive forces will assist in legal matters, discussions, and debates.

Leisure

Expansion feels great, and travel, short trips, and outings are most welcome. A competitive spirit excites any sports event.

Talk things out when necessary.

Romance can be very passionate.

Good days for outings; even with cloudy skies the air still feels somewhat warm. Drying effect, get plenty to drink.

Health

Sensitive body parts:

Thighs and Veins

All measures taken to flush out and detoxify the sensitive body parts are very effective.

Scarring is less severe.

Teeth: Removal of tartar and amalgam. Best for fillings, crowns, and dentures!

Blood-purifying, detoxifying herbal infusions and tea.

Sensitive sense organs.

Pains often arise in the sciatic nerve, veins, the small of the back, and thighs.

Avoid overstraining the body with unusual physical activities.

○ *Full Moon: Avoid any surgery and vaccination if possible.*

Body Care

Aromas, scents: Calendula (Marigold), Geranium, Rosemary

Prepare home-made ointments and cosmetics.

Apply detoxing facial and body care.

Treatments of bumps and pimples on the skin, and exfoliating procedures.

Removing body hair.

Correction of the nail bed.

Massages that serve to relax, ease tension, and detoxify.

Reflexology massage.

Removal of callused skin.

Treating obstinate athlete's foot, nail fungus, and warts.

Garden/Nature

Plant part:

Fruit

Sowing plants and vegetables that grow below ground.

Dig over/plow to prepare soil for planting.

Trimming and cutting back plants.

Pruning of fruit trees and bushes.

Cultivating grains, particularly corn.

Fertilize grains, vegetables, and fruit.

Combating pests above ground.

Weeding.

Gather herbs (roots) for vein diseases.

Avoid hoeing and harrowing.

Start a compost heap.

○ *Full Moon: Weather and climate changes. Herbs are most powerful.*

Housework

Housework is dealt with much more successfully, efficiently, and effortlessly.

Problem stains are removed readily.

Dry cleaning.

Thoroughly clean wooden and parquet floors, metals, china, etc.

Cleaning, polishing, and waterproofing shoes.

Combating mold.

Ventilate rooms sufficiently. Air beds.

Suitable for making cheese.

Freezing fruit and vegetables.

Baking bread, cakes, and cookies (use more leavening agent).

○ *Full Moon: Avoid doing laundry, cleaning windows, making preserves, painting.*

Nutrition

Food quality:

Protein

Beans, peas, corn, tomatoes, pumpkin, lentils, soybeans, cucumber, eggplant, zucchini, berries, fruit, chili, bell pepper, figs, avocado, melon, olives.

Weight associated with overeating is less likely. If underweight, eat larger portions.

Cleansing and detox diets. Fruit and juice days.

Flush out poisons. Treatment for drug abuse.

○ *Full Moon: A day of fasting.*

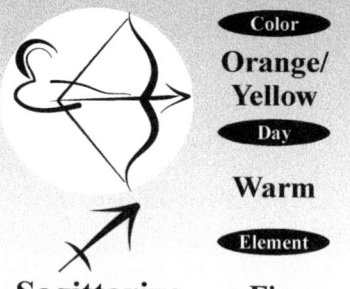

Sagittarius

Color
Orange/ Yellow

Day
Warm

Element
Fire

6:56 PM PDT
8:56 PM CDT
9:56 PM EDT

11 Wednesday

○ **Full Moon** 12:45 AM PDT, 2:45 AM CDT, 3:45 AM EDT
No meat.

J U N E

Positive affirmation:
"I trust in my inner guidance."

Turning Point
Transition of descending to ascending forces. Both forces are at work and neutralize each other.

detox
remove
be active
Waning Moon

Success

Career and business are in the foreground now and thinking becomes clear and serious, but somewhat inflexible.

Perseverance and reasoning assist in financial matters, planning, and contracts.

The values of tradition, authority, and discipline impact our endeavors.

Leisure

Money is not likely to be wasted in a shopping spree.

Many are drawn to enjoy cultural events.

The earth feels cold to the touch, so take slightly warmer clothes.

Health

Sensitive body parts:
Knees, Joints, Bones, Skin

All measures taken to flush out and detoxify the sensitive body parts are very effective.

Good for surgery, except on the sensitive body parts (see above), shoulders, arms, hands, and lungs. Scarring is less severe.

Teeth: Removal of tartar and amalgam. Best for fillings, crowns, and dentures!

Blood-purifying, detoxifying herbal infusions and teas.

Sensitive blood circulation.

Avoid overstraining bones and knees, and apply gentle stretching exercises only.

Problems with meniscus: Don't overstrain.

Dress slightly warmer.

High blood pressure: Avoid salty foods.

Massages, lymphatic therapy, and chiropractic treatment to release blockages.

Body Care

Aromas, scents:
Cedar, Juniper

Prepare home-made ointments and cosmetics.

Apply detoxing facial and body care.

Treatments of bumps and pimples on the skin, and exfoliating procedures.

Remove body hair, it may not grow back.

Correction of the nail bed.

Massages that serve to relax, ease tension, and detoxify.

Reflexology massage.

Treating obstinate athlete's foot, nail fungus, and warts.

Cutting and filing toenails and fingernails will make the nails grow stronger over time.

Garden/Nature

Plant part:
Root

Sowing and planting root vegetables and winter vegetables

Weeding. Harrowing weeds. Dig over to prepare soil. Trimming and cutting back plants.
Clear and thin out plants, forest edges, and hedges.
Plant cuttings.
Spread fertilizer and manure.
Start a compost heap.
Combat vermin.

Fertilize flowers with poorly formed roots.

Mulching.

Harvest produce is suitable for storage. Harvest root vegetables.

Gather herbs (roots) for bone, joint, and skin diseases.

Housework

Housework is dealt with much more successfully, efficiently, and effortlessly.

Problem stains are removed readily.

Best for doing laundry! Reduce on laundry detergent, support the environment.

Avoid dry cleaning, as the fabric may develop unwanted glossy blotches.

Thoroughly clean wooden and parquet floors, metals, china etc.

Cleaning, polishing, and waterproofing shoes.

Combating mold.

Air rooms only briefly.

Painting.

Preserving root vegetables. Slice cabbage now to ferment into sauerkraut.

Nutrition

Food quality:
Salt

Garlic, carrots, red beets, reddish, rutabaga, sugar beet, celery, potatoes, onions, kohlrabi.

Weight associated with overeating is less likely. If underweight, eat larger portions.

Cleansing and detox diets. Fruit and juice days.

Flush out poisons. Treatment for drug abuse.

Avoid large quantities of salty foods like bacon, ham, salted herring, fatty cheese, and the like. Avoid heavy and greasy foods.

It is not ignorance but knowledge which is the mother of wonder.
Joseph Wood Krutch

Capricorn

Color
Yellow

Day
Cool

Element
Earth

12 Thursday

13 Friday

No meat. Cutting and filing toenails and fingernails.

J U N E

Harvest Time
Ascending forces! Sap is rising, enhancing plant growth above ground, resulting in the most juicy fruits and vegetables.

detox remove be active

Waning Moon

Success

Inspiration, optimism, and impatience. Rational thinking, creativity and imagination spark new ideas and inspire planning for the future.

Shying away from routine tasks people will feel more drawn to anything new.

Instead of gridlocked structures choose new possibilities.

Leisure

Inspiration and optimism will boost friendship, social gatherings, and parties.

Express your creativity and imagination. Dwell in dreams and utopian ideas. It is easier now to perceive intuitive thoughts.

Health

Sensitive body parts:

Lower Legs, Veins

All measures taken to flush out and detoxify the sensitive body parts are very effective.

Good for surgery, except on the sensitive body parts (see above), shoulders, arms, hands, and lungs. Scarring is less severe.

Teeth: Removal of tartar and amalgam. Best for fillings, crowns, and dentures!

Blood-purifying, detoxifying herbal infusions and teas.

Sensitive glandular system.

Avoid inflammation of the veins. Apply ointments to lower legs, and rest legs in a raised position.

Varicose veins: Avoid long periods of standing.

While exercising go easy on the ankles.

Sensitivity to light, so bring your sunglasses along.

Body Care

Aromas, scents: Cyclamen, Peach, Wild Roses

Prepare home-made ointments and cosmetics.

Apply detoxing facial and body care.

Treatments of bumps and pimples on the skin, and exfoliating procedures.

Removing body hair.

Correction of the nail bed.

Massages that serve to relax, ease tension, and detoxify.

Reflexology massage.

Removal of callused skin.

Treating obstinate athlete's foot, nail fungus, and warts.

Garden/Nature

Plant part:

Flower

Fertilize flowers that no longer bloom.

Dig over/plow to prepare soil for planting.

Trimming and cutting back plants.

Hoeing and harrowing; weeds can be left to rot.

Pest control.

Start a compost heap.

Avoid watering plants.

Avoid transplanting sprouts.

Harvested produce is well suitable for storage.

Gather herbs (roots) for vein diseases.

Housework

Housework is dealt with much more successfully, efficiently, and effortlessly.

Problem stains are removed readily.

Best for doing laundry! Reduce on laundry detergent, support the environment.

Dry cleaning.

Clean and store seasonal clothing.

Best suited for a spring cleaning: Thoroughly clean wooden and parquet floors, metals, china etc.

Cleaning windows and glass.

Cleaning, polishing, and waterproofing shoes.

Combating mold.

Ventilate rooms thoroughly.

Baking bread, cakes, and cookies (add more leavening agent).

Making preserves.

Painting.

Nutrition

Food quality:

Fat

Cauliflower, artichoke, broccoli, sunflower seeds, flax seeds, nuts, rose hip, elder.

Weight associated with overeating is less likely. If underweight, eat larger portions.

Cleansing and detox diets. Fruit and juice days.

Flush out poisons. Treatment for drug abuse.

Pay attention to any particularly tempting foods today: Most likely the "wrong" things taste best.

High cholesterol: eat a low fat diet.

Grace is the beauty of form under the influence of freedom.
Friedrich Schiller

Color

Bright/ Dark Blue

Day

Air/Light

Element

Aquarius   **Air**

4:01 AM PDT
6:01 AM CDT
7:01 AM EDT

14 Saturday
Flag Day (US)

15 Sunday
Father's Day

11:10 AM PDT
1:10 PM CDT
2:10 PM EDT

16 Monday

J   U   N   E

Positive affirmation:
"I trust my inner guidance."

Harvest Time
Ascending forces! Sap is rising, enhancing plant growth above ground, resulting in the most juicy fruits and vegetables.

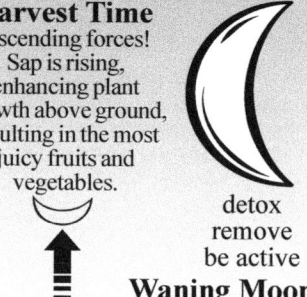

detox
remove
be active

Waning Moon

Success

Sensibility, intuition, and helpfulness.

Where possible, retreating is more favorable than dealing with business matters.

Dissolve restrictions, be patient and wait. Be aware that people can be more easily influenced.

Leisure

Your helpfulness will boost friendships.

Enjoy dancing or swimming, or watch a movie that will inspire your fantasies and imagination.

Retreat, relax, and recover.

Romance can be gentle and coziness will prevail.

If you plan outdoor excursions, be prepared for a shower here and there.

Health

Sensitive body parts:

Feet and Toes

All measures taken to flush out and detoxify the sensitive body parts are very effective.

Good for surgical operations except those on the sensitive body parts (see above), shoulders, arms, hands, and lungs.
Scarring is less severe.

Teeth: Removal of tartar and amalgam. Best for fillings, crowns, and dentures!

Blood-purifying, detoxifying herbal infusions and teas.

Sensitive nervous system.

Drugs have a much stronger effect on your body. Monitor closely what you put into your body.

Lymphatic therapy.

Sluggishness or fatigue may occur in the transition into the next Zodiac sign of Aries.

Body Care

Aromas, scents: Magnolia, Amaryllis, Clary Sage

Prepare home-made ointments and cosmetics.

Apply detoxing facial and body care.

Treatments of bumps and pimples on the skin, and exfoliating procedures.

Removing body hair.

Correction of the nail bed.

Massages that serve to relax, ease tension, and detoxify. Reflexology massage. Carry out with special care, people are more sensitive.

Removal of callused skin.

Treating obstinate athlete's foot, nail fungus, and warts.

Foot bath.

No haircuts, hair becomes shaggy and unmanageable.
Avoid washing your hair.

Garden/Nature

Plant part:

Leaf

Water plants.

Fertilize flowers.

Sow plants and vegetables that grow below ground, potatoes, leaf vegetables, and lettuce.

Dig over/plow to prepare soil for planting.
Trimming and cutting back plants.
Start a compost heap.

Mowing lawns.

Pest control. Weeding.

Harvested produce should be consumed as soon as possible.

Gather herbs for foot complaints.

Weeding on 6/18 before noon will help prevent weeds from growing back.

Housework

Housework is dealt with much more successfully, efficiently, and effortlessly.

Problem stains are removed readily.

Best for doing laundry! Reduce on laundry detergent, support the environment.

Dry cleaning.

Clean and store seasonal clothing.

Thoroughly clean wooden and parquet floors, metals, china etc.

Cleaning, polishing, and waterproofing shoes.

Combating mold.

Ventilate rooms briefly and rapidly.

Avoid painting.

Preserving and storing should be avoided.

Nutrition

Food quality:

Carbohydrate

Lettuce, spinach, lamb's lettuce, Endive, parsley, leek, cabbage (Brussels sprouts, kale, Chinese cabbage), all leafy herbs, asparagus, mushrooms, cress, Swiss chard, rhubarb.

Weight associated with overeating is less likely. If underweight, eat larger portions.

Cleansing and detox diets. Fruit and juice days.

Flush out poisons. Treatment for drug abuse.

Caffeine, alcohol, drugs, certain foods, and stimulants have a much stronger effect.

If you want to conquer fear, don't sit at home and think about it. Go out and get busy.
Dale Carnegie

Pisces

| Color |
| **Blueish White** |
| Day |
| **Wetness** |
| Element |

Water

17 Tuesday

4:09 PM PDT
6:09 PM CDT ⟩ ♓ → ♈
7:09 PM EDT

18 Wednesday

☽ **Half Moon.** No meat.

J U N E

Positive affirmation:
"I trust my inner guidance."

Harvest Time
Ascending forces! Sap is rising, enhancing plant growth above ground, resulting in the most juicy fruits and vegetables.

detox remove be active

Waning Moon

Success

Things get going and the way straight ahead seems the best.

People feel energetic, courageous, assertive, and at times anxious.

Good time for meetings and sales talks but impatience and selfishness do not favor teamwork.

Leisure

An enterprising spirit and spontaneity move people to enjoy outings, sports, competitions, cultural events, and travels.

Romance can be very passionate.

Good days for outings, even with cloudy skies the air still feels somewhat warm. Drying effect, get plenty to drink.

Health

Sensitive body parts:

Head, Brain, Eyes

All measures taken to flush out and detoxify the sensitive body parts are very effective.

Good for surgery, except on the sensitive body parts (see above), shoulders, arms, hands, and lungs.

Scarring is less severe.

Teeth: Removal of tartar and amalgam. Best for fillings, crowns, and dentures! Avoiding treatment of periodontitis and gums.

Blood-purifying, detoxifying herbal infusions and teas.

Sensitive sense organs.

If you suffer from migraines drink plenty of water, and avoid coffee, chocolate, and sugar.

Body Care

Aromas, scents: Cloves, Peppermint, Thyme

Prepare home-made ointments and cosmetics.

Apply detoxing facial and body care.

Treatments of bumps and pimples on the skin, and exfoliating procedures.

Removing body hair.

Correction of the nail bed.

Massages that serve to relax, ease tension, and detoxify.

Reflexology massage.

Removal of callused skin.

Treating obstinate athlete's foot, nail fungus, and warts.

Eye compresses to relieve strained eyes.

Any kind of hair care.

Garden/Nature

Plant part:

Fruit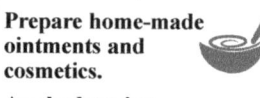

Sowing plants and vegetables that grow below ground.

Sowing and planting anything that is supposed to grow fast. Sowing and planting fruit and tomatoes.

Dig over/plow the soil to prepare for planting.

Spreading manure. Fertilizing grains, vegetables, and fruit.

Weeding. Pest control.

Pruning of fruit trees and bushes.

Harvesting and storing grains, vegetables, potatoes, fruits, and tomatoes.

Start a compost heap.

Gather herbs (roots) for eye complaints and headaches.

Day off on 6/19.

Housework

Housework is dealt with much more successfully, efficiently, and effortlessly.

Problem stains are removed readily.

Best for doing laundry!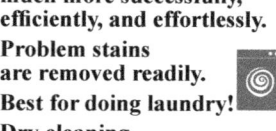

Dry cleaning.

Clean and store seasonal clothing.

Thoroughly clean wooden and parquet floors, metals, china, etc.

Cleaning windows and glass.

Cleaning, polishing, and waterproofing shoes.

Combating mold.

Ventilate rooms sufficiently. Air beds.

Suitable for making cheese.

Preserving and freezing fruit and vegetables.

Baking bread, cakes, and cookies (use more leavening agent).

Painting.

Nutrition

Food quality:

Protein

Beans, peas, corn, tomatoes, pumpkin, lentils, soybeans, cucumber, eggplant, zucchini, berries, fruit, chili, bell pepper, figs, avocado, melon, olives.

Weight associated with overeating is less likely. If underweight, eat larger portions.

Cleansing and detox diets. Fruit and juice days.

Flush out poisons. Treatment for drug abuse.

Drink plenty of water.

The dog that trots about finds a bone.
Golda Meir

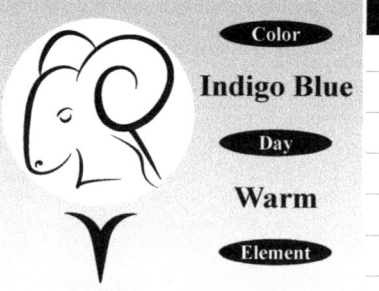

Color

Indigo Blue

Day

Warm

Element

Aries   **Fire**

6:56 PM PDT
8:56 PM CDT
9:56 PM EDT
♈ → ♉

19 **Thursday**
Juneteenth, Corpus Christi

20 **Friday**
Summer Solstice

No meat. Cutting and filing toenails and fingernails.

J U N E

Positive affirmation:
"I trust my inner guidance."

Harvest Time
Ascending forces! Sap is rising, enhancing plant growth above ground, resulting in the most juicy fruits and vegetables.

detox
remove
be active

Waning Moon

Success

Realism and material security are important. Persistence comes easy, thoughts and reactions are slower.

Assess financial areas.

Conservative tendencies may make people want to stay away from risk taking.

Leisure

Relax at a picnic/feast. Enjoy culinary pleasures and hobbies.

The earth feels cold to the touch, so take slightly warmer clothes.

Health

Sensitive body parts:

Head and Neck

All measures taken to flush out and detoxify the sensitive body parts are very effective.

Good for surgery, except on the sensitive body parts (see above), shoulders, arms, hands, and lungs. Scarring is severe.

Teeth: Removal of tartar and amalgam. Best for fillings, crowns, and dentures! Avoiding treatment of periodontitis and gums.

Blood-purifying, detoxifying herbal infusions and teas.

Sensitive blood circulation.

Organs of speech, jaws, teeth, tonsils, thyroid gland, neck, and vocal chords get easily affected. Keep neck warm. On cold days ears should be protected. Sensitivity to noise.

High blood pressure: Avoid salty foods.

Massages, lymphatic therapy, and chiropractic treatment to release blockages.

Body Care

Aromas, scents: Geranium, Jasmine, Rose

Prepare home-made ointments and cosmetics.

Apply detoxing facial and body care.

Treatments of bumps and pimples on the skin, and exfoliating procedures.

Removing body hair.

Correction of the nail bed.

Massages that serve to relax, ease tension, and detoxify.

Reflexology massage.

Removal of callused skin.

Treating obstinate athlete's foot, nail fungus, and warts.

Garden/Nature

Plant part: ✂

Root

Sow plants and vegetables that grow below ground.

Everything grows slowly and lasts well.

Dig over to prepare soil.

Trimming/cutting back plants. Weeding. Mulching.

Start a compost heap.

Combat vermin found in the soil.

Spread fertilizer and liquid manure.

Fertilize flowers with poorly formed roots.

Harvested produce is well suited for storage. Harvesting root vegetables.

Gather herbs (roots) for sinus issues, sore throat, and ear complaints.

Housework

Housework is dealt with much more successfully, efficiently, and effortlessly.

Problem stains are removed readily.

Best for doing laundry! Reduce on laundry detergent, support the environment.

Dry cleaning.

Clean and store seasonal clothing.

Thoroughly clean wooden and parquet floors, metals, china etc.

Cleaning, polishing, and waterproofing shoes.

Combating mold.

Air rooms only briefly.

Painting.

Preserving root vegetables.

Nutrition

Food quality:

Salt

Garlic, carrots, red beets, reddish, rutabaga, sugar beet, celery, potatoes, onions, kohlrabi.

Weight associated with overeating is less likely. If underweight, eat larger portions.

Cleansing and detox diets. Fruit and juice days.

Flush out poisons. Treatment for drug abuse.

Avoid large quantities of salty foods like bacon, ham, salted herring, fatty cheese, and the like.

Always do your best. What you plant now, you will harvest later.
Og Mandino

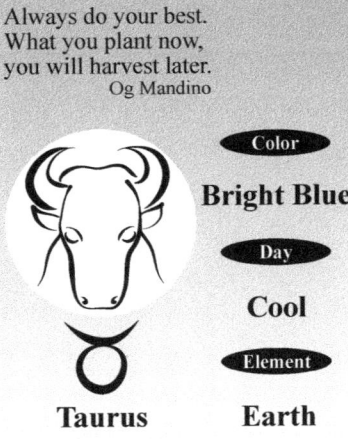

Color — Bright Blue

Day — Cool

Element — Earth

Taurus

21 Saturday National Indigenous People Day (CAN)

22 Sunday

J U N E

Harvest Time
Ascending forces! Sap is rising, enhancing plant growth above ground, resulting in the most juicy fruits and vegetables.

detox remove be active

Waning Moon

Success

Open mindedness and curiosity. A changeable and hectic time.

Good time for talking, negotiating, networking, and exchanging ideas as well as for meetings of a nonbinding nature, conferences, and studies.

Leisure

Good time for family gatherings, parties, and short trips.

People enjoy stimulating their minds with reading and studying. Attending theater performances is a preferred enjoyment. Enhance friendships.

Stretching exercises.

Be prepared for sudden changes in weather or climate.

Health

Sensitive body parts:
Shoulders, Arms, Hands, Lungs

All measures taken to flush out and detoxify the sensitive body parts are very effective.

Good for surgery, except on the sensitive body parts (see above), chest, stomach, liver, and gallbladder. Scarring is less severe.

Teeth: Removal of tartar and amalgam. Best for fillings, crowns, and dentures! Avoid having any teeth pulled.

Blood-purifying, detoxifying herbal infusions and teas.

Sensitive glandular system.

Make sure you are dressed warm enough in cool weather.

Exercises for shoulders. Breathing exercises.

Sensitivity to light, bring your sunglasses along.

Massages, lymphatic therapy, and chiropractic treatment to release blockages.

Body Care

Aromas, scents:
Lavender, Lemon Balm, Magnolia, Verbena

Prepare home-made ointments and cosmetics.

Apply detoxing facial and body care.

Treatments of bumps and pimples on the skin, and exfoliating procedures.

Removing body hair.

Correction of the nail bed.

Massages that serve to relax, ease tension, and detoxify.

Reflexology massage.

Removal of callused skin.

Treating obstinate athlete's foot, nail fungus, and warts.

Garden/Nature

Plant part:
Flower

Sow plants and vegetables that grow below ground.

Trimming and cutting back plants.

Start a compost heap.

Weeding. Pest control.

Fertilize flowers that no longer bloom.

Avoid watering plants.

Changes in weather are more likely.

Gather herbs (roots) for tensions in the shoulder and lung complaints.

Housework

Housework is dealt with much more successfully, efficiently, and effortlessly.

Problem stains are removed readily.

Best for doing laundry! Reduce on laundry detergent, support the environment.

Dry cleaning.

Clean and store seasonal clothing.

Thoroughly clean wooden and parquet floors, metals, china etc.

Cleaning windows and glass.

Cleaning, polishing, and waterproofing shoes.

Combating mold.

Ventilate rooms thoroughly.

Baking bread, cakes, and cookies (add more leavening agent).

Making preserves.

Painting.

Nutrition

Food quality:
Fat

Cauliflower, artichoke, broccoli, sunflower seeds, flax seeds, nuts, rose hip, elder.

Weight associated with overeating is less likely. If underweight, eat larger portions.

Cleansing and detox diets. Fruit and juice days.

Flush out poisons. Treatment for drug abuse.

Pay attention to any particularly tempting foods today: Most likely the "wrong" things taste best.

High cholesterol: eat a low fat diet.

Music expresses that which cannot be said and on which it is impossible to be silent.
Victor Hugo

Color
Light Blue

Day
Air/Light

Element

Gemini   **Air**

8:45 PM PDT
10:45 PM CDT
11:45 PM EDT

23 Monday

24 Tuesday

J U N E

Positive affirmation:
"I trust my inner guidance."

Turning Point
Transition of ascending to descending forces. Both forces are at work and neutralize each other.

detox
remove
be active
Waning Moon

Success

Feelings, sensitivity, and cooperativeness. Many are overly sensitive, so beware of treading on someone's toes.

Be cautious if you are easily influenced.

During negotiations make use of the cognitive ability of your senses.

● *New Moon: Confirm your resolutions. Finalize new decisions. Drop bad habits.*

Leisure

Relax within your close family.

Retreat to your safe haven and enjoy your fantasy while reading or listening to music. The inner world becomes more colorful than the outer.

Romance can be gentle. Deep feelings will prevail.

If you plan outdoor excursions, be prepared for a shower here and there.

Health

Sensitive body parts:
Chest, Lungs, Liver, Stomach, Gall Bladder

All measures taken to supply nutrient materials and strengthen the sensitive body parts are very effective.

Healing ointments are easily absorbed.

Sensitive nervous system.

Be cautious with alcohol since the liver is very sensitive.

Stomach could play up and cause gas and heartburn.

Rheumatism: Don't air bedding outside, damp will remain in the bedding.

Lymphatic therapy.

● *New Moon: Avoid any surgery if possible.*

Body Care

Aromas, scents:
Lilac, Lilies of the Valley, Lilies, Violets

Treatments with firming and moisturizing creams are more effective.

Massages that serve to regenerate, and strengthen, perhaps aided with beneficial massage oils.

Correcting and cutting ingrown nails.

No haircuts, hair becomes shaggy and unmanageable. Avoid washing your hair.

Garden/Nature

Plant part:
Leaf

Watering all indoor and outdoor plants.

Sow plants, herbs, and vegetables that grow and flourish above ground, leaf vegetables (no lettuce).

Transplanting.

Trimming and cutting back plants. Avoid pruning fruit trees and bushes.

Cut trees, garlands, pick flowers to dry; they will last longer.

Sowing and mowing lawns.

Setting up a compost heap.

Gather herbs for bronchitis, stomach, liver, and gall bladder complaints.

Unfavorable for harvesting, storing, and preserving.

● *New Moon: Change of weather is likely. Care for sickly plants.*

Housework

Light housework only.

Ventilate rooms briefly and rapidly. Don't air mattresses.

Any dirt and spots are easily removed in the laundry.

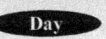

Avoid painting, as paint will take very long to dry.

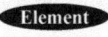

Nutrition

Food quality:
Carbohydrate

Lettuce, spinach, lamb's lettuce, Endive, parsley, leek, cabbage (Brussels sprouts, kale, Chinese cabbage), all leafy herbs, asparagus, mushrooms, cress, Swiss chard, rhubarb.

Weight gain: avoid indulging in rich foods. If overweight, eat smaller portions and avoid carbohydrates. Moodiness may make you want to eat more than is healthy.

Supply nutrient materials to strengthen the body. Focus on foods that contain essential minerals and vitamins. Stimulants and vitamins are more effective.

If you get stomach troubles easily, avoid heavy meals.

● *New Moon: A day of fasting.*

Positive affirmation:
"I trust the power of inner peace."

gather strength
rest, recover
buildup
Waxing Moon

Planting Time
Descending forces! Sap is drawn downward, enhancing root formation. Best days for sowing, planting, and transplanting.

25 Wednesday

● New Moon 3:33 AM PDT, 5:33 AM CDT, 6:33 AM EDT
No meat.

26 Thursday
Rath Yatra

J U N E

Do not speak of your happiness to one less fortunate than yourself.
Plutarch

Color
Green

Day
Wetness

Element
Water

Cancer

Success

Determination reigns, and risks are taken more often. Master your tasks with more self-confidence and creativity.

Limits appear to be more easily surmountable.

Auspicious day for sales, advertising, and publicity.

Leisure

Zest for life is in the air. People want to have a fun time, enjoy parties, musical events, movies, etc.

Possessive feelings can harm a relationship. Romance can be very passionate.

Outings: even with cloudy skies the air still feels somewhat warm. Drying effect, get plenty to drink.

Danger of sudden storms, not only in the sky.

Health

Sensitive body parts:
Heart, Back, Diaphragm, Circulation, Arteries

All measures taken to supply nutrient materials and strengthen the sensitive body parts are very effective.

Healing ointments are easily absorbed.

Sensitive sense organs.

Back and heart problems are more likely to occur.

Avoid over straining of the heart and circulation with unusual physical activities.

Expect sleepless nights.

Body Care

Aromas, scents:
Hibiscus, Oleander, Rose

Treatments with firming and moisturizing creams are more effective.

Massages that serve to regenerate, and strengthen, perhaps aided with beneficial massage oils.

Correcting and cutting ingrown nails.

Good days for haircuts, hair becomes stronger. But be aware that if you get a perm, curls will become quite frizzy. Baby's first haircut.

Garden/Nature

Plant part:
Fruit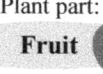

Sow plants and vegetables that grow and flourish above ground. Sowing and planting fruit. Also sow and plant vegetables that are highly perishable. Plant trees and bushes. Sow lawns.

Transplanting. Grafting onto fruit trees.

Trimming and cutting back plants.

Best for cultivating grains on wet fields.

Dig over/plow to prepare soil for planting.

Setting up a compost heap.

Not suitable for fertilizing.

Harvested produce should be consumed as soon as possible.

Gather herbs for heart and circulation complaints.

Housework

Light housework only.

Ventilate sufficiently.

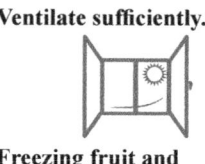

Freezing fruit and vegetables.

Baking bread, cakes, and cookies. Dough rises faster. (Except on New Moon)

Suitable for making cheese.

Avoid painting.

Nutrition

Food quality:
Protein

Beans, peas, corn, tomatoes, pumpkin, lentils, soybeans, cucumber, eggplant, zucchini, berries, fruit, chili, bell pepper, figs, avocado, melon, olives.

Weight gain: avoid indulging in rich foods. If overweight, eat smaller portions.

Supply nutrient materials to strengthen the body. Focus on foods that contain essential minerals and vitamins.

Stimulants and vitamins are more effective.

Positive affirmation:
"I trust the power of inner peace."

Planting Time
Descending forces! Sap is drawn downward, enhancing root formation. Best days for sowing, planting, and transplanting.

gather strength
rest, recover
buildup
Waxing Moon

♋ ➤ ♌ 11:06 PM PDT Thursday
1:06 AM CDT
2:06 AM EDT

27 Friday
Muharram

No meat. Cutting and filing toenails and fingernails.

28 Saturday

The soul that sees beauty may sometimes walk alone.
Johann Wolfgang von Goethe

Color: **Green**
Day: **Warm**
Element: **Fire**

♌ **Leo**

J U N E

Success

Good time for details, organization, routine, concentration, and duty.

Take care of financial and administrative tasks.

Prepare for future success now with realistic and critical assessment.

Leisure

Enjoy a nature walk.

Good time for health regimes. Improve your health with stretching exercises and yoga.

The earth feels cold to the touch, so take slightly warmer clothes.

Health

Sensitive body parts:
Digestive Organs, Nerves, Spleen, Pancreas

All measures taken to supply nutrient materials and strengthen the sensitive body parts are very effective.

Healing ointments are easily absorbed.

Sensitive blood circulation.

For a sensitive digestive system, a wholesome diet is recommended.

Dress slightly warmer.

High blood pressure: Avoid salty foods.

Massages, lymphatic therapy, and chiropractic treatment to release blockages.

Body Care

Aromas, scents: Lavender, Spruce Needles, Sage, Meadow Flowers

Treatments with firming and moisturizing creams are more effective.

Massages that serve to regenerate, and strengthen, perhaps aided with beneficial massage oils.

Correcting and cutting ingrown nails.

Best for haircuts because it retains its shape longer. Perms turn out best. Hair dyes applied now, will look more vibrant.

Garden/Nature

Plant part: **Root**

Best for sowing and planting, except lettuce.

Plant trees which are supposed to grow very tall. Plant hedges and bushes that are meant to grow very fast.

Sowing lawns.

Planting and re-potting balcony and indoor plants.

Transplanting.

Trimming and cutting back plants.

Planting cuttings.

Start a compost heap.

Avoid harvesting and storing.

Gather herbs (roots) for digestive organs, pancreas, and nervous complaints.

Housework

Light housework only.

Air rooms only briefly.

Making pickles, preserves, and cheese yields suboptimal results and should be avoided.

Nutrition

Food quality: **Salt**

Garlic, carrots, red beets, reddish, rutabaga, sugar beet, celery, potatoes, onions, kohlrabi.

Weight gain: avoid indulging in rich foods. If overweight, eat smaller portions.

Supply nutrient materials to strengthen the body. Focus on foods that contain essential minerals and vitamins.

Stimulants and vitamins are more effective.

Avoid large quantities of salty foods like bacon, ham, salted herring, fatty cheese, and the like. Avoid heavy and greasy foods.

Positive affirmation:
"I trust the power of inner peace."

Planting Time
Descending forces! Sap is drawn downward, enhancing root formation. Best days for sowing, planting, and transplanting.

gather strength rest, recover buildup
Waxing Moon

Ω → ♍   4:45 AM PDT / 6:45 AM CDT / 7:45 AM EDT

2:18 PM PDT / 4:18 PM CDT / 5:18 PM EDT   ♍ → ♎

29 Sunday

30 Monday

1 Tuesday
Canada Day (US)

J U N E / J U L Y

Happiness is the harvest of a quiet eye.
Austin O'Malley

Color: **Yellow**
Day: **Cool**
Element: **Earth**

♍ **Virgo**

Success

The artistic instinct rules, but so, too, does indecisiveness. The forces swing back and forth until equilibrium is achieved.

It's easy to reach compromises with tactful sensitivity.

A sense of judgment will support legal matters.

Leisure

Pursuit for harmony and cooperativeness supports good times in romance, friendship, and partnership.

Enjoy cultural events. Relax and get pampered with a spa treatment.

Romance can be passionate yet sensitive.

Health

Sensitive body parts:

Hips, Kidneys, Bladder

All measures taken to supply nutrient materials and strengthen the sensitive body parts are very effective.

Healing ointments are easily absorbed.

Sensitive glandular system.

Take special care to keep the area of bladder and kidneys warm.

Apply special exercises for the hip region.

Avoid having any teeth pulled.

Sensitivity to light, bring your sunglasses along.

Body Care

Aromas, scents: Roses, Violets, Daffodils

Treatments with firming and moisturizing creams are more effective.

Massages that serve to regenerate, and strengthen, perhaps aided with beneficial massage oils.

Correcting and cutting ingrown nails.

Hair dyes applied now, will look more vibrant.

Garden/Nature

Plant part:

Flower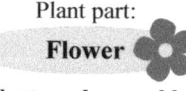

Sow plants and vegetables that grow and flourish above ground, specially flowers, and medicinal herbs.

Transplanting.

Trimming and cutting back plants.

Avoid watering plants.

Start a compost heap.

Harvested produce should be consumed as soon as possible.

Gather herbs for kidneys, gall bladder, and hip complaints.

Day off on 7/2.

Housework

Light housework only.

Ventilate rooms thoroughly.

Baking cakes and cookies. Dough rises faster. (Except on New Moon)

Nutrition

Food quality:

Fat

Cauliflower, artichoke, broccoli, sunflower seeds, flax seeds, nuts, rose hip, elder.

Weight gain: avoid indulging in rich foods. If overweight, eat smaller portions.

Supply nutrient materials to strengthen the body. Focus on foods that contain essential minerals and vitamins.

Stimulants and vitamins are more effective.

Pay attention to any particularly tempting foods today: Most likely the "wrong" things taste best.

High cholesterol: eat a low fat diet.

Positive affirmation:
"I trust the power of inner peace."

Planting Time
Descending forces! Sap is drawn downward, enhancing root formation. Best days for sowing, planting, and transplanting.

gather strength rest, recover buildup

Waxing Moon

2 Wednesday

☾ **Half Moon.** No meat.

3 Thursday

J U L Y

Having family responsibilities and concerns just has to make you a more understanding person.
Sandra Day O'Connor

Color
Orange

Day
Air/Light

Element
Air

Libra

Success

Critical and superstitious behavior emerges, especially pertaining to money.

A penetrating power will strengthen your capacity to act.

An increased perception opens our interest for the essentials and helps to discover hidden potentials.

Leisure

Relax within your close family, with meditation, and relaxation exercises.

A longing to feel safe will be nurtured if you focus on habits and rituals. An increased sensitivity will help to enjoy every moment.

Romance can be very passionate.

If you plan outdoor excursions, be prepared for a shower here and there.

Health

Sensitive body parts:

Sex organs, Ureter

All measures taken to supply nutrient materials and strengthen the sensitive body parts are very effective.

Healing ointments are easily absorbed. Applying herbal ointments to the shoulders for rheumatic gout and alike.

Sensitive nervous system.

Female disorders: As a preventative measure apply hip baths using yarrow.

Pregnancy: Avoid any exertion, miscarriages are more likely.

Keep region of the pelvis, kidneys, and feet warm to prevent infection of the bladder and kidneys.

Lymphatic therapy.

Body Care

Aromas, scents: Anemone, Cornflower Oregano, Thuja

Treatments with firming and moisturizing creams are more effective.

Massages that serve to regenerate, and strengthen, perhaps aided with beneficial massage oils.

Correcting and cutting ingrown nails.

Hair dyes applied now, will look more vibrant.

Garden/Nature

Plant part:

Leaf

Watering all indoor and outdoor plants.

Sow plants, herbs, and vegetables that grow and flourish above ground, leaf vegetables (no lettuce).

Sowing, planting, harvesting, and drying every kind of medicinal herbs.

Transplanting.

Trimming and cutting back plants.
Combating slugs and snails.
Mowing lawns.

Start a compost heap.

Avoid pruning fruit trees and bushes. Avoid cutting down any trees.

Harvested produce should be consumed as soon as possible.

Housework

Light housework only.

Ventilate rooms briefly and rapidly. Don't air mattresses.

Any dirt and spots are easily removed in the laundry.

Avoid painting, as paint will take very long to dry.

Nutrition

Food quality:

Carbohydrate

Lettuce, spinach, lamb's lettuce, Endive, parsley, leek, cabbage (Brussels sprouts, kale, Chinese cabbage), all leafy herbs, asparagus, mushrooms, cress, Swiss chard, rhubarb.

Weight gain: avoid indulging in rich foods. If overweight, eat smaller portions and avoid carbohydrates.

Supply nutrient materials to strengthen the body. Focus on foods that contain essential minerals and vitamins. Stimulants and vitamins are more effective.

Positive affirmation:
"I trust the power of inner peace."

Planting Time
Descending forces! Sap is drawn downward, enhancing root formation. Best days for sowing, planting, and transplanting.

gather strength rest, recover buildup
Waxing Moon

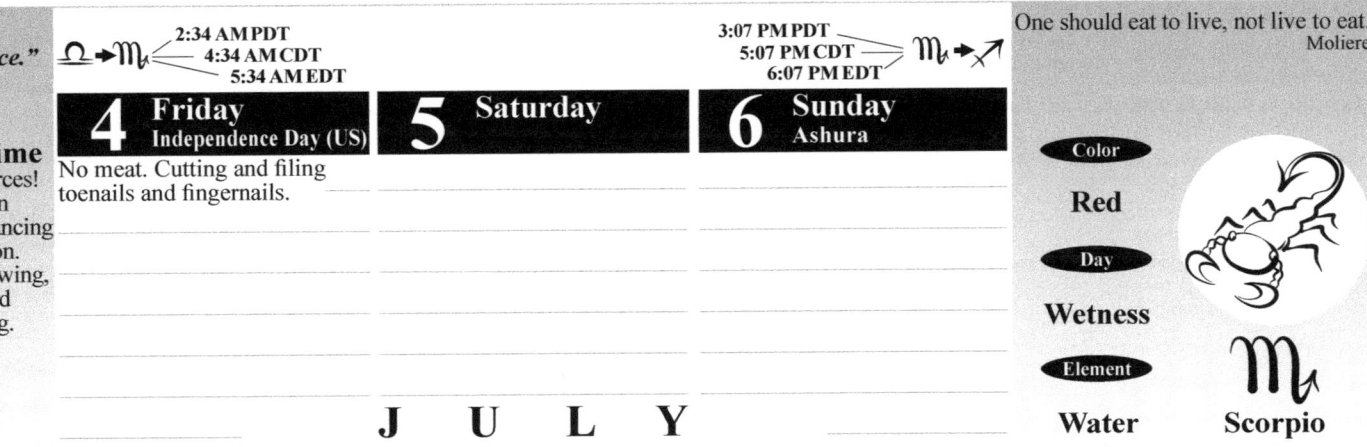

2:34 AM PDT
4:34 AM CDT
5:34 AM EDT

3:07 PM PDT
5:07 PM CDT
6:07 PM EDT

4 Friday Independence Day (US)

5 Saturday

6 Sunday Ashura

No meat. Cutting and filing toenails and fingernails.

J U L Y

One should eat to live, not live to eat.
Moliere

Color
Red

Day

Wetness

Element

Water   **Scorpio**

Success

Inquisitiveness and exuberant inspiration lead to new horizons. Insight and love for truth reign.

Bringing together is more important than splitting asunder.

Expansive forces will assist in legal matters, discussions, and debates.

Leisure

Expansion feels great, and travel, short trips, and outings are most welcome. A competitive spirit excites any sports event.

Talk things out when necessary.

Romance can be very passionate.

Good days for outings; even with cloudy skies the air still feels somewhat warm. Drying effect, get plenty to drink.

Health

Sensitive body parts:

Thighs and Veins

All measures taken to supply nutrient materials and strengthen the sensitive body parts are very effective.

Healing ointments are easily absorbed.

Sensitive sense organs.

Pains often arise in the sciatic nerve, veins, the small of the back, and thighs.

Avoid overstraining the body with unusual physical activities.

Body Care

Aromas, scents: Calendula (Marigold), Geranium, Rosemary

Treatments with firming and moisturizing creams are more effective.

Massages that serve to regenerate, and strengthen, perhaps aided with beneficial massage oils.

Correcting and cutting ingrown nails.

Hair dyes applied now, will look more vibrant.

Garden/Nature

Plant part:

Fruit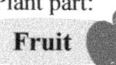

Sow plants and vegetables that grow and flourish above ground.

Sowing and planting fruit and vegetables that grow tall, and tomatoes, but no lettuce.

Transplanting.

Grafting onto fruit trees.

Cultivating grains, particularly corn.

Gather herbs for vein diseases.

Housework

Light housework only.

Ventilate sufficiently.

Freezing fruit and vegetables.

Baking bread, cakes, and cookies. Dough rises faster. (Except on New Moon)

Suitable for making cheese.

Making preserves.

Nutrition

Food quality:

Protein

Beans, peas, corn, tomatoes, pumpkin, lentils, soybeans, cucumber, eggplant, zucchini, berries, fruit, chili, bell pepper, figs, avocado, melon, olives.

Weight gain: avoid indulging in rich foods. If overweight, eat smaller portions.

Supply nutrient materials to strengthen the body. Focus on foods that contain essential minerals and vitamins.

Stimulants and vitamins are more effective.

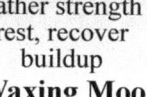

Turning Point

Transition of descending to ascending forces. Both forces are at work and neutralize each other.

gather strength
rest, recover
buildup

Waxing Moon

7 Monday

8 Tuesday

J U L Y

Earth laughs in flowers.
Ralph Waldo Emerson

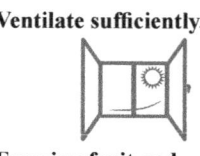

Color
Orange/Yellow

Day
Warm

Element
Fire

Sagittarius

Success

Career and business are in the foreground now and thinking becomes clear and serious, but somewhat inflexible.

Perseverance and reasoning assist in financial matters, planning, and contracts.

The values of tradition, authority, and discipline impact our endeavors.

Leisure

Money is not likely to be wasted in a shopping spree.

Many are drawn to enjoy cultural events.

The earth feels cold to the touch, so take slightly warmer clothes.

Health

Sensitive body parts:

Knees, Joints, Bones, Skin

All measures taken to supply nutrient materials and strengthen the sensitive body parts are very effective.

Healing ointments are easily absorbed.

Sensitive blood circulation.

Avoid overstraining bones and knees, and apply gentle stretching exercises only.

Problems with meniscus: Don't overstrain.

Dress slightly warmer.

High blood pressure: Avoid salty foods.

Massages, lymphatic therapy, and chiropractic treatment to release blockages.

○ *Full Moon: Avoid any surgery and vaccination if possible.*

Body Care

Aromas, scents:

Cedar, Juniper

Treatments with firming and moisturizing creams are more effective.

Massages that serve to regenerate, and strengthen, perhaps aided with beneficial massage oils.

Correcting and cutting ingrown nails.

Every kind of skin care is beneficial.

Cutting and filing toenails and fingernails will make the nails grow stronger over time.

Hair dyes applied now, will look more vibrant.

Garden/Nature

Plant part:

Root

Sow plants, herbs, and vegetables that grow and flourish above ground.

Transplanting.

Harvest produce is suitable for storage. Harvest root vegetables.

Gather herbs for bone, joint, and skin diseases.

○ *Full Moon: Weather and climate changes. Herbs are most powerful.*

Housework

Light housework only.

Air rooms only briefly.

Preserving root vegetables.

Avoid dry cleaning, as the fabric may develop unwanted glossy blotches.

○ *Full Moon: Avoid doing laundry, cleaning windows, making preserves, painting.*

Discover more about the lunar cycle and it's effects in the reference book "Nature's Daily Guide". ISBN 978-0-9854637-8-6

Nutrition

Food quality:

Salt

Garlic, carrots, red beets, reddish, rutabaga, sugar beet, celery, potatoes, onions, kohlrabi.

Weight gain: avoid indulging in rich foods. If overweight, eat smaller portions.

Supply nutrient materials to strengthen the body. Focus on foods that contain essential minerals and vitamins.

Stimulants and vitamins are more effective.

Avoid large quantities of salty foods like bacon, ham, salted herring, fatty cheese, and the like. Avoid heavy and greasy foods.

○ *Full Moon: A day of fasting.*

Positive affirmation:
"I trust the power of inner peace."

Harvest Time
Ascending forces! Sap is rising, enhancing plant growth above ground, resulting in the most juicy fruits and vegetables.

gather strength rest, recover buildup
Waxing Moon

1:56 AM PDT
3:56 AM CDT
4:56 AM EDT

9 Wednesday

No meat.

10 Thursday

○ **Full Moon** 3:38 PM PDT, 5:38 PM CDT, 6:38 PM EDT

J U L Y

It is during our darkest moments that we must focus to see the light.
Aristotle Onassis

Color
Yellow

Day
Cool

Element
Earth

Capricorn

Success

Career and business are in the foreground now and thinking becomes clear and serious, but somewhat inflexible.

Perseverance and reasoning assist in financial matters, planning, and contracts.

The values of tradition, authority, and discipline impact our endeavors.

Leisure

Money is not likely to be wasted in a shopping spree.

Many are drawn to enjoy cultural events.

The earth feels cold to the touch, so take slightly warmer clothes.

Health

Sensitive body parts:

Knees, Joints, Bones, Skin

All measures taken to flush out and detoxify the sensitive body parts are very effective.

Scarring is less severe.

Teeth: Removal of tartar and amalgam. Best for fillings, crowns, and dentures!

Blood-purifying, detoxifying herbal infusions and teas.

Sensitive blood circulation.

Avoid overstraining bones and knees, and apply gentle stretching exercises only.

Problems with meniscus: Don't overstrain.

Dress slightly warmer.

High blood pressure: Avoid salty foods.

Massages, lymphatic therapy, and chiropractic treatment to release blockages.

Body Care

Aromas, scents:

Cedar, Juniper

Prepare home-made ointments and cosmetics.

Apply detoxing facial and body care.

Treatments of bumps and pimples on the skin, and exfoliating procedures.

Remove body hair, it may not grow back.

Correction of the nail bed.

Massages that serve to relax, ease tension, and detoxify.

Reflexology massage.

Treating obstinate athlete's foot, nail fungus, and warts.

Cutting and filing toenails and fingernails will make the nails grow stronger over time.

Garden/Nature

Plant part:

Root

Sowing and planting root vegetables and winter vegetables

Weeding. Harrowing weeds. Dig over to prepare soil. Trimming and cutting back plants.
Clear and thin out plants, forest edges, and hedges. Plant cuttings.
Spread fertilizer and manure.
Start a compost heap.
Combat vermin.

Fertilize flowers with poorly formed roots.

Mulching.

Harvest produce is suitable for storage. Harvest root vegetables.

Gather herbs (roots) for bone, joint, and skin diseases.

Housework

Housework is dealt with much more successfully, efficiently, and effortlessly.

Problem stains are removed readily.

Best for doing laundry! Reduce on laundry detergent, support the environment.

Avoid dry cleaning, as the fabric may develop unwanted glossy blotches.

Thoroughly clean wooden and parquet floors, metals, china etc.

Cleaning, polishing, and waterproofing shoes.

Combating mold.

Air rooms only briefly.

Painting.

Preserving root vegetables. Slice cabbage now to ferment into sauerkraut.

Nutrition

Food quality:

Salt

Garlic, carrots, red beets, reddish, rutabaga, sugar beet, celery, potatoes, onions, kohlrabi.

Weight associated with overeating is less likely. If underweight, eat larger portions.

Cleansing and detox diets. Fruit and juice days.

Flush out poisons. Treatment for drug abuse.

Avoid large quantities of salty foods like bacon, ham, salted herring, fatty cheese, and the like. Avoid heavy and greasy foods.

What great thing would you attempt if you knew you could not fail?
Robert H. Schuller

10:22 AM PDT
12:22 PM CDT
1:22 PM EDT

11 Friday

No meat. Cutting and filing toenails and fingernails.

Positive affirmation:
"I trust the power of inner peace."

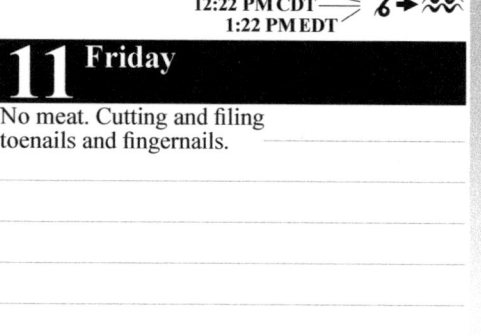

Harvest Time
Ascending forces! Sap is rising, enhancing plant growth above ground, resulting in the most juicy fruits and vegetables.

detox remove be active

Waning Moon

Color
Yellow

Day
Cool

Element
Earth

Capricorn

J U L Y

Success

Inspiration, optimism, and impatience. Rational thinking, creativity and imagination spark new ideas and inspire planning for the future.

Shying away from routine tasks people will feel more drawn to anything new.

Instead of gridlocked structures choose new possibilities.

Leisure

Inspiration and optimism will boost friendship, social gatherings, and parties.

Express your creativity and imagination. Dwell in dreams and utopian ideas. It is easier now to perceive intuitive thoughts.

Health

Sensitive body parts:

Lower Legs, Veins

All measures taken to flush out and detoxify the sensitive body parts are very effective.

Good for surgery, except on the sensitive body parts (see above), chest, lungs, stomach, liver, and gallbladder. Scarring is less severe.

Teeth: Removal of tartar and amalgam. Best for fillings, crowns, and dentures!

Blood-purifying, detoxifying herbal infusions and teas.

Sensitive glandular system.

Avoid inflammation of the veins. Apply ointments to lower legs, and rest legs in a raised position.

Varicose veins: Avoid long periods of standing.

While exercising go easy on the ankles.

Sensitivity to light, so bring your sunglasses along.

Body Care

Aromas, scents: Cyclamen, Peach, Wild Roses

Prepare home-made ointments and cosmetics.

Apply detoxing facial and body care.

Treatments of bumps and pimples on the skin, and exfoliating procedures.

Removing body hair.

Correction of the nail bed.

Massages that serve to relax, ease tension, and detoxify.

Reflexology massage.

Removal of callused skin.

Treating obstinate athlete's foot, nail fungus, and warts.

Garden/Nature

Plant part:

Flower

Fertilize flowers that no longer bloom.

Dig over/plow to prepare soil for planting.

Trimming and cutting back plants.

Hoeing and harrowing; weeds can be left to rot.

Pest control.

Start a compost heap.

Avoid watering plants.

Avoid transplanting sprouts.

Harvested produce is well suitable for storage.

Gather herbs (roots) for vein diseases.

Housework

Housework is dealt with much more successfully, efficiently, and effortlessly.

Problem stains are removed readily.

Best for doing laundry! Reduce on laundry detergent, support the environment.

Dry cleaning.

Clean and store seasonal clothing.

Best suited for a spring cleaning: Thoroughly clean wooden and parquet floors, metals, china etc.

Cleaning windows and glass.

Cleaning, polishing, and waterproofing shoes.

Combating mold.

Ventilate rooms thoroughly.

Baking bread, cakes, and cookies (add more leavening agent).

Making preserves.

Painting.

Nutrition

Food quality:

Fat

Cauliflower, artichoke, broccoli, sunflower seeds, flax seeds, nuts, rose hip, elder.

Weight associated with overeating is less likely. If underweight, eat larger portions.

Cleansing and detox diets. Fruit and juice days.

Flush out poisons. Treatment for drug abuse.

Pay attention to any particularly tempting foods today: Most likely the "wrong" things taste best.

High cholesterol: eat a low fat diet.

Every moment and every event of every man's life on earth plants something in his soul.
Thomas Merton

Color

Bright/ Dark Blue

Day

Air/Light

Element

Aquarius　　　**Air**

4:46 PM PDT
6:46 PM CDT ⟩ ≋ → ⟩⟨
7:46 PM EDT

12 Saturday

13 Sunday

J　U　L　Y

Harvest Time
Ascending forces! Sap is rising, enhancing plant growth above ground, resulting in the most juicy fruits and vegetables.

detox remove be active

Waning Moon

Success

Sensibility, intuition, and helpfulness.

Where possible, retreating is more favorable than dealing with business matters.

Dissolve restrictions, be patient and wait. Be aware that people can be more easily influenced.

Leisure

Your helpfulness will boost friendships.

Enjoy dancing or swimming, or watch a movie that will inspire your fantasies and imagination.

Retreat, relax, and recover.

Romance can be gentle and coziness will prevail.

If you plan outdoor excursions, be prepared for a shower here and there.

Health

Sensitive body parts:

Feet and Toes

All measures taken to flush out and detoxify the sensitive body parts are very effective.

Good for surgical operations except those on the sensitive body parts (see above), chest, lungs, stomach, liver, and gallbladder.
Scarring is less severe.

Teeth: Removal of tartar and amalgam. Best for fillings, crowns, and dentures!

Blood-purifying, detoxifying herbal infusions and teas.

Sensitive nervous system.

Drugs have a much stronger effect on your body.
Monitor closely what you put into your body.

Lymphatic therapy.

Sluggishness or fatigue may occur in the transition into the next Zodiac sign of Aries.

Body Care

Aromas, scents:
Magnolia, Amaryllis, Clary Sage

Prepare home-made ointments and cosmetics.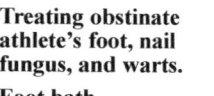

Apply detoxing facial and body care.

Treatments of bumps and pimples on the skin, and exfoliating procedures.

Removing body hair.

Correction of the nail bed.

Massages that serve to relax, ease tension, and detoxify. Reflexology massage. Carry out with special care, people are more sensitive.

Removal of callused skin.

Treating obstinate athlete's foot, nail fungus, and warts.

Foot bath.

No haircuts, hair becomes shaggy and unmanageable.
Avoid washing your hair.

Garden/Nature

Plant part:

Leaf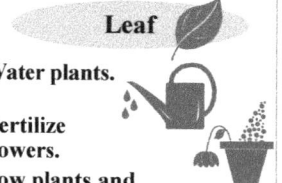

Water plants.

Fertilize flowers.

Sow plants and vegetables that grow below ground, potatoes, leaf vegetables, and lettuce.

Dig over/plow to prepare soil for planting.
Trimming and cutting back plants.
Start a compost heap.

Mowing lawns.

Pest control. Weeding.

Harvested produce should be consumed as soon as possible.

Gather herbs for foot complaints.

Housework

Housework is dealt with much more successfully, efficiently, and effortlessly.

Problem stains are removed readily.

Best for doing laundry! Reduce on laundry detergent, support the environment.

Dry cleaning.

Clean and store seasonal clothing.

Thoroughly clean wooden and parquet floors, metals, china etc.

Cleaning, polishing, and waterproofing shoes.

Combating mold.

Ventilate rooms briefly and rapidly.

Avoid painting.

Preserving and storing should be avoided.

Nutrition

Food quality:

Carbohydrate

Lettuce, spinach, lamb's lettuce, Endive, parsley, leek, cabbage (Brussels sprouts, kale, Chinese cabbage), all leafy herbs, asparagus, mushrooms, cress, Swiss chard, rhubarb.

Weight associated with overeating is less likely. If underweight, eat larger portions.

Cleansing and detox diets. Fruit and juice days.

Flush out poisons. Treatment for drug abuse.

Caffeine, alcohol, drugs, certain foods, and stimulants have a much stronger effect.

A good garden may have some weeds.
Thomas Fuller

Pisces

Color
Blueish White

Day
Wetness

Element

Water

9:33 PM PDT
11:33 PM CDT
Wednesday 12:33 AM EDT

14 Monday

15 Tuesday

J U L Y

Positive affirmation:
"I trust the power of inner peace."

Harvest Time
Ascending forces! Sap is rising, enhancing plant growth above ground, resulting in the most juicy fruits and vegetables.

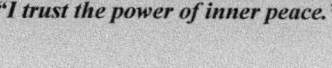

detox
remove
be active
Waning Moon

Success

Things get going and the way straight ahead seems the best.

People feel energetic, courageous, assertive, and at times anxious.

Good time for meetings and sales talks but impatience and selfishness do not favor teamwork.

Leisure

An enterprising spirit and spontaneity move people to enjoy outings, sports, competitions, cultural events, and travels.

Romance can be very passionate.

Good days for outings, even with cloudy skies the air still feels somewhat warm. Drying effect, get plenty to drink.

Health

Sensitive body parts:

Head, Brain, Eyes

All measures taken to flush out and detoxify the sensitive body parts are very effective.

Good for surgery, except on the sensitive body parts (see above), chest, lungs, stomach, liver, and gallbladder.

Scarring is less severe.

Teeth: Removal of tartar and amalgam. Best for fillings, crowns, and dentures! Avoiding treatment of periodontitis and gums.

Blood-purifying, detoxifying herbal infusions and teas.

Sensitive sense organs.

If you suffer from migraines drink plenty of water, and avoid coffee, chocolate, and sugar.

Body Care

Aromas, scents:
Cloves, Peppermint, Thyme

Prepare home-made ointments and cosmetics.

Apply detoxing facial and body care.

Treatments of bumps and pimples on the skin, and exfoliating procedures.

Removing body hair.

Correction of the nail bed.

Massages that serve to relax, ease tension, and detoxify.

Reflexology massage.

Removal of callused skin.

Treating obstinate athlete's foot, nail fungus, and warts.

Eye compresses to relieve strained eyes.

Any kind of hair care.

Garden/Nature

Plant part:

Fruit

Sowing plants and vegetables that grow below ground.

Sowing and planting anything that is supposed to grow fast. Sowing and planting fruit and tomatoes.

Dig over/plow the soil to prepare for planting.

Spreading manure. Fertilizing grains, vegetables, and fruit.

Weeding. Pest control.

Pruning of fruit trees and bushes.

Harvesting and storing grains, vegetables, potatoes, fruits, and tomatoes.

Start a compost heap.

Gather herbs (roots) for eye complaints and headaches.

Day off on 7/16.

Housework

Housework is dealt with much more successfully, efficiently, and effortlessly.

Problem stains are removed readily.

Best for doing laundry!

Dry cleaning.

Clean and store seasonal clothing.

Thoroughly clean wooden and parquet floors, metals, china, etc.

Cleaning windows and glass.

Cleaning, polishing, and waterproofing shoes.

Combating mold.

Ventilate rooms sufficiently. Air beds.

Suitable for making cheese.

Preserving and freezing fruit and vegetables.

Baking bread, cakes, and cookies (use more leavening agent).

Painting.

Nutrition

Food quality:

Protein

Beans, peas, corn, tomatoes, pumpkin, lentils, soybeans, cucumber, eggplant, zucchini, berries, fruit, chili, bell pepper, figs, avocado, melon, olives.

Weight associated with overeating is less likely. If underweight, eat larger portions.

Cleansing and detox diets. Fruit and juice days.

Flush out poisons. Treatment for drug abuse.

Drink plenty of water.

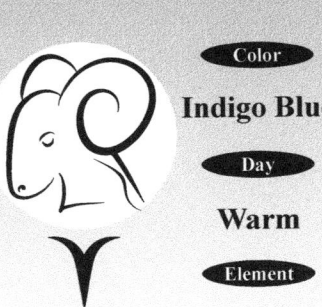

Aries — Fire

Color: **Indigo Blue**

Day: **Warm**

Element: **Fire**

Looking after my health today gives me a better hope for tomorrow.
Anne Wilson Schaef

16 Wednesday
No meat.

17 Thursday
☾ Half Moon.

J U L Y

Harvest Time
Ascending forces! Sap is rising, enhancing plant growth above ground, resulting in the most juicy fruits and vegetables.

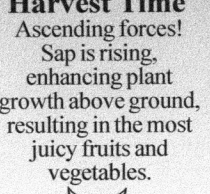

detox remove be active

Waning Moon

Success

Realism and material security are important. Persistence comes easy, thoughts and reactions are slower.

Assess financial areas.

Conservative tendencies may make people want to stay away from risk taking.

Leisure

Relax at a picnic/feast. Enjoy culinary pleasures and hobbies.

The earth feels cold to the touch, so take slightly warmer clothes.

Health

Sensitive body parts:

Head and Neck

All measures taken to flush out and detoxify the sensitive body parts are very effective.

Good for surgery, except on the sensitive body parts (see above), chest, lungs, stomach, liver, and gallbladder. Scarring is less severe.

Teeth: Removal of tartar and amalgam. Best for fillings, crowns, and dentures! Avoiding treatment of periodontitis and gums.

Blood-purifying, detoxifying herbal infusions and teas.

Sensitive blood circulation.

Organs of speech, jaws, teeth, tonsils, thyroid gland, neck, and vocal chords get easily affected. Keep neck warm. On cold days ears should be protected. Sensitivity to noise.

High blood pressure: Avoid salty foods.

Massages, lymphatic therapy, and chiropractic treatment to release blockages.

Body Care

Aromas, scents: Geranium, Jasmine, Rose

Prepare home-made ointments and cosmetics.

Apply detoxing facial and body care.

Treatments of bumps and pimples on the skin, and exfoliating procedures.

Removing body hair.

Correction of the nail bed.

Massages that serve to relax, ease tension, and detoxify.

Reflexology massage.

Removal of callused skin.

Treating obstinate athlete's foot, nail fungus, and warts.

Garden/Nature

Plant part:

Root

Sow plants and vegetables that grow below ground.

Everything grows slowly and lasts well.

Dig over to prepare soil.

Trimming/cutting back plants. Weeding. Mulching.

Start a compost heap.

Combat vermin found in the soil.

Spread fertilizer and liquid manure.

Fertilize flowers with poorly formed roots.

Harvested produce is well suited for storage. Harvesting root vegetables.

Gather herbs (roots) for sinus issues, sore throat, and ear complaints.

Housework

Housework is dealt with much more successfully, efficiently, and effortlessly.

Problem stains are removed readily.

Best for doing laundry! Reduce on laundry detergent, support the environment.

Dry cleaning.

Clean and store seasonal clothing.

Thoroughly clean wooden and parquet floors, metals, china etc.

Cleaning, polishing, and waterproofing shoes.

Combating mold.

Air rooms only briefly.

Painting.

Preserving root vegetables.

Nutrition

Food quality:

Salt

Garlic, carrots, red beets, reddish, rutabaga, sugar beet, celery, potatoes, onions, kohlrabi.

Weight associated with overeating is less likely. If underweight, eat larger portions.

Cleansing and detox diets. Fruit and juice days.

Flush out poisons. Treatment for drug abuse.

Avoid large quantities of salty foods like bacon, ham, salted herring, fatty cheese, and the like.

The more man meditates upon good thoughts, the better will be his world and the world at large.
Confucius

Color
Bright Blue

Day
Cool

Element

Taurus   **Earth**

♈ → ♉   1:00 AM PDT
3:00 AM CDT
4:00 AM EDT

18 Friday

No meat. Cutting and filing toenails and fingernails.

19 Saturday

J U L Y

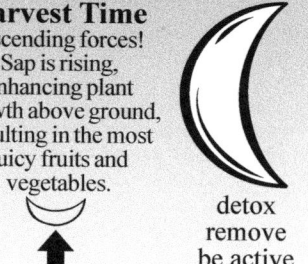

Harvest Time
Ascending forces! Sap is rising, enhancing plant growth above ground, resulting in the most juicy fruits and vegetables.

detox
remove
be active
Waning Moon

Success

Open mindedness and curiosity. A changeable and hectic time.

Good time for talking, negotiating, networking, and exchanging ideas as well as for meetings of a nonbinding nature, conferences, and studies.

Leisure

Good time for family gatherings, parties, and short trips.

People enjoy stimulating their minds with reading and studying. Attending theater performances is a preferred enjoyment. Enhance friendships.

Stretching exercises.

Be prepared for sudden changes in weather or climate.

Health

Sensitive body parts:

Shoulders, Arms, Hands, Lungs

All measures taken to flush out and detoxify the sensitive body parts are very effective.

Good for surgery, except on the sensitive body parts (see above), chest, stomach, liver, and gallbladder.
Scarring is less severe.

Teeth: Removal of tartar and amalgam. Best for fillings, crowns, and dentures! Avoid having any teeth pulled.

Blood-purifying, detoxifying herbal infusions and teas.

Sensitive glandular system.

Make sure you are dressed warm enough in cool weather.

Exercises for shoulders. Breathing exercises.

Sensitivity to light, bring your sunglasses along.

Massages, lymphatic therapy, and chiropractic treatment to release blockages.

Body Care

Aromas, scents:
Lavender, Lemon Balm, Magnolia, Verbena

Prepare home-made ointments and cosmetics.

Apply detoxing facial and body care.

Treatments of bumps and pimples on the skin, and exfoliating procedures.

Removing body hair.

Correction of the nail bed.

Massages that serve to relax, ease tension, and detoxify.

Reflexology massage.

Removal of callused skin.

Treating obstinate athlete's foot, nail fungus, and warts.

Garden/Nature

Plant part:
Flower

Sow plants and vegetablesthat grow below ground.

Trimming and cutting back plants.

Start a compost heap.

Weeding. Pest control.

Fertilize flowers that no longer bloom.

Avoid watering plants.

Changes in weather are more likely.

Gather herbs (roots) for tensions in the shoulder and lung complaints.

Housework

Housework is dealt with much more successfully, efficiently, and effortlessly.

Problem stains are removed readily.

Best for doing laundry! Reduce on laundry detergent, support the environment.

Dry cleaning.

Clean and store seasonal clothing.

Thoroughly clean wooden and parquet floors, metals, china etc.

Cleaning windows and glass.

Cleaning, polishing, and waterproofing shoes.

Combating mold.

Ventilate rooms thoroughly.

Baking bread, cakes, and cookies (add more leavening agent).

Making preserves.

Painting.

Nutrition

Food quality:
Fat

Cauliflower, artichoke, broccoli, sunflower seeds, flax seeds, nuts, rose hip, elder.

Weight associated with overeating is less likely. If underweight, eat larger portions.

Cleansing and detox diets. Fruit and juice days.

Flush out poisons. Treatment for drug abuse.

Pay attention to any particularly tempting foods today: Most likely the "wrong" things taste best.

High cholesterol: eat a low fat diet.

Anything you're good at contributes to happiness.
Bertrand Russell

Gemini

Color
Light Blue

Day
Air/Light

Element

Air

☿→♊ 3:32 AM PDT
5:32 AM CDT
6:32 AM EDT

20 Sunday

21 Monday

J U L Y

Turning Point
Transition of ascending to descending forces. Both forces are at work and neutralize each other.

detox
remove
be active

Waning Moon

Success

Feelings, sensitivity, and cooperativeness. Many are overly sensitive, so beware of treading on someone's toes.

Be cautious if you are easily influenced.

During negotiations make use of the cognitive ability of your senses.

Leisure

Relax within your close family.

Retreat to your safe haven and enjoy your fantasy while reading or listening to music. The inner world becomes more colorful than the outer.

Romance can be gentle. Deep feelings will prevail.

If you plan outdoor excursions, be prepared for a shower here and there.

Health

Sensitive body parts:
Chest, Lungs, Liver, Stomach, Gall Bladder

All measures taken to flush out and detoxify the sensitive body parts are very effective.

Scarring is less severe.

Teeth: Removal of tartar and amalgam. Best for fillings, crowns, and dentures!

Blood-purifying, detoxifying herbal infusions and teas.

Sensitive nervous system.

Be cautious with alcohol since the liver is very sensitive.

Stomach could play up and cause gas and heartburn.

Rheumatism: Don't air bedding outside, damp will remain in the bedding.

Lymphatic therapy.

Body Care

Aromas, scents:
Lilac, Lilies of the Valley, Lilies, Violets

Prepare home-made ointments and cosmetics.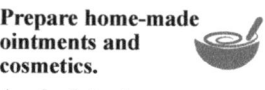

Apply detoxing facial and body care.

Treatments of bumps and pimples on the skin, and exfoliating procedures.

Removing body hair.

Correction of the nail bed.

Massages that serve to relax, ease tension, and detoxify.

Reflexology massage.

Removal of callused skin.

Treating obstinate athlete's foot, nail fungus, and warts.

No haircuts, hair becomes shaggy and unmanageable. Avoid washing your hair.

Garden/Nature

Plant part:
Leaf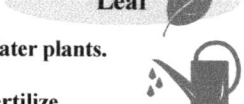

Water plants.

Fertilize flowers.

Sow plants and vegetables that grow below ground, leaf vegetables, and lettuce.

Dig over/plow to prepare soil for planting.

Trimming and cutting back plants. Transplanting. Weeding.

Combating pests above ground.

Start a compost heap.

Mowing lawns.

Gather herbs (roots) for bronchitis, stomach, liver, and gall bladder complaints.

Unfavorable for harvesting, storing, and preserving.

Housework

Housework is dealt with much more successfully, efficiently, and effortlessly.

Problem stains are removed readily.

Best for doing laundry! Reduce on laundry detergent, support the environment.

Dry cleaning.

Thoroughly clean wooden and parquet floors, metals, china etc.

Cleaning, polishing, and waterproofing shoes.

Combating mold.

Ventilate rooms briefly and rapidly.

Avoid painting.

Nutrition

Food quality:
Carbohydrate

Lettuce, spinach, lamb's lettuce, Endive, parsley, leek, cabbage (Brussels sprouts, kale, Chinese cabbage), all leafy herbs, asparagus, mushrooms, cress, Swiss chard, rhubarb.

Weight associated with overeating is less likely. If underweight, eat larger portions.

Moodiness may make you want to eat more than is healthy. If overweight avoid carbohydrates.

Cleansing and detox diets. Fruit and juice days.

Flush out poisons. Treatment for drug abuse.

If you get stomach troubles easily, avoid heavy meals.

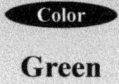

Color	**Green**
Day	**Wetness**
Element	**Cancer**

Cancer **Water**

II → 69 5:27 AM PDT
         7:27 AM CDT
         8:27 AM EDT

22 Tuesday

23 Wednesday
No meat.

J U L Y

Planting Time
Descending forces! Sap is drawn downward, enhancing root formation. Best days for sowing, planting, and transplanting.

detox
remove
be active
Waning Moon

Success

Determination reigns, and risks are taken more often. Master your tasks with more self-confidence and creativity.

Limits appear to be more easily surmountable.

Auspicious day for sales, advertising, and publicity.

● *New Moon: Confirm your resolutions. Finalize new decisions. Drop bad habits.*

Leisure

Zest for life is in the air. People want to have a fun time, enjoy parties, musical events, movies, etc.

Possessive feelings can harm a relationship. Romance can be very passionate.

Outings: even with cloudy skies the air still feels somewhat warm. Drying effect, get plenty to drink.

Danger of sudden storms, not only in the sky.

Health

Sensitive body parts:
Heart, Back, Diaphragm, Circulation, Arteries

All measures taken to flush out and detoxify the sensitive body parts are very effective.

Scarring is less severe.

Teeth: Removal of tartar and amalgam. Best for fillings, crowns, and dentures!

Blood-purifying, detoxifying herbal infusions and teas.

Sensitive sense organs.

Back and heart problems are more likely to occur.

Avoid overstraining of the heart and circulation with unusual physical activities.

Expect sleepless nights.

● *New Moon: Avoid any surgery if possible.*

Body Care

Aromas, scents:
Hibiscus, Oleander, Rose

Prepare home-made ointments and cosmetics.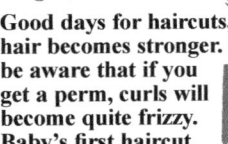

Apply detoxing facial and body care.

Treatments of bumps and pimples on the skin, and exfoliating procedures.

Removing body hair.

Correction of the nail bed.

Massages that serve to relax, ease tension, and detoxify.

Reflexology massage.

Removal of callused skin.

Treating obstinate athlete's foot, nail fungus, and warts.

Good days for haircuts, hair becomes stronger. But be aware that if you get a perm, curls will become quite frizzy. Baby's first haircut.

Garden/Nature

Plant part:
Fruit

Sowing plants and vegetables that grow below ground.

Sowing and planting fruit. Also sow and plant vegetables that are highly perishable. Plant trees and bushes. Sow lawns.

Dig over/plow to prepare soil for planting.

Trimming and cutting back plants. Pruning of fruit trees and bushes.

Transplanting. Not suitable for fertilizing. Weeding. Pest Control.

Harvested produce should be consumed as soon as possible.

Gather herbs (roots) for heart and circulation complaints.

Start compost heap.

● *New Moon: Change of weather is likely. Care for sickly plants.*

Housework

Housework is dealt with much more successfully, efficiently, and effortlessly.

Problem stains are removed readily.

Best for doing laundry!

Dry cleaning.

Thoroughly clean wooden and parquet floors, metals, china, etc.

Cleaning windows and glass.

Cleaning, polishing, and waterproofing shoes.

Combating mold.

Ventilate rooms sufficiently. Air beds.

Suitable for making cheese.

Preserving and freezing fruit and vegetables.

Baking bread, cakes, and cookies (use more leavening agent).

Avoid painting.

Nutrition

Food quality:
Protein

Beans, peas, corn, tomatoes, pumpkin, lentils, soybeans, cucumber, eggplant, zucchini, berries, fruit, chili, bell pepper, figs, avocado, melon, olives.

Weight associated with overeating is less likely. If underweight, eat larger portions.

Cleansing and detox diets. Fruit and juice days.

Flush out poisons. Treatment for drug abuse.

● *New Moon: A day of fasting.*

Always continue the climb. It is possible for you to do whatever you choose, if you first get to know who you are and are willing to work with a power that is greater than ourselves to do it.
Ella Wheeler Wilcox

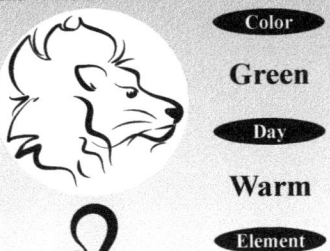

● Color
Green

● Day
Warm

● Element
Fire

♌ **Leo**

7:30 AM PDT
9:30 AM CDT
10:30 AM EDT

24 Thursday
● New Moon 12:12 PM PDT, 2:12 PM CDT, 3:12 PM EDT

J U L Y

Planting Time
Descending forces! Sap is drawn downward, enhancing root formation. Best days for sowing, planting, and transplanting.

detox
remove
be active
Waning Moon

Success

Determination reigns, and risks are taken more often. Master your tasks with more self-confidence and creativity.

Limits appear to be more easily surmountable.

Auspicious day for sales, advertising, and publicity.

Leisure

Zest for life is in the air. People want to have a fun time, enjoy parties, musical events, movies, etc.

Possessive feelings can harm a relationship. Romance can be very passionate.

Outings: even with cloudy skies the air still feels somewhat warm. Drying effect, get plenty to drink.

Danger of sudden storms, not only in the sky.

Health

Sensitive body parts:
Heart, Back, Diaphragm, Circulation, Arteries

All measures taken to supply nutrient materials and strengthen the sensitive body parts are very effective.

Healing ointments are easily absorbed.

Sensitive sense organs.

Back and heart problems are more likely to occur.

Avoid over straining of the heart and circulation with unusual physical activities.

Expect sleepless nights.

Body Care

Aromas, scents:
Hibiscus, Oleander, Rose

Treatments with firming and moisturizing creams are more effective.

Massages that serve to regenerate, and strengthen, perhaps aided with beneficial massage oils.

Correcting and cutting ingrown nails.

Good days for haircuts, hair becomes stronger. But be aware that if you get a perm, curls will become quite frizzy. Baby's first haircut.

Garden/Nature

Plant part:
Fruit

Sow plants and vegetables that grow and flourish above ground. Sowing and planting fruit. Also sow and plant vegetables that are highly perishable. Plant trees and bushes. Sow lawns.

Transplanting. Grafting onto fruit trees.

Trimming and cutting back plants.

Best for cultivating grains on wet fields.

Dig over/plow to prepare soil for planting.

Setting up a compost heap.

Not suitable for fertilizing.

Harvested produce should be consumed as soon as possible.

Gather herbs for heart and circulation complaints.

Housework

Light housework only.

Ventilate sufficiently.

Freezing fruit and vegetables.

Baking bread, cakes, and cookies. Dough rises faster. (Except on New Moon)

Suitable for making cheese.

Avoid painting.

Nutrition

Food quality:
Protein

Beans, peas, corn, tomatoes, pumpkin, lentils, soybeans, cucumber, eggplant, zucchini, berries, fruit, chili, bell pepper, figs, avocado, melon, olives.

Weight gain: avoid indulging in rich foods. If overweight, eat smaller portions.

Supply nutrient materials to strengthen the body. Focus on foods that contain essential minerals and vitamins.

Stimulants and vitamins are more effective.

Positive affirmation:
"I trust my intuition."

Planting Time
Descending forces! Sap is drawn downward, enhancing root formation. Best days for sowing, planting, and transplanting.

gather strength rest, recover buildup
Waxing Moon

25 Friday
No meat. Cutting and filing toenails and fingernails.

1:57 PM PDT
3:57 PM CDT ⟩ ♌ ➤ ♍
4:57 PM EDT

26 Saturday

If your happiness depends on what somebody else does, I guess you do have a problem.
Richard Bach

Color — **Green**

Day — **Warm**

Element — **Fire**

Leo ♌

J U L Y

Success

Good time for details, organization, routine, concentration, and duty.

Take care of financial and administrative tasks.

Prepare for future success now with realistic and critical assessment.

Leisure

Enjoy a nature walk.

Good time for health regimes. Improve your health with stretching exercises and yoga.

The earth feels cold to the touch, so take slightly warmer clothes.

Health

Sensitive body parts:

Digestive Organs, Nerves, Spleen, Pancreas

All measures taken to supply nutrient materials and strengthen the sensitive body parts are very effective.

Healing ointments are easily absorbed.

Sensitive blood circulation.

For a sensitive digestive system, a wholesome diet is recommended.

Dress slightly warmer.

High blood pressure: Avoid salty foods.

Massages, lymphatic therapy, and chiropractic treatment to release blockages.

Body Care

Aromas, scents: Lavender, Spruce Needles, Sage, Meadow Flowers

Treatments with firming and moisturizing creams are more effective.

Massages that serve to regenerate, and strengthen, perhaps aided with beneficial massage oils.

Correcting and cutting ingrown nails.

Best for haircuts because it retains its shape longer. Perms turn out best. Hair dyes applied now, will look more vibrant.

Garden/Nature

Plant part:

Root

Best for sowing and planting, except lettuce.

Plant trees which are supposed to grow very tall. Plant hedges and bushes that are meant to grow very fast.

Sowing lawns.

Planting and re-potting balcony and indoor plants.

Transplanting.

Trimming and cutting back plants.

Planting cuttings.

Start a compost heap.

Avoid harvesting and storing.

Gather herbs (roots) for digestive organs, pancreas, and nervous complaints.

Housework

Light housework only.

Air rooms only briefly.

Making pickles, preserves, and cheese yields suboptimal results and should be avoided.

Nutrition

Food quality:

Salt

Garlic, carrots, red beets, reddish, rutabaga, sugar beet, celery, potatoes, onions, kohlrabi.

Weight gain: avoid indulging in rich foods. If overweight, eat smaller portions.

Supply nutrient materials to strengthen the body. Focus on foods that contain essential minerals and vitamins.

Stimulants and vitamins are more effective.

Avoid large quantities of salty foods like bacon, ham, salted herring, fatty cheese, and the like. Avoid heavy and greasy foods.

Positive affirmation:
"I trust my intuition."

Planting Time
Descending forces! Sap is drawn downward, enhancing root formation. Best days for sowing, planting, and transplanting.

gather strength rest, recover buildup

Waxing Moon

27 Sunday
Parent's Day

28 Monday

J U L Y

For every person who has ever lived there has come, at last, a spring he will never see. Glory then in the springs that are yours.
Pam Brown

Color
Yellow

Day
Cool

Element
Earth

 **Virgo**

Success

The artistic instinct rules, but so, too, does indecisiveness. The forces swing back and forth until equilibrium is achieved.

It's easy to reach compromises with tactful sensitivity.

A sense of judgment will support legal matters.

Leisure

Pursuit for harmony and cooperativeness supports good times in romance, friendship, and partnership.

Enjoy cultural events. Relax and get pampered with a spa treatment.

Romance can be passionate yet sensitive.

Health

Sensitive body parts:

Hips, Kidneys, Bladder

All measures taken to supply nutrient materials and strengthen the sensitive body parts are very effective.

Healing ointments are easily absorbed.

Sensitive glandular system.

Take special care to keep the area of bladder and kidneys warm.

Apply special exercises for the hip region.

Avoid having any teeth pulled.

Sensitivity to light, bring your sunglasses along.

Body Care

Aromas, scents: Roses, Violets, Daffodils

Treatments with firming and moisturizing creams are more effective.

Massages that serve to regenerate, and strengthen, perhaps aided with beneficial massage oils.

Correcting and cutting ingrown nails.

Hair dyes applied now, will look more vibrant.

Garden/Nature

Plant part:

Flower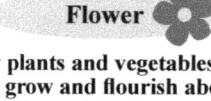

Sow plants and vegetables that grow and flourish above ground, specially flowers, and medicinal herbs.

Transplanting.

Trimming and cutting back plants.

Avoid watering plants.

Start a compost heap.

Harvested produce should be consumed as soon as possible.

Gather herbs for kidneys, gall bladder, and hip complaints.

Day off on 7/30.

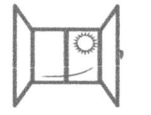

Housework

Light housework only.

Ventilate rooms thoroughly.

Baking cakes and cookies. Dough rises faster. (Except on New Moon)

Nutrition

Food quality:

Fat

Cauliflower, artichoke, broccoli, sunflower seeds, flax seeds, nuts, rose hip, elder.

Weight gain: avoid indulging in rich foods. If overweight, eat smaller portions.

Supply nutrient materials to strengthen the body. Focus on foods that contain essential minerals and vitamins.

Stimulants and vitamins are more effective.

Pay attention to any particularly tempting foods today: Most likely the "wrong" things taste best.

High cholesterol: eat a low fat diet.

Positive affirmation:
"I trust my intuition."

Planting Time
Descending forces! Sap is drawn downward, enhancing root formation. Best days for sowing, planting, and transplanting.

gather strength rest, recover buildup
Waxing Moon

♏→♎ 10:44 PM PDT Monday
12:44 AM CDT
1:44 AM EDT

10:26 AM PDT ♎→♏
12:26 PM CDT
1:26 PM EDT

29 Tuesday

30 Wednesday
No meat.

31 Thursday

J U L Y

Nothing is impossible, the word itself says 'I'm possible'!
Audrey Hepburn

Color
Orange

Day
Air/Light

Element
Air

Libra

Success

Critical and superstitious behavior emerges, especially pertaining to money.

A penetrating power will strengthen your capacity to act.

An increased perception opens our interest for the essentials and helps to discover hidden potentials.

Leisure

Relax within your close family, with meditation, and relaxation exercises.

A longing to feel safe will be nurtured if you focus on habits and rituals. An increased sensitivity will help to enjoy every moment.

Romance can be very passionate.

If you plan outdoor excursions, be prepared for a shower here and there.

Health

Sensitive body parts:

Sex organs, Ureter

All measures taken to supply nutrient materials and strengthen the sensitive body parts are very effective.

Healing ointments are easily absorbed. Applying herbal ointments to the shoulders for rheumatic gout and alike.

Sensitive nervous system.

Female disorders: As a preventative measure apply hip baths using yarrow.

Pregnancy: Avoid any exertion, miscarriages are more likely.

Keep region of the pelvis, kidneys, and feet warm to prevent infection of the bladder and kidneys.

Lymphatic therapy.

Body Care

Aromas, scents:
Anemone, Cornflower
Oregano, Thuja

Treatments with firming and moisturizing creams are more effective.

Massages that serve to regenerate, and strengthen, perhaps aided with beneficial massage oils.

Correcting and cutting ingrown nails.

Hair dyes applied now, will look more vibrant.

Garden/Nature

Plant part:

Leaf

Watering all indoor and outdoor plants.

Sow plants, herbs, and vegetables that grow and flourish above ground, leaf vegetables (no lettuce).

Sowing, planting, harvesting, and drying every kind of medicinal herbs.

Transplanting.

Trimming and cutting back plants.

Combating slugs and snails. Mowing lawns.

Start a compost heap.

Avoid pruning fruit trees and bushes. Avoid cutting down any trees.

Harvested produce should be consumed as soon as possible.

Housework

Light housework only.

Ventilate rooms briefly and rapidly. Don't air mattresses.

Any dirt and spots are easily removed in the laundry.

Avoid painting, as paint will take very long to dry.

Nutrition

Food quality:

Carbohydrate

Lettuce, spinach, lamb's lettuce, Endive, parsley, leek, cabbage (Brussels sprouts, kale, Chinese cabbage), all leafy herbs, asparagus, mushrooms, cress, Swiss chard, rhubarb.

Weight gain: avoid indulging in rich foods. If overweight, eat smaller portions and avoid carbohydrates.

Supply nutrient materials to strengthen the body. Focus on foods that contain essential minerals and vitamins. Stimulants and vitamins are more effective.

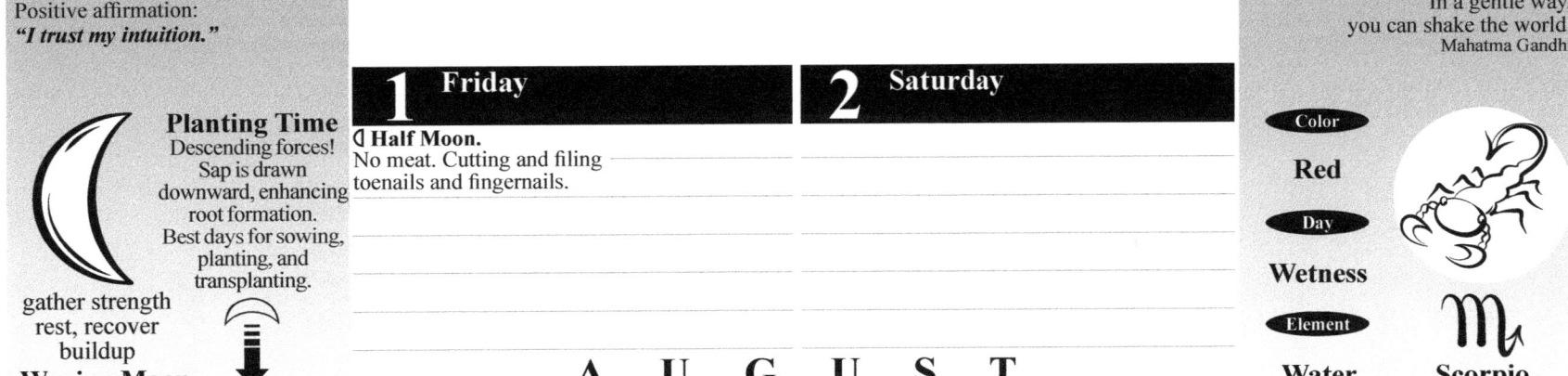

Positive affirmation:
"I trust my intuition."

Planting Time
Descending forces! Sap is drawn downward, enhancing root formation. Best days for sowing, planting, and transplanting.

gather strength rest, recover buildup
Waxing Moon

1 Friday
☽ Half Moon.
No meat. Cutting and filing toenails and fingernails.

2 Saturday

A U G U S T

In a gentle way, you can shake the world.
Mahatma Gandhi

Color
Red

Day

Wetness

Element

Water   Scorpio

Success

Inquisitiveness and exuberant inspiration lead to new horizons. Insight and love for truth reign.

Bringing together is more important than splitting asunder.

Expansive forces will assist in legal matters, discussions, and debates.

Leisure

Expansion feels great, and travel, short trips, and outings are most welcome. A competitive spirit excites any sports event.

Talk things out when necessary.

Romance can be very passionate.

Good days for outings; even with cloudy skies the air still feels somewhat warm. Drying effect, get plenty to drink.

Health

Sensitive body parts:

Thighs and Veins

All measures taken to supply nutrient materials and strengthen the sensitive body parts are very effective.

Healing ointments are easily absorbed.

Sensitive sense organs.

Pains often arise in the sciatic nerve, veins, the small of the back, and thighs.

Avoid overstraining the body with unusual physical activities.

Body Care

Aromas, scents: Calendula (Marigold), Geranium, Rosemary

Treatments with firming and moisturizing creams are more effective.

Massages that serve to regenerate, and strengthen, perhaps aided with beneficial massage oils.

Correcting and cutting ingrown nails.

Hair dyes applied now, will look more vibrant.

Garden/Nature

Plant part:

Fruit

Sow plants and vegetables that grow and flourish above ground.

Sowing and planting fruit and vegetables that grow tall, and tomatoes, but no lettuce.

Transplanting.

Grafting onto fruit trees.

Cultivating grains, particularly corn.

Gather herbs for vein diseases.

Housework

Light housework only.

Ventilate sufficiently.

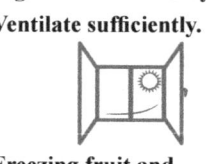

Freezing fruit and vegetables.

Baking bread, cakes, and cookies. Dough rises faster. (Except on New Moon)

Suitable for making cheese.

Making preserves.

Nutrition

Food quality:

Protein

Beans, peas, corn, tomatoes, pumpkin, lentils, soybeans, cucumber, eggplant, zucchini, berries, fruit, chili, bell pepper, figs, avocado, melon, olives.

Weight gain: avoid indulging in rich foods. If overweight, eat smaller portions.

Supply nutrient materials to strengthen the body. Focus on foods that contain essential minerals and vitamins.

Stimulants and vitamins are more effective.

Positive affirmation:
"I trust my intuition."

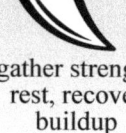

Turning Point

Transition of descending to ascending forces. Both forces are at work and neutralize each other.

gather strength
rest, recover
buildup

Waxing Moon

♏ → ♐
11:02 PM PDT Saturday
1:02 AM CDT
2:02 AM EDT

3 **Sunday** Tisha B'Av, Friendship Day

4 **Monday**

10:05 AM PDT
12:05 PM CDT
1:05 PM EDT
♐ → ♑

5 **Tuesday**

Life is like riding a bicycle. To keep your balance, you must keep moving.
Albert Einstein

Color
Orange/Yellow

Day
Warm

Element
Fire

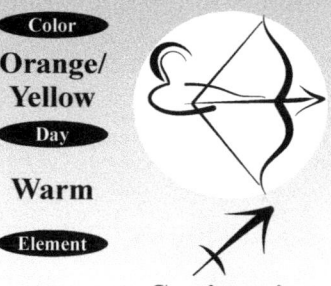

Sagittarius

A U G U S T

Success

Career and business are in the foreground now and thinking becomes clear and serious, but somewhat inflexible.

Perseverance and reasoning assist in financial matters, planning, and contracts.

The values of tradition, authority, and discipline impact our endeavors.

Leisure

Money is not likely to be wasted in a shopping spree.

Many are drawn to enjoy cultural events.

The earth feels cold to the touch, so take slightly warmer clothes.

Health

Sensitive body parts:

Knees, Joints, Bones, Skin

All measures taken to supply nutrient materials and strengthen the sensitive body parts are very effective.

Healing ointments are easily absorbed.

Sensitive blood circulation.

Avoid overstraining bones and knees, and apply gentle stretching exercises only.

Problems with meniscus: Don't overstrain.

Dress slightly warmer.

High blood pressure: Avoid salty foods.

Massages, lymphatic therapy, and chiropractic treatment to release blockages.

Body Care

Aromas, scents:

Cedar, Juniper

Treatments with firming and moisturizing creams are more effective.

Massages that serve to regenerate, and strengthen, perhaps aided with beneficial massage oils.

Correcting and cutting ingrown nails.

Every kind of skin care is beneficial.

Cutting and filing toenails and fingernails will make the nails grow stronger over time.

Hair dyes applied now, will look more vibrant.

Garden/Nature

Plant part:

Root

Sow plants, herbs, and vegetables that grow and flourish above ground.

Transplanting.

Harvest produce is suitable for storage. Harvest root vegetables.

Gather herbs for bone, joint, and skin diseases.

Housework

Light housework only.

Air rooms only briefly.

Preserving root vegetables.

Avoid dry cleaning, as the fabric may develop unwanted glossy blotches.

Nutrition

Food quality:

Salt

Garlic, carrots, red beets, reddish, rutabaga, sugar beet, celery, potatoes, onions, kohlrabi.

Weight gain: avoid indulging in rich foods. If overweight, eat smaller portions.

Supply nutrient materials to strengthen the body. Focus on foods that contain essential minerals and vitamins.

Stimulants and vitamins are more effective.

Avoid large quantities of salty foods like bacon, ham, salted herring, fatty cheese, and the like. Avoid heavy and greasy foods.

Positive affirmation:
"I trust my intuition."

Harvest Time
Ascending forces! Sap is rising, enhancing plant growth above ground, resulting in the most juicy fruits and vegetables.

gather strength rest, recover buildup
Waxing Moon

6:19 PM PDT
8:19 PM CDT
9:19 PM EDT

6 Wednesday

No meat.

7 Thursday

A U G U S T

Forgiveness is the giving, and so the receiving, of life.
George MacDonald

Color
Yellow

Day

Cool

Element

Earth   **Capricorn**

Success

Inspiration, optimism, and impatience. Rational thinking, creativity and imagination spark new ideas and inspire planning for the future.

Shying away from routine tasks people will feel more drawn to anything new.

Instead of gridlocked structures choose new possibilities.

Leisure

Inspiration and optimism will boost friendship, social gatherings, and parties.

Express your creativity and imagination. Dwell in dreams and utopian ideas. It is easier now to perceive intuitive thoughts.

Health

Sensitive body parts:

Lower Legs, Veins

All measures taken to supply nutrient materials and strengthen the sensitive body parts are very effective.

Healing ointments are easily absorbed.

Sensitive glandular system.

Avoid inflammation of the veins. Apply ointments to lower legs, and rest legs in a raised position.

Varicose veins: Avoid long periods of standing.

While exercising go easy on the ankles.

Sensitivity to light, so bring your sunglasses along.

Body Care

Aromas, scents: Cyclamen, Peach, Wild Roses

Treatments with firming and moisturizing creams are more effective.

Massages that serve to regenerate, and strengthen, perhaps aided with beneficial massage oils.

Correcting and cutting ingrown nails.

Hair dyes applied now, will look more vibrant.

Garden/Nature

Plant part:

Flower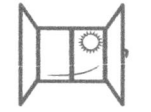

Avoid watering plants.

Harvested produce is well suitable for storage.

Gather herbs for vein diseases.

Housework

Light housework only.

Ventilate rooms thoroughly.

Baking cakes and cookies. Dough rises faster. (Except on New Moon)

Making preserves.

Nutrition

Food quality:

Fat

Cauliflower, artichoke, broccoli, sunflower seeds, flax seeds, nuts, rose hip, elder.

Weight gain: avoid indulging in rich foods. If overweight, eat smaller portions.

Supply nutrient materials to strengthen the body. Focus on foods that contain essential minerals and vitamins.

Stimulants and vitamins are more effective.

Pay attention to any particularly tempting foods today: Most likely the "wrong" things taste best.

High cholesterol: eat a low fat diet.

Positive affirmation:
"I trust my intuition."

Harvest Time
Ascending forces! Sap is rising, enhancing plant growth above ground, resulting in the most juicy fruits and vegetables.

gather strength rest, recover buildup
Waxing Moon

8 Friday
Raksha Bandhan
No meat. Cutting and filing toenails and fingernails.

A U G U S T

It is health that is real wealth and not pieces of gold and silver.
Mahatma Gandhi

Color
Bright/ Dark Blue

Day
Air/Light

Element

Air   Aquarius

Success

Inspiration, optimism, and impatience. Rational thinking, creativity and imagination spark new ideas and inspire planning for the future.

Shying away from routine tasks people will feel more drawn to anything new.

Instead of gridlocked structures choose new possibilities.

Leisure

Inspiration and optimism will boost friendship, social gatherings, and parties.

Express your creativity and imagination. Dwell in dreams and utopian ideas. It is easier now to perceive intuitive thoughts.

Health

Sensitive body parts:

Lower Legs, Veins

All measures taken to flush out and detoxify the sensitive body parts are very effective.

Scarring is less severe.

Teeth: Removal of tartar and amalgam. Best for fillings, crowns, and dentures!

Blood-purifying, detoxifying herbal infusions and teas.

Sensitive glandular system.

Avoid inflammation of the veins. Apply ointments to lower legs, and rest legs in a raised position.

Varicose veins: Avoid long periods of standing.

While exercising go easy on the ankles.

Sensitivity to light, so bring your sunglasses along.

○ *Full Moon: Avoid any surgery and vaccination if possible.*

Body Care

Aromas, scents: Cyclamen, Peach, Wild Roses

Prepare home-made ointments and cosmetics.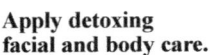

Apply detoxing facial and body care.

Treatments of bumps and pimples on the skin, and exfoliating procedures.

Removing body hair.

Correction of the nail bed.

Massages that serve to relax, ease tension, and detoxify.

Reflexology massage.

Removal of callused skin.

Treating obstinate athlete's foot, nail fungus, and warts.

Garden/Nature

Plant part:

Flower

Fertilize flowers that no longer bloom.

Dig over/plow to prepare soil for planting.

Trimming and cutting back plants.

Hoeing and harrowing; weeds can be left to rot.

Pest control.

Start a compost heap.

Avoid watering plants.

Avoid transplanting sprouts.

Harvested produce is well suitable for storage.

Gather herbs (roots) for vein diseases.

○ *Full Moon: Weather and climate changes. Herbs are most powerful.*

Housework

Housework is dealt with much more successfully, efficiently, and effortlessly.

Problem stains are removed readily.

Dry cleaning.

Clean and store seasonal clothing.

Best suited for a spring cleaning: Thoroughly clean wooden and parquet floors, metals, china etc.

Cleaning, polishing, and waterproofing shoes.

Combating mold.

Ventilate rooms thoroughly.

Baking bread, cakes, and cookies (add more leavening agent).

○ *Full Moon: Avoid doing laundry, cleaning windows, making preserves, painting.*

Nutrition

Food quality:

Fat

Cauliflower, artichoke, broccoli, sunflower seeds, flax seeds, nuts, rose hip, elder.

Weight associated with overeating is less likely. If underweight, eat larger portions.

Cleansing and detox diets. Fruit and juice days.

Flush out poisons. Treatment for drug abuse.

Pay attention to any particularly tempting foods today: Most likely the "wrong" things taste best.

High cholesterol: eat a low fat diet.

○ *Full Moon: A day of fasting.*

Everything is blooming most recklessly; if it were voices instead of colors, there would be an unbelievable shrieking into the heart of the night.
Rainer Maria Rilke

Color
Bright/ Dark Blue

Day
Air/Light

Element

Aquarius　　**Air**

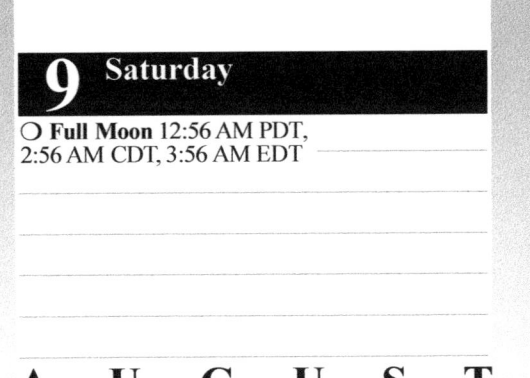

9 Saturday

○ **Full Moon** 12:56 AM PDT, 2:56 AM CDT, 3:56 AM EDT

A U G U S T

Positive affirmation:
"I trust my intuition."

Harvest Time
Ascending forces! Sap is rising, enhancing plant growth above ground, resulting in the most juicy fruits and vegetables.

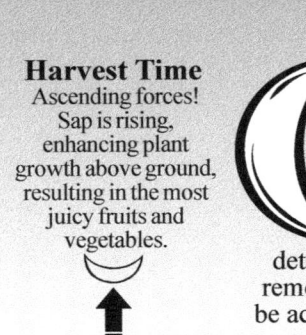

detox remove be active

Waning Moon

Success

Sensibility, intuition, and helpfulness.

Where possible, retreating is more favorable than dealing with business matters.

Dissolve restrictions, be patient and wait. Be aware that people can be more easily influenced.

Leisure

Your helpfulness will boost friendships.

Enjoy dancing or swimming, or watch a movie that will inspire your fantasies and imagination.

Retreat, relax, and recover.

Romance can be gentle and coziness will prevail.

If you plan outdoor excursions, be prepared for a shower here and there.

Health

Sensitive body parts:

Feet and Toes

All measures taken to flush out and detoxify the sensitive body parts are very effective.

Good for surgical operations except those on the sensitive body parts (see above), heart, back, diaphragm, circulation, and arteries.
Scarring is less severe.

Teeth: Removal of tartar and amalgam. Best for fillings, crowns, and dentures!

Blood-purifying, detoxifying herbal infusions and teas.

Sensitive nervous system.

Drugs have a much stronger effect on your body. Monitor closely what you put into your body.

Lymphatic therapy.

Sluggishness or fatigue may occur in the transition into the next Zodiac sign of Aries.

Body Care

Aromas, scents:
Magnolia, Amaryllis, Clary Sage

Prepare home-made ointments and cosmetics.

Apply detoxing facial and body care.

Treatments of bumps and pimples on the skin, and exfoliating procedures.

Removing body hair.

Correction of the nail bed.

Massages that serve to relax, ease tension, and detoxify. Reflexology massage. Carry out with special care, people are more sensitive.

Removal of callused skin.

Treating obstinate athlete's foot, nail fungus, and warts.

Foot bath.

No haircuts, hair becomes shaggy and unmanageable.
Avoid washing your hair.

Garden/Nature

Plant part:

Leaf

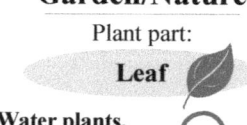

Water plants.

Fertilize flowers.

Sow plants and vegetables that grow below ground, potatoes, leaf vegetables, and lettuce.

Dig over/plow to prepare soil for planting.
Trimming and cutting back plants.
Start a compost heap.

Mowing lawns.

Pest control. Weeding.

Harvested produce should be consumed as soon as possible.

Gather herbs for foot complaints.

Housework

Housework is dealt with much more successfully, efficiently, and effortlessly.

Problem stains are removed readily.

Best for doing laundry! Reduce on laundry detergent, support the environment.

Dry cleaning.

Clean and store seasonal clothing.

Thoroughly clean wooden and parquet floors, metals, china etc.

Cleaning, polishing, and waterproofing shoes.

Combating mold.

Ventilate rooms briefly and rapidly.

Avoid painting.

Preserving and storing should be avoided.

Nutrition

Food quality:

Carbohydrate

Lettuce, spinach, lamb's lettuce, Endive, parsley, leek, cabbage (Brussels sprouts, kale, Chinese cabbage), all leafy herbs, asparagus, mushrooms, cress, Swiss chard, rhubarb.

Weight associated with overeating is less likely. If underweight, eat larger portions.

Cleansing and detox diets. Fruit and juice days.

Flush out poisons. Treatment for drug abuse.

Caffeine, alcohol, drugs, certain foods, and stimulants have a much stronger effect.

Act as if what you do makes a difference. It does.
William James

Color
Blueish White

Day

Wetness

Element

 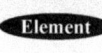

Pisces   Water

11:51 PM PDT Saturday
1:51 AM CDT
2:51 AM EDT

10 Sunday

11 Monday

A U G U S T

Harvest Time
Ascending forces! Sap is rising, enhancing plant growth above ground, resulting in the most juicy fruits and vegetables.

detox remove be active

Waning Moon

Success

Things get going and the way straight ahead seems the best.

People feel energetic, courageous, assertive, and at times anxious.

Good time for meetings and sales talks but impatience and selfishness do not favor teamwork.

Leisure

An enterprising spirit and spontaneity move people to enjoy outings, sports, competitions, cultural events, and travels.

Romance can be very passionate.

Good days for outings, even with cloudy skies the air still feels somewhat warm. Drying effect, get plenty to drink.

Health

Sensitive body parts:

Head, Brain, Eyes

All measures taken to flush out and detoxify the sensitive body parts are very effective.

Good for surgery, except on the sensitive body parts (see above), heart, diaphragm, back, circulation, and arteries.

Scarring is less severe.

Teeth: Removal of tartar and amalgam. Best for fillings, crowns, and dentures! Avoiding treatment of periodontitis and gums.

Blood-purifying, detoxifying herbal infusions and teas.

Sensitive sense organs.

If you suffer from migraines drink plenty of water, and avoid coffee, chocolate, and sugar.

Body Care

Aromas, scents: Cloves, Peppermint, Thyme

Prepare home-made ointments and cosmetics.

Apply detoxing facial and body care.

Treatments of bumps and pimples on the skin, and exfoliating procedures.

Removing body hair.

Correction of the nail bed.

Massages that serve to relax, ease tension, and detoxify.

Reflexology massage.

Removal of callused skin.

Treating obstinate athlete's foot, nail fungus, and warts.

Eye compresses to relieve strained eyes.

Any kind of hair care.

Garden/Nature

Plant part:

Fruit

Sowing plants and vegetables that grow below ground.

Sowing and planting anything that is supposed to grow fast. Sowing and planting fruit and tomatoes.

Dig over/plow the soil to prepare for planting.

Spreading manure. Fertilizing grains, vegetables, and fruit.

Weeding. Pest control.

Pruning of fruit trees and bushes.

Harvesting and storing grains, vegetables, potatoes, fruits, and tomatoes.

Start a compost heap.

Gather herbs (roots) for eye complaints and headaches.

Day off on 8/13.

Housework

Housework is dealt with much more successfully, efficiently, and effortlessly.

Problem stains are removed readily.

Best for doing laundry!

Dry cleaning.

Clean and store seasonal clothing.

Thoroughly clean wooden and parquet floors, metals, china, etc.

Cleaning windows and glass.

Cleaning, polishing, and waterproofing shoes.

Combating mold.

Ventilate rooms sufficiently. Air beds.

Suitable for making cheese.

Preserving and freezing fruit and vegetables.

Baking bread, cakes, and cookies (use more leavening agent).

Painting.

Nutrition

Food quality:

Protein

Beans, peas, corn, tomatoes, pumpkin, lentils, soybeans, cucumber, eggplant, zucchini, berries, fruit, chili, bell pepper, figs, avocado, melon, olives.

Weight associated with overeating is less likely. If underweight, eat larger portions.

Cleansing and detox diets. Fruit and juice days.

Flush out poisons. Treatment for drug abuse.

Drink plenty of water.

If music be the food of love, play on.
William Shakespeare

✵ → ♈

3:34 AM PDT
5:34 AM CDT
6:34 AM EDT

Color

Indigo Blue

Day

Warm

Element

Aries **Fire**

12 Tuesday	**13** Wednesday
	No meat.

A U G U S T

Positive affirmation:
"I trust my intuition."

Harvest Time
Ascending forces! Sap is rising, enhancing plant growth above ground, resulting in the most juicy fruits and vegetables.

detox remove be active

Waning Moon

Success

Realism and material security are important. Persistence comes easy, thoughts and reactions are slower.

Assess financial areas.

Conservative tendencies may make people want to stay away from risk taking.

Leisure

Relax at a picnic/feast. Enjoy culinary pleasures and hobbies.

The earth feels cold to the touch, so take slightly warmer clothes.

Health

Sensitive body parts:

Head and Neck

All measures taken to flush out and detoxify the sensitive body parts are very effective.

Good for surgery, except on the sensitive body parts (see above), heart, back, circulation, and arteries. Scarring is less severe.

Teeth: Removal of tartar and amalgam. Best for fillings, crowns, and dentures! Avoiding treatment of periodontitis and gums.

Blood-purifying, detoxifying herbal infusions and teas.

Sensitive blood circulation.

Organs of speech, jaws, teeth, tonsils, thyroid gland, neck, and vocal chords get easily affected. Keep neck warm. On cold days ears should be protected. Sensitivity to noise.

High blood pressure: Avoid salty foods.

Massages, lymphatic therapy, and chiropractic treatment to release blockages.

Body Care

Aromas, scents: Geranium, Jasmine, Rose

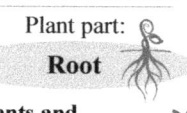

Prepare home-made ointments and cosmetics.

Apply detoxing facial and body care.

Treatments of bumps and pimples on the skin, and exfoliating procedures.

Removing body hair.

Correction of the nail bed.

Massages that serve to relax, ease tension, and detoxify.

Reflexology massage.

Removal of callused skin.

Treating obstinate athlete's foot, nail fungus, and warts.

Garden/Nature

Plant part:

Root

Sow plants and vegetables that grow below ground.

Everything grows slowly and lasts well.

Dig over to prepare soil.

Trimming/cutting back plants. Weeding. Mulching.

Start a compost heap.

Combat vermin found in the soil.

Spread fertilizer and liquid manure.

Fertilize flowers with poorly formed roots.

Harvested produce is well suited for storage. Harvesting root vegetables.

Gather herbs (roots) for sinus issues, sore throat, and ear complaints.

Housework

Housework is dealt with much more successfully, efficiently, and effortlessly.

Problem stains are removed readily.

Best for doing laundry! Reduce on laundry detergent, support the environment.

Dry cleaning.

Clean and store seasonal clothing.

Thoroughly clean wooden and parquet floors, metals, china etc.

Cleaning, polishing, and waterproofing shoes.

Combating mold.

Air rooms only briefly.

Painting.

Preserving root vegetables.

Nutrition

Food quality:

Salt

Garlic, carrots, red beets, reddish, rutabaga, sugar beet, celery, potatoes, onions, kohlrabi.

Weight associated with overeating is less likely. If underweight, eat larger portions.

Cleansing and detox diets. Fruit and juice days.

Flush out poisons. Treatment for drug abuse.

Avoid large quantities of salty foods like bacon, ham, salted herring, fatty cheese, and the like.

An effort made for the happiness of others lifts above ourselves.
Lydia M. Child

Color — **Bright Blue**

Day — **Cool**

Element — **Earth**

Taurus

♈ ➔ ♉ 6:23 AM PDT
8:23 AM CDT
9:23 AM EDT

14 Thursday

15 Friday
Assumption of Mary
No meat. Cutting and filing toenails and fingernails.

A U G U S T

Harvest Time
Ascending forces! Sap is rising, enhancing plant growth above ground, resulting in the most juicy fruits and vegetables.

detox
remove
be active

Waning Moon

Success

Open mindedness and curiosity. A changeable and hectic time.

Good time for talking, negotiating, networking, and exchanging ideas as well as for meetings of a nonbinding nature, conferences, and studies.

Leisure

Good time for family gatherings, parties, and short trips.

People enjoy stimulating their minds with reading and studying. Attending theater performances is a preferred enjoyment. Enhance friendships.

Stretching exercises.

Be prepared for sudden changes in weather or climate.

Health

Sensitive body parts:
Shoulders, Arms, Hands, Lungs

All measures taken to flush out and detoxify the sensitive body parts are very effective.

Good for surgery, except on the sensitive body parts (see above), heart, back, diaphragm, circulation, arteries. Scarring is less severe.

Teeth: Removal of tartar and amalgam. Best for fillings, crowns, and dentures! Avoid having any teeth pulled.

Blood-purifying, detoxifying herbal infusions and teas.

Sensitive glandular system.

Make sure you are dressed warm enough in cool weather.

Exercises for shoulders. Breathing exercises.

Sensitivity to light, bring your sunglasses along.

Massages, lymphatic therapy, and chiropractic treatment to release blockages.

Body Care

Aromas, scents:
Lavender, Lemon Balm, Magnolia, Verbena

Prepare home-made ointments and cosmetics.

Apply detoxing facial and body care.

Treatments of bumps and pimples on the skin, and exfoliating procedures.

Removing body hair.

Correction of the nail bed.

Massages that serve to relax, ease tension, and detoxify.

Reflexology massage.

Removal of callused skin.

Treating obstinate athlete's foot, nail fungus, and warts.

Garden/Nature

Plant part:
Flower

Sow plants and vegetablesthat grow below ground.

Trimming and cutting back plants.

Start a compost heap.

Weeding. Pest control.

Fertilize flowers that no longer bloom.

Avoid watering plants.

Changes in weather are more likely.

Gather herbs (roots) for tensions in the shoulder and lung complaints.

Housework

Housework is dealt with much more successfully, efficiently, and effortlessly.

Problem stains are removed readily.

Best for doing laundry! Reduce on laundry detergent, support the environment.

Dry cleaning.

Clean and store seasonal clothing.

Thoroughly clean wooden and parquet floors, metals, china etc.

Cleaning windows and glass.

Cleaning, polishing, and waterproofing shoes.

Combating mold.

Ventilate rooms thoroughly.

Baking bread, cakes, and cookies (add more leavening agent).

Making preserves.

Painting.

Nutrition

Food quality:
Fat

Cauliflower, artichoke, broccoli, sunflower seeds, flax seeds, nuts, rose hip, elder.

Weight associated with overeating is less likely. If underweight, eat larger portions.

Cleansing and detox diets. Fruit and juice days.

Flush out poisons. Treatment for drug abuse.

Pay attention to any particularly tempting foods today: Most likely the "wrong" things taste best.

High cholesterol: eat a low fat diet.

Charity begins at home, but should not end there.
Thomas Fuller

Color
Light Blue

Day
Air/Light

Element

Gemini   **Air**

♂ → ♊   9:02 AM PDT
11:02 AM CDT
12:02 PM EDT

12:06 PM PDT
2:06 PM CDT
3:06 PM EDT   ♊ → ♋

16 Saturday Krishna Janmashtani

☽ Half Moon.

17 Sunday

18 Monday

A U G U S T

Turning Point
Transition of ascending to descending forces. Both forces are at work and neutralize each other.

detox remove be active
Waning Moon

Success

Feelings, sensitivity, and cooperativeness. Many are overly sensitive, so beware of treading on someone's toes.

Be cautious if you are easily influenced.

During negotiations make use of the cognitive ability of your senses.

Leisure

Relax within your close family.

Retreat to your safe haven and enjoy your fantasy while reading or listening to music. The inner world becomes more colorful than the outer.

Romance can be gentle. Deep feelings will prevail.

If you plan outdoor excursions, be prepared for a shower here and there.

Health

Sensitive body parts:
Chest, Lungs, Liver, Stomach, Gall Bladder

All measures taken to flush out and detoxify the sensitive body parts are very effective.

Good for surgical operations except those on the sensitive body parts (see above), heart, diaphragm, back, circulation, and arteries.
Scarring is less severe.

Teeth: Removal of tartar and amalgam. Best for fillings, crowns, and dentures!

Blood-purifying, detoxifying herbal infusions and teas.

Sensitive nervous system.

Be cautious with alcohol since the liver is very sensitive.

Stomach could play up and cause gas and heartburn.

Rheumatism: Don't air bedding outside, damp will remain in the bedding.

Lymphatic therapy.

Body Care

Aromas, scents:
Lilac, Lilies of the Valley, Lilies, Violets

Prepare home-made ointments and cosmetics.

Apply detoxing facial and body care.

Treatments of bumps and pimples on the skin, and exfoliating procedures.

Removing body hair.

Correction of the nail bed.

Massages that serve to relax, ease tension, and detoxify.

Reflexology massage.

Removal of callused skin.

Treating obstinate athlete's foot, nail fungus, and warts.

No haircuts, hair becomes shaggy and unmanageable. Avoid washing your hair.

Garden/Nature

Plant part:
Leaf

Water plants.

Fertilize flowers.

Sow plants and vegetables that grow below ground, leaf vegetables, and lettuce.

Dig over/plow to prepare soil for planting.

Trimming and cutting back plants. Transplanting. Weeding.

Combating pests above ground.

Start a compost heap.

Mowing lawns.

Gather herbs (roots) for bronchitis, stomach, liver, and gall bladder complaints.

Unfavorable for harvesting, storing, and preserving.

Housework

Housework is dealt with much more successfully, efficiently, and effortlessly.

Problem stains are removed readily.

Best for doing laundry! Reduce on laundry detergent, support the environment.

Dry cleaning.

Thoroughly clean wooden and parquet floors, metals, china etc.

Cleaning, polishing, and waterproofing shoes.

Combating mold.

Ventilate rooms briefly and rapidly.

Avoid painting.

Nutrition

Food quality:
Carbohydrate

Lettuce, spinach, lamb's lettuce, Endive, parsley, leek, cabbage (Brussels sprouts, kale, Chinese cabbage), all leafy herbs, asparagus, mushrooms, cress, Swiss chard, rhubarb.

Weight associated with overeating is less likely. If underweight, eat larger portions.

Moodiness may make you want to eat more than is healthy. If overweight avoid carbohydrates.

Cleansing and detox diets. Fruit and juice days.

Flush out poisons. Treatment for drug abuse.

If you get stomach troubles easily, avoid heavy meals.

Maybe a person's time would be as well spent raising food as raising money to buy food.
Frank Howard Clark

Color — **Green**

Day — **Wetness**

Element — **Water**

Cancer

4:18 PM PDT
6:18 PM CDT
7:18 PM EDT

19 Tuesday

20 Wednesday
No meat.

A U G U S T

Positive affirmation:
"I trust my intuition."

Planting Time
Descending forces! Sap is drawn downward, enhancing root formation. Best days for sowing, planting, and transplanting.

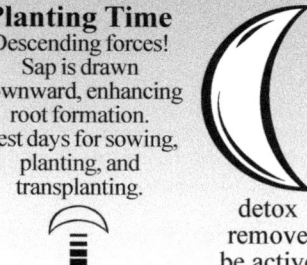

detox
remove
be active
Waning Moon

Success

Determination reigns, and risks are taken more often. Master your tasks with more self-confidence and creativity.

Limits appear to be more easily surmountable.

Auspicious day for sales, advertising, and publicity.

Leisure

Zest for life is in the air. People want to have a fun time, enjoy parties, musical events, movies, etc.

Possessive feelings can harm a relationship. Romance can be very passionate.

Outings: even with cloudy skies the air still feels somewhat warm. Drying effect, get plenty to drink.

Danger of sudden storms, not only in the sky.

Health

Sensitive body parts:
Heart, Back, Diaphragm, Circulation, Arteries

All measures taken to flush out and detoxify the sensitive body parts are very effective.

Good for surgery, except on the sensitive body parts (see above).
Scarring is less severe.

Teeth: Removal of tartar and amalgam. Best for fillings, crowns, and dentures!

Blood-purifying, detoxifying herbal infusions and teas.

Sensitive sense organs.

Back and heart problems are more likely to occur.

Avoid overstraining of the heart and circulation with unusual physical activities.

Expect sleepless nights.

Body Care

Aromas, scents:
Hibiscus, Oleander, Rose

Prepare home-made ointments and cosmetics.

Apply detoxing facial and body care.

Treatments of bumps and pimples on the skin, and exfoliating procedures.

Removing body hair.

Correction of the nail bed.

Massages that serve to relax, ease tension, and detoxify.

Reflexology massage.

Removal of callused skin.

Treating obstinate athlete's foot, nail fungus, and warts.

Good days for haircuts, hair becomes stronger. But be aware that if you get a perm, curls will become quite frizzy. Baby's first haircut.

Garden/Nature

Plant part:
Fruit

Sowing plants and vegetables that grow below ground.

Sowing and planting fruit. Also sow and plant vegetables that are highly perishable. Plant trees and bushes. Sow lawns.

Dig over/plow to prepare soil for planting.

Trimming and cutting back plants. Pruning of fruit trees and bushes.

Transplanting.

Not suitable for fertilizing.

Weeding. Pest Control.

Harvested produce should be consumed as soon as possible.

Gather herbs (roots) for heart and circulation complaints.

Start compost heap.

Housework

Housework is dealt with much more successfully, efficiently, and effortlessly.

Problem stains are removed readily.

Best for doing laundry!

Dry cleaning.

Thoroughly clean wooden and parquet floors, metals, china, etc.

Cleaning windows and glass.

Cleaning, polishing, and waterproofing shoes.

Combating mold.

Ventilate rooms sufficiently. Air beds.

Suitable for making cheese.

Preserving and freezing fruit and vegetables.

Baking bread, cakes, and cookies (use more leavening agent).

Avoid painting.

Nutrition

Food quality:
Protein

Beans, peas, corn, tomatoes, pumpkin, lentils, soybeans, cucumber, eggplant, zucchini, berries, fruit, chili, bell pepper, figs, avocado, melon, olives.

Weight associated with overeating is less likely. If underweight, eat larger portions.

Cleansing and detox diets. Fruit and juice days.

Flush out poisons. Treatment for drug abuse.

Of life's two chief prizes, beauty and truth, I found the first in a loving heart and the second in a laborer's hand.
Khalil Gibran

Color: **Green**

Day: **Warm**

Element: **Fire**

Leo

21 Thursday
Senior Citizens Day

22 Friday
No meat. Cutting and filing toenails and fingernails.

A U G U S T

Planting Time
Descending forces! Sap is drawn downward, enhancing root formation. Best days for sowing, planting, and transplanting.

detox remove be active

Waning Moon

Success

Good time for details, organization, routine, concentration, and duty.

Take care of financial and administrative tasks.

Prepare for future success now with realistic and critical assessment.

● *New Moon: Confirm your resolutions. Finalize new decisions. Drop bad habits.*

Leisure

Enjoy a nature walk.

Good time for health regimes. Improve your health with stretching exercises and yoga.

The earth feels cold to the touch, so take slightly warmer clothes.

Health

Sensitive body parts:
Digestive Organs, Nerves, Spleen, Pancreas

All measures taken to supply nutrient materials and strengthen the sensitive body parts are very effective.

Healing ointments are easily absorbed.

Sensitive blood circulation.

For a sensitive digestive system, a wholesome diet is recommended.

Dress slightly warmer.

High blood pressure: Avoid salty foods.

Massages, lymphatic therapy, and chiropractic treatment to release blockages.

● *New Moon: Avoid any surgery if possible.*

Body Care

Aromas, scents:
Lavender, Spruce Needles, Sage, Meadow Flowers

Treatments with firming and moisturizing creams are more effective.

Massages that serve to regenerate, and strengthen, perhaps aided with beneficial massage oils.

Correcting and cutting ingrown nails.

Best for haircuts because it retains its shape longer. Perms turn out best. Hair dyes applied now, will look more vibrant.

Garden/Nature

Plant part:
Root

Best for sowing and planting, except lettuce.

Plant trees which are supposed to grow very tall. Plant hedges and bushes that are meant to grow very fast.

Sowing lawns.

Planting and re-potting balcony and indoor plants.

Transplanting.

Trimming and cutting back plants.

Planting cuttings.

Start a compost heap.

Avoid harvesting and storing.

Gather herbs (roots) for digestive organs, pancreas, and nervous complaints.

● *New Moon: Change of weather is likely. Care for sickly plants.*

Housework

Light housework only.

Air rooms only briefly.

Making pickles, preserves, and cheese yields suboptimal results and should be avoided.

Nutrition

Food quality:
Salt

Garlic, carrots, red beets, reddish, rutabaga, sugar beet, celery, potatoes, onions, kohlrabi.

Weight gain: avoid indulging in rich foods. If overweight, eat smaller portions.

Supply nutrient materials to strengthen the body. Focus on foods that contain essential minerals and vitamins.

Stimulants and vitamins are more effective.

Avoid large quantities of salty foods like bacon, ham, salted herring, fatty cheese, and the like. Avoid heavy and greasy foods.

● *New Moon: A day of fasting.*

Positive affirmation:
"I trust to be able to accomplish all my tasks."

Planting Time
Descending forces! Sap is drawn downward, enhancing root formation. Best days for sowing, planting, and transplanting.

gather strength rest, recover buildup
Waxing Moon

Ω → ♍ ← 10:25 PM PDT Friday
           12:25 AM CDT
           1:25 AM EDT

23 Saturday

● **New Moon** 11:08 PM PDT Friday, 1:08 AM CDT, 2:08 AM EDT

24 Sunday

Beauty is a manifestation of secret natural laws, which otherwise would have been hidden from us forever.
Johann Wolfgang von Goethe

Color
Yellow

Day
Cool

Element
Earth

♍ **Virgo**

A U G U S T

Success

The artistic instinct rules, but so, too, does indecisiveness. The forces swing back and forth until equilibrium is achieved.

It's easy to reach compromises with tactful sensitivity.

A sense of judgment will support legal matters.

Leisure

Pursuit for harmony and cooperativeness supports good times in romance, friendship, and partnership.

Enjoy cultural events. Relax and get pampered with a spa treatment.

Romance can be passionate yet sensitive.

Health

Sensitive body parts:

Hips, Kidneys, Bladder

All measures taken to supply nutrient materials and strengthen the sensitive body parts are very effective.

Healing ointments are easily absorbed.

Sensitive glandular system.

Take special care to keep the area of bladder and kidneys warm.

Apply special exercises for the hip region.

Avoid having any teeth pulled.

Sensitivity to light, bring your sunglasses along.

Body Care

Aromas, scents: Roses, Violets, Daffodils

Treatments with firming and moisturizing creams are more effective.

Massages that serve to regenerate, and strengthen, perhaps aided with beneficial massage oils.

Correcting and cutting ingrown nails.

Hair dyes applied now, will look more vibrant.

Garden/Nature

Plant part:

Flower

Sow plants and vegetables that grow and flourish above ground, specially flowers, and medicinal herbs.

Transplanting.

Trimming and cutting back plants.

Avoid watering plants.

Start a compost heap.

Harvested produce should be consumed as soon as possible.

Gather herbs for kidneys, gall bladder, and hip complaints.

Day off on 8/26.

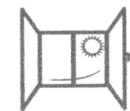

Housework

Light housework only.

Ventilate rooms thoroughly.

Baking cakes and cookies. Dough rises faster. (Except on New Moon)

Nutrition

Food quality:

Fat

Cauliflower, artichoke, broccoli, sunflower seeds, flax seeds, nuts, rose hip, elder.

Weight gain: avoid indulging in rich foods. If overweight, eat smaller portions.

Supply nutrient materials to strengthen the body. Focus on foods that contain essential minerals and vitamins.

Stimulants and vitamins are more effective.

Pay attention to any particularly tempting foods today: Most likely the "wrong" things taste best.

High cholesterol: eat a low fat diet.

Positive affirmation:
"I trust to be able to accomplish all my tasks."

Planting Time
Descending forces! Sap is drawn downward, enhancing root formation. Best days for sowing, planting, and transplanting.

gather strength rest, recover buildup
Waxing Moon

♍→♎ 7:09 AM PDT / 9:09 AM CDT / 10:09 AM EDT

25 Monday

26 Tuesday Ganesh Charturthi, Women's Equality Day

6:28 PM PDT / 8:28 PM CDT / 9:28 PM EDT ♎→♏

27 Wednesday

No meat.

A U G U S T

Man never made any material as resilient as the human spirit.
Bern Williams

 Color
Orange

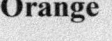 Day
Air/Light

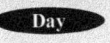 Element

Air

 Libra

Success

Critical and superstitious behavior emerges, especially pertaining to money.

A penetrating power will strengthen your capacity to act.

An increased perception opens our interest for the essentials and helps to discover hidden potentials.

Leisure

Relax within your close family, with meditation, and relaxation exercises.

A longing to feel safe will be nurtured if you focus on habits and rituals. An increased sensitivity will help to enjoy every moment.

Romance can be very passionate.

If you plan outdoor excursions, be prepared for a shower here and there.

Health

Sensitive body parts:

Sex organs, Ureter

All measures taken to supply nutrient materials and strengthen the sensitive body parts are very effective.

Healing ointments are easily absorbed. Applying herbal ointments to the shoulders for rheumatic gout and alike.

Sensitive nervous system.

Female disorders: As a preventative measure apply hip baths using yarrow.

Pregnancy: Avoid any exertion, miscarriages are more likely.

Keep region of the pelvis, kidneys, and feet warm to prevent infection of the bladder and kidneys.

Lymphatic therapy.

Body Care

Aromas, scents:
Anemone, Cornflower
Oregano, Thuja

Treatments with firming and moisturizing creams are more effective.

Massages that serve to regenerate, and strengthen, perhaps aided with beneficial massage oils.

Correcting and cutting ingrown nails.

Hair dyes applied now, will look more vibrant.

Garden/Nature

Plant part:

Leaf

Watering all indoor and outdoor plants.

Sow plants, herbs, and vegetables that grow and flourish above ground, leaf vegetables (no lettuce).

Sowing, planting, harvesting, and drying every kind of medicinal herbs.

Transplanting.

Trimming and cutting back plants.
Combating slugs and snails.
Mowing lawns.

Start a compost heap.

Avoid pruning fruit trees and bushes. Avoid cutting down any trees.

Harvested produce should be consumed as soon as possible.

Housework

Light housework only.

Ventilate rooms briefly and rapidly. Don't air mattresses.

Any dirt and spots are easily removed in the laundry.

Avoid painting, as paint will take very long to dry.

Nutrition

Food quality:

Carbohydrate

Lettuce, spinach, lamb's lettuce, Endive, parsley, leek, cabbage (Brussels sprouts, kale, Chinese cabbage), all leafy herbs, asparagus, mushrooms, cress, Swiss chard, rhubarb.

Weight gain: avoid indulging in rich foods. If overweight, eat smaller portions and avoid carbohydrates.

Supply nutrient materials to strengthen the body. Focus on foods that contain essential minerals and vitamins. Stimulants and vitamins are more effective.

Positive affirmation:
"I trust to be able to accomplish all my tasks."

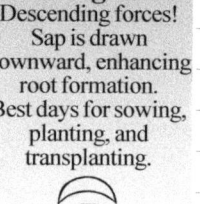

Planting Time
Descending forces!
Sap is drawn downward, enhancing root formation.
Best days for sowing, planting, and transplanting.

gather strength rest, recover buildup
Waxing Moon

28 Thursday

29 Friday
No meat. Cutting and filing toenails and fingernails.

Happiness resides not in possessions, and not in gold, happiness dwells in the soul.
Democritus

Color
Red

Day

Wetness

Element

Water

Scorpio

A U G U S T

Success

Inquisitiveness and exuberant inspiration lead to new horizons. Insight and love for truth reign.

Bringing together is more important than splitting asunder.

Expansive forces will assist in legal matters, discussions, and debates.

Leisure

Expansion feels great, and travel, short trips, and outings are most welcome. A competitive spirit excites any sports event.

Talk things out when necessary.

Romance can be very passionate.

Good days for outings; even with cloudy skies the air still feels somewhat warm. Drying effect, get plenty to drink.

Health

Sensitive body parts:

Thighs and Veins

All measures taken to supply nutrient materials and strengthen the sensitive body parts are very effective.

Healing ointments are easily absorbed.

Sensitive sense organs.

Pains often arise in the sciatic nerve, veins, the small of the back, and thighs.

Avoid overstraining the body with unusual physical activities.

Body Care

Aromas, scents: Calendula (Marigold), Geranium, Rosemary

Treatments with firming and moisturizing creams are more effective.

Massages that serve to regenerate, and strengthen, perhaps aided with beneficial massage oils.

Correcting and cutting ingrown nails.

Hair dyes applied now, will look more vibrant.

Garden/Nature

Plant part:

Fruit

Sow plants and vegetables that grow and flourish above ground.

Sowing and planting fruit and vegetables that grow tall, and tomatoes, but no lettuce.

Transplanting.

Grafting onto fruit trees.

Cultivating grains, particularly corn.

Gather herbs for vein diseases.

Housework

Light housework only.

Ventilate sufficiently.

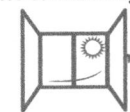

Freezing fruit and vegetables.

Baking bread, cakes, and cookies. Dough rises faster. (Except on New Moon)

Suitable for making cheese.

Making preserves.

Nutrition

Food quality:

Protein

Beans, peas, corn, tomatoes, pumpkin, lentils, soybeans, cucumber, eggplant, zucchini, berries, fruit, chili, bell pepper, figs, avocado, melon, olives.

Weight gain: avoid indulging in rich foods. If overweight, eat smaller portions.

Supply nutrient materials to strengthen the body. Focus on foods that contain essential minerals and vitamins.

Stimulants and vitamins are more effective.

Positive affirmation:
"I trust to be able to accomplish all my tasks."

Turning Point
Transition of descending to ascending forces. Both forces are at work and neutralize each other.

gather strength rest, recover buildup
Waxing Moon

♏ ➜ ♐
7:06 AM PDT
9:06 AM CDT
10:06 AM EDT

30 Saturday

31 Sunday

☾ Half Moon.

6:46 PM PDT
8:46 PM CDT
9:46 PM EDT
♐ ➜ ♑

1 Monday
Labor Day

AUGUST/SEPTEMBER

Clouds come floating into my life, no longer to carry rain or usher storm, but to add color to my sunset sky.
Rabindranath Tagore

Color
Orange/ Yellow

Day
Warm

Element
Fire

Sagittarius

Success

Career and business are in the foreground now and thinking becomes clear and serious, but somewhat inflexible.

Perseverance and reasoning assist in financial matters, planning, and contracts.

The values of tradition, authority, and discipline impact our endeavors.

Leisure

Money is not likely to be wasted in a shopping spree.

Many are drawn to enjoy cultural events.

The earth feels cold to the touch, so take slightly warmer clothes.

Health

Sensitive body parts:

Knees, Joints, Bones, Skin

All measures taken to supply nutrient materials and strengthen the sensitive body parts are very effective.

Healing ointments are easily absorbed.

Sensitive blood circulation.

Avoid overstraining bones and knees, and apply gentle stretching exercises only.

Problems with meniscus: Don't overstrain.

Dress slightly warmer.

High blood pressure: Avoid salty foods.

Massages, lymphatic therapy, and chiropractic treatment to release blockages.

Body Care

Aromas, scents:

Cedar, Juniper

Treatments with firming and moisturizing creams are more effective.

Massages that serve to regenerate, and strengthen, perhaps aided with beneficial massage oils.

Correcting and cutting ingrown nails.

Every kind of skin care is beneficial.

Cutting and filing toenails and fingernails will make the nails grow stronger over time.

Hair dyes applied now, will look more vibrant.

Garden/Nature

Plant part:

Root

Sow plants, herbs, and vegetables that grow and flourish above ground.

Transplanting.

Harvest produce is suitable for storage. Harvest root vegetables.

Gather herbs for bone, joint, and skin diseases.

Housework

Light housework only.

Air rooms only briefly.

Preserving root vegetables.

Avoid dry cleaning, as the fabric may develop unwanted glossy blotches.

Nutrition

Food quality:

Salt

Garlic, carrots, red beets, reddish, rutabaga, sugar beet, celery, potatoes, onions, kohlrabi.

Weight gain: avoid indulging in rich foods. If overweight, eat smaller portions.

Supply nutrient materials to strengthen the body. Focus on foods that contain essential minerals and vitamins.

Stimulants and vitamins are more effective.

Avoid large quantities of salty foods like bacon, ham, salted herring, fatty cheese, and the like. Avoid heavy and greasy foods.

Positive affirmation:
"I trust to be able to accomplish all my tasks."

Harvest Time
Ascending forces! Sap is rising, enhancing plant growth above ground, resulting in the most juicy fruits and vegetables.

gather strength rest, recover buildup
Waxing Moon

2 Tuesday

3 Wednesday

No meat.

Forgiveness is the fragrance that the violet sheds on the heel that has crushed it.
Mark Twain

Color
Yellow

Day
Cool

Element
Earth

Capricorn

S E P T E M B E R

Success

Inspiration, optimism, and impatience. Rational thinking, creativity and imagination spark new ideas and inspire planning for the future.

Shying away from routine tasks people will feel more drawn to anything new.

Instead of gridlocked structures choose new possibilities.

Leisure

Inspiration and optimism will boost friendship, social gatherings, and parties.

Express your creativity and imagination. Dwell in dreams and utopian ideas. It is easier now to perceive intuitive thoughts.

Health

Sensitive body parts:

Lower Legs, Veins

All measures taken to supply nutrient materials and strengthen the sensitive body parts are very effective.

Healing ointments are easily absorbed.

Sensitive glandular system.

Avoid inflammation of the veins. Apply ointments to lower legs, and rest legs in a raised position.

Varicose veins: Avoid long periods of standing.

While exercising go easy on the ankles.

Sensitivity to light, so bring your sunglasses along.

Body Care

Aromas, scents: Cyclamen, Peach, Wild Roses

Treatments with firming and moisturizing creams are more effective.

Massages that serve to regenerate, and strengthen, perhaps aided with beneficial massage oils.

Correcting and cutting ingrown nails.

Hair dyes applied now, will look more vibrant.

Garden/Nature

Plant part:

Flower

Avoid watering plants.

Harvested produce is well suitable for storage.

Gather herbs for vein diseases.

Housework

Light housework only.

Ventilate rooms thoroughly.

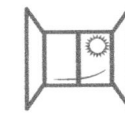

Baking cakes and cookies. Dough rises faster. (Except on New Moon)

Making preserves.

Nutrition

Food quality:

Fat

Cauliflower, artichoke, broccoli, sunflower seeds, flax seeds, nuts, rose hip, elder.

Weight gain: avoid indulging in rich foods. If overweight, eat smaller portions.

Supply nutrient materials to strengthen the body. Focus on foods that contain essential minerals and vitamins.

Stimulants and vitamins are more effective.

Pay attention to any particularly tempting foods today: Most likely the "wrong" things taste best.

High cholesterol: eat a low fat diet.

Positive affirmation:
"There is a solution for every problem."

Harvest Time
Ascending forces! Sap is rising, enhancing plant growth above ground, resulting in the most juicy fruits and vegetables.

gather strength rest, recover buildup
Waxing Moon

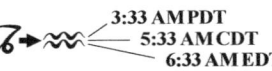
3:33 AM PDT
5:33 AM CDT
6:33 AM EDT

4 Thursday

5 Friday
The Prophet's Birthday
No meat. Cutting and filing toenails and fingernails.

S E P T E M B E R

Health is the vital principle of bliss, and exercise, of health.
James Thomsont

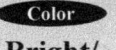 Color
Bright/ Dark Blue

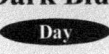 Day
Air/Light

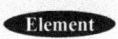 Element

Air   **Aquarius**

Success

Sensibility, intuition, and helpfulness.

Where possible, retreating is more favorable than dealing with business matters.

Dissolve restrictions, be patient and wait. Be aware that people can be more easily influenced.

Leisure

Your helpfulness will boost friendships.

Enjoy dancing or swimming, or watch a movie that will inspire your fantasies and imagination.

Retreat, relax, and recover.

Romance can be gentle and coziness will prevail.

If you plan outdoor excursions, be prepared for a shower here and there.

Health

Sensitive body parts:

Feet and Toes

All measures taken to supply nutrient materials and strengthen the sensitive body parts are very effective.

Healing ointments are easily absorbed.

Sensitive nervous system.

Drugs have a much stronger effect on your body. Monitor closely what you put into your body.

Lymphatic therapy.

Sluggishness or fatigue may occur in the transition into the next Zodiac sign of Aries.

○ *Full Moon: Avoid any surgery and vaccination if possible.*

Body Care

Aromas, scents:
Magnolia, Amaryllis, Clary Sage

Treatments with firming and moisturizing creams are more effective.

Massages that serve to regenerate, and strengthen, perhaps aided with beneficial massage oils. Reflexology massage. Carry out with special care, people are more sensitive.

Correcting and cutting ingrown nails.

Foot bath.

No haircuts, hair becomes shaggy and unmanageable. Avoid washing your hair. Dandruff could develop.

Garden/Nature

Plant part:

Leaf

Watering all indoor and outdoor plants.

Sow plants, herbs, and vegetables that grow and flourish above ground, and leaf vegetables.

Transplanting.

Mowing lawns.

Avoid pruning fruit trees and bushes.

Harvested produce should be consumed as soon as possible.

Gather herbs for foot complaints.

○ *Full Moon: Weather and climate changes. Herbs are most powerful.*

Housework

Light housework only.

Ventilate rooms briefly and rapidly. Don't air mattresses.

○ *Full Moon: Avoid doing laundry, cleaning windows, making preserves, painting.*

Nutrition

Food quality:

Carbohydrate

Lettuce, spinach, lamb's lettuce, Endive, parsley, leek, cabbage (Brussels sprouts, kale, Chinese cabbage), all leafy herbs, asparagus, mushrooms, cress, Swiss chard, rhubarb.

Weight gain: avoid indulging in rich foods. If overweight, eat smaller portions and avoid carbohydrates.

Supply nutrient materials to strengthen the body. Focus on foods that contain essential minerals and vitamins.

Caffeine, alcohol, drugs, certain foods, and stimulants have a much stronger effect.

○ *Full Moon: A day of fasting.*

Positive affirmation:
"I trust to be able to accomplish all my tasks."

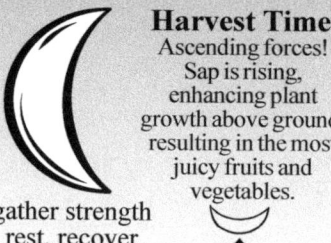

Harvest Time
Ascending forces! Sap is rising, enhancing plant growth above ground, resulting in the most juicy fruits and vegetables.

gather strength
rest, recover
buildup
Waxing Moon

≈ → ⬈ 8:56 AM PDT
→ 10:56 AM CDT
11:56 AM EDT

6 **Saturday**

7 **Sunday**
National Grandparents Day (US)

○ **Full Moon** 11:10 AM PDT,
1:10 PM CDT, 2:10 PM EDT

Complete peace equally reigns between two mental waves.
Swami Sivananda

Color
Blueish White

Day

Wetness

Element

Water

Pisces

S E P T E M B E R

Success

Sensibility, intuition, and helpfulness.

Where possible, retreating is more favorable than dealing with business matters.

Dissolve restrictions, be patient and wait. Be aware that people can be more easily influenced.

Leisure

Your helpfulness will boost friendships.

Enjoy dancing or swimming, or watch a movie that will inspire your fantasies and imagination.

Retreat, relax, and recover.

Romance can be gentle and coziness will prevail.

If you plan outdoor excursions, be prepared for a shower here and there.

Health

Sensitive body parts:

Feet and Toes

All measures taken to flush out and detoxify the sensitive body parts are very effective.

Scarring is less severe.

Teeth: Removal of tartar and amalgam. Best for fillings, crowns, and dentures!

Blood-purifying, detoxifying herbal infusions and teas.

Sensitive nervous system.

Drugs have a much stronger effect on your body. Monitor closely what you put into your body.

Lymphatic therapy.

Sluggishness or fatigue may occur in the transition into the next Zodiac sign of Aries.

Body Care

Aromas, scents: Magnolia, Amaryllis, Clary Sage

Prepare home-made ointments and cosmetics.

Apply detoxing facial and body care.

Treatments of bumps and pimples on the skin, and exfoliating procedures.

Removing body hair.

Correction of the nail bed.

Massages that serve to relax, ease tension, and detoxify. Reflexology massage. Carry out with special care, people are more sensitive.

Removal of callused skin.

Treating obstinate athlete's foot, nail fungus, and warts.

Foot bath.

No haircuts, hair becomes shaggy and unmanageable.
Avoid washing your hair.

Garden/Nature

Plant part:

Leaf

Water plants.

Fertilize flowers.

Sow plants and vegetables that grow below ground, potatoes, leaf vegetables, and lettuce.

Dig over/plow to prepare soil for planting.
Trimming and cutting back plants.
Start a compost heap.

Mowing lawns.

Pest control. Weeding.

Harvested produce should be consumed as soon as possible.

Gather herbs for foot complaints.

Housework

Housework is dealt with much more successfully, efficiently, and effortlessly.

Problem stains are removed readily.

Best for doing laundry! Reduce on laundry detergent, support the environment.

Dry cleaning.

Clean and store seasonal clothing.

Thoroughly clean wooden and parquet floors, metals, china etc.

Cleaning, polishing, and waterproofing shoes.

Combating mold.

Ventilate rooms briefly and rapidly.

Avoid painting.

Preserving and storing should be avoided.

Nutrition

Food quality:

Carbohydrate

Lettuce, spinach, lamb's lettuce, Endive, parsley, leek, cabbage (Brussels sprouts, kale, Chinese cabbage), all leafy herbs, asparagus, mushrooms, cress, Swiss chard, rhubarb.

Weight associated with overeating is less likely. If underweight, eat larger portions.

Cleansing and detox diets. Fruit and juice days.

Flush out poisons. Treatment for drug abuse.

Caffeine, alcohol, drugs, certain foods, and stimulants have a much stronger effect.

Make a home for yourself inside your own head.
You'll find what you need to furnish it – memory, friends
you can trust, love of learning, and other such things.
Tad Williams

Color

Blueish White

Day

Wetness

Element

Pisces **Water**

11:38 AM PDT
1:38 PM CDT ⟶ ⟩(⟶ ↑
2:38 PM EDT

8 Monday

S E P T E M B E R

Harvest Time
Ascending forces!
Sap is rising,
enhancing plant
growth above ground,
resulting in the most
juicy fruits and
vegetables.

detox
remove
be active

Waning Moon

Success

Things get going and the way straight ahead seems the best.

People feel energetic, courageous, assertive, and at times anxious.

Good time for meetings and sales talks but impatience and selfishness do not favor teamwork.

Leisure

An enterprising spirit and spontaneity move people to enjoy outings, sports, competitions, cultural events, and travels.

Romance can be very passionate.

Good days for outings, even with cloudy skies the air still feels somewhat warm. Drying effect, get plenty to drink.

Health

Sensitive body parts:

Head, Brain, Eyes

All measures taken to flush out and detoxify the sensitive body parts are very effective.

Good for surgery, except on the sensitive body parts (see above), digestive organs, nerves, spleen, and pancreas.

Scarring is less severe.

Teeth: Removal of tartar and amalgam. Best for fillings, crowns, and dentures! Avoiding treatment of periodontitis and gums.

Blood-purifying, detoxifying herbal infusions and teas.

Sensitive sense organs.

If you suffer from migraines drink plenty of water, and avoid coffee, chocolate, and sugar.

Body Care

Aromas, scents:
Cloves, Peppermint, Thyme

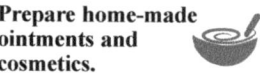

Prepare home-made ointments and cosmetics.

Apply detoxing facial and body care.

Treatments of bumps and pimples on the skin, and exfoliating procedures.

Removing body hair.

Correction of the nail bed.

Massages that serve to relax, ease tension, and detoxify.

Reflexology massage.

Removal of callused skin.

Treating obstinate athlete's foot, nail fungus, and warts.

Eye compresses to relieve strained eyes.

Any kind of hair care.

Garden/Nature

Plant part:
Fruit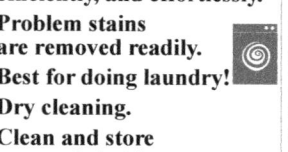

Sowing plants and vegetables that grow below ground.

Sowing and planting anything that is supposed to grow fast. Sowing and planting fruit and tomatoes.

Dig over/plow the soil to prepare for planting.

Spreading manure. Fertilizing grains, vegetables, and fruit.

Weeding. Pest control.

Pruning of fruit trees and bushes.

Harvesting and storing grains, vegetables, potatoes, fruits, and tomatoes.

Start a compost heap.

Gather herbs (roots) for eye complaints and headaches.

Day off on 9/9.

Housework

Housework is dealt with much more successfully, efficiently, and effortlessly.

Problem stains are removed readily.

Best for doing laundry!

Dry cleaning.

Clean and store seasonal clothing.

Thoroughly clean wooden and parquet floors, metals, china, etc.

Cleaning windows and glass.

Cleaning, polishing, and waterproofing shoes.

Combating mold.

Ventilate rooms sufficiently. Air beds.

Suitable for making cheese.

Preserving and freezing fruit and vegetables.

Baking bread, cakes, and cookies (use more leavening agent).

Painting.

Nutrition

Food quality:
Protein

Beans, peas, corn, tomatoes, pumpkin, lentils, soybeans, cucumber, eggplant, zucchini, berries, fruit, chili, bell pepper, figs, avocado, melon, olives.

Weight associated with overeating is less likely. If underweight, eat larger portions.

Cleansing and detox diets. Fruit and juice days.

Flush out poisons. Treatment for drug abuse.

Drink plenty of water.

After silence, that which comes nearest to expressing the inexpressible is music.
Aldous Huxley

Color
Indigo Blue

Day

Warm

Element

Aries   **Fire**

1:04 PM PDT
3:04 PM CDT
4:04 PM EDT

9 Tuesday

10 Wednesday
No meat.

Harvest Time
Ascending forces! Sap is rising, enhancing plant growth above ground, resulting in the most juicy fruits and vegetables.

detox remove be active

Waning Moon

SEPTEMBER

Success

Realism and material security are important. Persistence comes easy, thoughts and reactions are slower.

Assess financial areas.

Conservative tendencies may make people want to stay away from risk taking.

Leisure

Relax at a picnic/feast. Enjoy culinary pleasures and hobbies.

The earth feels cold to the touch, so take slightly warmer clothes.

Health

Sensitive body parts:

Head and Neck

All measures taken to flush out and detoxify the sensitive body parts are very effective.

Good for surgery, except on the sensitive body parts (see above), digestive organs, nerves, spleen, and pancreas. Scarring is less severe.

Teeth: Removal of tartar and amalgam. Best for fillings, crowns, and dentures! Avoiding treatment of periodontitis and gums.

Blood-purifying, detoxifying herbal infusions and teas.

Sensitive blood circulation.

Organs of speech, jaws, teeth, tonsils, thyroid gland, neck, and vocal chords get easily affected. Keep neck warm. On cold days ears should be protected. Sensitivity to noise.

High blood pressure: Avoid salty foods.

Massages, lymphatic therapy, and chiropractic treatment to release blockages.

Body Care

Aromas, scents: Geranium, Jasmine, Rose

Prepare home-made ointments and cosmetics.

Apply detoxing facial and body care.

Treatments of bumps and pimples on the skin, and exfoliating procedures.

Removing body hair.

Correction of the nail bed.

Massages that serve to relax, ease tension, and detoxify.

Reflexology massage.

Removal of callused skin.

Treating obstinate athlete's foot, nail fungus, and warts.

Garden/Nature

Plant part:

Root

Sow plants and vegetables that grow below ground.

Everything grows slowly and lasts well.

Dig over to prepare soil.

Trimming/cutting back plants. Weeding. Mulching.

Start a compost heap.

Combat vermin found in the soil.

Spread fertilizer and liquid manure.

Fertilize flowers with poorly formed roots.

Harvested produce is well suited for storage. Harvesting root vegetables.

Gather herbs (roots) for sinus issues, sore throat, and ear complaints.

Housework

Housework is dealt with much more successfully, efficiently, and effortlessly.

Problem stains are removed readily.

Best for doing laundry! Reduce on laundry detergent, support the environment.

Dry cleaning.

Clean and store seasonal clothing.

Thoroughly clean wooden and parquet floors, metals, china etc.

Cleaning, polishing, and waterproofing shoes.

Combating mold.

Air rooms only briefly.

Painting.

Preserving root vegetables.

Nutrition

Food quality:

Salt

Garlic, carrots, red beets, reddish, rutabaga, sugar beet, celery, potatoes, onions, kohlrabi.

Weight associated with overeating is less likely. If underweight, eat larger portions.

Cleansing and detox diets. Fruit and juice days.

Flush out poisons. Treatment for drug abuse.

Avoid large quantities of salty foods like bacon, ham, salted herring, fatty cheese, and the like.

Always leave something to wish for; otherwise you will be miserable from your very happiness.
Baltasar Gracian

Bright Blue — Color

Cool — Day

Earth — Element

Taurus

11 Thursday
Patriot Day (US)

2:39 PM PDT
4:39 PM CDT ⟩ ♉ ➔ ♊
5:39 PM EDT

12 Friday

No meat. Cutting and filing toenails and fingernails.

SEPTEMBER

Positive affirmation:
"I trust to be able to accomplish all my tasks."

Harvest Time
Ascending forces! Sap is rising, enhancing plant growth above ground, resulting in the most juicy fruits and vegetables.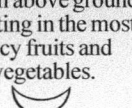

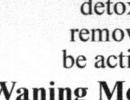

detox
remove
be active

Waning Moon

Success

Open mindedness and curiosity. A changeable and hectic time.

Good time for talking, negotiating, networking, and exchanging ideas as well as for meetings of a nonbinding nature, conferences, and studies.

Leisure

Good time for family gatherings, parties, and short trips.

People enjoy stimulating their minds with reading and studying. Attending theater performances is a preferred enjoyment. Enhance friendships.

Stretching exercises.

Be prepared for sudden changes in weather or climate.

Health

Sensitive body parts:

Shoulders, Arms, Hands, Lungs

All measures taken to flush out and detoxify the sensitive body parts are very effective.
Good for surgery, except on the sensitive body parts (see above), digestive organs, nerves, spleen, pancreas. Scarring is less severe.
Teeth: Removal of tartar and amalgam. Best for fillings, crowns, and dentures! Avoid having any teeth pulled.
Blood-purifying, detoxifying herbal infusions and teas. Sensitive glandular system. Make sure you are dressed warm enough in cool weather.
Exercises for shoulders. Breathing exercises. Sensitivity to light, bring your sunglasses along. Massages, lymphatic therapy, and chiropractic treatment to release blockages.

Body Care

Aromas, scents: Lavender, Lemon Balm, Magnolia, Verbena

Prepare home-made ointments and cosmetics.

Apply detoxing facial and body care.

Treatments of bumps and pimples on the skin, and exfoliating procedures.

Removing body hair.

Correction of the nail bed.

Massages that serve to relax, ease tension, and detoxify.

Reflexology massage.

Removal of callused skin.

Treating obstinate athlete's foot, nail fungus, and warts.

Garden/Nature

Plant part:

Flower

Sow plants and vegetablesthat grow below ground.

Trimming and cutting back plants.

Start a compost heap.

Weeding. Pest control.

Fertilize flowers that no longer bloom.

Avoid watering plants.

Changes in weather are more likely.

Gather herbs (roots) for tensions in the shoulder and lung complaints.

Housework

Housework is dealt with much more successfully, efficiently, and effortlessly.

Problem stains are removed readily.

Best for doing laundry! Reduce on laundry detergent, support the environment.

Dry cleaning.

Clean and store seasonal clothing.

Thoroughly clean wooden and parquet floors, metals, china etc.

Cleaning windows and glass.

Cleaning, polishing, and waterproofing shoes.

Combating mold.

Ventilate rooms thoroughly.

Baking bread, cakes, and cookies (add more leavening agent).

Making preserves.

Painting.

Nutrition

Food quality:

Fat

Cauliflower, artichoke, broccoli, sunflower seeds, flax seeds, nuts, rose hip, elder.

Weight associated with overeating is less likely. If underweight, eat larger portions.

Cleansing and detox diets. Fruit and juice days.

Flush out poisons. Treatment for drug abuse.

Pay attention to any particularly tempting foods today: Most likely the "wrong" things taste best.

High cholesterol: eat a low fat diet.

Growth itself contains the germ of happiness.
Pearl S. Buck

Color
Light Blue

Day
Air/Light

Element

Gemini   **Air**

5:31 PM PDT
7:31 PM CDT ⟹ Ⅱ ➔ ♋
8:31 PM EDT

13 Saturday

14 Sunday

☽ Half Moon.

SEPTEMBER

Positive affirmation:
"I trust to be able to accomplish all my tasks."

Turning Point
Transition of ascending to descending forces. Both forces are at work and neutralize each other.

detox
remove
be active
Waning Moon

Success

Feelings, sensitivity, and cooperativeness. Many are overly sensitive, so beware of treading on someone's toes.

Be cautious if you are easily influenced.

During negotiations make use of the cognitive ability of your senses.

Leisure

Relax within your close family.

Retreat to your safe haven and enjoy your fantasy while reading or listening to music. The inner world becomes more colorful than the outer.

Romance can be gentle. Deep feelings will prevail.

If you plan outdoor excursions, be prepared for a shower here and there.

Health

Sensitive body parts:
Chest, Lungs, Liver, Stomach, Gall Bladder

All measures taken to flush out and detoxify the sensitive body parts are very effective.

Good for surgical operations except those on the sensitive body parts (see above), digestive organs, nerves, spleen, pancreas. Scarring is less severe.

Teeth: Removal of tartar and amalgam. Best for fillings, crowns, and dentures!

Blood-purifying, detoxifying herbal infusions and teas.

Sensitive nervous system.

Be cautious with alcohol since the liver is very sensitive.

Stomach could play up and cause gas and heartburn.

Rheumatism: Don't air bedding outside, damp will remain in the bedding.

Lymphatic therapy.

Body Care

Aromas, scents:
Lilac, Lilies of the Valley, Lilies, Violets

Prepare home-made ointments and cosmetics.

Apply detoxing facial and body care.

Treatments of bumps and pimples on the skin, and exfoliating procedures.

Removing body hair.

Correction of the nail bed.

Massages that serve to relax, ease tension, and detoxify.

Reflexology massage.

Removal of callused skin.

Treating obstinate athlete's foot, nail fungus, and warts.

No haircuts, hair becomes shaggy and unmanageable. Avoid washing your hair.

Garden/Nature

Plant part:
Leaf

Water plants.

Fertilize flowers.

Sow plants and vegetables that grow below ground, leaf vegetables, and lettuce.

Dig over/plow to prepare soil for planting.

Trimming and cutting back plants. Transplanting. Weeding.

Combating pests above ground.

Start a compost heap.

Mowing lawns.

Gather herbs (roots) for bronchitis, stomach, liver, and gall bladder complaints.

Unfavorable for harvesting, storing, and preserving.

Housework

Housework is dealt with much more successfully, efficiently, and effortlessly.

Problem stains are removed readily.

Best for doing laundry! Reduce on laundry detergent, support the environment.

Dry cleaning.

Thoroughly clean wooden and parquet floors, metals, china etc.

Cleaning, polishing, and waterproofing shoes.

Combating mold.

Ventilate rooms briefly and rapidly.

Avoid painting.

Nutrition

Food quality:
Carbohydrate

Lettuce, spinach, lamb's lettuce, Endive, parsley, leek, cabbage (Brussels sprouts, kale, Chinese cabbage), all leafy herbs, asparagus, mushrooms, cress, Swiss chard, rhubarb.

Weight associated with overeating is less likely. If underweight, eat larger portions.

Moodiness may make you want to eat more than is healthy. If overweight avoid carbohydrates.

Cleansing and detox diets. Fruit and juice days.

Flush out poisons. Treatment for drug abuse.

If you get stomach troubles easily, avoid heavy meals.

Food for the body is not enough. There must be food for the soul.
Dorothy Day

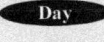 Color
Green

Day
Wetness

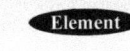 Element
Cancer   **Water**

15 Monday

16 Tuesday

S E P T E M B E R

Planting Time
Descending forces! Sap is drawn downward, enhancing root formation. Best days for sowing, planting, and transplanting.

detox remove be active
Waning Moon

Success

Determination reigns, and risks are taken more often. Master your tasks with more self-confidence and creativity.

Limits appear to be more easily surmountable.

Auspicious day for sales, advertising, and publicity.

Leisure

Zest for life is in the air. People want to have a fun time, enjoy parties, musical events, movies, etc.

Possessive feelings can harm a relationship. Romance can be very passionate.

Outings: even with cloudy skies the air still feels somewhat warm. Drying effect, get plenty to drink.

Danger of sudden storms, not only in the sky.

Health

Sensitive body parts:
Heart, Back, Diaphragm, Circulation, Arteries

All measures taken to flush out and detoxify the sensitive body parts are very effective.

Good for surgery, except on the sensitive body parts (see above), digestive organs, nerves, spleen, pancreas. Scarring is less severe.

Teeth: Removal of tartar and amalgam. Best for fillings, crowns, and dentures!

Blood-purifying, detoxifying herbal infusions and teas.

Sensitive sense organs.

Back and heart problems are more likely to occur.

Avoid overstraining of the heart and circulation with unusual physical activities.

Expect sleepless nights.

Body Care

Aromas, scents:
Hibiscus, Oleander, Rose

Prepare home-made ointments and cosmetics.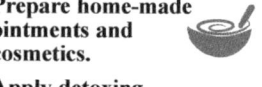

Apply detoxing facial and body care.

Treatments of bumps and pimples on the skin, and exfoliating procedures.

Removing body hair.

Correction of the nail bed.

Massages that serve to relax, ease tension, and detoxify.

Reflexology massage.

Removal of callused skin.

Treating obstinate athlete's foot, nail fungus, and warts.

Good days for haircuts, hair becomes stronger. But be aware that if you get a perm, curls will become quite frizzy. Baby's first haircut.

Garden/Nature

Plant part:
Fruit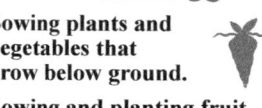

Sowing plants and vegetables that grow below ground.

Sowing and planting fruit. Also sow and plant vegetables that are highly perishable. Plant trees and bushes. Sow lawns.

Dig over/plow to prepare soil for planting.

Trimming and cutting back plants. Pruning of fruit trees and bushes.

Transplanting.

Not suitable for fertilizing.

Weeding. Pest Control.

Harvested produce should be consumed as soon as possible.

Gather herbs (roots) for heart and circulation complaints.

Start compost heap.

Housework

Housework is dealt with much more successfully, efficiently, and effortlessly.

Problem stains are removed readily.

Best for doing laundry!

Dry cleaning.

Thoroughly clean wooden and parquet floors, metals, china, etc.

Cleaning windows and glass.

Cleaning, polishing, and waterproofing shoes.

Combating mold.

Ventilate rooms sufficiently. Air beds.

Suitable for making cheese.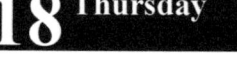

Preserving and freezing fruit and vegetables.

Baking bread, cakes, and cookies (use more leavening agent).

Avoid painting.

Nutrition

Food quality:
Protein

Beans, peas, corn, tomatoes, pumpkin, lentils, soybeans, cucumber, eggplant, zucchini, berries, fruit, chili, bell pepper, figs, avocado, melon, olives.

Weight associated with overeating is less likely. If underweight, eat larger portions.

Cleansing and detox diets. Fruit and juice days.

Flush out poisons. Treatment for drug abuse.

In every man's heart there is a secret nerve that answers to the vibrations of beauty.
Christopher Morley

Leo

Color	**Green**
Day	**Warm**
Element	**Fire**

10:21 PM PDT Tuesday
12:21 AM CDT
1:21 AM EDT

17 Wednesday
No meat.

18 Thursday

Positive affirmation:
"I trust to be able to accomplish all my tasks."

Planting Time
Descending forces! Sap is drawn downward, enhancing root formation. Best days for sowing, planting, and transplanting.

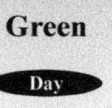

detox remove be active
Waning Moon

S E P T E M B E R

Success

Good time for details, organization, routine, concentration, and duty.

Take care of financial and administrative tasks.

Prepare for future success now with realistic and critical assessment.

● *New Moon: Confirm your resolutions. Finalize new decisions. Drop bad habits.*

Leisure

Enjoy a nature walk.

Good time for health regimes. Improve your health with stretching exercises and yoga.

The earth feels cold to the touch, so take slightly warmer clothes.

Health

Sensitive body parts:
Digestive Organs, Nerves, Spleen, Pancreas

All measures taken to flush out and detoxify the sensitive body parts are very effective.
Scarring is less severe.
Teeth: Removal of tartar and amalgam. Best for fillings, crowns, and dentures!
Avoiding treatment of periodontitis and gums.
Blood-purifying, detoxifying herbal infusions and teas.
Sensitive blood circulation.

For a sensitive digestive system, a wholesome diet is recommended.
Dress slightly warmer.
High blood pressure: Avoid salty foods.
Massages, lymphatic therapy, and chiropractic treatment to release blockages.

● *New Moon: Avoid any surgery if possible.*

Body Care

Aromas, scents: Lavender, Spruce Needles, Sage, Meadow Flowers

Prepare home-made ointments and cosmetics.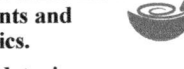

Apply detoxing facial and body care.

Treatments of bumps and pimples on the skin, and exfoliating procedures.

Removing body hair.

Correction of the nail bed.

Massages that serve to relax, ease tension, and detoxify.

Reflexology massage.

Removal of callused skin.

Treating obstinate athlete's foot, nail fungus, and warts.

Best for haircuts because it retains its shape longer. Perms turn out best.

Garden/Nature

Plant part:
Root

Best for sowing and planting, except lettuce.
Plant trees which are supposed to grow very tall. Plant hedges and bushes that are meant to grow very fast.
Planting and re-potting balcony and indoor plants.
Dig over/plow to prepare soil for planting.
Trimming and cutting back plants. Planting cuttings.
Spread fertilizer and manure. Fertilize flowers with poorly formed roots.
Start a compost heap.
Transplanting. Mulching.
Weeding. Pest control (vermin in the soil).
Avoid harvesting and storing.
Gather herbs (roots) for digestive organs, pancreas, and nervous complaints.

● *New Moon: Change of weather is likely. Care for sickly plants.*

Housework

Housework is dealt with much more successfully, efficiently, and effortlessly.
Problem stains are removed readily.
Best for doing laundry! Reduce on laundry detergent, support the environment.
Dry cleaning.
Thoroughly clean wooden and parquet floors, metals, china etc.
Cleaning, polishing, and waterproofing shoes.
Combating mold.
Air rooms only briefly.
Painting.
Making pickles, preserves, and cheese yields suboptimal results and should be avoided.

Nutrition

Food quality:
Salt

Garlic, carrots, red beets, reddish, rutabaga, sugar beet, celery, potatoes, onions, kohlrabi.

Weight associated with overeating is less likely. If underweight, eat larger portions.

Cleansing and detox diets. Fruit and juice days.

Flush out poisons. Treatment for drug abuse.

Avoid large quantities of salty foods like bacon, ham, salted herring, fatty cheese, and the like. Avoid heavy and greasy foods.

● *New Moon: A day of fasting.*

Beauty in things exists in the mind which contemplates them.
David Hume

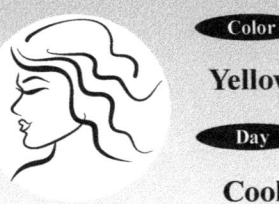

♍ Virgo

Color Yellow
Day Cool
Element Earth

♌ → ♍ 5:24 AM PDT / 7:24 AM CDT / 8:24 AM EDT

19 Friday
No meat. Cutting and filing toenails and fingernails.

20 Saturday

2:42 PM PDT / 4:42 PM CDT / 5:42 PM EDT ♍ → ♎

21 Sunday
● **New Moon** 11:55 AM PDT 1:55 PM CDT, 2:55 PM EDT
Lunar Eclipse 11:43 AM PDT 1:43 PM CDT, 2:43 PM EDT

S E P T E M B E R

Planting Time
Descending forces! Sap is drawn downward, enhancing root formation. Best days for sowing, planting, and transplanting.

detox remove be active
Waning Moon

Success

The artistic instinct rules, but so, too, does indecisiveness. The forces swing back and forth until equilibrium is achieved.

It's easy to reach compromises with tactful sensitivity.

A sense of judgment will support legal matters.

Leisure

Pursuit for harmony and cooperativeness supports good times in romance, friendship, and partnership.

Enjoy cultural events. Relax and get pampered with a spa treatment.

Romance can be passionate yet sensitive.

Health

Sensitive body parts:

Hips, Kidneys, Bladder

All measures taken to supply nutrient materials and strengthen the sensitive body parts are very effective.

Healing ointments are easily absorbed.

Sensitive glandular system.

Take special care to keep the area of bladder and kidneys warm.

Apply special exercises for the hip region.

Avoid having any teeth pulled.

Sensitivity to light, bring your sunglasses along.

Body Care

Aromas, scents:
Roses, Violets, Daffodils

Treatments with firming and moisturizing creams are more effective.

Massages that serve to regenerate, and strengthen, perhaps aided with beneficial massage oils.

Correcting and cutting ingrown nails.

Hair dyes applied now, will look more vibrant.

Garden/Nature

Plant part:

Flower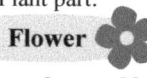

Sow plants and vegetables that grow and flourish above ground, specially flowers, and medicinal herbs.

Transplanting.

Trimming and cutting back plants.

Avoid watering plants.

Start a compost heap.

Harvested produce should be consumed as soon as possible.

Gather herbs for kidneys, gall bladder, and hip complaints.

Day off on 9/22.

Housework

Light housework only.

Ventilate rooms thoroughly.

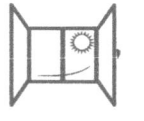

Baking cakes and cookies. Dough rises faster. (Except on New Moon)

Nutrition

Food quality:

Fat

Cauliflower, artichoke, broccoli, sunflower seeds, flax seeds, nuts, rose hip, elder.

Weight gain: avoid indulging in rich foods. If overweight, eat smaller portions.

Supply nutrient materials to strengthen the body. Focus on foods that contain essential minerals and vitamins.

Stimulants and vitamins are more effective.

Pay attention to any particularly tempting foods today: Most likely the "wrong" things taste best.

High cholesterol: eat a low fat diet.

Positive affirmation:
"I trust the wisdom derived from inner silence."

Planting Time
Descending forces! Sap is drawn downward, enhancing root formation. Best days for sowing, planting, and transplanting.

gather strength rest, recover buildup
Waxing Moon

22 Monday
Fall Equinox, Navratri

23 Tuesday
Rosh Hashanah

Change brings opportunity.
Nido Qubein

Color
Orange

Day
Air/Light

Element
Air

Libra

S E P T E M B E R

Success

Critical and superstitious behavior emerges, especially pertaining to money.

A penetrating power will strengthen your capacity to act.

An increased perception opens our interest for the essentials and helps to discover hidden potentials.

Leisure

Relax within your close family, with meditation, and relaxation exercises.

A longing to feel safe will be nurtured if you focus on habits and rituals. An increased sensitivity will help to enjoy every moment.

Romance can be very passionate.

If you plan outdoor excursions, be prepared for a shower here and there.

Health

Sensitive body parts:

Sex organs, Ureter

All measures taken to supply nutrient materials and strengthen the sensitive body parts are very effective.

Healing ointments are easily absorbed. Applying herbal ointments to the shoulders for rheumatic gout and alike.

Sensitive nervous system.

Female disorders: As a preventative measure apply hip baths using yarrow.

Pregnancy: Avoid any exertion, miscarriages are more likely.

Keep region of the pelvis, kidneys, and feet warm to prevent infection of the bladder and kidneys.

Lymphatic therapy.

Body Care

Aromas, scents:
Anemone, Cornflower
Oregano, Thuja

Treatments with firming and moisturizing creams are more effective.

Massages that serve to regenerate, and strengthen, perhaps aided with beneficial massage oils.

Correcting and cutting ingrown nails.

Hair dyes applied now, will look more vibrant.

Garden/Nature

Plant part:

 Leaf

Watering all indoor and outdoor plants.

Sow plants, herbs, and vegetables that grow and flourish above ground, leaf vegetables (no lettuce).

Sowing, planting, harvesting, and drying every kind of medicinal herbs.

Transplanting.

Trimming and cutting back plants.
Combating slugs and snails.
Mowing lawns.

Start a compost heap.

Avoid pruning fruit trees and bushes. Avoid cutting down any trees.

Harvested produce should be consumed as soon as possible.

Housework

Light housework only.

Ventilate rooms briefly and rapidly. Don't air mattresses.

Any dirt and spots are easily removed in the laundry.

Avoid painting, as paint will take very long to dry.

Nutrition

Food quality:

Carbohydrate

Lettuce, spinach, lamb's lettuce, Endive, parsley, leek, cabbage (Brussels sprouts, kale, Chinese cabbage), all leafy herbs, asparagus, mushrooms, cress, Swiss chard, rhubarb.

Weight gain: avoid indulging in rich foods. If overweight, eat smaller portions and avoid carbohydrates.

Supply nutrient materials to strengthen the body. Focus on foods that contain essential minerals and vitamins. Stimulants and vitamins are more effective.

Positive affirmation:
"I trust the wisdom derived from inner silence."

Planting Time
Descending forces!
Sap is drawn downward, enhancing root formation.
Best days for sowing, planting, and transplanting.

gather strength
rest, recover
buildup
Waxing Moon

♎→♏ 12:01 AM PDT
2:01 AM CDT
3:01 AM EDT

24 Wednesday

No meat.

25 Thursday

2:38 PM PDT
4:38 PM CDT → ♏→♐
5:38 PM EDT

26 Friday

No meat. Cutting and filing toenails and fingernails.

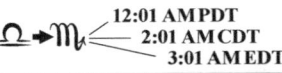

S E P T E M B E R

Happiness is not something you postpone for the future; it is something you design for the present.
Jim Rohn

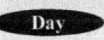 Color
Red

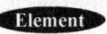 Day
Wetness

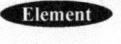 Element
Water

♏
Scorpio

Success

Inquisitiveness and exuberant inspiration lead to new horizons. Insight and love for truth reign.

Bringing together is more important than splitting asunder.

Expansive forces will assist in legal matters, discussions, and debates.

Leisure

Expansion feels great, and travel, short trips, and outings are most welcome. A competitive spirit excites any sports event.

Talk things out when necessary.

Romance can be very passionate.

Good days for outings; even with cloudy skies the air still feels somewhat warm. Drying effect, get plenty to drink.

Health

Sensitive body parts:

Thighs and Veins

All measures taken to supply nutrient materials and strengthen the sensitive body parts are very effective.

Healing ointments are easily absorbed.

Sensitive sense organs.

Pains often arise in the sciatic nerve, veins, the small of the back, and thighs.

Avoid overstraining the body with unusual physical activities.

Body Care

Aromas, scents: Calendula (Marigold), Geranium, Rosemary

Treatments with firming and moisturizing creams are more effective.

Massages that serve to regenerate, and strengthen, perhaps aided with beneficial massage oils.

Correcting and cutting ingrown nails.

Hair dyes applied now, will look more vibrant.

Garden/Nature

Plant part:

Fruit

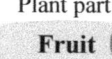

Sow plants and vegetables that grow and flourish above ground.

Sowing and planting fruit and vegetables that grow tall, and tomatoes, but no lettuce.

Transplanting.

Grafting onto fruit trees.

Cultivating grains, particularly corn.

Gather herbs for vein diseases.

Housework

Light housework only.

Ventilate sufficiently.

Freezing fruit and vegetables.

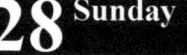

Baking bread, cakes, and cookies. Dough rises faster. (Except on New Moon)

Suitable for making cheese.

Making preserves.

Nutrition

Food quality:

Protein

Beans, peas, corn, tomatoes, pumpkin, lentils, soybeans, cucumber, eggplant, zucchini, berries, fruit, chili, bell pepper, figs, avocado, melon, olives.

Weight gain: avoid indulging in rich foods. If overweight, eat smaller portions.

Supply nutrient materials to strengthen the body. Focus on foods that contain essential minerals and vitamins.

Stimulants and vitamins are more effective.

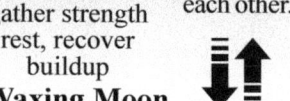

Turning Point

Transition of descending to ascending forces. Both forces are at work and neutralize each other.

gather strength rest, recover buildup

Waxing Moon

27 Saturday

28 Sunday

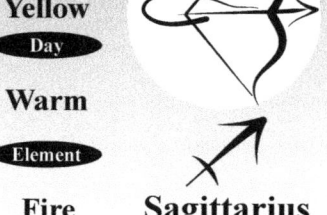

Color
Orange/ Yellow

Day
Warm

Element
Fire

Sagittarius

S E P T E M B E R

Success

Career and business are in the foreground now and thinking becomes clear and serious, but somewhat inflexible.

Perseverance and reasoning assist in financial matters, planning, and contracts.

The values of tradition, authority, and discipline impact our endeavors.

Leisure

Money is not likely to be wasted in a shopping spree.

Many are drawn to enjoy cultural events.

The earth feels cold to the touch, so take slightly warmer clothes.

Health

Sensitive body parts:

Knees, Joints, Bones, Skin

All measures taken to supply nutrient materials and strengthen the sensitive body parts are very effective.

Healing ointments are easily absorbed.

Sensitive blood circulation.

Avoid overstraining bones and knees, and apply gentle stretching exercises only.

Problems with meniscus: Don't overstrain.

Dress slightly warmer.

High blood pressure: Avoid salty foods.

Massages, lymphatic therapy, and chiropractic treatment to release blockages.

Body Care

Aromas, scents:

Cedar, Juniper

Treatments with firming and moisturizing creams are more effective.

Massages that serve to regenerate, and strengthen, perhaps aided with beneficial massage oils.

Correcting and cutting ingrown nails.

Every kind of skin care is beneficial.

Cutting and filing toenails and fingernails will make the nails grow stronger over time.

Hair dyes applied now, will look more vibrant.

Garden/Nature

Plant part:

Root

Sow plants, herbs, and vegetables that grow and flourish above ground.

Transplanting.

Harvest produce is suitable for storage. Harvest root vegetables.

Gather herbs for bone, joint, and skin diseases.

Housework

Light housework only.

Air rooms only briefly.

Preserving root vegetables.

Avoid dry cleaning, as the fabric may develop unwanted glossy blotches.

Nutrition

Food quality:

Salt

Garlic, carrots, red beets, reddish, rutabaga, sugar beet, celery, potatoes, onions, kohlrabi.

Weight gain: avoid indulging in rich foods. If overweight, eat smaller portions.

Supply nutrient materials to strengthen the body. Focus on foods that contain essential minerals and vitamins.

Stimulants and vitamins are more effective.

Avoid large quantities of salty foods like bacon, ham, salted herring, fatty cheese, and the like. Avoid heavy and greasy foods.

Positive affirmation:
"I trust the wisdom derived from inner silence. "

Harvest Time
Ascending forces! Sap is rising, enhancing plant growth above ground, resulting in the most juicy fruits and vegetables.

gather strength rest, recover buildup
Waxing Moon

12:56 AM PDT
2:56 AM CDT
3:56 AM EDT

29 Monday
☽ Half Moon.

30 Tuesday

12:53 PM PDT
2:53 PM CDT
3:53 PM EDT

1 Wednesday
Dussehra
No meat.

SEPTEMBER/OCTOBER

Forgiveness is a virtue of the brave.
Indira Gandhi

Color
Yellow

Day
Cool

Element
Earth

Capricorn

Success

Inspiration, optimism, and impatience. Rational thinking, creativity and imagination spark new ideas and inspire planning for the future.

Shying away from routine tasks people will feel more drawn to anything new.

Instead of gridlocked structures choose new possibilities.

Leisure

Inspiration and optimism will boost friendship, social gatherings, and parties.

Express your creativity and imagination. Dwell in dreams and utopian ideas. It is easier now to perceive intuitive thoughts.

Health

Sensitive body parts:

Lower Legs, Veins

All measures taken to supply nutrient materials and strengthen the sensitive body parts are very effective.

Healing ointments are easily absorbed.

Sensitive glandular system.

Avoid inflammation of the veins. Apply ointments to lower legs, and rest legs in a raised position.

Varicose veins: Avoid long periods of standing.

While exercising go easy on the ankles.

Sensitivity to light, so bring your sunglasses along.

Body Care

Aromas, scents:
Cyclamen, Peach, Wild Roses

Treatments with firming and moisturizing creams are more effective.

Massages that serve to regenerate, and strengthen, perhaps aided with beneficial massage oils.

Correcting and cutting ingrown nails.

Hair dyes applied now, will look more vibrant.

Garden/Nature

Plant part:

Flower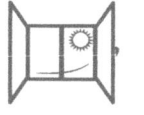

Avoid watering plants.

Harvested produce is well suitable for storage.

Gather herbs for vein diseases.

Housework

Light housework only.

Ventilate rooms thoroughly.

Baking cakes and cookies. Dough rises faster. (Except on New Moon)

Making preserves.

Nutrition

Food quality:

Fat

Cauliflower, artichoke, broccoli, sunflower seeds, flax seeds, nuts, rose hip, elder.

Weight gain: avoid indulging in rich foods. If overweight, eat smaller portions.

Supply nutrient materials to strengthen the body. Focus on foods that contain essential minerals and vitamins.

Stimulants and vitamins are more effective.

Pay attention to any particularly tempting foods today: Most likely the "wrong" things taste best.

High cholesterol: eat a low fat diet.

Positive affirmation:
"I trust the wisdom derived from inner silence."

Harvest Time
Ascending forces! Sap is rising, enhancing plant growth above ground, resulting in the most juicy fruits and vegetables.

gather strength rest, recover buildup
Waxing Moon

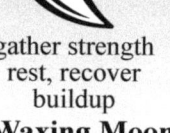

2 **Thursday**
Yom Kippur

7:08 PM PDT
9:08 PM CDT
10:08 PM EDT
≈ →)(

3 **Friday**

No meat. Cutting and filing toenails and fingernails.

The real and lasting victories are those of peace, and not of war.
Ralph Waldo Emerson

Color
Bright/ Dark Blue

Day
Air/Light

Element

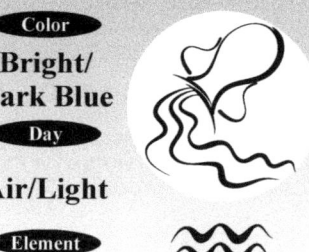

Air   Aquarius

O C T O B E R

Success

Sensibility, intuition, and helpfulness.

Where possible, retreating is more favorable than dealing with business matters.

Dissolve restrictions, be patient and wait. Be aware that people can be more easily influenced.

Leisure

Your helpfulness will boost friendships.

Enjoy dancing or swimming, or watch a movie that will inspire your fantasies and imagination.

Retreat, relax, and recover.

Romance can be gentle and coziness will prevail.

If you plan outdoor excursions, be prepared for a shower here and there.

Health

Sensitive body parts:

Feet and Toes

All measures taken to supply nutrient materials and strengthen the sensitive body parts are very effective.

Healing ointments are easily absorbed.

Sensitive nervous system.

Drugs have a much stronger effect on your body. Monitor closely what you put into your body.

Lymphatic therapy.

Sluggishness or fatigue may occur in the transition into the next Zodiac sign of Aries.

Body Care

Aromas, scents:
Magnolia, Amaryllis, Clary Sage

Treatments with firming and moisturizing creams are more effective.

Massages that serve to regenerate, and strengthen, perhaps aided with beneficial massage oils. Reflexology massage. Carry out with special care, people are more sensitive.

Correcting and cutting ingrown nails.

Foot bath.

No haircuts, hair becomes shaggy and unmanageable. Avoid washing your hair. Dandruff could develop.

Garden/Nature

Plant part:

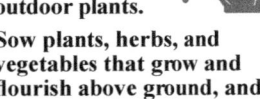 **Leaf**

Watering all indoor and outdoor plants.

Sow plants, herbs, and vegetables that grow and flourish above ground, and leaf vegetables.

Transplanting.

Mowing lawns.

Avoid pruning fruit trees and bushes.

Harvested produce should be consumed as soon as possible.

Gather herbs for foot complaints.

Housework

Light housework only.

Ventilate rooms briefly and rapidly. Don't air mattresses.

Any dirt and spots are easily removed in the laundry.

Avoid painting, as paint will take very long to dry.

Preserving and storing should be avoided.

Nutrition

Food quality:

Carbohydrate

Lettuce, spinach, lamb's lettuce, Endive, parsley, leek, cabbage (Brussels sprouts, kale, Chinese cabbage), all leafy herbs, asparagus, mushrooms, cress, Swiss chard, rhubarb.

Weight gain: avoid indulging in rich foods. If overweight, eat smaller portions and avoid carbohydrates.

Supply nutrient materials to strengthen the body. Focus on foods that contain essential minerals and vitamins.

Caffeine, alcohol, drugs, certain foods, and stimulants have a much stronger effect.

Positive affirmation:
"I trust the wisdom derived from inner silence."

Harvest Time
Ascending forces! Sap is rising, enhancing plant growth above ground, resulting in the most juicy fruits and vegetables.

gather strength
rest, recover
buildup
Waxing Moon

9:49 PM PDT
11:49 PM CDT ⟩ ✲ → ♈
Monday 12:49 AM EDT

4 Saturday
Feast of Francis of Assisi

5 Sunday

O C T O B E R

An eye for an eye only ends up making the whole world blind.
Mahatma Gandhi

Color
Blueish White
Day
Wetness
Element

Water

 Pisces

Success

Things get going and the way straight ahead seems the best.

People feel energetic, courageous, assertive, and at times anxious.

Good time for meetings and sales talks but impatience and selfishness do not favor teamwork.

Leisure

An enterprising spirit and spontaneity move people to enjoy outings, sports, competitions, cultural events, and travels.

Romance can be very passionate.

Good days for outings, even with cloudy skies the air still feels somewhat warm. Drying effect, get plenty to drink.

Health

Sensitive body parts:

Head, Brain, Eyes

All measures taken to supply nutrient materials and strengthen the sensitive body parts are very effective.

Healing ointments are easily absorbed.

Sensitive sense organs.

If you suffer from migraines drink plenty of water, and avoid coffee, chocolate, and sugar.

○ *Full Moon: Avoid any surgery and vaccination if possible.*

Body Care

Aromas, scents:
Cloves, Peppermint, Thyme

Treatments with firming and moisturizing creams are more effective.

Massages that serve to regenerate, and strengthen, perhaps aided with beneficial massage oils.

Correcting and cutting ingrown nails.

Eye compresses for strained eyes.

Any kind of hair care. Hair dyes applied now, will look more vibrant.

Garden/Nature

Plant part:

Fruit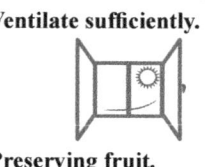

Sow plants and vegetables that grow and flourish above ground, especially fruit and tomatoes.

Sowing and planting anything that is supposed to grow fast and for immediate use.

Grafting onto fruit trees.

Cultivating grains.

Transplanting.

Harvesting and storing grains, vegetables, potatoes, fruit, and tomatoes.

Gather herbs for eye complaints and headaches.

Day off on 10/6.

○ *Full Moon: Weather and climate changes. Herbs are most powerful.*

Housework

Light housework only.

Ventilate sufficiently.

Preserving fruit.

Freezing fruit and vegetables.

Baking bread, cakes, and cookies. Dough rises faster. (Except on New Moon)

Suitable for making cheese.

○ *Full Moon: Avoid doing laundry, cleaning windows, making preserves, painting.*

Nutrition

Food quality:

Protein

Beans, peas, corn, tomatoes, pumpkin, lentils, soybeans, cucumber, eggplant, zucchini, berries, fruit, chili, bell pepper, figs, avocado, melon, olives.

Weight gain: avoid indulging in rich foods. If overweight, eat smaller portions.

Supply nutrient materials to strengthen the body. Focus on foods that contain essential minerals and vitamins.

Stimulants and vitamins are more effective.

Drink plenty of water.

○ *Full Moon: A day of fasting.*

Positive affirmation:
"I trust the wisdom derived from inner silence."

Harvest Time
Ascending forces! Sap is rising, enhancing plant growth above ground, resulting in the most juicy fruits and vegetables.

gather strength rest, recover buildup
Waxing Moon

6 Monday

○ **Full Moon** 8:49 PM PDT, 10:49 PM CDT, 11:49 PM EDT

O C T O B E R

A garden must combine the poetic and the mysterious with a feeling of serenity and joy.
Luis Barragan

Color
Indigo Blue

Day
Warm

Element

Fire   Aries

Success

Things get going and the way straight ahead seems the best.

People feel energetic, courageous, assertive, and at times anxious.

Good time for meetings and sales talks but impatience and selfishness do not favor teamwork.

Leisure

An enterprising spirit and spontaneity move people to enjoy outings, sports, competitions, cultural events, and travels.

Romance can be very passionate.

Good days for outings, even with cloudy skies the air still feels somewhat warm. Drying effect, get plenty to drink.

Health

Sensitive body parts:

Head, Brain, Eyes

All measures taken to flush out and detoxify the sensitive body parts are very effective.

Scarring is less severe.

Teeth: Removal of tartar and amalgam. Best for fillings, crowns, and dentures! Avoiding treatment of periodontitis and gums.

Blood-purifying, detoxifying herbal infusions and teas.

Sensitive sense organs.

If you suffer from migraines drink plenty of water, and avoid coffee, chocolate, and sugar.

Body Care

Aromas, scents: Cloves, Peppermint, Thyme

Prepare home-made ointments and cosmetics.

Apply detoxing facial and body care.

Treatments of bumps and pimples on the skin, and exfoliating procedures.

Removing body hair.

Correction of the nail bed.

Massages that serve to relax, ease tension, and detoxify.

Reflexology massage.

Removal of callused skin.

Treating obstinate athlete's foot, nail fungus, and warts.

Eye compresses to relieve strained eyes.

Any kind of hair care.

Garden/Nature

Plant part:

Fruit

Sowing plants and vegetables that grow below ground.

Sowing and planting anything that is supposed to grow fast. Sowing and planting fruit and tomatoes.

Dig over/plow the soil to prepare for planting.

Spreading manure. Fertilizing grains, vegetables, and fruit.

Weeding. Pest control.

Pruning of fruit trees and bushes.

Harvesting and storing grains, vegetables, potatoes, fruits, and tomatoes.

Start a compost heap.

Gather herbs (roots) for eye complaints and headaches.

Housework

Housework is dealt with much more successfully, efficiently, and effortlessly.

Problem stains are removed readily.

Dry cleaning.

Clean and store seasonal clothing.

Thoroughly clean wooden and parquet floors, metals, china, etc.

Cleaning, polishing, and waterproofing shoes.

Combating mold.

Ventilate rooms sufficiently. Air beds.

Suitable for making cheese.

Freezing fruit and vegetables.

Baking bread, cakes, and cookies (use more leavening agent).

Nutrition

Food quality:

Protein

Beans, peas, corn, tomatoes, pumpkin, lentils, soybeans, cucumber, eggplant, zucchini, berries, fruit, chili, bell pepper, figs, avocado, melon, olives.

Weight associated with overeating is less likely. If underweight, eat larger portions.

Cleansing and detox diets. Fruit and juice days.

Flush out poisons. Treatment for drug abuse.

Drink plenty of water.

Cheerfulness is the best promoter of health and is as friendly to the mind as to the body.
Joseph Addison

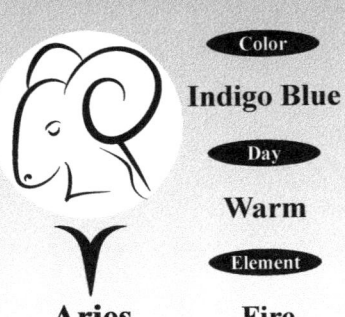

Color

Indigo Blue

Day

Warm

Element

Aries **Fire**

7 Tuesday
Shukkot

O C T O B E R

Harvest Time
Ascending forces! Sap is rising, enhancing plant growth above ground, resulting in the most juicy fruits and vegetables.

detox remove be active

Waning Moon

Success

Realism and material security are important. Persistence comes easy, thoughts and reactions are slower.

Assess financial areas.

Conservative tendencies may make people want to stay away from risk taking.

Leisure

Relax at a picnic/feast. Enjoy culinary pleasures and hobbies.

The earth feels cold to the touch, so take slightly warmer clothes.

Health

Sensitive body parts:

Head and Neck

All measures taken to flush out and detoxify the sensitive body parts are very effective.

Good for surgery, except on the sensitive body parts (see above), hips, kidneys, and bladder.
Scarring is less severe.
Teeth: Removal of tartar and amalgam. Best for fillings, crowns, and dentures!
Avoiding treatment of periodontitis and gums.
Blood-purifying, detoxifying herbal infusions and teas.
Sensitive blood circulation.
Organs of speech, jaws, teeth, tonsils, thyroid gland, neck, and vocal chords get easily affected. Keep neck warm. On cold days ears should be protected. Sensitivity to noise.
High blood pressure: Avoid salty foods.
Massages, lymphatic therapy, and chiropractic treatment to release blockages.

Body Care

Aromas, scents: Geranium, Jasmine, Rose

Prepare home-made ointments and cosmetics.

Apply detoxing facial and body care.

Treatments of bumps and pimples on the skin, and exfoliating procedures.

Removing body hair.

Correction of the nail bed.

Massages that serve to relax, ease tension, and detoxify.

Reflexology massage.

Removal of callused skin.

Treating obstinate athlete's foot, nail fungus, and warts.

Garden/Nature

Plant part:

Root

Sow plants and vegetables that grow below ground.

Everything grows slowly and lasts well.

Dig over to prepare soil.

Trimming/cutting back plants. Weeding. Mulching.

Start a compost heap.

Combat vermin found in the soil.

Spread fertilizer and liquid manure.

Fertilize flowers with poorly formed roots.

Harvested produce is well suited for storage.
Harvesting root vegetables.

Gather herbs (roots) for sinus issues, sore throat, and ear complaints.

Housework

Housework is dealt with much more successfully, efficiently, and effortlessly.

Problem stains are removed readily.

Best for doing laundry! Reduce on laundry detergent, support the environment.

Dry cleaning.

Clean and store seasonal clothing.

Thoroughly clean wooden and parquet floors, metals, china etc.

Cleaning, polishing, and waterproofing shoes.

Combating mold.

Air rooms only briefly.

Painting.

Preserving root vegetables.

Nutrition

Food quality:

Salt

Garlic, carrots, red beets, reddish, rutabaga, sugar beet, celery, potatoes, onions, kohlrabi.

Weight associated with overeating is less likely. If underweight, eat larger portions.

Cleansing and detox diets. Fruit and juice days.

Flush out poisons. Treatment for drug abuse.

Avoid large quantities of salty foods like bacon, ham, salted herring, fatty cheese, and the like.

All who joy would win must share it. Happiness was born a twin.
Lord Byron

Taurus

Color — **Bright Blue**

Day — **Cool**

Element — **Earth**

10:14 PM PDT Thursday
12:14 AM CDT
1:14 AM EDT

8 Wednesday

No meat.

9 Thursday

O C T O B E R

Positive affirmation:
"I trust the wisdom derived from inner silence."

Harvest Time
Ascending forces! Sap is rising, enhancing plant growth above ground, resulting in the most juicy fruits and vegetables.

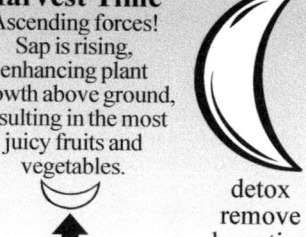

detox
remove
be active

Waning Moon

Success

Open mindedness and curiosity. A changeable and hectic time.

Good time for talking, negotiating, networking, and exchanging ideas as well as for meetings of a nonbinding nature, conferences, and studies.

Leisure

Good time for family gatherings, parties, and short trips.

People enjoy stimulating their minds with reading and studying. Attending theater performances is a preferred enjoyment. Enhance friendships.

Stretching exercises.

Be prepared for sudden changes in weather or climate.

Health

Sensitive body parts:

Shoulders, Arms, Hands, Lungs

All measures taken to flush out and detoxify the sensitive body parts are very effective.

Good for surgery, except on the sensitive body parts (see above), hips, kidneys, and bladder.
Scarring is less severe.

Teeth: Removal of tartar and amalgam. Best for fillings, crowns, and dentures! Avoid having any teeth pulled.

Blood-purifying, detoxifying herbal infusions and teas.

Sensitive glandular system.

Make sure you are dressed warm enough in cool weather.

Exercises for shoulders. Breathing exercises.

Sensitivity to light, bring your sunglasses along.

Massages, lymphatic therapy, and chiropractic treatment to release blockages.

Body Care

Aromas, scents: Lavender, Lemon Balm, Magnolia, Verbena

Prepare home-made ointments and cosmetics.

Apply detoxing facial and body care.

Treatments of bumps and pimples on the skin, and exfoliating procedures.

Removing body hair.

Correction of the nail bed.

Massages that serve to relax, ease tension, and detoxify.

Reflexology massage.

Removal of callused skin.

Treating obstinate athlete's foot, nail fungus, and warts.

Garden/Nature

Plant part:

Flower

Sow plants and vegetablesthat grow below ground.

Trimming and cutting back plants.

Start a compost heap.

Weeding. Pest control.

Fertilize flowers that no longer bloom.

Avoid watering plants.

Changes in weather are more likely.

Gather herbs (roots) for tensions in the shoulder and lung complaints.

Housework

Housework is dealt with much more successfully, efficiently, and effortlessly.

Problem stains are removed readily.

Best for doing laundry! Reduce on laundry detergent, support the environment.

Dry cleaning.

Clean and store seasonal clothing.

Thoroughly clean wooden and parquet floors, metals, china etc.

Cleaning windows and glass.

Cleaning, polishing, and waterproofing shoes.

Combating mold.

Ventilate rooms thoroughly.

Baking bread, cakes, and cookies (add more leavening agent).

Making preserves.

Painting.

Nutrition

Food quality:

Fat

Cauliflower, artichoke, broccoli, sunflower seeds, flax seeds, nuts, rose hip, elder.

Weight associated with overeating is less likely. If underweight, eat larger portions.

Cleansing and detox diets. Fruit and juice days.

Flush out poisons. Treatment for drug abuse.

Pay attention to any particularly tempting foods today: Most likely the "wrong" things taste best.

High cholesterol: eat a low fat diet.

Happiness is like those palaces in fairy tales whose gates are guarded by dragons: we must fight in order to conquer it.
Alexandre Dumas

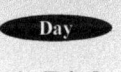 Color

Light Blue

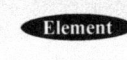 Day

Air/Light

Element

Gemini **Air**

♉ ➤ ♊ 10:13 PM PDT Thursday
12:13 AM CDT
1:13 AM EDT

10 Friday

No meat. Cutting and filing toenails and fingernails.

11 Saturday

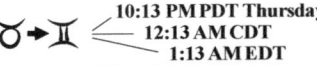 O C T O B E R

Positive affirmation:
"I trust the wisdom derived from inner silence."

Turning Point

Transition of ascending to descending forces. Both forces are at work and neutralize each other.

detox remove be active

Waning Moon

Success

Feelings, sensitivity, and cooperativeness. Many are overly sensitive, so beware of treading on someone's toes.

Be cautious if you are easily influenced.

During negotiations make use of the cognitive ability of your senses.

Leisure

Relax within your close family.

Retreat to your safe haven and enjoy your fantasy while reading or listening to music. The inner world becomes more colorful than the outer.

Romance can be gentle. Deep feelings will prevail.

If you plan outdoor excursions, be prepared for a shower here and there.

Health

Sensitive body parts:
Chest, Lungs, Liver, Stomach, Gall Bladder

All measures taken to flush out and detoxify the sensitive body parts are very effective.

Good for surgical operations except those on the sensitive body parts (see above), hips, kidneys, and bladder. Scarring is less severe.

Teeth: Removal of tartar and amalgam. Best for fillings, crowns, and dentures!

Blood-purifying, detoxifying herbal infusions and teas.

Sensitive nervous system.

Be cautious with alcohol since the liver is very sensitive.

Stomach could play up and cause gas and heartburn.

Rheumatism: Don't air bedding outside, damp will remain in the bedding.

Lymphatic therapy.

Body Care

Aromas, scents:
Lilac, Lilies of the Valley, Lilies, Violets

Prepare home-made ointments and cosmetics.

Apply detoxing facial and body care.

Treatments of bumps and pimples on the skin, and exfoliating procedures.

Removing body hair.

Correction of the nail bed.

Massages that serve to relax, ease tension, and detoxify.

Reflexology massage.

Removal of callused skin.

Treating obstinate athlete's foot, nail fungus, and warts.

No haircuts, hair becomes shaggy and unmanageable. Avoid washing your hair.

Garden/Nature

Plant part:
Leaf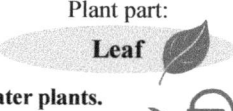

Water plants.

Fertilize flowers.

Sow plants and vegetables that grow below ground, leaf vegetables, and lettuce.

Dig over/plow to prepare soil for planting.

Trimming and cutting back plants. Transplanting. Weeding.

Combating pests above ground.

Start a compost heap.

Mowing lawns.

Gather herbs (roots) for bronchitis, stomach, liver, and gall bladder complaints.

Unfavorable for harvesting, storing, and preserving.

Housework

Housework is dealt with much more successfully, efficiently, and effortlessly.

Problem stains are removed readily.

Best for doing laundry! Reduce on laundry detergent, support the environment.

Dry cleaning.

Thoroughly clean wooden and parquet floors, metals, china etc.

Cleaning, polishing, and waterproofing shoes.

Combating mold.

Ventilate rooms briefly and rapidly.

Avoid painting.

Nutrition

Food quality:
Carbohydrate

Lettuce, spinach, lamb's lettuce, Endive, parsley, leek, cabbage (Brussels sprouts, kale, Chinese cabbage), all leafy herbs, asparagus, mushrooms, cress, Swiss chard, rhubarb.

Weight associated with overeating is less likely. If underweight, eat larger portions.

Moodiness may make you want to eat more than is healthy. If overweight avoid carbohydrates.

Cleansing and detox diets. Fruit and juice days.

Flush out poisons. Treatment for drug abuse.

If you get stomach troubles easily, avoid heavy meals.

Cultivation to the mind is as necessary as food to the body.
Marcus Tullius Cicero

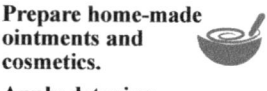 11:38 PM PDT Saturday
1:38 AM CDT
2:38 AM EDT

12 Sunday

13 Monday Columbus Day (US), Thanksgiving Day (CAN)

☽ Half Moon.

Positive affirmation:
"I trust the wisdom derived from inner silence."

Planting Time
Descending forces! Sap is drawn downward, enhancing root formation. Best days for sowing, planting, and transplanting.

detox
remove
be active

Waning Moon

  Color **Green** Day **Wetness** Element

Cancer Water

O C T O B E R

Success

Determination reigns, and risks are taken more often. Master your tasks with more self-confidence and creativity.

Limits appear to be more easily surmountable.

Auspicious day for sales, advertising, and publicity.

Leisure

Zest for life is in the air. People want to have a fun time, enjoy parties, musical events, movies, etc.

Possessive feelings can harm a relationship. Romance can be very passionate.

Outings: even with cloudy skies the air still feels somewhat warm. Drying effect, get plenty to drink.

Danger of sudden storms, not only in the sky.

Health

Sensitive body parts:
Heart, Back, Diaphragm, Circulation, Arteries

All measures taken to flush out and detoxify the sensitive body parts are very effective.

Good for surgery, except on the sensitive body parts (see above), hips, kidneys, and bladder. Scarring is less severe.

Teeth: Removal of tartar and amalgam. Best for fillings, crowns, and dentures!

Blood-purifying, detoxifying herbal infusions and teas.

Sensitive sense organs.

Back and heart problems are more likely to occur.

Avoid overstraining of the heart and circulation with unusual physical activities.

Expect sleepless nights.

Body Care

Aromas, scents:
Hibiscus, Oleander, Rose

Prepare home-made ointments and cosmetics.

Apply detoxing facial and body care.

Treatments of bumps and pimples on the skin, and exfoliating procedures.

Removing body hair.

Correction of the nail bed.

Massages that serve to relax, ease tension, and detoxify.

Reflexology massage.

Removal of callused skin.

Treating obstinate athlete's foot, nail fungus, and warts.

Good days for haircuts, hair becomes stronger. But be aware that if you get a perm, curls will become quite frizzy. Baby's first haircut.

Garden/Nature

Plant part:
Fruit

Sowing plants and vegetables that grow below ground.

Sowing and planting fruit. Also sow and plant vegetables that are highly perishable. Plant trees and bushes. Sow lawns.

Dig over/plow to prepare soil for planting.

Trimming and cutting back plants. Pruning of fruit trees and bushes.

Transplanting.

Not suitable for fertilizing.

Weeding. Pest Control.

Harvested produce should be consumed as soon as possible.

Gather herbs (roots) for heart and circulation complaints.

Start compost heap.

Housework

Housework is dealt with much more successfully, efficiently, and effortlessly.

Problem stains are removed readily.

Best for doing laundry!

Dry cleaning.

Thoroughly clean wooden and parquet floors, metals, china, etc.

Cleaning windows and glass.

Cleaning, polishing, and waterproofing shoes.

Combating mold.

Ventilate rooms sufficiently. Air beds.

Suitable for making cheese.

Preserving and freezing fruit and vegetables.

Baking bread, cakes, and cookies (use more leavening agent).

Avoid painting.

Nutrition

Food quality:
Protein

Beans, peas, corn, tomatoes, pumpkin, lentils, soybeans, cucumber, eggplant, zucchini, berries, fruit, chili, bell pepper, figs, avocado, melon, olives.

Weight associated with overeating is less likely. If underweight, eat larger portions.

Cleansing and detox diets. Fruit and juice days.

Flush out poisons. Treatment for drug abuse.

Heat cannot be separated from fire, or beauty from The Eternal.
Dante Alighieri

Color	**Green**
Day	**Warm**
Element	

Leo — **Fire**

3:48 AM PDT
5:48 AM CDT
6:48 AM EDT
♋ → ♌

11:07 AM PDT
1:07 PM CDT
2:07 PM EDT
♌ → ♍

14 Tuesday
Shemini Atzeret

15 Wednesday
Simchat Torah
No meat.

16 Thursday

O C T O B E R

Planting Time
Descending forces! Sap is drawn downward, enhancing root formation. Best days for sowing, planting, and transplanting.

detox
remove
be active
Waning Moon

Success

Good time for details, organization, routine, concentration, and duty.

Take care of financial and administrative tasks.

Prepare for future success now with realistic and critical assessment.

Leisure

Enjoy a nature walk.

Good time for health regimes. Improve your health with stretching exercises and yoga.

The earth feels cold to the touch, so take slightly warmer clothes.

Health

Sensitive body parts:
Digestive Organs, Nerves, Spleen, Pancreas

All measures taken to flush out and detoxify the sensitive body parts are very effective.

Good for surgery, except on the sensitive body parts (see above), hips, kidneys, and bladder.
Scarring is less severe.

Teeth: Removal of tartar and amalgam. Best for fillings, crowns, and dentures!
Avoiding treatment of periodontitis and gums.

Blood-purifying, detoxifying herbal infusions and teas.

Sensitive blood circulation.

For a sensitive digestive system, a wholesome diet is recommended.

Dress slightly warmer.

High blood pressure: Avoid salty foods.

Massages, lymphatic therapy, and chiropractic treatment to release blockages.

Body Care

Aromas, scents:
Lavender, Spruce Needles, Sage, Meadow Flowers

Prepare home-made ointments and cosmetics.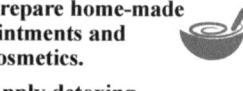

Apply detoxing facial and body care.

Treatments of bumps and pimples on the skin, and exfoliating procedures.

Removing body hair.

Correction of the nail bed.

Massages that serve to relax, ease tension, and detoxify.

Reflexology massage.

Removal of callused skin.

Treating obstinate athlete's foot, nail fungus, and warts.

Best for haircuts because it retains its shape longer.
Perms turn out best.

Garden/Nature

Plant part: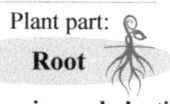
Root

Best for sowing and planting, except lettuce.

Plant trees which are supposed to grow very tall. Plant hedges and bushes that are meant to grow very fast.

Planting and re-potting balcony and indoor plants.

Dig over/plow to prepare soil for planting.

Trimming and cutting back plants. Planting cuttings.

Spread fertilizer and manure. Fertilize flowers with poorly formed roots.

Start a compost heap.

Transplanting. Mulching.

Weeding. Pest control (vermin in the soil).

Avoid harvesting and storing.

Gather herbs (roots) for digestive organs, pancreas, and nervous complaints.

Housework

Housework is dealt with much more successfully, efficiently, and effortlessly.

Problem stains are removed readily.

Best for doing laundry! Reduce on laundry detergent, support the environment.

Dry cleaning.

Thoroughly clean wooden and parquet floors, metals, china etc.

Cleaning, polishing, and waterproofing shoes.

Combating mold.

Air rooms only briefly.

Painting.

Making pickles, preserves, and cheese yields suboptimal results and should be avoided.

Nutrition

Food quality:
Salt

Garlic, carrots, red beets, reddish, rutabaga, sugar beet, celery, potatoes, onions, kohlrabi.

Weight associated with overeating is less likely. If underweight, eat larger portions.

Cleansing and detox diets. Fruit and juice days.

Flush out poisons. Treatment for drug abuse.

Avoid large quantities of salty foods like bacon, ham, salted herring, fatty cheese, and the like. Avoid heavy and greasy foods.

Beauty doesn't need ornaments. Softness can't bear the weight of ornaments.
Munshi Premchand

Color
Yellow

Day
Cool

Element
Earth

Virgo ♍

9:03 PM PDT
11:03 PM CDT
Sunday 12:03 AM EDT
♍ → ♎

17 Friday
No meat. Cutting and filing toenails and fingernails.

18 Saturday

O C T O B E R

Positive affirmation:
"I trust the wisdom derived from inner silence."

Planting Time
Descending forces! Sap is drawn downward, enhancing root formation. Best days for sowing, planting, and transplanting.

detox
remove
be active
Waning Moon

Success

The artistic instinct rules, but so, too, does indecisiveness. The forces swing back and forth until equilibrium is achieved.

It's easy to reach compromises with tactful sensitivity.

A sense of judgment will support legal matters.

Leisure

Pursuit for harmony and cooperativeness supports good times in romance, friendship, and partnership.

Enjoy cultural events. Relax and get pampered with a spa treatment.

Romance can be passionate yet sensitive.

Health

Sensitive body parts:
Hips, Kidneys, Bladder

All measures taken to flush out and detoxify the sensitive body parts are very effective.

Good for surgery, except on the sensitive body parts (see above).
Scarring is less severe.

Teeth: Removal of tartar and amalgam. Best for fillings, crowns, and dentures! Avoid treatment of periodontitis and gums, avoid pulling teeth.

Blood-purifying, detoxifying herbal infusions and teas.

Sensitive glandular system.

Take special care to keep the area of the bladder and kidneys warm.

Apply special exercises for the hip region.

Sensitivity to light, so bring your sunglasses along.

Body Care

Aromas, scents:
Roses, Violets, Daffodils

Prepare home-made ointments and cosmetics.

Apply detoxing facial and body care.

Treatments of bumps and pimples on the skin, and exfoliating procedures.

Removing body hair.

Correction of the nail bed.

Massages that serve to relax, ease tension, and detoxify.

Reflexology massage.

Removal of callused skin.

Treating obstinate athlete's foot, nail fungus, and warts.

Garden/Nature

Plant part:
Flower

Sow plants and vegetables that grow below ground.

Dig over/plow to prepare soil for planting.

Trimming and cutting back plants.

Start a compost heap.

Weeding. Pest control.

Fertilize flowers that no longer bloom.

Transplanting.

Avoid watering plants.

Harvested produce should be consumed as soon as possible.

Gather herbs (roots) for kidneys, gall bladder and hip complaints.

Day off on 10/19.

Housework

Housework is dealt with much more successfully, efficiently, and effortlessly.

Problem stains are removed readily.

Best for doing laundry! Reduce on laundry detergent, support the environment.

Dry cleaning.

Clean and store seasonal clothing.

Thoroughly clean wooden and parquet floors, metals, china etc.

Cleaning windows and glass.

Cleaning, polishing, and waterproofing shoes.

Combating mold.

Ventilate rooms thoroughly.

Baking bread, cakes, and cookies (add more leavening agent).

Making preserves.

Painting.

Nutrition

Food quality:
Fat

Cauliflower, artichoke, broccoli, sunflower seeds, flax seeds, nuts, rose hip, elder.

Weight associated with overeating is less likely. If underweight, eat larger portions.

Cleansing and detox diets. Fruit and juice days.

Flush out poisons. Treatment for drug abuse.

Pay attention to any particularly tempting foods today: Most likely the "wrong" things taste best.

High cholesterol: eat a low fat diet.

Change alone is eternal, perpetual, immortal.
Arthur Schopenhauer

Color
Orange

Day
Air/Light

Element

Libra   **Air**

19 Sunday

20 Monday

O C T O B E R

Planting Time
Descending forces! Sap is drawn downward, enhancing root formation. Best days for sowing, planting, and transplanting.

detox
remove
be active
Waning Moon

Success

Critical and superstitious behavior emerges, especially pertaining to money.

A penetrating power will strengthen your capacity to act.

An increased perception opens our interest for the essentials and helps to discover hidden potentials.

● *New Moon: Confirm your resolutions. Finalize new decisions. Drop bad habits.*

Leisure

Relax within your close family, with meditation, and relaxation exercises.

A longing to feel safe will be nurtured if you focus on habits and rituals. An increased sensitivity will help to enjoy every moment.

Romance can be very passionate.

If you plan outdoor excursions, be prepared for a shower here and there.

Health

Sensitive body parts:

Sex organs, Ureter

All measures taken to flush out and detoxify the sensitive body parts are very effective.

Scarring is less severe.

Teeth: Removal of tartar and amalgam. Best for fillings, crowns, and dentures!

Blood-purifying, detoxifying herbal infusions and teas.

Sensitive nervous system.

Female disorders: As a preventative measure apply hip baths using yarrow.

Pregnancy: Avoid any exertion, miscarriages are more likely.

Keep region of the pelvis, kidneys, and feet warm to prevent infection of the bladder and kidneys.

Lymphatic therapy.

● *New Moon: Avoid any surgery if possible.*

Body Care

Aromas, scents:
Anemone, Cornflower
Oregano, Thuja

Prepare home-made ointments and cosmetics.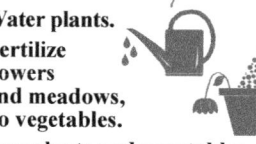

Apply detoxing facial and body care.

Treatments of bumps and pimples on the skin, and exfoliating procedures.

Removing body hair.

Correction of the nail bed.

Massages that serve to relax, ease tension, and detoxify.

Reflexology massage.

Removal of callused skin.

Treating obstinate athlete's foot, nail fungus, and warts.

Garden/Nature

Plant part:

Leaf

Water plants.

Fertilize flowers and meadows, no vegetables.

Sow plants and vegetables that grow below ground, leaf vegetables, and lettuce.

Sowing, planting, harvesting, and drying every kind of medicinal herbs.

Dig over/plow to prepare soil for planting.

Trimming and cutting back plants. Transplanting. Weeding. Pest control. Start a compost heap.

Mowing lawns.

Harvested produce should be consumed as soon as possible.

Avoid cutting down trees, danger of bark beetles.

● *New Moon: Change of weather is likely. Care for sickly plants.*

Housework

Housework is dealt with much more successfully, efficiently, and effortlessly.

Problem stains are removed readily.

Best for doing laundry! Reduce on laundry detergent, support the environment.

Dry cleaning.

Thoroughly clean wooden and parquet floors, metals, china etc.

Cleaning, polishing, and waterproofing shoes.

Combating mold.

Ventilate rooms briefly and rapidly.

Avoid painting.

Nutrition

Food quality:

Carbohydrate

Lettuce, spinach, lamb's lettuce, Endive, parsley, leek, cabbage (Brussels sprouts, kale, Chinese cabbage), all leafy herbs, asparagus, mushrooms, cress, Swiss chard, rhubarb.

Weight associated with overeating is less likely. If underweight, eat larger portions.

Cleansing and detox diets. Fruit and juice days.

Flush out poisons. Treatment for drug abuse.

● *New Moon: A day of fasting.*

A compliment is something like a kiss through a veil.
Victor Hugo

Color

Red

Day

Wetness

Element

Scorpio **Water**

Ω ➜ ♏
8:43 AM PDT
10:43 AM CDT
11:43 AM EDT

21 Tuesday
Diwali

● New Moon 5:26 PM PDT, 7:26 PM CDT, 8:26 PM EDT

O C T O B E R

Positive affirmation:
"I trust that I can be there for others."

Planting Time
Descending forces! Sap is drawn downward, enhancing root formation. Best days for sowing, planting, and transplanting.

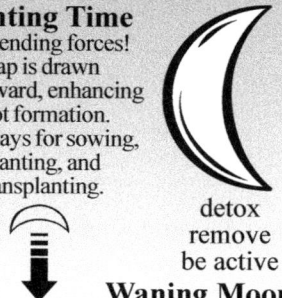

detox
remove
be active

Waning Moon

Success

Critical and superstitious behavior emerges, especially pertaining to money.

A penetrating power will strengthen your capacity to act.

An increased perception opens our interest for the essentials and helps to discover hidden potentials.

Leisure

Relax within your close family, with meditation, and relaxation exercises.

A longing to feel safe will be nurtured if you focus on habits and rituals. An increased sensitivity will help to enjoy every moment.

Romance can be very passionate.

If you plan outdoor excursions, be prepared for a shower here and there.

Health

Sensitive body parts:

Sex organs, Ureter

All measures taken to supply nutrient materials and strengthen the sensitive body parts are very effective.

Healing ointments are easily absorbed. Applying herbal ointments to the shoulders for rheumatic gout and alike.

Sensitive nervous system.

Female disorders: As a preventative measure apply hip baths using yarrow.

Pregnancy: Avoid any exertion, miscarriages are more likely.

Keep region of the pelvis, kidneys, and feet warm to prevent infection of the bladder and kidneys.

Lymphatic therapy.

Body Care

Aromas, scents:
Anemone, Cornflower
Oregano, Thuja

Treatments with firming and moisturizing creams are more effective.

Massages that serve to regenerate, and strengthen, perhaps aided with beneficial massage oils.

Correcting and cutting ingrown nails.

Hair dyes applied now, will look more vibrant.

Garden/Nature

Plant part:

Leaf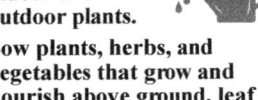

Watering all indoor and outdoor plants.

Sow plants, herbs, and vegetables that grow and flourish above ground, leaf vegetables (no lettuce).

Sowing, planting, harvesting, and drying every kind of medicinal herbs.

Transplanting.

Trimming and cutting back plants.

Combating slugs and snails. Mowing lawns.

Start a compost heap.

Avoid pruning fruit trees and bushes. Avoid cutting down any trees.

Harvested produce should be consumed as soon as possible.

Housework

Light housework only.

Ventilate rooms briefly and rapidly. Don't air mattresses.

Any dirt and spots are easily removed in the laundry.

Avoid painting, as paint will take very long to dry.

Nutrition

Food quality:

Carbohydrate

Lettuce, spinach, lamb's lettuce, Endive, parsley, leek, cabbage (Brussels sprouts, kale, Chinese cabbage), all leafy herbs, asparagus, mushrooms, cress, Swiss chard, rhubarb.

Weight gain: avoid indulging in rich foods. If overweight, eat smaller portions and avoid carbohydrates.

Supply nutrient materials to strengthen the body. Focus on foods that contain essential minerals and vitamins. Stimulants and vitamins are more effective.

Positive affirmation:
"I trust that I can be there for others."

Planting Time
Descending forces!
Sap is drawn downward, enhancing root formation.
Best days for sowing, planting, and transplanting.

gather strength rest, recover buildup
Waxing Moon

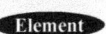

22 Wednesday

No meat.

9:20 PM PDT
11:20 PM CDT
Friday 12:20 PM EDT

23 Thursday

O C T O B E R

Forgive your enemies, but never forget their names.
John F. Kennedy

Color
Red

Day

Wetness

Element

Water

Scorpio

Success

Inquisitiveness and exuberant inspiration lead to new horizons. Insight and love for truth reign.

Bringing together is more important than splitting asunder.

Expansive forces will assist in legal matters, discussions, and debates.

Leisure

Expansion feels great, and travel, short trips, and outings are most welcome. A competitive spirit excites any sports event.

Talk things out when necessary.

Romance can be very passionate.

Good days for outings; even with cloudy skies the air still feels somewhat warm. Drying effect, get plenty to drink.

Health

Sensitive body parts:

Thighs and Veins

All measures taken to supply nutrient materials and strengthen the sensitive body parts are very effective.

Healing ointments are easily absorbed.

Sensitive sense organs.

Pains often arise in the sciatic nerve, veins, the small of the back, and thighs.

Avoid overstraining the body with unusual physical activities.

Body Care

Aromas, scents: Calendula (Marigold), Geranium, Rosemary

Treatments with firming and moisturizing creams are more effective.

Massages that serve to regenerate, and strengthen, perhaps aided with beneficial massage oils.

Correcting and cutting ingrown nails.

Hair dyes applied now, will look more vibrant.

Garden/Nature

Plant part:

Fruit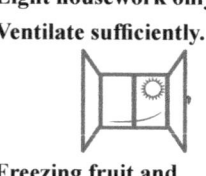

Sow plants and vegetables that grow and flourish above ground.

Sowing and planting fruit and vegetables that grow tall, and tomatoes, but no lettuce.

Transplanting.

Grafting onto fruit trees.

Cultivating grains, particularly corn.

Gather herbs for vein diseases.

Housework

Light housework only.

Ventilate sufficiently.

Freezing fruit and vegetables.

Baking bread, cakes, and cookies. Dough rises faster. (Except on New Moon)

Suitable for making cheese.

Making preserves.

Nutrition

Food quality:

Protein

Beans, peas, corn, tomatoes, pumpkin, lentils, soybeans, cucumber, eggplant, zucchini, berries, fruit, chili, bell pepper, figs, avocado, melon, olives.

Weight gain: avoid indulging in rich foods. If overweight, eat smaller portions.

Supply nutrient materials to strengthen the body. Focus on foods that contain essential minerals and vitamins.

Stimulants and vitamins are more effective.

Positive affirmation:
"I trust that I can be there for others."

Turning Point

Transition of descending to ascending forces. Both forces are at work and neutralize each other.

gather strength
rest, recover
buildup
Waxing Moon

24 Friday
No meat. Cutting and filing toenails and fingernails.

25 Saturday

Color
Orange/Yellow

Day
Warm

Element
Fire

Sagittarius

O C T O B E R

Success

Career and business are in the foreground now and thinking becomes clear and serious, but somewhat inflexible.

Perseverance and reasoning assist in financial matters, planning, and contracts.

The values of tradition, authority, and discipline impact our endeavors.

Leisure

Money is not likely to be wasted in a shopping spree.

Many are drawn to enjoy cultural events.

The earth feels cold to the touch, so take slightly warmer clothes.

Health

Sensitive body parts:

Knees, Joints, Bones, Skin

All measures taken to supply nutrient materials and strengthen the sensitive body parts are very effective.

Healing ointments are easily absorbed.

Sensitive blood circulation.

Avoid overstraining bones and knees, and apply gentle stretching exercises only.

Problems with meniscus: Don't overstrain.

Dress slightly warmer.

High blood pressure: Avoid salty foods.

Massages, lymphatic therapy, and chiropractic treatment to release blockages.

Body Care

Aromas, scents:

Cedar, Juniper

Treatments with firming and moisturizing creams are more effective.

Massages that serve to regenerate, and strengthen, perhaps aided with beneficial massage oils.

Correcting and cutting ingrown nails.

Every kind of skin care is beneficial.

Cutting and filing toenails and fingernails will make the nails grow stronger over time.

Hair dyes applied now, will look more vibrant.

Garden/Nature

Plant part:

Root

Sow plants, herbs, and vegetables that grow and flourish above ground.

Transplanting.

Harvest produce is suitable for storage. Harvest root vegetables.

Gather herbs for bone, joint, and skin diseases.

Housework

Light housework only.

Air rooms only briefly.

Preserving root vegetables.

Avoid dry cleaning, as the fabric may develop unwanted glossy blotches.

Nutrition

Food quality:

Salt

Garlic, carrots, red beets, reddish, rutabaga, sugar beet, celery, potatoes, onions, kohlrabi.

Weight gain: avoid indulging in rich foods. If overweight, eat smaller portions.

Supply nutrient materials to strengthen the body. Focus on foods that contain essential minerals and vitamins.

Stimulants and vitamins are more effective.

Avoid large quantities of salty foods like bacon, ham, salted herring, fatty cheese, and the like. Avoid heavy and greasy foods.

Positive affirmation:
"I trust that I can be there for others."

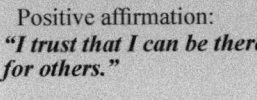

Harvest Time
Ascending forces! Sap is rising, enhancing plant growth above ground, resulting in the most juicy fruits and vegetables.

gather strength rest, recover buildup
Waxing Moon

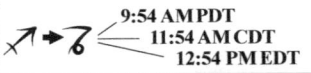

9:54 AM PDT
11:54 AM CDT
12:54 PM EDT

26 Sunday

27 Monday

8:56 PM PDT
10:56 PM CDT
11:56 PM EDT

28 Tuesday

O C T O B E R

The secret of improved plant breeding, apart from scientific knowledge, is love.
Luther Burbank

 Color
Yellow

 Day

Cool

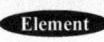 Element

Earth

Capricorn

Success

Inspiration, optimism, and impatience. Rational thinking, creativity and imagination spark new ideas and inspire planning for the future.

Shying away from routine tasks people will feel more drawn to anything new.

Instead of gridlocked structures choose new possibilities.

Leisure

Inspiration and optimism will boost friendship, social gatherings, and parties.

Express your creativity and imagination. Dwell in dreams and utopian ideas. It is easier now to perceive intuitive thoughts.

Health

Sensitive body parts:

Lower Legs, Veins

All measures taken to supply nutrient materials and strengthen the sensitive body parts are very effective.

Healing ointments are easily absorbed.

Sensitive glandular system.

Avoid inflammation of the veins. Apply ointments to lower legs, and rest legs in a raised position.

Varicose veins: Avoid long periods of standing.

While exercising go easy on the ankles.

Sensitivity to light, so bring your sunglasses along.

Body Care

Aromas, scents:
Cyclamen, Peach, Wild Roses

Treatments with firming and moisturizing creams are more effective.

Massages that serve to regenerate, and strengthen, perhaps aided with beneficial massage oils.

Correcting and cutting ingrown nails.

Hair dyes applied now, will look more vibrant.

Garden/Nature

Plant part:

 **Flower**

Avoid watering plants.

Harvested produce is well suitable for storage.

Gather herbs for vein diseases.

Housework

Light housework only.

Ventilate rooms thoroughly.

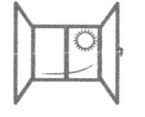

Baking cakes and cookies. Dough rises faster. (Except on New Moon)

Making preserves.

Nutrition

Food quality:

Fat

Cauliflower, artichoke, broccoli, sunflower seeds, flax seeds, nuts, rose hip, elder.

Weight gain: avoid indulging in rich foods. If overweight, eat smaller portions.

Supply nutrient materials to strengthen the body. Focus on foods that contain essential minerals and vitamins.

Stimulants and vitamins are more effective.

Pay attention to any particularly tempting foods today: Most likely the "wrong" things taste best.

High cholesterol: eat a low fat diet.

Positive affirmation:
"I trust that I can be there for others."

Harvest Time
Ascending forces! Sap is rising, enhancing plant growth above ground, resulting in the most juicy fruits and vegetables.

gather strength rest, recover buildup
Waxing Moon

29 Wednesday

☽ **Half Moon.** No meat.

30 Thursday

Your body hears everything your mind says.
Naomi Judd

Color
Bright/ Dark Blue

Day
Air/Light

Element
Air

Aquarius

O C T O B E R

Success

Sensibility, intuition, and helpfulness.

Where possible, retreating is more favorable than dealing with business matters.

Dissolve restrictions, be patient and wait. Be aware that people can be more easily influenced.

Leisure

Your helpfulness will boost friendships.

Enjoy dancing or swimming, or watch a movie that will inspire your fantasies and imagination.

Retreat, relax, and recover.

Romance can be gentle and coziness will prevail.

If you plan outdoor excursions, be prepared for a shower here and there.

Health

Sensitive body parts:

Feet and Toes

All measures taken to supply nutrient materials and strengthen the sensitive body parts are very effective.

Healing ointments are easily absorbed.

Sensitive nervous system.

Drugs have a much stronger effect on your body. Monitor closely what you put into your body.

Lymphatic therapy.

Sluggishness or fatigue may occur in the transition into the next Zodiac sign of Aries.

Body Care

Aromas, scents: Magnolia, Amaryllis, Clary Sage

Treatments with firming and moisturizing creams are more effective.

Massages that serve to regenerate, and strengthen, perhaps aided with beneficial massage oils. Reflexology massage. Carry out with special care, people are more sensitive.

Correcting and cutting ingrown nails.

Foot bath.

No haircuts, hair becomes shaggy and unmanageable. Avoid washing your hair. Dandruff could develop.

Garden/Nature

Plant part:

Leaf

Watering all indoor and outdoor plants.

Sow plants, herbs, and vegetables that grow and flourish above ground, and leaf vegetables.

Transplanting.

Mowing lawns.

Avoid pruning fruit trees and bushes.

Harvested produce should be consumed as soon as possible.

Gather herbs for foot complaints.

Housework

Light housework only.

Ventilate rooms briefly and rapidly. Don't air mattresses.

Any dirt and spots are easily removed in the laundry.

Avoid painting, as paint will take very long to dry.

Preserving and storing should be avoided.

Nutrition

Food quality:

Carbohydrate

Lettuce, spinach, lamb's lettuce, Endive, parsley, leek, cabbage (Brussels sprouts, kale, Chinese cabbage), all leafy herbs, asparagus, mushrooms, cress, Swiss chard, rhubarb.

Weight gain: avoid indulging in rich foods. If overweight, eat smaller portions and avoid carbohydrates.

Supply nutrient materials to strengthen the body. Focus on foods that contain essential minerals and vitamins.

Caffeine, alcohol, drugs, certain foods, and stimulants have a much stronger effect.

Positive affirmation:
"I trust that I can be there for others."

Harvest Time
Ascending forces! Sap is rising, enhancing plant growth above ground, resulting in the most juicy fruits and vegetables.

gather strength rest, recover buildup
Waxing Moon

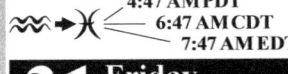

≈≈→⤳ 4:47 AM PDT
6:47 AM CDT
7:47 AM EDT

31 Friday
Halloween

No meat. Cutting and filing toenails and fingernails.

1 Saturday
All Saint's Day

OCTOBER/NOVEMBER

Man needs difficulties; they are necessary for health.
Carl Jung

 Color
Blueish White
 Day
Wetness
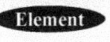 Element

Water

Pisces

Success

Things get going and the way straight ahead seems the best.

People feel energetic, courageous, assertive, and at times anxious.

Good time for meetings and sales talks but impatience and selfishness do not favor teamwork.

Leisure

An enterprising spirit and spontaneity move people to enjoy outings, sports, competitions, cultural events, and travels.

Romance can be very passionate.

Good days for outings, even with cloudy skies the air still feels somewhat warm. Drying effect, get plenty to drink.

Health

Sensitive body parts:

Head, Brain, Eyes

All measures taken to supply nutrient materials and strengthen the sensitive body parts are very effective.

Healing ointments are easily absorbed.

Sensitive sense organs.

If you suffer from migraines drink plenty of water, and avoid coffee, chocolate, and sugar.

Body Care

Aromas, scents: Cloves, Peppermint, Thyme

Treatments with firming and moisturizing creams are more effective.

Massages that serve to regenerate, and strengthen, perhaps aided with beneficial massage oils.

Correcting and cutting ingrown nails.

Eye compresses for strained eyes.

Any kind of hair care. Hair dyes applied now, will look more vibrant.

Garden/Nature

Plant part:

Fruit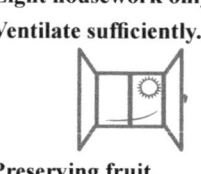

Sow plants and vegetables that grow and flourish above ground, especially fruit and tomatoes.

Sowing and planting anything that is supposed to grow fast and for immediate use.

Grafting onto fruit trees.

Cultivating grains.

Transplanting.

Harvesting and storing grains, vegetables, potatoes, fruit, and tomatoes.

Gather herbs for eye complaints and headaches.

Day off on 11/3.

Housework

Light housework only.
Ventilate sufficiently.

Preserving fruit.

Freezing fruit and vegetables.

Baking bread, cakes, and cookies. Dough rises faster. (Except on New Moon)

Suitable for making cheese.

Nutrition

Food quality:

Protein

Beans, peas, corn, tomatoes, pumpkin, lentils, soybeans, cucumber, eggplant, zucchini, berries, fruit, chili, bell pepper, figs, avocado, melon, olives.

Weight gain: avoid indulging in rich foods. If overweight, eat smaller portions.

Supply nutrient materials to strengthen the body. Focus on foods that contain essential minerals and vitamins.

Stimulants and vitamins are more effective.

Drink plenty of water.

Positive affirmation:
"I trust that I can be there for others."

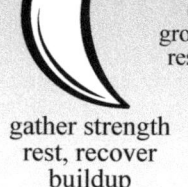

Harvest Time
Ascending forces! Sap is rising, enhancing plant growth above ground, resulting in the most juicy fruits and vegetables.

gather strength rest, recover buildup
Waxing Moon

♓ → ♈
7:41 AM PST
9:41 AM CST
10:41 AM EST

2 **Sunday** All Soul's Day, Daylight Saving Time ends

3 **Monday**

N O V E M B E R

A well-developed sense of humor is the pole that adds balance to your steps as you walk the tightrope of life.
William Arthur Ward

Color
Indigo Blue

Day
Warm

Element
Fire

Aries ♈

Success

Realism and material security are important. Persistence comes easy, thoughts and reactions are slower.

Assess financial areas.

Conservative tendencies may make people want to stay away from risk taking.

Leisure

Relax at a picnic/feast. Enjoy culinary pleasures and hobbies.

The earth feels cold to the touch, so take slightly warmer clothes.

Health

Sensitive body parts:

Head and Neck

All measures taken to supply nutrient materials and strengthen the sensitive body parts are very effective.

Healing ointments are easily absorbed.

Sensitive blood circulation.

Organs of speech, jaws, teeth, tonsils, thyroid gland, neck, and vocal chords get easily affected. Keep neck warm. On cold days ears should be protected. Sensitivity to noise.

High blood pressure: Avoid salty foods.

Massages, lymphatic therapy, and chiropractic treatment to release blockages.

Body Care

Aromas, scents: Geranium, Jasmine, Rose

Treatments with firming and moisturizing creams are more effective.

Massages that serve to regenerate, and strengthen, perhaps aided with beneficial massage oils.

Correcting and cutting ingrown nails.

Hair dyes applied now, will look more vibrant.

Garden/Nature

Plant part:

Root

Sow plants, herbs, and vegetables that grow and flourish above ground.

Sowing and planting trees, bushes, hedges, and root vegetables. Everything grows slowly and lasts well.

Transplanting.

Harvesting and storing root vegetables. Harvested produce is well suited for storage.

Gather herbs for sinus issues, sore throat, and ear complaints.

Housework

Light housework only.

Air rooms only briefly.

Preserving root vegetables.

Nutrition

Food quality:

Salt

Garlic, carrots, red beets, reddish, rutabaga, sugar beet, celery, potatoes, onions, kohlrabi.

Weight gain: avoid indulging in rich foods. If overweight, eat smaller portions.

Supply nutrient materials to strengthen the body. Focus on foods that contain essential minerals and vitamins.

Stimulants and vitamins are more effective.

Avoid large quantities of salty foods like bacon, ham, salted herring, fatty cheese, and the like.

Positive affirmation:
"I trust that I can be there for others."

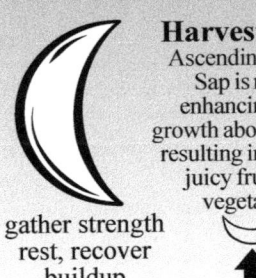

Harvest Time
Ascending forces!
Sap is rising, enhancing plant growth above ground, resulting in the most juicy fruits and vegetables.

gather strength
rest, recover
buildup
Waxing Moon

8:17 AM PST
♓ → ♈ 10:17 AM CST
11:17 AM EST

4 Tuesday

N O V E M B E R

Happiness is itself a kind of gratitude.
Joseph Wood Krutch

Color
Bright Blue

Day
Cool

Element
Earth

Taurus

Success

Realism and material security are important. Persistence comes easy, thoughts and reactions are slower.

Assess financial areas.

Conservative tendencies may make people want to stay away from risk taking.

Leisure

Relax at a picnic/feast. Enjoy culinary pleasures and hobbies.

The earth feels cold to the touch, so take slightly warmer clothes.

Health

Sensitive body parts:

Head and Neck

All measures taken to flush out and detoxify the sensitive body parts are very effective. Scarring is less severe. Teeth: Removal of tartar and amalgam. Best for fillings, crowns, and dentures! Avoiding treatment of periodontitis and gums. Blood-purifying, detoxifying herbal infusions and teas. Sensitive blood circulation. Organs of speech, jaws, teeth, tonsils, thyroid gland, neck, and vocal chords get easily affected. Keep neck warm. On cold days ears should be protected. Sensitivity to noise. High blood pressure: Avoid salty foods. Massages, lymphatic therapy, and chiropractic treatment to release blockages.

○ *Full Moon: Avoid any surgery and vaccination if possible.*

Body Care

Aromas, scents: Geranium, Jasmine, Rose

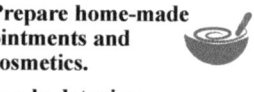

Prepare home-made ointments and cosmetics.

Apply detoxing facial and body care.

Treatments of bumps and pimples on the skin, and exfoliating procedures.

Removing body hair.

Correction of the nail bed.

Massages that serve to relax, ease tension, and detoxify.

Reflexology massage.

Removal of callused skin.

Treating obstinate athlete's foot, nail fungus, and warts.

Garden/Nature

Plant part:

Root

Sow plants and vegetables that grow below ground.

Everything grows slowly and lasts well.

Dig over to prepare soil.

Trimming/cutting back plants. Weeding. Mulching.

Start a compost heap.

Combat vermin found in the soil.

Spread fertilizer and liquid manure.

Fertilize flowers with poorly formed roots.

Harvested produce is well suited for storage. Harvesting root vegetables.

Gather herbs (roots) for sinus issues, sore throat, and ear complaints.

○ *Full Moon: Weather and climate changes. Herbs are most powerful.*

Housework

Housework is dealt with much more successfully, efficiently, and effortlessly.

Problem stains are removed readily.

Dry cleaning.

Clean and store seasonal clothing.

Thoroughly clean wooden and parquet floors, metals, china etc.

Cleaning, polishing, and waterproofing shoes.

Combating mold.

Air rooms only briefly.

○ *Full Moon: Avoid doing laundry, cleaning windows, making preserves, painting.*

Nutrition

Food quality:

Salt

Garlic, carrots, red beets, reddish, rutabaga, sugar beet, celery, potatoes, onions, kohlrabi.

Weight associated with overeating is less likely. If underweight, eat larger portions.

Cleansing and detox diets. Fruit and juice days.

Flush out poisons. Treatment for drug abuse.

Avoid large quantities of salty foods like bacon, ham, salted herring, fatty cheese, and the like.

○ *Full Moon: A day of fasting.*

Well done is better than well said.
Benjamin Franklin

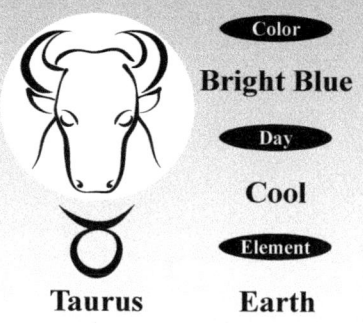

Color
Bright Blue

Day
Cool

Element

Taurus   **Earth**

5 Wednesday

○ **Full Moon** 5:20 AM PST, 7:20 AM CST, 8:20 AM EST
No meat.

N O V E M B E R

Positive affirmation:
"I trust that I can be there for others."

Harvest Time
Ascending forces! Sap is rising, enhancing plant growth above ground, resulting in the most juicy fruits and vegetables.

detox
remove
be active
Waning Moon

Success

Open mindedness and curiosity. A changeable and hectic time.

Good time for talking, negotiating, networking, and exchanging ideas as well as for meetings of a nonbinding nature, conferences, and studies.

Leisure

Good time for family gatherings, parties, and short trips.

People enjoy stimulating their minds with reading and studying. Attending theater performances is a preferred enjoyment. Enhance friendships.

Stretching exercises.

Be prepared for sudden changes in weather or climate.

Health

Sensitive body parts:
Shoulders, Arms, Hands, Lungs

All measures taken to flush out and detoxify the sensitive body parts are very effective.

Good for surgery, except on the sensitive body parts (see above), sex organs, and ureter.
Scarring is less severe.

Teeth: Removal of tartar and amalgam. Best for fillings, crowns, and dentures! Avoid having any teeth pulled.

Blood-purifying, detoxifying herbal infusions and teas.

Sensitive glandular system.

Make sure you are dressed warm enough in cool weather.

Exercises for shoulders. Breathing exercises.

Sensitivity to light, bring your sunglasses along.

Massages, lymphatic therapy, and chiropractic treatment to release blockages.

Body Care

Aromas, scents:
Lavender, Lemon Balm, Magnolia, Verbena

Prepare home-made ointments and cosmetics.

Apply detoxing facial and body care.

Treatments of bumps and pimples on the skin, and exfoliating procedures.

Removing body hair.

Correction of the nail bed.

Massages that serve to relax, ease tension, and detoxify.

Reflexology massage.

Removal of callused skin.

Treating obstinate athlete's foot, nail fungus, and warts.

Garden/Nature

Plant part:
Flower

Sow plants and vegetablesthat grow below ground.

Trimming and cutting back plants.

Start a compost heap.

Weeding. Pest control.

Fertilize flowers that no longer bloom.

Avoid watering plants.

Changes in weather are more likely.

Gather herbs (roots) for tensions in the shoulder and lung complaints.

Housework

Housework is dealt with much more successfully, efficiently, and effortlessly.

Problem stains are removed readily.

Best for doing laundry! Reduce on laundry detergent, support the environment.

Dry cleaning.

Clean and store seasonal clothing.

Thoroughly clean wooden and parquet floors, metals, china etc.

Cleaning windows and glass.

Cleaning, polishing, and waterproofing shoes.

Combating mold.

Ventilate rooms thoroughly.

Baking bread, cakes, and cookies (add more leavening agent).

Making preserves.

Painting.

Nutrition

Food quality:
Fat

Cauliflower, artichoke, broccoli, sunflower seeds, flax seeds, nuts, rose hip, elder.

Weight associated with overeating is less likely. If underweight, eat larger portions.

Cleansing and detox diets. Fruit and juice days.

Flush out poisons. Treatment for drug abuse.

Pay attention to any particularly tempting foods today: Most likely the "wrong" things taste best.

High cholesterol: eat a low fat diet.

A crust eaten in peace is better than a banquet partaken in anxiety.
Aesop

Gemini — **Air**

Color	**Light Blue**
Day	**Air/Light**
Element	

☿ → ♊ 7:22 AM PST
9:22 AM CST
10:22 AM EST

6 Thursday

7 Friday

No meat. Cutting and filing toenails and fingernails.

N O V E M B E R

Positive affirmation:
"I trust that I can be there for others."

Turning Point

Transition of ascending to descending forces. Both forces are at work and neutralize each other.

detox
remove
be active

Waning Moon

Success

Feelings, sensitivity, and cooperativeness. Many are overly sensitive, so beware of treading on someone's toes.

Be cautious if you are easily influenced.

During negotiations make use of the cognitive ability of your senses.

Leisure

Relax within your close family.

Retreat to your safe haven and enjoy your fantasy while reading or listening to music. The inner world becomes more colorful than the outer.

Romance can be gentle. Deep feelings will prevail.

If you plan outdoor excursions, be prepared for a shower here and there.

Health

Sensitive body parts:
Chest, Lungs, Liver, Stomach, Gall Bladder

All measures taken to flush out and detoxify the sensitive body parts are very effective.

Good for surgical operations except those on the sensitive body parts (see above), sex organs, and ureter. Scarring is less severe.

Teeth: Removal of tartar and amalgam. Best for fillings, crowns, and dentures!

Blood-purifying, detoxifying herbal infusions and teas.

Sensitive nervous system.

Be cautious with alcohol since the liver is very sensitive.

Stomach could play up and cause gas and heartburn.

Rheumatism: Don't air bedding outside, damp will remain in the bedding.

Lymphatic therapy.

Body Care

Aromas, scents:
Lilac, Lilies of the Valley, Lilies, Violets

Prepare home-made ointments and cosmetics.

Apply detoxing facial and body care.

Treatments of bumps and pimples on the skin, and exfoliating procedures.

Removing body hair.

Correction of the nail bed.

Massages that serve to relax, ease tension, and detoxify.

Reflexology massage.

Removal of callused skin.

Treating obstinate athlete's foot, nail fungus, and warts.

No haircuts, hair becomes shaggy and unmanageable. Avoid washing your hair.

Garden/Nature

Plant part:
Leaf

Water plants.

Fertilize flowers.

Sow plants and vegetables that grow below ground, leaf vegetables, and lettuce.

Dig over/plow to prepare soil for planting.

Trimming and cutting back plants. Transplanting. Weeding.

Combating pests above ground.

Start a compost heap.

Mowing lawns.

Gather herbs (roots) for bronchitis, stomach, liver, and gall bladder complaints.

Unfavorable for harvesting, storing, and preserving.

Housework

Housework is dealt with much more successfully, efficiently, and effortlessly.

Problem stains are removed readily.

Best for doing laundry! Reduce on laundry detergent, support the environment.

Dry cleaning.

Thoroughly clean wooden and parquet floors, metals, china etc.

Cleaning, polishing, and waterproofing shoes.

Combating mold.

Ventilate rooms briefly and rapidly.

Avoid painting.

Nutrition

Food quality:
Carbohydrate

Lettuce, spinach, lamb's lettuce, Endive, parsley, leek, cabbage (Brussels sprouts, kale, Chinese cabbage), all leafy herbs, asparagus, mushrooms, cress, Swiss chard, rhubarb.

Weight associated with overeating is less likely. If underweight, eat larger portions.

Moodiness may make you want to eat more than is healthy. If overweight avoid carbohydrates.

Cleansing and detox diets. Fruit and juice days.

Flush out poisons. Treatment for drug abuse.

If you get stomach troubles easily, avoid heavy meals.

Flowers are a proud assertion that a ray of beauty out values all the utilities of the world.
Ralph Waldo Emerson

♋ Cancer

Color	**Green**
Day	**Wetness**
Element	**Water**

Ⅱ → ♋ 7:07 AM PST
9:07 AM CST
10:07 AM EST

8 Saturday

9 Sunday

N O V E M B E R

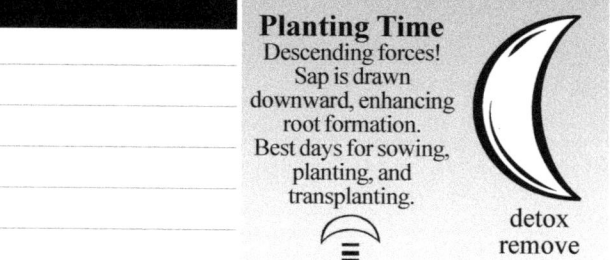

Planting Time
Descending forces! Sap is drawn downward, enhancing root formation. Best days for sowing, planting, and transplanting.

detox
remove
be active
Waning Moon

Success

Determination reigns, and risks are taken more often. Master your tasks with more self-confidence and creativity.

Limits appear to be more easily surmountable.

Auspicious day for sales, advertising, and publicity.

Leisure

Zest for life is in the air. People want to have a fun time, enjoy parties, musical events, movies, etc.

Possessive feelings can harm a relationship. Romance can be very passionate.

Outings: even with cloudy skies the air still feels somewhat warm. Drying effect, get plenty to drink.

Danger of sudden storms, not only in the sky.

Health

Sensitive body parts:
Heart, Back, Diaphragm, Circulation, Arteries

All measures taken to flush out and detoxify the sensitive body parts are very effective.

Good for surgery, except on the sensitive body parts (see above), sex organs, and ureter.
Scarring is less severe.

Teeth: Removal of tartar and amalgam. Best for fillings, crowns, and dentures!

Blood-purifying, detoxifying herbal infusions and teas.

Sensitive sense organs.

Back and heart problems are more likely to occur.

Avoid overstraining of the heart and circulation with unusual physical activities.

Expect sleepless nights.

Body Care

Aromas, scents:
Hibiscus, Oleander, Rose

Prepare home-made ointments and cosmetics.

Apply detoxing facial and body care.

Treatments of bumps and pimples on the skin, and exfoliating procedures.

Removing body hair.

Correction of the nail bed.

Massages that serve to relax, ease tension, and detoxify.

Reflexology massage.

Removal of callused skin.

Treating obstinate athlete's foot, nail fungus, and warts.

Good days for haircuts, hair becomes stronger. But be aware that if you get a perm, curls will become quite frizzy. Baby's first haircut.

Garden/Nature

Plant part:
Fruit

Sowing plants and vegetables that grow below ground.

Sowing and planting fruit. Also sow and plant vegetables that are highly perishable. Plant trees and bushes. Sow lawns.

Dig over/plow to prepare soil for planting.

Trimming and cutting back plants. Pruning of fruit trees and bushes.

Transplanting.

Not suitable for fertilizing.

Weeding. Pest Control.

Harvested produce should be consumed as soon as possible.

Gather herbs (roots) for heart and circulation complaints.

Start compost heap.

Housework

Housework is dealt with much more successfully, efficiently, and effortlessly.

Problem stains are removed readily.

Best for doing laundry!

Dry cleaning.

Thoroughly clean wooden and parquet floors, metals, china, etc.

Cleaning windows and glass.

Cleaning, polishing, and waterproofing shoes.

Combating mold.

Ventilate rooms sufficiently.
Air beds.

Suitable for making cheese.

Preserving and freezing fruit and vegetables.

Baking bread, cakes, and cookies (use more leavening agent).

Avoid painting.

Nutrition

Food quality:
Protein

Beans, peas, corn, tomatoes, pumpkin, lentils, soybeans, cucumber, eggplant, zucchini, berries, fruit, chili, bell pepper, figs, avocado, melon, olives.

Weight associated with overeating is less likely. If underweight, eat larger portions.

Cleansing and detox diets. Fruit and juice days.

Flush out poisons. Treatment for drug abuse.

A thing of beauty is a joy forever:
its loveliness increases;
it will never pass into nothingness.
John Keats

Leo

Color **Green**
Day **Warm**
Element **Fire**

9:35 AM PST
11:35 AM CST
12:35 PM EST
♋ → ♌

10 Monday

11 Tuesday Veterans Day, Remembrance Day
☽ Half Moon.

12 Wednesday
No meat.

3:53 PM PST
5:53 PM CST
6:53 PM EST
♌ → ♍

N O V E M B E R

Planting Time
Descending forces!
Sap is drawn downward, enhancing root formation.
Best days for sowing, planting, and transplanting.

detox
remove
be active

Waning Moon

Success

Good time for details, organization, routine, concentration, and duty.

Take care of financial and administrative tasks.

Prepare for future success now with realistic and critical assessment.

Leisure

Enjoy a nature walk.

Good time for health regimes. Improve your health with stretching exercises and yoga.

The earth feels cold to the touch, so take slightly warmer clothes.

Health

Sensitive body parts:
Digestive Organs, Nerves, Spleen, Pancreas

All measures taken to flush out and detoxify the sensitive body parts are very effective.

Good for surgery, except on the sensitive body parts (see above), sex organs, and ureter. Scarring is less severe.

Teeth: Removal of tartar and amalgam. Best for fillings, crowns, and dentures! Avoiding treatment of periodontitis and gums.

Blood-purifying, detoxifying herbal infusions and teas.

Sensitive blood circulation.

For a sensitive digestive system, a wholesome diet is recommended.

Dress slightly warmer.

High blood pressure: Avoid salty foods.

Massages, lymphatic therapy, and chiropractic treatment to release blockages.

Body Care

Aromas, scents:
Lavender, Spruce Needles, Sage, Meadow Flowers

Prepare home-made ointments and cosmetics.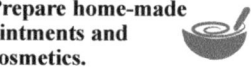

Apply detoxing facial and body care.

Treatments of bumps and pimples on the skin, and exfoliating procedures.

Removing body hair.

Correction of the nail bed.

Massages that serve to relax, ease tension, and detoxify.

Reflexology massage.

Removal of callused skin.

Treating obstinate athlete's foot, nail fungus, and warts.

Best for haircuts because it retains its shape longer. Perms turn out best.

Garden/Nature

Plant part:
Root

Best for sowing and planting, except lettuce.

Plant trees which are supposed to grow very tall. Plant hedges and bushes that are meant to grow very fast.

Planting and re-potting balcony and indoor plants.

Dig over/plow to prepare soil for planting.

Trimming and cutting back plants. Planting cuttings.

Spread fertilizer and manure. Fertilize flowers with poorly formed roots.

Start a compost heap.

Transplanting. Mulching.

Weeding. Pest control (vermin in the soil).

Avoid harvesting and storing.

Gather herbs (roots) for digestive organs, pancreas, and nervous complaints.

Housework

Housework is dealt with much more successfully, efficiently, and effortlessly.

Problem stains are removed readily.

Best for doing laundry! Reduce on laundry detergent, support the environment.

Dry cleaning.

Thoroughly clean wooden and parquet floors, metals, china etc.

Cleaning, polishing, and waterproofing shoes.

Combating mold.

Air rooms only briefly.

Painting.

Making pickles, preserves, and cheese yields suboptimal results and should be avoided.

Nutrition

Food quality:
Salt

Garlic, carrots, red beets, reddish, rutabaga, sugar beet, celery, potatoes, onions, kohlrabi.

Weight associated with overeating is less likely. If underweight, eat larger portions.

Cleansing and detox diets. Fruit and juice days.

Flush out poisons. Treatment for drug abuse.

Avoid large quantities of salty foods like bacon, ham, salted herring, fatty cheese, and the like. Avoid heavy and greasy foods.

Any change, even a change for the better, is always accompanied by drawbacks and discomforts.
Arnold Bennett

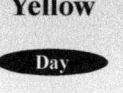
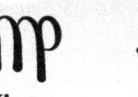

Color
Yellow

Day
Cool

Element
Earth

Virgo

13 Thursday

14 Friday
No meat. Cutting and filing toenails and fingernails.

Planting Time
Descending forces! Sap is drawn downward, enhancing root formation. Best days for sowing, planting, and transplanting.

detox
remove
be active
Waning Moon

NOVEMBER

Success

The artistic instinct rules, but so, too, does indecisiveness. The forces swing back and forth until equilibrium is achieved.

It's easy to reach compromises with tactful sensitivity.

A sense of judgment will support legal matters.

Leisure

Pursuit for harmony and cooperativeness supports good times in romance, friendship, and partnership.

Enjoy cultural events. Relax and get pampered with a spa treatment.

Romance can be passionate yet sensitive.

Health

Sensitive body parts:

Hips, Kidneys, Bladder

All measures taken to flush out and detoxify the sensitive body parts are very effective.

Good for surgery, except on the sensitive body parts (see above), sex organs, and ureter.
Scarring is less severe.

Teeth: Removal of tartar and amalgam. Best for fillings, crowns, and dentures! Avoid treatment of periodontitis and gums, avoid pulling teeth.

Blood-purifying, detoxifying herbal infusions and teas.

Sensitive glandular system.

Take special care to keep the area of the bladder and kidneys warm.

Apply special exercises for the hip region.

Sensitivity to light, so bring your sunglasses along.

Body Care

Aromas, scents: Roses, Violets, Daffodils

Prepare home-made ointments and cosmetics.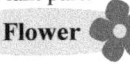

Apply detoxing facial and body care.

Treatments of bumps and pimples on the skin, and exfoliating procedures.

Removing body hair.

Correction of the nail bed.

Massages that serve to relax, ease tension, and detoxify.

Reflexology massage.

Removal of callused skin.

Treating obstinate athlete's foot, nail fungus, and warts.

Garden/Nature

Plant part:

Flower

Sow plants and vegetables that grow below ground.

Dig over/plow to prepare soil for planting.

Trimming and cutting back plants.

Start a compost heap.

Weeding. Pest control.

Fertilize flowers that no longer bloom.

Transplanting.

Avoid watering plants.

Harvested produce should be consumed as soon as possible.

Gather herbs (roots) for kidneys, gall bladder and hip complaints.

Day off on 11/16.

Housework

Housework is dealt with much more successfully, efficiently, and effortlessly.

Problem stains are removed readily.

Best for doing laundry! Reduce on laundry detergent, support the environment.

Dry cleaning.

Clean and store seasonal clothing.

Thoroughly clean wooden and parquet floors, metals, china etc.

Cleaning windows and glass.

Cleaning, polishing, and waterproofing shoes.

Combating mold.

Ventilate rooms thoroughly.

Baking bread, cakes, and cookies (add more leavening agent).

Making preserves.

Painting.

Nutrition

Food quality:

Fat

Cauliflower, artichoke, broccoli, sunflower seeds, flax seeds, nuts, rose hip, elder.

Weight associated with overeating is less likely. If underweight, eat larger portions.

Cleansing and detox diets. Fruit and juice days.

Flush out poisons. Treatment for drug abuse.

Pay attention to any particularly tempting foods today: Most likely the "wrong" things taste best.

High cholesterol: eat a low fat diet.

A mind that is stretched by a new experience can never go back to its old dimensions.
Oliver Wendell Holmes, Jr.

Color

Orange

Day

Air/Light

Element

Libra　　**Air**

ᴍ♍→♎ 1:45 AM PST / 3:45 AM CST / 4:45 AM EST

15 Saturday

16 Sunday

1:46 PM PST / 3:46 PM CST / 4:46 PM EST ♎→♏

17 Monday

N O V E M B E R

Positive affirmation:
"I trust that I can be there for others."

Planting Time
Descending forces!
Sap is drawn downward, enhancing root formation.
Best days for sowing, planting, and transplanting.

detox remove be active

Waning Moon

Success

Critical and superstitious behavior emerges, especially pertaining to money.

A penetrating power will strengthen your capacity to act.

An increased perception opens our interest for the essentials and helps to discover hidden potentials.

Leisure

Relax within your close family, with meditation, and relaxation exercises.

A longing to feel safe will be nurtured if you focus on habits and rituals. An increased sensitivity will help to enjoy every moment.

Romance can be very passionate.

If you plan outdoor excursions, be prepared for a shower here and there.

Health

Sensitive body parts:

Sex organs, Ureter

All measures taken to flush out and detoxify the sensitive body parts are very effective.

Good for surgical operations except those on the sensitive body parts (see above). Scarring is less severe.

Teeth: Removal of tartar and amalgam. Best for fillings, crowns, and dentures!

Blood-purifying, detoxifying herbal infusions and teas.

Sensitive nervous system.

Female disorders: As a preventative measure apply hip baths using yarrow.

Pregnancy: Avoid any exertion, miscarriages are more likely.

Keep region of the pelvis, kidneys, and feet warm to prevent infection of the bladder and kidneys.

Lymphatic therapy.

Body Care

Aromas, scents:
Anemone, Cornflower
Oregano, Thuja

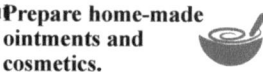

Prepare home-made ointments and cosmetics.

Apply detoxing facial and body care.

Treatments of bumps and pimples on the skin, and exfoliating procedures.

Removing body hair.

Correction of the nail bed.

Massages that serve to relax, ease tension, and detoxify.

Reflexology massage.

Removal of callused skin.

Treating obstinate athlete's foot, nail fungus, and warts.

Garden/Nature

Plant part:

Leaf

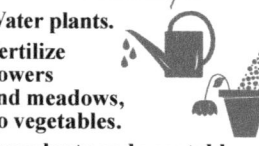

Water plants.

Fertilize flowers and meadows, no vegetables.

Sow plants and vegetables that grow below ground, leaf vegetables, and lettuce.

Sowing, planting, harvesting, and drying every kind of medicinal herbs.

Dig over/plow to prepare soil for planting.

Trimming and cutting back plants. Transplanting. Weeding. Pest control. Start a compost heap.

Mowing lawns.

Harvested produce should be consumed as soon as possible.

Avoid cutting down trees, danger of bark beetles.

Housework

Housework is dealt with much more successfully, efficiently, and effortlessly.

Problem stains are removed readily.

Best for doing laundry! Reduce on laundry detergent, support the environment.

Dry cleaning.

Thoroughly clean wooden and parquet floors, metals, china etc.

Cleaning, polishing, and waterproofing shoes.

Combating mold.

Ventilate rooms briefly and rapidly.

Avoid painting.

Nutrition

Food quality:

Carbohydrate

Lettuce, spinach, lamb's lettuce, Endive, parsley, leek, cabbage (Brussels sprouts, kale, Chinese cabbage), all leafy herbs, asparagus, mushrooms, cress, Swiss chard, rhubarb.

Weight associated with overeating is less likely. If underweight, eat larger portions.

Cleansing and detox diets. Fruit and juice days.

Flush out poisons. Treatment for drug abuse.

A house is not a home unless it contains food and fire for the mind as well as the body.
Benjamin Franklin

Color — **Red**

Day — **Wetness**

Element — **Water**

Scorpio ♏

18 Tuesday

19 Wednesday
No meat.

Planting Time
Descending forces! Sap is drawn downward, enhancing root formation. Best days for sowing, planting, and transplanting.

detox
remove
be active

Waning Moon

N O V E M B E R

Success

Inquisitiveness and exuberant inspiration lead to new horizons. Insight and love for truth reign.

Bringing together is more important than splitting asunder.

Expansive forces will assist in legal matters, discussions, and debates.

● *New Moon: Confirm your resolutions. Finalize new decisions. Drop bad habits.*

Leisure

Expansion feels great, and travel, short trips, and outings are most welcome. A competitive spirit excites any sports event.

Talk things out when necessary.

Romance can be very passionate.

Good days for outings; even with cloudy skies the air still feels somewhat warm. Drying effect, get plenty to drink.

Health

Sensitive body parts:

Thighs and Veins

All measures taken to supply nutrient materials and strengthen the sensitive body parts are very effective.

Healing ointments are easily absorbed.

Sensitive sense organs.

Pains often arise in the sciatic nerve, veins, the small of the back, and thighs.

Avoid overstraining the body with unusual physical activities.

● *New Moon: Avoid any surgery if possible.*

Body Care

Aromas, scents: Calendula (Marigold), Geranium, Rosemary

Treatments with firming and moisturizing creams are more effective.

Massages that serve to regenerate, and strengthen, perhaps aided with beneficial massage oils.

Correcting and cutting ingrown nails.

Hair dyes applied now, will look more vibrant.

Garden/Nature

Plant part:

Fruit

Sow plants and vegetables that grow and flourish above ground.

Sowing and planting fruit and vegetables that grow tall, and tomatoes, but no lettuce.

Transplanting.

Grafting onto fruit trees.

Cultivating grains, particularly corn.

Gather herbs for vein diseases.

● *New Moon: Change of weather is likely. Care for sickly plants.*

Housework

Light housework only.

Ventilate sufficiently.

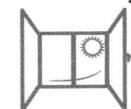

Freezing fruit and vegetables.

Baking bread, cakes, and cookies. Dough rises faster. (Except on New Moon)

Suitable for making cheese.

Making preserves.

Nutrition

Food quality:

Protein

Beans, peas, corn, tomatoes, pumpkin, lentils, soybeans, cucumber, eggplant, zucchini, berries, fruit, chili, bell pepper, figs, avocado, melon, olives.

Weight gain: avoid indulging in rich foods. If overweight, eat smaller portions.

Supply nutrient materials to strengthen the body. Focus on foods that contain essential minerals and vitamins.

Stimulants and vitamins are more effective.

● *New Moon: A day of fasting.*

Positive affirmation:
"I trust the power of positive thinking."

Turning Point

Transition of descending to ascending forces. Both forces are at work and neutralize each other.

gather strength rest, recover buildup

Waxing Moon

♏ ➔ ♐   2:27 AM PST
4:27 AM CST
5:27 AM EST

20 Thursday

● **New Moon** 10:48 PM PST Thursday, 12:48 AM CST, 1:48 AM EST

21 Friday

No meat. Cutting and filing toenails and fingernails.

2:54 PM PST
4:54 PM CST ➔ ♐ ➔ ♑
5:54 PM EST

22 Saturday

N O V E M B E R

Always forgive your enemies — nothing annoys them so much.
Oscar Wilde

 Color
Orange/ Yellow

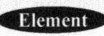 Day
Warm

Element
Fire

Sagittarius

Success

Career and business are in the foreground now and thinking becomes clear and serious, but somewhat inflexible.

Perseverance and reasoning assist in financial matters, planning, and contracts.

The values of tradition, authority, and discipline impact our endeavors.

Leisure

Money is not likely to be wasted in a shopping spree.

Many are drawn to enjoy cultural events.

The earth feels cold to the touch, so take slightly warmer clothes.

Health

Sensitive body parts:

Knees, Joints, Bones, Skin

All measures taken to supply nutrient materials and strengthen the sensitive body parts are very effective.

Healing ointments are easily absorbed.

Sensitive blood circulation.

Avoid overstraining bones and knees, and apply gentle stretching exercises only.

Problems with meniscus: Don't overstrain.

Dress slightly warmer.

High blood pressure: Avoid salty foods.

Massages, lymphatic therapy, and chiropractic treatment to release blockages.

Body Care

Aromas, scents:

Cedar, Juniper

Treatments with firming and moisturizing creams are more effective.

Massages that serve to regenerate, and strengthen, perhaps aided with beneficial massage oils.

Correcting and cutting ingrown nails.

Every kind of skin care is beneficial.

Cutting and filing toenails and fingernails will make the nails grow stronger over time.

Hair dyes applied now, will look more vibrant.

Garden/Nature

Plant part:

Root

Sow plants, herbs, and vegetables that grow and flourish above ground.

Transplanting.

Harvest produce is suitable for storage. Harvest root vegetables.

Gather herbs for bone, joint, and skin diseases.

Housework

Light housework only.

Air rooms only briefly.

Preserving root vegetables.

Avoid dry cleaning, as the fabric may develop unwanted glossy blotches.

Nutrition

Food quality:

Salt

Garlic, carrots, red beets, reddish, rutabaga, sugar beet, celery, potatoes, onions, kohlrabi.

Weight gain: avoid indulging in rich foods. If overweight, eat smaller portions.

Supply nutrient materials to strengthen the body. Focus on foods that contain essential minerals and vitamins.

Stimulants and vitamins are more effective.

Avoid large quantities of salty foods like bacon, ham, salted herring, fatty cheese, and the like. Avoid heavy and greasy foods.

Positive affirmation:
"I trust the power of positive thinking."

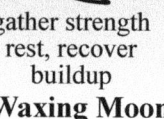

Harvest Time
Ascending forces! Sap is rising, enhancing plant growth above ground, resulting in the most juicy fruits and vegetables.

gather strength rest, recover buildup
Waxing Moon

23 Sunday

24 Monday

N O V E M B E R

Peace is a journey of a thousand miles and it must be taken one step at a time.
Lyndon B. Johnson

Color
Yellow

Day
Cool

Element
Earth

Capricorn

Success

Inspiration, optimism, and impatience. Rational thinking, creativity and imagination spark new ideas and inspire planning for the future.

Shying away from routine tasks people will feel more drawn to anything new.

Instead of gridlocked structures choose new possibilities.

Leisure

Inspiration and optimism will boost friendship, social gatherings, and parties.

Express your creativity and imagination. Dwell in dreams and utopian ideas. It is easier now to perceive intuitive thoughts.

Health

Sensitive body parts:

Lower Legs, Veins

All measures taken to supply nutrient materials and strengthen the sensitive body parts are very effective.

Healing ointments are easily absorbed.

Sensitive glandular system.

Avoid inflammation of the veins. Apply ointments to lower legs, and rest legs in a raised position.

Varicose veins: Avoid long periods of standing.

While exercising go easy on the ankles.

Sensitivity to light, so bring your sunglasses along.

Body Care

Aromas, scents: Cyclamen, Peach, Wild Roses

Treatments with firming and moisturizing creams are more effective.

Massages that serve to regenerate, and strengthen, perhaps aided with beneficial massage oils.

Correcting and cutting ingrown nails.

Hair dyes applied now, will look more vibrant.

Garden/Nature

Plant part:

Flower

Avoid watering plants.

Harvested produce is well suitable for storage.

Gather herbs for vein diseases.

Housework

Light housework only.

Ventilate rooms thoroughly.

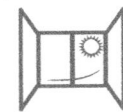

Baking cakes and cookies. Dough rises faster. (Except on New Moon)

Making preserves.

Nutrition

Food quality:

Fat

Cauliflower, artichoke, broccoli, sunflower seeds, flax seeds, nuts, rose hip, elder.

Weight gain: avoid indulging in rich foods. If overweight, eat smaller portions.

Supply nutrient materials to strengthen the body. Focus on foods that contain essential minerals and vitamins.

Stimulants and vitamins are more effective.

Pay attention to any particularly tempting foods today: Most likely the "wrong" things taste best.

High cholesterol: eat a low fat diet.

Positive affirmation:
"I trust the power of positive thinking."

Harvest Time
Ascending forces! Sap is rising, enhancing plant growth above ground, resulting in the most juicy fruits and vegetables.

gather strength rest, recover buildup
Waxing Moon

2:17 AM PST
4:17 AM CST
5:17 AM EST

25 Tuesday

26 Wednesday

No meat.

11:25 AM PST
1:25 PM CST
2:25 PM EST

27 Thursday
Thanksgiving (US)

N O V E M B E R

What is a weed? A plant whose virtues have never been discovered.
Paul Walker

Color
Bright/ Dark Blue

Day
Air/Light

Element

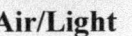

Air   **Aquarius**

Success

Sensibility, intuition, and helpfulness.

Where possible, retreating is more favorable than dealing with business matters.

Dissolve restrictions, be patient and wait. Be aware that people can be more easily influenced.

Leisure

Your helpfulness will boost friendships.

Enjoy dancing or swimming, or watch a movie that will inspire your fantasies and imagination.

Retreat, relax, and recover.

Romance can be gentle and coziness will prevail.

If you plan outdoor excursions, be prepared for a shower here and there.

Health

Sensitive body parts:

Feet and Toes

All measures taken to supply nutrient materials and strengthen the sensitive body parts are very effective.

Healing ointments are easily absorbed.

Sensitive nervous system.

Drugs have a much stronger effect on your body. Monitor closely what you put into your body.

Lymphatic therapy.

Sluggishness or fatigue may occur in the transition into the next Zodiac sign of Aries.

Body Care

Aromas, scents:
Magnolia, Amaryllis, Clary Sage

Treatments with firming and moisturizing creams are more effective.

Massages that serve to regenerate, and strengthen, perhaps aided with beneficial massage oils. Reflexology massage. Carry out with special care, people are more sensitive.

Correcting and cutting ingrown nails.

Foot bath.

No haircuts, hair becomes shaggy and unmanageable. Avoid washing your hair. Dandruff could develop.

Garden/Nature

Plant part:

Leaf

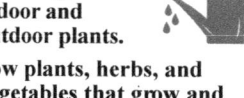

Watering all indoor and outdoor plants.

Sow plants, herbs, and vegetables that grow and flourish above ground, and leaf vegetables.

Transplanting.

Mowing lawns.

Avoid pruning fruit trees and bushes.

Harvested produce should be consumed as soon as possible.

Gather herbs for foot complaints.

Housework

Light housework only.

Ventilate rooms briefly and rapidly. Don't air mattresses.

Any dirt and spots are easily removed in the laundry.

Avoid painting, as paint will take very long to dry.

Preserving and storing should be avoided.

Nutrition

Food quality:

Carbohydrate

Lettuce, spinach, lamb's lettuce, Endive, parsley, leek, cabbage (Brussels sprouts, kale, Chinese cabbage), all leafy herbs, asparagus, mushrooms, cress, Swiss chard, rhubarb.

Weight gain: avoid indulging in rich foods. If overweight, eat smaller portions and avoid carbohydrates.

Supply nutrient materials to strengthen the body. Focus on foods that contain essential minerals and vitamins.

Caffeine, alcohol, drugs, certain foods, and stimulants have a much stronger effect.

Positive affirmation:
"I trust the power of positive thinking."

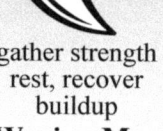

Harvest Time
Ascending forces! Sap is rising, enhancing plant growth above ground, resulting in the most juicy fruits and vegetables.

gather strength
rest, recover
buildup
Waxing Moon

5:08 PM PST
7:08 PM CST
8:08 PM EST

28 Friday

☽ **Half Moon.** No meat. Cutting and filing toenails and fingernails.

29 Saturday

You know, all that really matters is that the people you love are happy and healthy. Everything else is just sprinkles on the sundae.
Paul Walker

Color
Blueish White

Day
Wetness

Element
Water

Pisces

N O V E M B E R

Success

Things get going and the way straight ahead seems the best.

People feel energetic, courageous, assertive, and at times anxious.

Good time for meetings and sales talks but impatience and selfishness do not favor teamwork.

Leisure

An enterprising spirit and spontaneity move people to enjoy outings, sports, competitions, cultural events, and travels.

Romance can be very passionate.

Good days for outings, even with cloudy skies the air still feels somewhat warm. Drying effect, get plenty to drink.

Health

Sensitive body parts:

Head, Brain, Eyes

All measures taken to supply nutrient materials and strengthen the sensitive body parts are very effective.

Healing ointments are easily absorbed.

Sensitive sense organs.

If you suffer from migraines drink plenty of water, and avoid coffee, chocolate, and sugar.

Body Care

Aromas, scents:
Cloves, Peppermint, Thyme

Treatments with firming and moisturizing creams are more effective.

Massages that serve to regenerate, and strengthen, perhaps aided with beneficial massage oils.

Correcting and cutting ingrown nails.

Eye compresses for strained eyes.

Any kind of hair care. Hair dyes applied now, will look more vibrant.

Garden/Nature

Plant part:

Fruit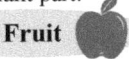

Sow plants and vegetables that grow and flourish above ground, especially fruit and tomatoes.

Sowing and planting anything that is supposed to grow fast and for immediate use.

Grafting onto fruit trees.

Cultivating grains.

Transplanting.

Harvesting and storing grains, vegetables, potatoes, fruit, and tomatoes.

Gather herbs for eye complaints and headaches.

Day off on 11/30.

Housework

Light housework only.

Ventilate sufficiently.

Preserving fruit.

Freezing fruit and vegetables.

Baking bread, cakes, and cookies. Dough rises faster. (Except on New Moon)

Suitable for making cheese.

Nutrition

Food quality:

Protein

Beans, peas, corn, tomatoes, pumpkin, lentils, soybeans, cucumber, eggplant, zucchini, berries, fruit, chili, bell pepper, figs, avocado, melon, olives.

Weight gain: avoid indulging in rich foods. If overweight, eat smaller portions.

Supply nutrient materials to strengthen the body. Focus on foods that contain essential minerals and vitamins.

Stimulants and vitamins are more effective.

Drink plenty of water.

Positive affirmation:
"I trust the power of positive thinking."

Harvest Time
Ascending forces! Sap is rising, enhancing plant growth above ground, resulting in the most juicy fruits and vegetables.

gather strength rest, recover buildup
Waxing Moon

30 Sunday
1. Advent

1 Monday

7:14 PM PST
9:14 PM CST
10:14 PM EST
♈ ➙ ♉

NOVEMBER/DECEMBER

A healthy outside starts from the inside.
Robert Urich

 Color
Indigo Blue

 Day
Warm

Element
Fire

Aries ♈

Success

Realism and material security are important. Persistence comes easy, thoughts and reactions are slower.

Assess financial areas.

Conservative tendencies may make people want to stay away from risk taking.

Leisure

Relax at a picnic/feast. Enjoy culinary pleasures and hobbies.

The earth feels cold to the touch, so take slightly warmer clothes.

Health

Sensitive body parts:

Head and Neck

All measures taken to supply nutrient materials and strengthen the sensitive body parts are very effective.

Healing ointments are easily absorbed.

Sensitive blood circulation.

Organs of speech, jaws, teeth, tonsils, thyroid gland, neck, and vocal chords get easily affected. Keep neck warm. On cold days ears should be protected. Sensitivity to noise.

High blood pressure: Avoid salty foods.

Massages, lymphatic therapy, and chiropractic treatment to release blockages.

Body Care

Aromas, scents: Geranium, Jasmine, Rose

Treatments with firming and moisturizing creams are more effective.

Massages that serve to regenerate, and strengthen, perhaps aided with beneficial massage oils.

Correcting and cutting ingrown nails.

Hair dyes applied now, will look more vibrant.

Garden/Nature

Plant part:

Root

Sow plants, herbs, and vegetables that grow and flourish above ground.

Sowing and planting trees, bushes, hedges, and root vegetables. Everything grows slowly and lasts well.

Transplanting.

Harvesting and storing root vegetables. Harvested produce is well suited for storage.

Gather herbs for sinus issues, sore throat, and ear complaints.

Housework

Light housework only.

Air rooms only briefly.

Preserving root vegetables.

Nutrition

Food quality:

Salt

Garlic, carrots, red beets, reddish, rutabaga, sugar beet, celery, potatoes, onions, kohlrabi.

Weight gain: avoid indulging in rich foods. If overweight, eat smaller portions.

Supply nutrient materials to strengthen the body. Focus on foods that contain essential minerals and vitamins.

Stimulants and vitamins are more effective.

Avoid large quantities of salty foods like bacon, ham, salted herring, fatty cheese, and the like.

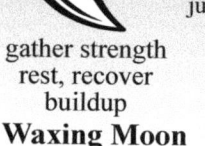

Harvest Time
Ascending forces! Sap is rising, enhancing plant growth above ground, resulting in the most juicy fruits and vegetables.

gather strength rest, recover buildup
Waxing Moon

2 Tuesday	**3** Wednesday
	No meat.

6:49 PM PST
8:49 PM CST ♉ → ♊
9:49 PM EST

A sense of humor is a major defense against minor troubles.
Mignon McLaughlin

Color
Bright Blue

Day
Cool

Element
Earth

Taurus

D E C E M B E R

Success

Open mindedness and curiosity. A changeable and hectic time.

Good time for talking, negotiating, networking, and exchanging ideas as well as for meetings of a nonbinding nature, conferences, and studies.

Leisure

Good time for family gatherings, parties, and short trips.

People enjoy stimulating their minds with reading and studying. Attending theater performances is a preferred enjoyment. Enhance friendships.

Stretching exercises.

Be prepared for sudden changes in weather or climate.

Health

Sensitive body parts:

Shoulders, Arms, Hands, Lungs

All measures taken to supply nutrient materials and strengthen the sensitive body parts are very effective.

Healing ointments are easily absorbed. Applying herbal ointments to the shoulders for rheumatic gout and alike.

Sensitive glandular system.

Make sure you are dressed warm enough in cool weather.

Exercises for shoulders. Breathing exercises.

Avoid having any teeth pulled.

Sensitivity to light, bring your sunglasses along.

Massages, lymphatic therapy, and chiropractic treatment to release blockages.

○ *Full Moon: Avoid any surgery and vaccination if possible.*

Body Care

Aromas, scents: Lavender, Lemon Balm, Magnolia, Verbena

Treatments with firming and moisturizing creams are more effective.

Massages that serve to regenerate, and strengthen, perhaps aided with beneficial massage oils.

Correcting and cutting ingrown nails.

Hair dyes applied now, will look more vibrant.

Garden/Nature

Plant part:

 **Flower**

Sow plants, herbs, and vegetables that grow and flourish above ground.

Sowing and planting any creeping or climbing plants, flowers, and medicinal herbs.

Transplanting.

Avoid watering plants.

Gather herbs for tensions in the shoulder and lung complaints.

Changes in weather are more likely.

○ *Full Moon: Weather and climate changes. Herbs are most powerful.*

Housework

Light housework only.

Ventilate rooms thoroughly.

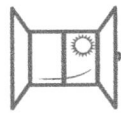

Making preserves.

Baking cakes and cookies. Dough rises faster. (Except on New Moon)

○ *Full Moon: Avoid doing laundry, cleaning windows, making preserves, painting.*

Nutrition

Food quality:

Fat

Cauliflower, artichoke, broccoli, sunflower seeds, flax seeds, nuts, rose hip, elder.

Weight gain: avoid indulging in rich foods. If overweight, eat smaller portions.

Supply nutrient materials to strengthen the body. Focus on foods that contain essential minerals and vitamins.

Stimulants and vitamins are more effective.

Pay attention to any particularly tempting foods today: Most likely the "wrong" things taste best.

High cholesterol: eat a low fat diet.

○ *Full Moon: A day of fasting.*

Positive affirmation:
"I trust the power of positive thinking."

Turning Point

Transition of ascending to descending forces. Both forces are at work and neutralize each other.

gather strength rest, recover buildup
Waxing Moon

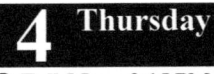

4 Thursday

○ **Full Moon** 3:15 PM PST, 5:15 PM CST, 6:15 PM EST

D E C E M B E R

Happiness depends upon ourselves.
Aristotle

 Color
Light Blue

 Day
Air/Light

Element

Air   **Gemini**

Success

Open mindedness and curiosity. A changeable and hectic time.

Good time for talking, negotiating, networking, and exchanging ideas as well as for meetings of a nonbinding nature, conferences, and studies.

Leisure

Good time for family gatherings, parties, and short trips.

People enjoy stimulating their minds with reading and studying. Attending theater performances is a preferred enjoyment. Enhance friendships.

Stretching exercises.

Be prepared for sudden changes in weather or climate.

Health

Sensitive body parts:

Shoulders, Arms, Hands, Lungs

All measures taken to flush out and detoxify the sensitive body parts are very effective.

Scarring is less severe.

Teeth: Removal of tartar and amalgam. Best for fillings, crowns, and dentures! Avoid having any teeth pulled.

Blood-purifying, detoxifying herbal infusions and teas.

Sensitive glandular system.

Make sure you are dressed warm enough in cool weather.

Exercises for shoulders. Breathing exercises.

Sensitivity to light, bring your sunglasses along.

Massages, lymphatic therapy, and chiropractic treatment to release blockages.

Body Care

Aromas, scents: Lavender, Lemon Balm, Magnolia, Verbena

Prepare home-made ointments and cosmetics.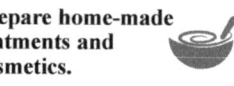

Apply detoxing facial and body care.

Treatments of bumps and pimples on the skin, and exfoliating procedures.

Removing body hair.

Correction of the nail bed.

Massages that serve to relax, ease tension, and detoxify.

Reflexology massage.

Removal of callused skin.

Treating obstinate athlete's foot, nail fungus, and warts.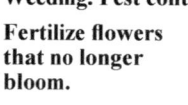

Garden/Nature

Plant part:

Flower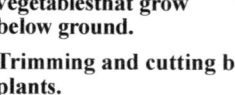

Sow plants and vegetables that grow below ground.

Trimming and cutting back plants.

Start a compost heap.

Weeding. Pest control.

Fertilize flowers that no longer bloom.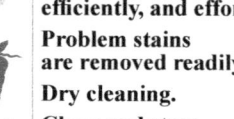

Avoid watering plants.

Changes in weather are more likely.

Gather herbs (roots) for tensions in the shoulder and lung complaints.

Housework

Housework is dealt with much more successfully, efficiently, and effortlessly.

Problem stains are removed readily.

Dry cleaning.

Clean and store seasonal clothing.

Thoroughly clean wooden and parquet floors, metals, china etc.

Cleaning, polishing, and waterproofing shoes.

Combating mold.

Ventilate rooms thoroughly.

Baking bread, cakes, and cookies (add more leavening agent).

Nutrition

Food quality:

Fat

Cauliflower, artichoke, broccoli, sunflower seeds, flax seeds, nuts, rose hip, elder.

Weight associated with overeating is less likely. If underweight, eat larger portions.

Cleansing and detox diets. Fruit and juice days.

Flush out poisons. Treatment for drug abuse.

Pay attention to any particularly tempting foods today: Most likely the "wrong" things taste best.

High cholesterol: eat a low fat diet.

We are learning, too, that the love of beauty is one of Nature's greatest healers.
Ellsworth Huntington

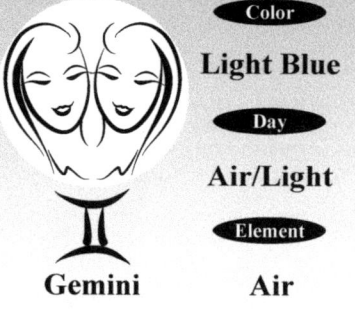

Color

Light Blue

Day

Air/Light

Element

Gemini   **Air**

5:55 PM PST
7:55 PM CST
8:55 PM EST

5 **Friday**

No meat. Cutting and filing toenails and fingernails.

D E C E M B E R

Turning Point

Transition of ascending to descending forces. Both forces are at work and neutralize each other.

detox
remove
be active

Waning Moon

Success

Feelings, sensitivity, and cooperativeness. Many are overly sensitive, so beware of treading on someone's toes.

Be cautious if you are easily influenced.

During negotiations make use of the cognitive ability of your senses.

Leisure

Relax within your close family.

Retreat to your safe haven and enjoy your fantasy while reading or listening to music. The inner world becomes more colorful than the outer.

Romance can be gentle. Deep feelings will prevail.

If you plan outdoor excursions, be prepared for a shower here and there.

Health

Sensitive body parts:
Chest, Lungs, Liver, Stomach, Gall Bladder

All measures taken to flush out and detoxify the sensitive body parts are very effective.

Good for surgical operations except those on the sensitive body parts (see above), thighs, and veins.
Scarring is less severe.

Teeth: Removal of tartar and amalgam. Best for fillings, crowns, and dentures!

Blood-purifying, detoxifying herbal infusions and teas.

Sensitive nervous system.

Be cautious with alcohol since the liver is very sensitive.

Stomach could play up and cause gas and heartburn.

Rheumatism: Don't air bedding outside, damp will remain in the bedding.

Lymphatic therapy.

Body Care

Aromas, scents:
Lilac, Lilies of the Valley, Lilies, Violets

Prepare home-made ointments and cosmetics.

Apply detoxing facial and body care.

Treatments of bumps and pimples on the skin, and exfoliating procedures.

Removing body hair.

Correction of the nail bed.

Massages that serve to relax, ease tension, and detoxify.

Reflexology massage.

Removal of callused skin.

Treating obstinate athlete's foot, nail fungus, and warts.

No haircuts, hair becomes shaggy and unmanageable.
Avoid washing your hair.

Garden/Nature

Plant part:
Leaf

Water plants.

Fertilize flowers.

Sow plants and vegetables that grow below ground, leaf vegetables, and lettuce.

Dig over/plow to prepare soil for planting.

Trimming and cutting back plants. Transplanting. Weeding.

Combating pests above ground.

Start a compost heap.

Mowing lawns.

Gather herbs (roots) for bronchitis, stomach, liver, and gall bladder complaints.

Unfavorable for harvesting, storing, and preserving.

Housework

Housework is dealt with much more successfully, efficiently, and effortlessly.

Problem stains are removed readily.

Best for doing laundry! Reduce on laundry detergent, support the environment.

Dry cleaning.

Thoroughly clean wooden and parquet floors, metals, china etc.

Cleaning, polishing, and waterproofing shoes.

Combating mold.

Ventilate rooms briefly and rapidly.

Avoid painting.

Nutrition

Food quality:
Carbohydrate

Lettuce, spinach, lamb's lettuce, Endive, parsley, leek, cabbage (Brussels sprouts, kale, Chinese cabbage), all leafy herbs, asparagus, mushrooms, cress, Swiss chard, rhubarb.

Weight associated with overeating is less likely. If underweight, eat larger portions.

Moodiness may make you want to eat more than is healthy. If overweight avoid carbohydrates.

Cleansing and detox diets. Fruit and juice days.

Flush out poisons. Treatment for drug abuse.

If you get stomach troubles easily, avoid heavy meals.

Tolerance becomes a crime when applied to evil.
Thomas Mann

Color
Green

Day
Wetness

Element

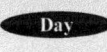

Cancer — **Water**

6 Saturday
St. Nicholas

7 Sunday 2. Advent
Pearl Harbor Remembrance Day (US)

6:49 PM PST
8:49 PM CST
9:49 PM EST

D E C E M B E R

Positive affirmation:
"I trust the power of positive thinking."

Planting Time
Descending forces! Sap is drawn downward, enhancing root formation. Best days for sowing, planting, and transplanting.

detox
remove
be active

Waning Moon

Success

Determination reigns, and risks are taken more often. Master your tasks with more self-confidence and creativity.

Limits appear to be more easily surmountable.

Auspicious day for sales, advertising, and publicity.

Leisure

Zest for life is in the air. People want to have a fun time, enjoy parties, musical events, movies, etc.

Possessive feelings can harm a relationship. Romance can be very passionate.

Outings: even with cloudy skies the air still feels somewhat warm. Drying effect, get plenty to drink.

Danger of sudden storms, not only in the sky.

Health

Sensitive body parts:
Heart, Back, Diaphragm, Circulation, Arteries

All measures taken to flush out and detoxify the sensitive body parts are very effective.

Good for surgery, except on the sensitive body parts (see above), thighs, and veins.

Scarring is less severe.

Teeth: Removal of tartar and amalgam. Best for fillings, crowns, and dentures!

Blood-purifying, detoxifying herbal infusions and teas.

Sensitive sense organs.

Back and heart problems are more likely to occur.

Avoid overstraining of the heart and circulation with unusual physical activities.

Expect sleepless nights.

Body Care

Aromas, scents:
Hibiscus, Oleander, Rose

Prepare home-made ointments and cosmetics.

Apply detoxing facial and body care.

Treatments of bumps and pimples on the skin, and exfoliating procedures.

Removing body hair.

Correction of the nail bed.

Massages that serve to relax, ease tension, and detoxify.

Reflexology massage.

Removal of callused skin.

Treating obstinate athlete's foot, nail fungus, and warts.

Good days for haircuts, hair becomes stronger. But be aware that if you get a perm, curls will become quite frizzy. Baby's first haircut.

Garden/Nature

Plant part:
Fruit

Sowing plants and vegetables that grow below ground.

Sowing and planting fruit. Also sow and plant vegetables that are highly perishable. Plant trees and bushes. Sow lawns.

Dig over/plow to prepare soil for planting.

Trimming and cutting back plants. Pruning of fruit trees and bushes.

Transplanting.

Not suitable for fertilizing.

Weeding. Pest Control.

Harvested produce should be consumed as soon as possible.

Gather herbs (roots) for heart and circulation complaints.

Start compost heap.

Housework

Housework is dealt with much more successfully, efficiently, and effortlessly.

Problem stains are removed readily.

Best for doing laundry!

Dry cleaning.

Thoroughly clean wooden and parquet floors, metals, china, etc.

Cleaning windows and glass.

Cleaning, polishing, and waterproofing shoes.

Combating mold.

Ventilate rooms sufficiently. Air beds.

Suitable for making cheese.

Preserving and freezing fruit and vegetables.

Baking bread, cakes, and cookies (use more leavening agent).

Avoid painting.

Nutrition

Food quality:
Protein

Beans, peas, corn, tomatoes, pumpkin, lentils, soybeans, cucumber, eggplant, zucchini, berries, fruit, chili, bell pepper, figs, avocado, melon, olives.

Weight associated with overeating is less likely. If underweight, eat larger portions.

Cleansing and detox diets. Fruit and juice days.

Flush out poisons. Treatment for drug abuse.

Goodness is beauty in the best estate.
Christopher Marlowe

Color — Green

Day — Warm

Element — Fire

Leo

8 Monday

9 Tuesday

D E C E M B E R

Planting Time
Descending forces! Sap is drawn downward, enhancing root formation. Best days for sowing, planting, and transplanting.

detox
remove
be active

Waning Moon

Success

Good time for details, organization, routine, concentration, and duty.

Take care of financial and administrative tasks.

Prepare for future success now with realistic and critical assessment.

Leisure

Enjoy a nature walk.

Good time for health regimes. Improve your health with stretching exercises and yoga.

The earth feels cold to the touch, so take slightly warmer clothes.

Health

Sensitive body parts:
Digestive Organs, Nerves, Spleen, Pancreas

All measures taken to flush out and detoxify the sensitive body parts are very effective.

Good for surgery, except on the sensitive body parts (see above), thighs, and veins. Scarring is less severe.

Teeth: Removal of tartar and amalgam. Best for fillings, crowns, and dentures! Avoiding treatment of periodontitis and gums.

Blood-purifying, detoxifying herbal infusions and teas.

Sensitive blood circulation.

For a sensitive digestive system, a wholesome diet is recommended.

Dress slightly warmer.

High blood pressure: Avoid salty foods.

Massages, lymphatic therapy, and chiropractic treatment to release blockages.

Body Care

Aromas, scents:
Lavender, Spruce Needles, Sage, Meadow Flowers

Prepare home-made ointments and cosmetics.

Apply detoxing facial and body care.

Treatments of bumps and pimples on the skin, and exfoliating procedures.

Removing body hair.

Correction of the nail bed.

Massages that serve to relax, ease tension, and detoxify.

Reflexology massage.

Removal of callused skin.

Treating obstinate athlete's foot, nail fungus, and warts.

Best for haircuts because it retains its shape longer. Perms turn out best.

Garden/Nature

Plant part:
Root

Best for sowing and planting, except lettuce.

Plant trees which are supposed to grow very tall. Plant hedges and bushes that are meant to grow very fast.

Planting and re-potting balcony and indoor plants.

Dig over/plow to prepare soil for planting.

Trimming and cutting back plants. Planting cuttings.

Spread fertilizer and manure. Fertilize flowers with poorly formed roots.

Start a compost heap.

Transplanting. Mulching.

Weeding. Pest control (vermin in the soil).

Avoid harvesting and storing.

Gather herbs (roots) for digestive organs, pancreas, and nervous complaints.

Housework

Housework is dealt with much more successfully, efficiently, and effortlessly.

Problem stains are removed readily.

Best for doing laundry! Reduce on laundry detergent, support the environment.

Dry cleaning.

Thoroughly clean wooden and parquet floors, metals, china etc.

Cleaning, polishing, and waterproofing shoes.

Combating mold.

Air rooms only briefly.

Painting.

Making pickles, preserves, and cheese yields suboptimal results and should be avoided.

Nutrition

Food quality:
Salt

Garlic, carrots, red beets, reddish, rutabaga, sugar beet, celery, potatoes, onions, kohlrabi.

Weight associated with overeating is less likely. If underweight, eat larger portions.

Cleansing and detox diets. Fruit and juice days.

Flush out poisons. Treatment for drug abuse.

Avoid large quantities of salty foods like bacon, ham, salted herring, fatty cheese, and the like. Avoid heavy and greasy foods.

The mind has exactly the same power as the hands; not merely to grasp the world, but to change it.
Colin Wilson

♍

Virgo

Color
Yellow

Day
Cool

Element
Earth

♌ → ♍   11:21 PM PST Tuesday
1:21 AM CST
2:21 AM EST

10 Wednesday

No meat.

11 Thursday

☾ Half Moon.

D E C E M B E R

Planting Time
Descending forces!
Sap is drawn downward, enhancing root formation.
Best days for sowing, planting, and transplanting.

detox
remove
be active
Waning Moon

Success

The artistic instinct rules, but so, too, does indecisiveness. The forces swing back and forth until equilibrium is achieved.

It's easy to reach compromises with tactful sensitivity.

A sense of judgment will support legal matters.

Leisure

Pursuit for harmony and cooperativeness supports good times in romance, friendship, and partnership.

Enjoy cultural events. Relax and get pampered with a spa treatment.

Romance can be passionate yet sensitive.

Health

Sensitive body parts:

Hips, Kidneys, Bladder

All measures taken to flush out and detoxify the sensitive body parts are very effective.

Good for surgery, except on the sensitive body parts (see above), thighs, and veins. Scarring is less severe.

Teeth: Removal of tartar and amalgam. Best for fillings, crowns, and dentures! Avoid treatment of periodontitis and gums, avoid pulling teeth.

Blood-purifying, detoxifying herbal infusions and teas.

Sensitive glandular system.

Take special care to keep the area of the bladder and kidneys warm.

Apply special exercises for the hip region.

Sensitivity to light, so bring your sunglasses along.

Body Care

Aromas, scents: Roses, Violets, Daffodils

Prepare home-made ointments and cosmetics.

Apply detoxing facial and body care.

Treatments of bumps and pimples on the skin, and exfoliating procedures.

Removing body hair.

Correction of the nail bed.

Massages that serve to relax, ease tension, and detoxify.

Reflexology massage.

Removal of callused skin.

Treating obstinate athlete's foot, nail fungus, and warts.

Garden/Nature

Plant part:

Flower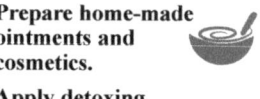

Sow plants and vegetables that grow below ground.

Dig over/plow to prepare soil for planting.

Trimming and cutting back plants.

Start a compost heap.

Weeding. Pest control.

Fertilize flowers that no longer bloom.

Transplanting.

Avoid watering plants.

Harvested produce should be consumed as soon as possible.

Gather herbs (roots) for kidneys, gall bladder and hip complaints.

Day off on 12/13.

Housework

Housework is dealt with much more successfully, efficiently, and effortlessly.

Problem stains are removed readily.

Best for doing laundry! Reduce on laundry detergent, support the environment.

Dry cleaning.

Clean and store seasonal clothing.

Thoroughly clean wooden and parquet floors, metals, china etc.

Cleaning windows and glass.

Cleaning, polishing, and waterproofing shoes.

Combating mold.

Ventilate rooms thoroughly.

Baking bread, cakes, and cookies (add more leavening agent).

Making preserves.

Painting.

Nutrition

Food quality:

Fat

Cauliflower, artichoke, broccoli, sunflower seeds, flax seeds, nuts, rose hip, elder.

Weight associated with overeating is less likely. If underweight, eat larger portions.

Cleansing and detox diets. Fruit and juice days.

Flush out poisons. Treatment for drug abuse.

Pay attention to any particularly tempting foods today: Most likely the "wrong" things taste best.

High cholesterol: eat a low fat diet.

Always remember that the future comes one day at a time.
Dean Acheson

Color — Orange

Day — Air/Light

Element

Libra   Air

8:08 AM PST
10:08 AM CST
11:08 AM EST

♍ ➤ ♎

7:52 PM PST
9:52 PM CST
10:52 PM EST

♎ ➤ ♏

12 Friday
No meat. Cutting and filing toenails and fingernails.

13 Saturday

14 Sunday
3. Advent

D E C E M B E R

Positive affirmation:
"I trust the power of positive thinking."

Planting Time
Descending forces! Sap is drawn downward, enhancing root formation. Best days for sowing, planting, and transplanting.

detox
remove
be active

Waning Moon

Success

Critical and superstitious behavior emerges, especially pertaining to money.

A penetrating power will strengthen your capacity to act.

An increased perception opens our interest for the essentials and helps to discover hidden potentials.

Leisure

Relax within your close family, with meditation, and relaxation exercises.

A longing to feel safe will be nurtured if you focus on habits and rituals. An increased sensitivity will help to enjoy every moment.

Romance can be very passionate.

If you plan outdoor excursions, be prepared for a shower here and there.

Health

Sensitive body parts:

Sex organs, Ureter

All measures taken to flush out and detoxify the sensitive body parts are very effective.

Good for surgical operations except those on the sensitive body parts (see above), thighs, and veins.
Scarring is less severe.

Teeth: Removal of tartar and amalgam. Best for fillings, crowns, and dentures!

Blood-purifying, detoxifying herbal infusions and teas.

Sensitive nervous system.

Female disorders: As a preventative measure apply hip baths using yarrow.

Pregnancy: Avoid any exertion, miscarriages are more likely.

Keep region of the pelvis, kidneys, and feet warm to prevent infection of the bladder and kidneys.

Lymphatic therapy.

Body Care

Aromas, scents:
Anemone, Cornflower
Oregano, Thuja

Prepare home-made ointments and cosmetics.

Apply detoxing facial and body care.

Treatments of bumps and pimples on the skin, and exfoliating procedures.

Removing body hair.

Correction of the nail bed.

Massages that serve to relax, ease tension, and detoxify.

Reflexology massage.

Removal of callused skin.

Treating obstinate athlete's foot, nail fungus, and warts.

Garden/Nature

Plant part:

Leaf

Water plants.

Fertilize flowers and meadows, no vegetables.

Sow plants and vegetables that grow below ground, leaf vegetables, and lettuce.

Sowing, planting, harvesting, and drying every kind of medicinal herbs.

Dig over/plow to prepare soil for planting.

Trimming and cutting back plants. Transplanting. Weeding. Pest control. Start a compost heap.

Mowing lawns.

Harvested produce should be consumed as soon as possible.

Avoid cutting down trees, danger of bark beetles.

Housework

Housework is dealt with much more successfully, efficiently, and effortlessly.

Problem stains are removed readily.

Best for doing laundry! Reduce on laundry detergent, support the environment.

Dry cleaning.

Thoroughly clean wooden and parquet floors, metals, china etc.

Cleaning, polishing, and waterproofing shoes.

Combating mold.

Ventilate rooms briefly and rapidly.

Avoid painting.

Nutrition

Food quality:

Carbohydrate

Lettuce, spinach, lamb's lettuce, Endive, parsley, leek, cabbage (Brussels sprouts, kale, Chinese cabbage), all leafy herbs, asparagus, mushrooms, cress, Swiss chard, rhubarb.

Weight associated with overeating is less likely. If underweight, eat larger portions.

Cleansing and detox diets. Fruit and juice days.

Flush out poisons. Treatment for drug abuse.

A successful man is one who can lay a firm foundation with the bricks others have thrown at him.
David Brinkley

Color

Red

Day

Wetness

Element

m

Scorpio **Water**

15 Monday
Hannukah Starts

16 Tuesday

Planting Time
Descending forces! Sap is drawn downward, enhancing root formation. Best days for sowing, planting, and transplanting.

detox
remove
be active

Waning Moon

D E C E M B E R

Success

Inquisitiveness and exuberant inspiration lead to new horizons. Insight and love for truth reign.

Bringing together is more important than splitting asunder.

Expansive forces will assist in legal matters, discussions, and debates.

● *New Moon: Confirm your resolutions. Finalize new decisions. Drop bad habits.*

Leisure

Expansion feels great, and travel, short trips, and outings are most welcome. A competitive spirit excites any sports event.

Talk things out when necessary.

Romance can be very passionate.

Good days for outings; even with cloudy skies the air still feels somewhat warm. Drying effect, get plenty to drink.

Health

Sensitive body parts:

Thighs and Veins

All measures taken to flush out and detoxify the sensitive body parts are very effective.

Scarring is less severe.

Teeth: Removal of tartar and amalgam. Best for fillings, crowns, and dentures!

Blood-purifying, detoxifying herbal infusions and tea.

Sensitive sense organs.

Pains often arise in the sciatic nerve, veins, the small of the back, and thighs.

Avoid overstraining the body with unusual physical activities.

● *New Moon: Avoid any surgery if possible.*

Body Care

Aromas, scents:
Calendula (Marigold), Geranium, Rosemary

Prepare home-made ointments and cosmetics.

Apply detoxing facial and body care.

Treatments of bumps and pimples on the skin, and exfoliating procedures.

Removing body hair.

Correction of the nail bed.

Massages that serve to relax, ease tension, and detoxify.

Reflexology massage.

Removal of callused skin.

Treating obstinate athlete's foot, nail fungus, and warts.

Garden/Nature

Plant part:

Fruit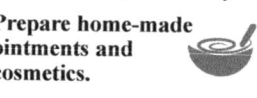

Sowing plants and vegetables that grow below ground.

Dig over/plow to prepare soil for planting.

Trimming and cutting back plants.
Pruning of fruit trees and bushes.

Cultivating grains, particularly corn.

Fertilize grains, vegetables, and fruit.

Combating pests above ground. Weeding.

Gather herbs (roots) for vein diseases.

Avoid hoeing and harrowing.

Start a compost heap.

● *New Moon: Change of weather is likely. Care for sickly plants.*

Housework

Housework is dealt with much more successfully, efficiently, and effortlessly.

Problem stains are removed readily.

Best for doing laundry!

Dry cleaning.

Thoroughly clean wooden and parquet floors, metals, china, etc.

Cleaning windows and glass.

Cleaning, polishing, and waterproofing shoes.

Combating mold.

Ventilate rooms sufficiently. Air beds.

Suitable for making cheese.

Preserving and freezing fruit and vegetables.

Baking bread, cakes, and cookies (use more leavening agent).

Painting.

Nutrition

Food quality:

Protein

Beans, peas, corn, tomatoes, pumpkin, lentils, soybeans, cucumber, eggplant, zucchini, berries, fruit, chili, bell pepper, figs, avocado, melon, olives.

Weight associated with overeating is less likely. If underweight, eat larger portions.

Cleansing and detox diets. Fruit and juice days.

Flush out poisons. Treatment for drug abuse.

● *New Moon: A day of fasting.*

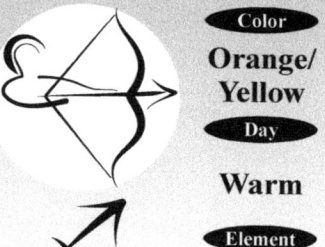

A heart makes a good home for the friend.
Yunus Emre

Color
Orange/ Yellow

Day

Warm

Element

Sagittarius   Fire

♏ → ♐
8:40 AM PST
10:40 AM CST
11:40 AM EST

17 Wednesday

No meat.

18 Thursday

8:54 PM PST
10:54 PM CST
11:54 PM EST
♐ → ♑

19 Friday

● New Moon 5:44 PM PST, 7:44 PM CST, 8:44 AM EST
No meat. Cutting and filing toenails and fingernails.

Positive affirmation:
"I trust the power of positive thinking."

Turning Point
Transition of descending to ascending forces. Both forces are at work and neutralize each other.

detox
remove
be active

Waning Moon

D E C E M B E R

Success

Career and business are in the foreground now and thinking becomes clear and serious, but somewhat inflexible.

Perseverance and reasoning assist in financial matters, planning, and contracts.

The values of tradition, authority, and discipline impact our endeavors.

Leisure

Money is not likely to be wasted in a shopping spree.

Many are drawn to enjoy cultural events.

The earth feels cold to the touch, so take slightly warmer clothes.

Health

Sensitive body parts:

Knees, Joints, Bones, Skin

All measures taken to supply nutrient materials and strengthen the sensitive body parts are very effective.

Healing ointments are easily absorbed.

Sensitive blood circulation.

Avoid overstraining bones and knees, and apply gentle stretching exercises only.

Problems with meniscus: Don't overstrain.

Dress slightly warmer.

High blood pressure: Avoid salty foods.

Massages, lymphatic therapy, and chiropractic treatment to release blockages.

Body Care

Aromas, scents:

Cedar, Juniper

Treatments with firming and moisturizing creams are more effective.

Massages that serve to regenerate, and strengthen, perhaps aided with beneficial massage oils.

Correcting and cutting ingrown nails.

Every kind of skin care is beneficial.

Cutting and filing toenails and fingernails will make the nails grow stronger over time.

Hair dyes applied now, will look more vibrant.

Garden/Nature

Plant part:

Root

Sow plants, herbs, and vegetables that grow and flourish above ground.

Transplanting.

Harvest produce is suitable for storage. Harvest root vegetables.

Gather herbs for bone, joint, and skin diseases.

Housework

Light housework only.

Air rooms only briefly.

Preserving root vegetables.

Avoid dry cleaning, as the fabric may develop unwanted glossy blotches.

Nutrition

Food quality:

Salt

Garlic, carrots, red beets, reddish, rutabaga, sugar beet, celery, potatoes, onions, kohlrabi.

Weight gain: avoid indulging in rich foods. If overweight, eat smaller portions.

Supply nutrient materials to strengthen the body. Focus on foods that contain essential minerals and vitamins.

Stimulants and vitamins are more effective.

Avoid large quantities of salty foods like bacon, ham, salted herring, fatty cheese, and the like. Avoid heavy and greasy foods.

Positive affirmation:
"I trust a life in harmony."

Harvest Time
Ascending forces! Sap is rising, enhancing plant growth above ground, resulting in the most juicy fruits and vegetables.

gather strength rest, recover buildup
Waxing Moon

20 Saturday	**21** Sunday Winter Solstice, 4. Advent

D E C E M B E R

Peace begins with a smile.
Mother Teresa

Color

Yellow

Day

Cool

Element

Earth

Capricorn

Success

Inspiration, optimism, and impatience. Rational thinking, creativity and imagination spark new ideas and inspire planning for the future.

Shying away from routine tasks people will feel more drawn to anything new.

Instead of gridlocked structures choose new possibilities.

Leisure

Inspiration and optimism will boost friendship, social gatherings, and parties.

Express your creativity and imagination. Dwell in dreams and utopian ideas. It is easier now to perceive intuitive thoughts.

Health

Sensitive body parts:

Lower Legs, Veins

All measures taken to supply nutrient materials and strengthen the sensitive body parts are very effective.

Healing ointments are easily absorbed.

Sensitive glandular system.

Avoid inflammation of the veins. Apply ointments to lower legs, and rest legs in a raised position.

Varicose veins: Avoid long periods of standing.

While exercising go easy on the ankles.

Sensitivity to light, so bring your sunglasses along.

Body Care

Aromas, scents:
Cyclamen, Peach, Wild Roses

Treatments with firming and moisturizing creams are more effective.

Massages that serve to regenerate, and strengthen, perhaps aided with beneficial massage oils.

Correcting and cutting ingrown nails.

Hair dyes applied now, will look more vibrant.

Garden/Nature

Plant part:

Flower

Avoid watering plants.

Harvested produce is well suitable for storage.

Gather herbs for vein diseases.

Housework

Light housework only.

Ventilate rooms thoroughly.

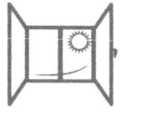

Baking cakes and cookies. Dough rises faster. (Except on New Moon)

Making preserves.

Nutrition

Food quality:

Fat

Cauliflower, artichoke, broccoli, sunflower seeds, flax seeds, nuts, rose hip, elder.

Weight gain: avoid indulging in rich foods. If overweight, eat smaller portions.

Supply nutrient materials to strengthen the body. Focus on foods that contain essential minerals and vitamins.

Stimulants and vitamins are more effective.

Pay attention to any particularly tempting foods today: Most likely the "wrong" things taste best.

High cholesterol: eat a low fat diet.

Positive affirmation:
"I trust a life in harmony."

Harvest Time
Ascending forces! Sap is rising, enhancing plant growth above ground, resulting in the most juicy fruits and vegetables.

gather strength rest, recover buildup
Waxing Moon

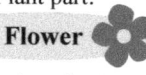
7:53 AM PST
9:53 AM CST
10:53 AM EST

22 Monday
Hannukah Final Day

23 Tuesday

5:10 PM PST
7:10 PM CST
8:10 PM EST

24 Wednesday
Christmas Eve

No meat.

Someone's sitting in the shade today because someone planted a tree a long time ago.
Les Brown

Color
Bright/ Dark Blue

Day
Air/Light

Element
Air

Aquarius

D E C E M B E R

Success

Sensibility, intuition, and helpfulness.

Where possible, retreating is more favorable than dealing with business matters.

Dissolve restrictions, be patient and wait. Be aware that people can be more easily influenced.

Leisure

Your helpfulness will boost friendships.

Enjoy dancing or swimming, or watch a movie that will inspire your fantasies and imagination.

Retreat, relax, and recover.

Romance can be gentle and coziness will prevail.

If you plan outdoor excursions, be prepared for a shower here and there.

Health

Sensitive body parts:

Feet and Toes

All measures taken to supply nutrient materials and strengthen the sensitive body parts are very effective.

Healing ointments are easily absorbed.

Sensitive nervous system.

Drugs have a much stronger effect on your body. Monitor closely what you put into your body.

Lymphatic therapy.

Sluggishness or fatigue may occur in the transition into the next Zodiac sign of Aries.

Body Care

Aromas, scents: Magnolia, Amaryllis, Clary Sage

Treatments with firming and moisturizing creams are more effective.

Massages that serve to regenerate, and strengthen, perhaps aided with beneficial massage oils. Reflexology massage. Carry out with special care, people are more sensitive.

Correcting and cutting ingrown nails.

Foot bath.

No haircuts, hair becomes shaggy and unmanageable. Avoid washing your hair. Dandruff could develop.

Garden/Nature

Plant part:

 Leaf

Watering all indoor and outdoor plants.

Sow plants, herbs, and vegetables that grow and flourish above ground, and leaf vegetables.

Transplanting.

Mowing lawns.

Avoid pruning fruit trees and bushes.

Harvested produce should be consumed as soon as possible.

Gather herbs for foot complaints.

Discover more about the lunar cycle and it's effects in the reference book "Nature's Daily Guide". ISBN 978-0-9854637-8-6

Nature's Daily Guide
The Influence of the Lunar Cycle

Housework

Light housework only.

Ventilate rooms briefly and rapidly. Don't air mattresses.

Any dirt and spots are easily removed in the laundry.

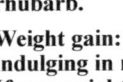

Avoid painting, as paint will take very long to dry.

Preserving and storing should be avoided.

Nutrition

Food quality:

Carbohydrate

Lettuce, spinach, lamb's lettuce, Endive, parsley, leek, cabbage (Brussels sprouts, kale, Chinese cabbage), all leafy herbs, asparagus, mushrooms, cress, Swiss chard, rhubarb.

Weight gain: avoid indulging in rich foods. If overweight, eat smaller portions and avoid carbohydrates.

Supply nutrient materials to strengthen the body. Focus on foods that contain essential minerals and vitamins.

Caffeine, alcohol, drugs, certain foods, and stimulants have a much stronger effect.

Positive affirmation:
"I trust a life in harmony."

Harvest Time
Ascending forces! Sap is rising, enhancing plant growth above ground, resulting in the most juicy fruits and vegetables.

gather strength
rest, recover
buildup
Waxing Moon

25 **Thursday**
Christmas Day

26 **Friday** Kwanzaa starts,
Boxing Day (CAN)

No meat. Cutting and filing toenails and fingernails.

What the public expects and what is healthy for an individual are two very different things.
Esther Williams

 Color

Blueish White

 Day

Wetness

Element

Water

Pisces

D E C E M B E R

Success

Things get going and the way straight ahead seems the best.

People feel energetic, courageous, assertive, and at times anxious.

Good time for meetings and sales talks but impatience and selfishness do not favor teamwork.

Leisure

An enterprising spirit and spontaneity move people to enjoy outings, sports, competitions, cultural events, and travels.

Romance can be very passionate.

Good days for outings, even with cloudy skies the air still feels somewhat warm. Drying effect, get plenty to drink.

Health

Sensitive body parts:

Head, Brain, Eyes

All measures taken to supply nutrient materials and strengthen the sensitive body parts are very effective.

Healing ointments are easily absorbed.

Sensitive sense organs.

If you suffer from migraines drink plenty of water, and avoid coffee, chocolate, and sugar.

Body Care

Aromas, scents: Cloves, Peppermint, Thyme

Treatments with firming and moisturizing creams are more effective.

Massages that serve to regenerate, and strengthen, perhaps aided with beneficial massage oils.

Correcting and cutting ingrown nails.

Eye compresses for strained eyes.

Any kind of hair care. Hair dyes applied now, will look more vibrant.

Garden/Nature

Plant part:

Fruit

Sow plants and vegetables that grow and flourish above ground, especially fruit and tomatoes.

Sowing and planting anything that is supposed to grow fast and for immediate use.

Grafting onto fruit trees.

Cultivating grains.

Transplanting.

Harvesting and storing grains, vegetables, potatoes, fruit, and tomatoes.

Gather herbs for eye complaints and headaches.

Day off on 12/27.

Housework

Light housework only.

Ventilate sufficiently.

Preserving fruit.

Freezing fruit and vegetables.

Baking bread, cakes, and cookies. Dough rises faster. (Except on New Moon)

Suitable for making cheese.

Nutrition

Food quality:

Protein

Beans, peas, corn, tomatoes, pumpkin, lentils, soybeans, cucumber, eggplant, zucchini, berries, fruit, chili, bell pepper, figs, avocado, melon, olives.

Weight gain: avoid indulging in rich foods. If overweight, eat smaller portions.

Supply nutrient materials to strengthen the body. Focus on foods that contain essential minerals and vitamins.

Stimulants and vitamins are more effective.

Drink plenty of water.

Positive affirmation:
"I trust a life in harmony."

Harvest Time
Ascending forces! Sap is rising, enhancing plant growth above ground, resulting in the most juicy fruits and vegetables.

gather strength
rest, recover
buildup
Waxing Moon

♓ → ♈ 12:03 AM PST
2:03 AM CST
3:03 AM EST

27 Saturday

☽ Half Moon.

28 Sunday

A healthy attitude is contagious but don't wait to catch it from others.
Be a carrier.
Tom Stoppard

Color
Indigo Blue

Day
Warm

Element

D E C E M B E R

Fire   Aries

Success

Realism and material security are important. Persistence comes easy, thoughts and reactions are slower.

Assess financial areas.

Conservative tendencies may make people want to stay away from risk taking.

Leisure

Relax at a picnic/feast. Enjoy culinary pleasures and hobbies.

The earth feels cold to the touch, so take slightly warmer clothes.

Health

Sensitive body parts:

Head and Neck

All measures taken to supply nutrient materials and strengthen the sensitive body parts are very effective.

Healing ointments are easily absorbed.

Sensitive blood circulation.

Organs of speech, jaws, teeth, tonsils, thyroid gland, neck, and vocal chords get easily affected. Keep neck warm. On cold days ears should be protected. Sensitivity to noise.

High blood pressure: Avoid salty foods.

Massages, lymphatic therapy, and chiropractic treatment to release blockages.

Body Care

Aromas, scents: Geranium, Jasmine, Rose

Treatments with firming and moisturizing creams are more effective.

Massages that serve to regenerate, and strengthen, perhaps aided with beneficial massage oils.

Correcting and cutting ingrown nails.

Hair dyes applied now, will look more vibrant.

Garden/Nature

Plant part:

Root

Sow plants, herbs, and vegetables that grow and flourish above ground.

Sowing and planting trees, bushes, hedges, and root vegetables. Everything grows slowly and lasts well.

Transplanting.

Harvesting and storing root vegetables. Harvested produce is well suited for storage.

Gather herbs for sinus issues, sore throat, and ear complaints.

Housework

Light housework only.

Air rooms only briefly.

Preserving root vegetables.

Nutrition

Food quality:

Salt

Garlic, carrots, red beets, reddish, rutabaga, sugar beet, celery, potatoes, onions, kohlrabi.

Weight gain: avoid indulging in rich foods. If overweight, eat smaller portions.

Supply nutrient materials to strengthen the body. Focus on foods that contain essential minerals and vitamins.

Stimulants and vitamins are more effective.

Avoid large quantities of salty foods like bacon, ham, salted herring, fatty cheese, and the like.

Positive affirmation:
"I trust a life in harmony."

Harvest Time
Ascending forces! Sap is rising, enhancing plant growth above ground, resulting in the most juicy fruits and vegetables.

gather strength rest, recover buildup
Waxing Moon

♈ ➜ ♉ ◄ 3:58 AM PST
5:58 AM CST
6:58 AM EST

29 Monday

30 Tuesday

D E C E M B E R

A person without a sense of humor is like a wagon without springs. It's jolted by every pebble on the road.
Henry Ward Beecher

 Color

Bright Blue

 Day

Cool

 Element

Earth   **Taurus**

Success

Open mindedness and curiosity. A changeable and hectic time.

Good time for talking, negotiating, networking, and exchanging ideas as well as for meetings of a nonbinding nature, conferences, and studies.

Leisure

Good time for family gatherings, parties, and short trips.

People enjoy stimulating their minds with reading and studying. Attending theater performances is a preferred enjoyment. Enhance friendships.

Stretching exercises.

Be prepared for sudden changes in weather or climate.

Health

Sensitive body parts:

Shoulders, Arms, Hands, Lungs

All measures taken to supply nutrient materials and strengthen the sensitive body parts are very effective.

Healing ointments are easily absorbed. Applying herbal ointments to the shoulders for rheumatic gout and alike.

Sensitive glandular system.

Make sure you are dressed warm enough in cool weather.

Exercises for shoulders. Breathing exercises.

Avoid having any teeth pulled.

Sensitivity to light, bring your sunglasses along.

Massages, lymphatic therapy, and chiropractic treatment to release blockages.

Body Care

Aromas, scents: Lavender, Lemon Balm, Magnolia, Verbena

Treatments with firming and moisturizing creams are more effective.

Massages that serve to regenerate, and strengthen, perhaps aided with beneficial massage oils.

Correcting and cutting ingrown nails.

Hair dyes applied now, will look more vibrant.

Garden/Nature

Plant part:

Flower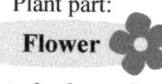

Sow plants, herbs, and vegetables that grow and flourish above ground.

Sowing and planting any creeping or climbing plants, flowers, and medicinal herbs.

Transplanting.

Avoid watering plants.

Gather herbs for tensions in the shoulder and lung complaints.

Changes in weather are more likely.

Housework

Light housework only.

Ventilate rooms thoroughly.

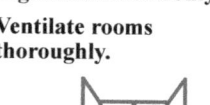

Making preserves.

Baking cakes and cookies. Dough rises faster. (Except on New Moon)

Nutrition

Food quality:

Fat

Cauliflower, artichoke, broccoli, sunflower seeds, flax seeds, nuts, rose hip, elder.

Weight gain: avoid indulging in rich foods. If overweight, eat smaller portions.

Supply nutrient materials to strengthen the body. Focus on foods that contain essential minerals and vitamins.

Stimulants and vitamins are more effective.

Pay attention to any particularly tempting foods today: Most likely the "wrong" things taste best.

High cholesterol: eat a low fat diet.

Positive affirmation:
"I trust a life in harmony."

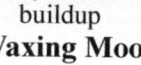

Turning Point
Transition of ascending to descending forces. Both forces are at work and neutralize each other.

gather strength rest, recover buildup
Waxing Moon

⬆⬇

♉ → ♊
5:14 AM PST
7:14 AM CST
8:14 AM EST

31 **Wednesday**
New Year's Eve

No meat.

1 **Thursday**
New Year's Day

Consistency requires you to be as ignorant today as you were a year ago.
Bernard Berenson

Color
Light Blue

Day
Air/Light

Element
Air

Gemini

DECEMBER/JANUARY